THE MAKING OF MODERN THEOLOGY
19TH AND 20TH CENTURY THEOLOGICAL TEXTS

This series of theological texts is designed to introduce a new generation of readers — theological students, students of religion, ordained ministers and the interested general reader — to the writings of some of those Christian theologians who, since the beginning of the 19th century, have had a formative influence on the development of Christian theology. Each volume in the series is intended to introduce the theologian, to trace the emergence of key or seminal ideas and insights, particularly within their social and historical context, and to show how they have contributed to the making of modern theology. The primary way in which this is done is by allowing the theologians chosen to address us in their own words.

There are three sections to each volume. The Introduction includes a short biography of the theologian, and an overview of his or her theology in relation to the texts which have been selected for study. The Texts, the bulk of each volume, are comprised largely of substantial edited selections from the theologian's writings. Each text is also introduced with information about its origin and its significance. The guiding rule in making the selection of texts has been the question: in what way has this particular theologian contributed to the shaping of contemporary theology? A Select Bibliography provides guidance for those who wish to read further both in the primary literature and in secondary sources.

Rudolf Bultmann 1884–1976

THE MAKING OF MODERN THEOLOGY

19TH AND 20TH CENTURY TEXTS

General Editor: John de Gruchy

RUDOLF BULTMANN

Interpreting Faith for the Modern Era

ROGER A. JOHNSON

COLLINS

Collins Liturgical Publications
8 Grafton Street, London W1X 3LA

Collins San Francisco
Icehouse One − 401
151 Union Street, San Francisco, CA 94111-1299

Collins Liturgical in Canada
c/o Novalis, Box 9700, Terminal,
375 Rideau St, Ottawa, Ontario K1G 4B4

Distributed in Ireland by
Educational Company of Ireland
21 Talbot Street, Dublin 1

Collins Liturgical Australia
PO Box 316, Blackburn, Victoria 3130

Collins Liturgical New Zealand
PO Box 1, Auckland

ISBN 0 00 599977 4 (paperback)
ISBN 0 00 599061 0 (cased)

First published 1987

Library of Congress Cataloging-in-Publication Data

Johnson, Roger A., 1930-
    Rudolf Bultmann: interpreting faith for the modern era.

    (The Making of modern theology)
    Bibliography: p.
    Includes index.
    1. Bultmann, Rudolf Karl, 1884-1976.   I. Title.   II. Series.
BX4827.B78J64   1987   230'.092'4   87-18256
ISBN 0-00-599061-0
ISBN 0-00-599977-4 (pbk.)

Index by Elizabeth Bernatowicz
Typographical design Colin Reed
Typeset by Swains (Glasgow) Limited
Printed in Great Britain by
Richard Clay Ltd, Bungay, Suffolk

CONTENTS

CONTENTS

ACKNOWLEDGMENTS

The publishers acknowledge with thanks permission to reproduce the following copyright texts from works by Rudolf Bultmann:

"Crisis of Faith" used by permission of the translator, Edward Hobbs.

Existence and Faith: Shorter Writings of Rudolf Bultmann, Schubert Ogden, trans. Copyright © 1960 by Meridian Books, Inc. Reprinted by arrangement with NAL Penguin Inc., New York, NY.

"Liberal Theology and the Latest Theological Movement", "What Does it Mean to Speak of God", "The Question of Wonder" from *Faith and Understanding,* Louise Pettibone Smith, trans. Copyright © 1969 by SCM Press Ltd. Reprinted by permission of SCM Press and Harper & Row, Publishers, Inc.

Jesus Christ and Mythology, Copyright © 1958 Rudolf Bultmann; copyright renewed 1986 Antje B. Lemke. Reprinted with the permission of Charles Scribner's Sons and T & T Clark Ltd.

"The Problem of Hermeneutics" from *New Testament and Mythology and Other Basic Writings,* selected, edited and translated by Schubert M. Ogden. English translation copyright © 1984 Fortress Press. Used by permission of Fortress Press and SCM Press.

Primitive Christianity in its Contemporary Setting, R. H. Fuller, trans., Meridian Books, 1957. Used by permission of Thames and Hudson Ltd.

"Karl Barth's *Epistle to the Romans in its Second Edition*" and "The Problem of a Theological Exegesis of the New Testament" from *The Beginnings of Dialectic Theology,* James M. Robinson, ed. (John Knox Press, 1968), trans. from *Anfänge der dialektischen Theologie Band II,* pub. by Chr. Kaiser, München, 1963. Used by permission of Chr. Kaiser Verlag.

"The Coming of the Kingdom of God: the Necessity for Decision" from *Jesus and the Word,* Louise Pettibone Smith and Erminie Huntress, trans. Copyright 1934 Charles Scribner's Sons. Reissued 1958. Reprinted with the permission of Charles Scribner's Sons.

"The Message of Jesus" and "The Relation between Theology and Proclamation" from *Theology of the New Testament*, Kendrick Grobel, trans. Copyright 1955 Charles Scribner's Sons; copyright © 1983 Antje B. Lemke. Reprinted with the permission of Charles Scribner's Sons.

"Sermon: Matthew 6:25-33" from *This World and Beyond: Marburg Sermons*, Harold Knight, trans. Copyright 1960 Charles Scribner's Sons and Lutterworth Press, Cambridge, and used with their permission.

INTRODUCTION

1

THE FORMATION OF
BULTMANN'S THEOLOGY

BIOGRAPHICAL SKETCH

Rudolf Karl Bultmann was born 20 August 1884 in a village of the duchy of Oldenburg.[1]* For several generations members of his family had served as pastors in the Lutheran tradition of the German Evangelical Church. His father was a pastor, who joined his son for annual gatherings of "The Friends of *Die Christliche Welt.*"[2] His maternal grandfather and paternal great-grandfather had also been pastors. While Bultmann became identified with the causes of "radical criticism" and "existentialism" during the early years of his theological career, he understood his own work to have its purpose in the service of church and theology and this, in part, was a legacy from his family.

By 1903, Bultmann had completed his final examinations for the *Gymnasium* at Oldenburg. He then went on to study theology, first at Tübingen University, then in Berlin, and finally at Marburg University. At Marburg, he first studied with Wilhelm Herrmann, whose theology Bultmann appropriated as the foundation and continuing core for his own position. There he also studied with Johannes Weiss, Professor of New Testament, who encouraged Bultmann to prepare himself for a future of research and teaching in this field.

He completed his first theological degree at Marburg in 1906, but returned to that same university in 1907 to begin his doctoral studies. In 1908, Wilhelm Heitmüller joined the Marburg faculty, and through him Bultmann became immersed in the work of the history-of-religions school. Heitmüller, along with the writings of Richard Reitzenstein and Wilhelm Bousset, taught Bultmann to understand the literature of the New Testament by comparing early Christianity with other reli-

---

* Footnotes indicated by figures are on pp. 332 ff.

gious movements of the same era: e.g., Jewish apocalyptic or Hellenistic Gnosticism. Bultmann himself made significant contributions to the work of this group, and not surprisingly, he was invited to succeed Heitmüller at Marburg University in 1921. For the next thirty years, Marburg University was Bultmann's academic home. Even after his retirement in 1951, he continued to be an active participant in Marburg theological discussions. He died in 1976.[3]

The formation of Bultmann's own theology can best be understood in terms of the theological issues which engaged his attention and that of the other scholars — New Testament historians, theologians and philosophers — with whom he was in dialogue.

BULTMANN'S CRITIQUE AND REVISION OF LIBERAL THEOLOGY: "THE HISTORICAL JESUS" AND NEW TESTAMENT ESCHATOLOGY*

While Bultmann completed his Ph.D. in 1910 and his post-doctoral dissertation in 1912, his publications between then and 1920 were few in number and not substantial. Then, in 1920, he began to produce a steady stream of books and essays which set forth fundamental new positions in both theology and New Testament studies. His productivity as an author continued from 1920 until long after his retirement in 1951. In the early twenties some of these writings embodied the results of technical New Testament research, such as his epoch-making *The History of the Synoptic Tradition* (1921); some were primarily oriented towards the theological concerns of Bultmann's generation, such as the sermon and several essays in the first section of readings. Others, from this same period, incorporated a surprising combination of technical New Testament competencies, in both literary analysis and research in religions of the Hellenistic era, with a new model of theological reflection. A 1920 article, "Ethical and Mystical Religion in Primitive Christianity", is a particularly important example of this combination. While the article is often confusing and overly technical, not suitable for inclusion in a book of readings such as this, it provides a useful focus for understanding the theological transition which Bultmann made in the second and third decades of this century.

This 1920 article was the first publication in which Bultmann criti-

---

* For texts, see below pp. 91-128.

cized Liberal Theology, the dominant Protestant theological movement of the nineteenth century.[4] He begins by noting how Liberal Theology understood the message of Jesus to be the essence of Christian faith. Paul, John and other New Testament authors extended this same message of Jesus, but only as mixed with "alien influences and complications".[5] According to New Testament scholarship before Bultmann, Jesus proclaimed a God who willed the good and whose message was a fit authority for the Christian conscience of modern people. Jesus also proclaimed God as the "forgiving power of grace", the one who saved the sinners while judging their sin (*ibid*.). Through the historical Jesus, Christians could apprehend God both as the law of moral life and a source of moral renewal in the midst of failure.

While Bultmann inherited this "theology of Jesus" from Liberal New Testament scholars, he also had come to recognize that the claim of this theology to be grounded in an historical Jesus was a fraud. Two different types of New Testament research led Bultmann to this conclusion. First, by 1920, when this essay was written, Bultmann had already completed the manuscript of *The History of the Synoptic Tradition* (1921). In that book, he utilized a new method of historical analysis ("Form History", usually translated Form Criticism) to distinguish the differing layers of oral tradition built into the three Synoptic Gospels (Mark, Matthew, and Luke). While individual fragments of Jesus' teachings had been gathered together in a layer of tradition rooted in Palestine, a unified "'life of Jesus' was first created by the Christ myth of the Hellenistic congregation" (*ibid., p. 223**). The Gospel of Mark is the first example of such a "life of Jesus", and in it, not only the unified form of the Christ myth, but also much of the content reflects the Hellenistic (Greek-speaking) church, far removed in time, language and culture from the Palestinian origins of Jesus. Bultmann therefore concluded that, in terms of available literary evidence, we are able to know very little about the so-called historical Jesus.

Second, as a result of historical studies which compared early Christianity with other religious movements of that period (like Hellenistic mystery religions or Gnosticism), Bultmann had to acknowledge that Christian faith did not appear until the emergence of the Hellenistic church. Followers of the so-called historical Jesus, as well as members of the earliest Palestinian congregations, belonged to a religious sect of Judaism, but not to the Christian church.

* In the Introduction, page references in italic refer to the edition cited in prior footnote. Non-italic page references refer to pages in this volume.

From the viewpoint of the historian the judgment must be made that "Christianity" as a self-sufficient, historical entity, a religious community with its own forms of myth and cult and communal life, begins with primitive Hellenistic Christianity (*ibid., p. 227*).

In brief, the results of New Testament research, his own and that of others, obliged Bultmann to repudiate prior efforts to ground Christian faith in an "historical Jesus". We do not have adequate evidence to establish clearly the life and personality of Jesus. Bultmann reiterates this judgment in *Jesus* (1926) and in publications as late as 1960, "The Relation of the Primitive Christian Kerygma to the Historical Jesus".[6] Even if we did have such evidence, a theology oriented towards the figure of Jesus would not be a Christian theology. For Christian theology is the explication of Christian faith, and that faith became a historical reality for the first time in the Hellenistic church, not the Jesus movement of Palestine. It is for this reason that Bultmann defines Jesus' proclamation of the Kingdom of God as "a presupposition for the theology of the New Testament rather than a part of that theology itself". That statement from *Theology of the New Testament* Volume I (1948) reflects Bultmann's consistent judgment concerning the role of Jesus in New Testament theology. Jesus proclaimed the Kingdom of God; subsequently, the kerygma of the Hellenistic church proclaimed Jesus as the crucified and risen Christ.

While studies of the New Testament led Bultmann to reject the historical foundation for the religion of Jesus advocated by Liberal Theology, his own sense of piety was also offended by this "Jesus theology". Two theological issues were particularly important for him. First, by 1920 Bultmann was already clear concerning the purpose of theology: to speak of God not as identified with some particular time of the past but as the power of the eternal to break into our present. Any theology which claims to bind God's revelation to some particular period of history, like the lifetime of Jesus of Nazareth, and then makes our apprehension of that past revelation dependent upon the results of historical criticism, violates faith's understanding of itself. Piety rightly rejects any effort to be made dependent upon "the most exact knowledge of history possible" (*ibid., p. 230*).

Second, in Bultmann's view, "the most serious error" of Liberal Theology was its "confusion of [religion with] a religiously colored moralism" (*ibid., p. 233*). Religion should not be understood as a body of moral teachings tinged with emotion, however often Liberal Theology had presented such a view. In faith, a believer submits himself or herself to a claim far more compelling than any moral ideal (*ibid., p. 233*). Believers are concerned with the fulfillment of their own being — not with the doing of certain moral deeds. In identifying God with the ideal of "The Good" and in limiting religious concerns to moral matters, Liberal Theology had lost what is distinctive to religion.

New Testament studies, combined with Bultmann's own sense of piety, thus provided the impetus for him to initiate a fundamental critique of Liberal Theology. However, the contribution of New Testament studies to Bultmann's new theology cannot be limited to their role in undermining established views, especially concerning the "historical Jesus"; through other studies of the New Testament, especially the work of Bultmann's mentor in this field, Johannes Weiss, Bultmann discovered an alternative understanding of God, a fundamental new paradigm, around which his later theology would grow and develop. In place of the "historical Jesus", no longer available as an object of historical inquiry, Weiss prompted Bultmann to explore the eschatological themes of the New Testament.

Eschatology means, literally, doctrine of the end, and in the case of the New Testament this means teachings concerning the last days, the end of history. For Bultmann in these early decades of the twentieth century — and since then for an increasingly large number of New Testament scholars — it became clear that the major figures of the New Testament expressed, in differing ways, an expectation of an imminent end to world history. Jesus' preaching of God's Kingdom, the epistles of Paul, the Gospel of Mark, and the Gospel of Matthew: all shared in common some form of eschatological expectation (*ibid., p. 227*). For Bultmann, this eschatology became the hard rock against which all theology had to be tested. It was so prominent in the New Testament proclamation of faith that modern theology either learned to understand Christian faith in this eschatological perspective or gave up any claim to speak of that faith. Yet, it was also clear that this eschatology appeared to be a source of embarrassment for modern Christians. The end of the world had not come in the lifetime of the early church. Nor did educated middle-class Christians feel particularly comfortable identifying themselves with a religion which announced the end of history.

Only as Bultmann became increasingly familiar with this eschatological perspective did he begin to appreciate its meaning for faith in the modern era. As we will see later, Bultmann came to understand modern culture as a seductive temptation to a false self-understanding. People of the modern era were particularly prone to believe that their own fulfillment as human beings was totally dependent upon some combination of worldly powers: their genetic inheritance, success in a career, or some combination of these and other tangible, visible forces of history. For Bultmann, this is an excessively simplified form of belief with destructive consequences for the individual and humanity as whole. Over against this sort of naive confidence in one's own resources stands the eschatological understanding of God in the New Testament. God stands in opposition to all structures of this world, God will unleash untold destructive powers to turn inside out the old and corrupt age, God is disclosed to believers always as a stranger, always in a relation of distance and tension; in the theological language of those early decades, God is best identified as "Wholly Other". Bultmann freely acknowledged that he borrowed this theological category from Rudolf Otto's book *The Idea of the Holy*. However, the phrase, "Wholly Other", increasingly came to express Bultmann's own interpretation of the eschatological understanding of God in the New Testament (*ibid., p. 234*).

In the next part of this introduction we will trace Bultmann's several uses of this theological term, "Wholly Other". For the moment, it is sufficient to recognize Bultmann's new understanding of God as a modern alternative for the "historical Jesus" advocated by Liberal Theology. In recognizing this fundamental turn in Bultmann's theology, it should be apparent that, for Bultmann, this development occurred within his continuing conversation with Liberal Theology. As he reminds us in the essay "Liberal Theology and the Newest Theological Movement", the new theology did not arise out of "a revival of orthodoxy [or] a repudiation of Liberal Theology . . . but as a discussion within it" (p. 65). He then goes on to acknowledge his indebtedness to Schleiermacher, the founding father of Liberal Theology, and to the critical spirit of free inquiry, nurtured by Liberal Theology. The "historical Jesus" was itself one of the early results of the critical historical research of Liberal Theology; further literary and historical studies, carried out within this same theological tradition, exposed this historical claim as a projection from nineteenth century ideals on to a vague, little known figure of first century Palestine. Similarly, it was not orthodox theology that uncovered New Testament eschatology and then struggled to make theological sense of it, but scholars from the tradition of Liberal Theology, like Bultmann's Marburg mentor, Johannes Weiss. Bultmann's own form-critical analysis of the Synoptic Gospels (1921) is another clear example of the spirit of Liberal Theology at work. While he repudiated certain elements in Liberal Theology, Bultmann consistently identified himself and his work with that larger theological movement.

While all of this may seem obvious in the latter decades of this century, in 1922 the situation was much less clear. In that year, Bultmann wrote a long review of the second edition of Karl Barth's *Epistle to the Romans* (1922) which inaugurated a brief theological alliance and long term friendship. This theological alliance came to be called "Dialectical Theology" and was identified with the work of Friedrich Gogarten, in addition to Barth and Bultmann. However, it was Barth who engaged Bultmann's theological attention throughout the whole of his career. In part, Bultmann found one aspect of his early theology represented in the early (mid 1920s) work of Barth. In part, Barth's rejection of Liberal Theology as a whole prompted Bultmann to defend it. In any case, Bultmann consistently perceived his own position between Liberal Theology, on the one hand, and Karl Barth, on the other. As a result, in this introduction to Bultmann, we will repeatedly bump up against the figure of Karl Barth.

From the beginning, these three theologians constituted an unlikely troika and their alliance was a fragile one. In the beginning, Bultmann and Gogarten appeared to have the most in common. Already by 1920 Bultmann was quoting Gogarten appreciatively, especially for his book *Religion weither* and his lectures at Eisenach.[7] In this same essay, Bultmann made only passing references to Karl Barth's *Epistle to the Romans* (first edition, 1919). He agreed with Barth's "religious criticism of culture" but, as for Barth's affirmations, he found little positive except "an arbitrary adaptation of the Pauline Christ myth" (*ibid., p. 232*).

This same pattern persists, even in Bultmann's more appreciative review of *Epistle to the Romans* (second edition, 1922): that is, agreement with Barth's critique of other positions and disagreement with his affirmations.[8] In the beginning and conclusion of this long review, Bultmann makes explicit his identification with the tradition of Liberal Theology. He begins by praising Barth, but in the language of Liberal Theology ("The book attempts to prove the independence and absolute nature of religion."). He links Barth's book with the founder of Liberal Theology, Friedrich Schleiermacher. In the conclusion, he faults Barth for failing to provide some way for understanding faith as one's own. In addition, as in his response to the first edition, Bultmann objects to Barth's arbitrary use of "the Pauline Christ myth", this time specifying how Barth has confused it with "the historical Jesus". In between this beginning and ending, Bultmann agrees with Barth's "polemic against historicism and psychologism" and any other effort to substitute some part of the world for the eschatological, "Wholly Other" God.

During the mid-twenties Barth and Bultmann were very much a minority among the more numerous and powerful defenders of Liberal Theology. They did actively support each other, especially during the years 1922 to 1926. Each lectured at the other's institution, brought students to attend the lectures of the other, used these brief visits to teach jointly morning seminar sessions, and intentionally sustained a common front against mutual enemies: e.g., both had agreed, at one of these events, that they would abstain from any public airing of differences which could be misused against Barth.

It would be a mistake, however, to construe this temporary alliance as founded on a firm foundation of shared theological convictions. Barth's father was as much a Calvinist in his theology as Bultmann's was Lutheran, and the two of them acknowledged the continuing role of these two Protestant traditions in their own differences. While both had studied with Wilhelm Herrmann, a nineteenth century Lutheran pietist theologian, only Bultmann appropriated Herrmann's theology as his own. In addition, only Bultmann was grounded in the critical discipline of biblical studies; only Bultmann had to espouse for himself the tradition of Liberal Theology because it provided the only context which had nourished such studies. In contrast, Barth never could appreciate why Bultmann, in his New Testament interpretations, was so concerned with historical distinctions. Not surprisingly, after the publication of *Jesus*(1926), Bultmann felt as if Barth had distanced himself from their dialogue, and that condition persisted until the early thirties, when the advent of Nazi political power brought them closer together again.

Thus, Bultmann's new theological position, first expressed in 1920, has to be understood in terms of the theological issues and New Testament dialogue partners formative for his own development. Bultmann's new position was most definitely not a variation from Barth, whose influence was negligible in its formation. Nor was it, directly, a response to World War I, though the disillusionment and confusion born of the war created a social context more open to Bultmann's new theology. Instead, the sources for Bultmann's theology were primarily the unresolved problems which he inherited in his chosen field of New Testament studies. How can the church continue to proclaim a faith, centered in the historical figure of Jesus, when historical knowledge of such a figure is no longer a reliable possibility? How can the church proclaim a message of faith congenial with the moral ideals of modern people when the New Testament is riddled with expectations for an end of history that never happened and must, in some sense, seem absurd to the modern believer? These were the urgent questions of faith and scholarship which Bultmann inherited from the work of his mentors. It was his genius to convert such apparent liabilities into new resources of strength for both New Testament scholarship and the preaching of the church.

2

MAIN THEMES IN BULTMANN'S THEOLOGY

GOD AS "WHOLLY OTHER"*

In Bultmann's 1917 sermon we hear some of the earliest echoes from New Testament eschatology. God is here proclaimed as "Wholly Other", a phrase Bultmann borrowed from Rudolf Otto but redefined to make his own. This theological category has at least three distinct uses in the early sermon and the writings of the early twenties. By the 1925 essay, "What Does it Mean to Speak of God?", Bultmann will have redefined this same category with a single meaning.

In the first instance, God is "Wholly Other" than he had been conceived to be in the theology and culture of the pre-World War I period.

> If we want to see God, then the first thing we should say to ourselves is that we may not see him as we have conceived him. We must remind ourselves that he may appear to be wholly other than the picture we have made of him (p. 48).

For Bultmann, and many others of his generation, pre-War Christian piety had made God appear to be too small, too comfortable. "God is greater . . . infinite . . . full of contradictions and riddles". World War I had exposed the falseness of the pre-War concept of God and in this religious-cultural crisis Bultmann discerned a situation analogous to that of the early Christians. In their eschatological hope they anticipated an overthrow of all established values and authorities, just as the younger generation of German intellectuals found the order and norms of their world called into question.

Second, God is "Wholly Other" than human work, morality, knowledge and all other expressions of human effort to know and control reality so as to win a secure existence. Bultmann calls upon his listeners to recognize the richness of religious experience.

> [Experience] means to perceive that miraculous forces hold sway in

---

* For texts, see below pp. 44-90.

the world, which we cannot reckon with, cannot enlist as mere factors in our work. It means to know that over and above our knowledge, our work, yes, and even our moral duty, there is something else — a fullness of life that streams in upon us completely as a gift, completely as grace (p. 48).

The opposition between the "Wholly Other" God and the human work-world is a fundamental theme in Bultmann's theology. In the theology of Wilhelm Herrmann, Bultmann first found a theological critique of the excesses and illusions attached to the bourgeois work ethos. The self-understanding of work, which seeks to win for the self a secure future, is not only a delusion but sin. Bultmann will develop this theme more extensively in his later writings. He will consistently set in opposition "justification by faith", a basic theological principle from Luther's Reformation, with "justification by work", meaning not the religious works of the Middle Ages criticized by Luther, but the middle-class work-ethos of the modern era.

Third, God is "Wholly Other" as one who may be known only through the free act of self-disclosure. We cannot ever know another person unless she discloses something of herself to us. If this is true for our knowledge of other people, how much more so is this true for our knowledge of God? Just as people may share themselves with us, without exhausting their own inner resources, so with God. Both hidden and revealed, God is not under our control or management, unlike the objects of our work-world.

In the essays from 1924 on "Liberal Theology and the Latest Theological Movement" and 1925 "What Does It Mean to Speak of God?", Bultmann formulates an understanding of God as "Wholly Other" which is distinct from all of the above and which becomes the stable core in his use of this image. "Wholly Other", in these two writings, is strictly a relational category which says more about the human condition than it does about God. In particular, Bultmann wants to exclude any sense of "Wholly Other" which could be construed in a metaphysical or speculative manner. The term does not mean that "God is something wholly different from man, a metaphysical being, a kind of an immaterial world" (1925, p. 83). Bultmann always rejects every effort to construe God as some sort of metaphysical object about which the human mind can construct theories of one sort or another. "Wholly Other" does not signify God's removal from the world inhabited by humans; it does not locate God in some realm of being distant from the reality in which we move and find our being. Indeed, we encounter God precisely as that determination of our reality which we cannot escape. But the truth of our human condition is that we do seek to avoid God. We would prefer to think and act as if we ourselves constituted the determining center of reality. To encounter God, therefore, is to find our pretension to self-sufficiency judged. God must be acknowledged as "Wholly Other", and not a congenial friend, because of our prior disposition to get along without God, to live out our wish of being god for ourselves. For us, God can be only "Wholly Other", encountering us not with a friendly "hello" but with a firm word of judgment.

The term Bultmann uses to describe the existential orientation depicted above is "sin". Bultmann does not identify sin with moral wrong-doing. Rather, for him, as for Paul, sin means a fundamental distortion of the human will and existence, the illusion of self-sufficiency. The opposite of sin is faith, not moral action of some sort. Sin is a specific theological category, meaning the presumption of people to live by and for themselves alone, that pride (*superbia*) which leads us to deny the finitude of our own existence and the reality of God's determining presence. After 1925, when Bultmann speaks of God as "Wholly Other", it will function solely as a relational theological category. Because of our sin, God can only be known as "Wholly Other". "To speak of God as the 'Wholly Other' has meaning, then, only if I have understood that the actual situation of man is the situation of the sinner" (p. 84).

Having begun this discussion of God as 'Wholly Other" with Bultmann's sermon referring explicitly to World War I, we need to conclude with the question: Is Bultmann's theology, with its turn away from the "historical Jesus" towards God as "Wholly Other", to be understood primarily as a response to the chaos and cultural disintegration that accompanied World War I? Did Bultmann reject the happy harmony of God and human endeavor, as depicted in his sermon recollections of earlier Pentecost celebrations and as presumed in Liberal Theology, only because of the multiple conflicts engendered by that war? If so, we might conclude that Bultmann's theology was appropriate for times of war or other situations of turmoil and disorder, but of less interest in the normal days in between such disruptions.

Bultmann, however, was clear that World War I played a relatively unimportant role in his personal development and in the formation of his theology. However, he did find himself preoccupied with the theological consequences of new research on "the historical Jesus" as well as the strange new eschatology of early Christianity. For Bultmann, these were the primary issues which shaped his early theology. As he wrote to a German pastor in 1926,

> I must be frank. The war was not a shattering experience for me. . . . So I do not believe that the war has influenced my theology. . . . My view is that if anyone is looking for the genesis of our theology he will find that internal discussion with the theology of our teachers plays an incomparably greater role than the impact of the war.[9]

In referring to "internal discussion . . . with our teachers", Bultmann is speaking of those problematic points of scholarship and faith, like "the historical Jesus" and New Testament eschatology. His eschatological understanding of God as "Wholly Other" grew out of his struggle with the most urgent questions of New Testament studies rather than his personal experience with the war.

EXISTENTIALIST INTERPRETATION OF SCRIPTURE*

While unresolved historical issues from New Testament studies provided the focus for Bultmann's earliest theological development, philosophical concerns soon played an increasing role in his work. The impetus for this new development was the arrival in 1923 at Marburg University of a new professor of philosophy, Martin Heidegger. Heidegger had been working on some theological authors, especially Paul and Luther, and quickly perceived Bultmann's expertise as a valuable resource for his own interests.[10] Bultmann, in turn, discovered in Heidegger a brilliant intellect committed to the development of a fundamental new form of philosophy which could provide an alternative to the several forms of philosophical Idealism long dominant in German thought. Their mutual interests quickly led them into regular discussions with each other, as well as jointly taught seminars. The impact of Heidegger's existentialism began to appear in Bultmann's writings by 1925; two years later, in 1927, Heidegger published *Being and Time*, one of the most influential sources of existentialist philosophy in the twentieth century. Heidegger left Marburg in 1928 for Freiburg University, but by that time, Bultmann had already integrated existentialism into his understanding of New Testament eschatology.[11]

It would be a mistake, however, to assume that Bultmann's existen-

---

* For texts, see below pp. 129-157.

tialism was simply an extension of Heidegger's philosophy into theology. It was not. Bultmann adapted Heidegger's philosophy to fit his own theological purposes. More specifically, Bultmann assimilated Heidegger's thought to an older philosophical-theological tradition called Marburg Neo-Kantianism.[12] While this tradition is not as well known as existentialism, it did play a formative role in modern theology. Martin Buber's religious philosophy of "I and Thou" grew out of Marburg Neo-Kantianism, as did Bultmann's theology. Bultmann's existentialism, therefore, is a distinctive version, all his own, with sources far older than his work with Heidegger in the mid-twenties.

Two pairs of contrasting concepts provide the most helpful guide to understanding Bultman's existentialism. The first is the contrast between "existential event" and "existentialist conceptuality", and the second is the opposition between an "existentialist conceptuality" and an "objectifying conceptuality".

Bultmann uses the word "existential" (in German, *existentiell*) to refer to an individual human being as responsible for his or her own future. What is existential is personal and expressed in an individual's self-understanding. By self-understanding, Bultmann refers to the ways in which each of us comes to terms with anxious concerns for his or her future. In speaking of existential self-understanding, Bultmann is often obliged to use first person singular pronouns. In contrast, existentialist (in German, *existential*) refers to a systematic body of philosophical concepts and a method of understanding human existence. Hence, existentialist is most often linked with "conceptuality". While these concepts were developed in order to explicate and illumine human existence (in contrast with things or the world in general), they do not refer directly to individual persons but to a body of thought. First person singular pronouns may be necessary in order to express an existential event, but would be inappropriate for elucidating the intricacies of existentialist thought.

The difference between these two can be illumined by using one of Bultmann's favorite examples, friendship. Someone may have devoted considerable intellectual effort to understanding the phenomenon of friendship. Such a person may have conducted extensive social-psychological research on patterns of friendship formation, written books and articles on the subject, and indeed be recognized as an expert on "friendship". However, a highly developed intellectual theory of friendship is quite different from the concrete experience of being befriended. For Bultmann, existentialist concepts are tools for thinking that are part of a very complex theoretical understanding of human existence. They are intellectual constructs, the results of disciplined reflection, and in that way are like a theory on friendship. In contrast, the experience of being befriended is an existential event. In my self-understanding, I may have formed a systematic mistrust of other people, viewing others primarily as potential threats to my own well being, and keeping them at some distance from myself. Then, in an unguarded moment, I found myself befriended. Such an event would impinge directly upon my understanding of self, others and world. I may know little about the theory of friendship formation, but I would know that my life was changed because now I had a friend and before I had none.

Bultmann uses this contrast between existential and existentialist to distinguish between "faith" and "theology". In faith, I confess that God has reached out to me in such a way as to change the way I understand the story of my life. In the light of that concrete moment, I find that my old understanding of myself is no longer adequate. For faith is as concrete and particular as the experience of friendship. Like friendship, faith presumes the initiative of another, in this case the "Wholly Other" God, and a change in my self-understanding. In this way, Bultmann consistently links faith with an existential decision of a particular person in a concrete situation. Faith cannot be understood as a body of true propositions to be believed.

Theology, in contrast, has the task of explicating the meaning of faith in a clear and coherent manner. For this purpose, theology needs an appropriate theoretical model, a conceptual scheme within which it can articulate its understanding of faith. In terms of our analogy, a public discussion of friendship requires more than the experience of being befriended; it also must be informed by the research and reflections of the specialist on "friendship". So it is with theology. Existentialist philosophy, like the specialist on friendship, has developed a complex and sophisticated understanding of its subject matter: in this case, human existence. While the naive reader of scripture has no need of existentialist concepts to hear the word of God, the theologian does need such a conceptuality in order to provide a scientific and disciplined understanding of faith.

The two essays in section three illustrate Bultmann's appropriation of existentialist concepts in two distinct stages: the first, "existential", and the second, "existentialist". The essay of 1925 is one of his earliest efforts to use existentialist philosophy in the service of theological exegesis, or explicating the meaning of biblical texts. His use of existentialism in this early essay is cautious and limited. He does not advocate the systematic use of an existentialist conceptuality, but addresses himself instead to the concrete self-understanding of the interpreter. In what frame of mind should one approach the task of explicating a text of scripture? With what expectations? What other life experiences are most like, and most unlike, interpreting a biblical text? For example, the biblical exegete should ask not only what did this text say or mean at the time it was written, but what does it mean, for me, now? Instead of assuming a posture of distance and control, the exegete should recognize the "problematic character of one's own existence". Instead of the impersonal, neutral relation of a natural scientist to an experiment, the exegete's relation to the subject matter of biblical texts is more like "an I to Thou, friend to friend, husband to wife, or father to child" (p. 134). In these personal relations, a genuine exchange occurs, one in which others make a claim upon us, we respond with our decisions, and through those decisions, become the persons that we are. So it is in the theological exegesis of biblical texts.

In later writings, Bultmann will increasingly come to repudiate the "existential", personalistic understanding of exegesis as proposed in the 1923 essay and summarized above. In the 1950 essay on hermeneutics (the science or principle of interpreting written texts), he admitted that he had not previously distinguished clearly between a scientific "existentialist" understanding of interpretation and a personal, "existential" exegesis (p. 338, note 32). In this later essay, he draws a sharp distinction between faith as an existential event and theology as a disciplined interpretation of faith, dependent upon existentialist concepts as tools of thought. This distinction is built into all his later writings. The exegesis of biblical texts which he proposes is one dependent upon the systematic use of existentialist concepts as the most appropriate, fitting or right concepts for the elucidation of faith.

To explicate Bultmann's judgment concerning existentialism as the most appropriate body of concepts or method of thinking for theology, it may be helpful to specify its inappropriate alternative. In choosing an existentialist conceptuality, what is Bultmann rejecting? What kind of thinking provides "inappropriate concepts" for interpreting biblical texts? Why does he judge one mode of thought to be more appropriate for theology than others?

Bultmann consistently identifies an objectifying conceptuality as the mode of thought inappropriate for theology. While natural science, especially mathematical physics, provided his primary model of an "objectifying" conceptuality, he extended this category far beyond the limits of the natural sciences. Psychology and history and a host of other human sciences are also "objectifying" modes of thought. Indeed, any mode of thought is objectifying which presupposes the subject-object dichotomy of post-Cartesian epistemology. When we imagine ourselves to be thinking subjects and the rest of reality around us to be a field of objects, with which we are not already connected, we are presuming an objectifying frame of reference.

Such a mode of thought has proven very useful, as the intellectual development of the modern West clearly indicates. It lends itself to problem-solving in many areas of human life. Why then should Bultmann be so suspicious of the use of this mode of thinking in theology? If it has worked well in the natural sciences, and contributed towards progress in the human sciences, why would it not prove equally useful in theology?

To answer this question we need to understand Bultmann's concept of objectifying in its philosophical origins. Bultmann inherited his understanding of objectifying thinking from his theological mentor, Wilhelm Herrmann.[13] It is rooted in a distinctive form of philosophical Idealism called Marburg Neo-Kantianism.[14] While we need not develop here the complexities of Neo-Kantianism, we do need to recognize its peculiar use of the term "objectifying". The word takes its origins from the verb, to objectify, because it designates the object-making activity of Reason. When Bultmann writes of an "objectifying" mode of thought, therefore, he does not refer to thinking that is oriented towards what is genuinely objective. Rather, he is speaking of a mental fabrication which provides a model for external reality, but which is not itself that reality. In light of this, it should be apparent why theology should not use an objectifying mode of thought to speak of God. For God is not our mental construct, but the One who is "Wholly Other" than we. To speak of God in concepts appropriate to a mere construct of Reason is to make God into an idol.

To answer this same question in terms more specific to Bultmann's theological development, an "objectifying" mode of thought is not appropriate to an eschatological faith. When I think in an objectifying way, I give a certain permanence to the objects of my thought, whether they are ideas or things, physical or spiritual. But eschatology apprehends God without any taint of permanence. God's word happens in a moment, an eschatological moment, which cannot be fitted into chron-

25

ological time. Similarly, God's action cannot be regarded as if it were one of the causal forces of this world; to do so is to deny the eschatological, other-worldly character of an act of God. Event, moment, act, encounter, decision; faith as a particular self-understanding manifest in behavior or action, but not as an item available for introspection: these are the characteristics of faith for an eschatological theology. No aspect of it belongs to an objectifying way of thinking. The presuppositions, concepts and methods of objectifying thought are thus alien to an eschatological faith, whereas an existentialist point of view and body of concepts are congruent with such a faith.

Later in this introduction, we shall have to pursue further developments in Bultmann's theological critique of objectifying. For example, objectifying reason has a prominent role in his view of modern culture; in that context he will argue that the source of all objectifying thinking is in our work and that the primary motive of work is to secure our future by our own efforts. Hence, objectifying thinking becomes tainted by its godless origins in work. Again, in Bultmann's proposal for demythologizing, we will once more be dealing with his criticism of any objectifying mode of thought. In good part, demythologizing simply means "deobjectifying", interpreting biblical speech of God consistently within the limits of an existentialist conceptuality so as to eliminate any objectifying thinking about God.[15] At this point, it is sufficient to recognize what he means by existentialist and objectifying conceptualities and why he chooses the one and rejects the other.

Having focused exclusively upon existentialist interpretation in this section, one important qualification is needed: Bultmann never claims that an existentialist interpretation can abandon historical methods of interpretation. In all his writings on exegesis, from the 1925 essay to his most mature publications, Bultmann consistently affirmed the necessity for a philologically based interpretation of documents in their own historical context. In 1925, he expressed the continuing role of historical considerations in theological exegesis as follows:

> The intent of such [existentialist] reflecton is not at all to dispose of all the old methods in favor of a new one, but only to ask how far the old methods can carry us in our concern for the reality of history (pp. 132-133).

In his 1950 essay, Bultmann identifies such an historical understanding of texts — that "all literary documents are historically conditioned by circumstances of time and place" — as a legacy of the Enlightenment (p. 139). To be sure, this principle of interpretation, when it became the sole principle for interpreting texts from the ancient world, ignored the subject matter of such documents, like their claim to speak of God or truth, and thus reduced all literature, philosophy and theology to the status of mere sources for the historical reconstruction of the past (p. 146). Bultmann sees his own work as a corrective of this "historicism", but he does not envision existentialist interpretation as rejecting these older rules of interpretation: "Beyond question, it [biblical interpretation] is subject first of all to the old hermeneutical rules of grammatical interpretation, formal analysis and explanation in terms of contemporary conditions" (p. 153). As will be apparent in reading Bultmann's actual interpretations of New Testament texts, he devotes considerable effort to understanding the subject matter in terms of its own historical context.

Finally, as in the prior readings, Bultmann's dialogue with Barth is very much evident in both of these essays on theological interpretation. Bultmann delivered the early essay in February 1925 as a lecture at Barth's University of Güttingen. Some of his language in this essay is more like Barth than at any other point of his career. In particular, he identifies his emerging existential understanding of exegesis with "objective" exegesis, a term Barth had used in his 1922 *Epistle to the Romans*. As previously described, when Bultmann uses any form of the word "objective" theologically, it has a pejorative meaning. His positive use of that term in 1925 is therefore strange and out of character. More typical is his critique of this way of speaking in his 1922 review of Barth:

> By wanting to use the talk about the "objective" to gain support for dogmas of old or new provenience, one makes faith into a work and God into an idol, and in truth, empties the objective of its character (p. 59).

Similarly, in both the 1924 essay on "Liberal Theology" and the 1925 essay on "Speaking of God", Bultmann described any speech of God as an "object" as both theologically confused and sinful. His use of "objective exegesis" in this 1925 essay is therefore an exception that reflects his particular affinity with Barth at this time.

In contrast, Barth appears in the 1950 essay only as an opponent with whom Bultmann must do battle. On the one hand, he defends himself against Barth's misunderstanding of existentialist interpretation as "statements about the inner life of a human being" (p. 156). On several prior occasions Bultmann had attempted to clarify this issue; for him, concrete human existence happens only through interaction with others and the environment. In Bultmann's view, Barth refused to understand him, just as he had consistently misunderstood their theological mentor, Wilhelm Herrmann. On the other hand, Bultmann attacks Barth's confused conceptuality in the latter's account of the resurrection of Jesus. What does it mean to claim that "stories . . . really happen [but are not]matters of historical fact?" (p. 156). In Bultmann's view, Barth brings to the interpretation of scripture a conceptuality still confused by the burden of an objectifying mode of thought, and the consequences appear as contradictions in his thought.[16]

KERYGMA: WORD OF GOD IN THE PROCLAMATION OF THE EARLY CHURCH*

Kerygma is a Greek word meaning proclamation. It originally signified the public announcement of a town crier or herald, such as calling out the names of victors in an Olympic game or issuing to citizens a summons to an official government assembly. In the New Testament, the word continues to designate a public proclamation, specifically, the preaching of the early church. The content of that message was the news of an eschatological salvation which God had initiated through the crucifixion and resurrection of Christ. However, the kerygma did not simply report the news of a salvation which had happened at some other time and place; instead, the kerygma was itself the means through which God's saving work was accomplished. Kerygma, then, means both the word of God, as expressed in the language of any time and place, and its specific historically conditioned formulation in the New Testament.

While earlier sections of this introduction have concentrated on historical and philosophical sources for Bultmann's theology, here we will be dealing with the most important theological source for his thought. Yet, as will soon be apparent, when we read Bultmann struggling with New Testament texts and their theological meaning, we find ourselves immersed, once again, in the historical and existentialist themes previously considered. For Bultmann's thought is an organic whole; while new elements can be identified as they are initially appropriated, in the actual doing of theology all of the elements come into play. Hence, in this discussion of Bultmann's understanding of the New Testament kerygma, we will focus first on the

* For texts, see below pp. 158-239.

impact of New Testament historical research and then, in examining his exegesis of Paul, turn to his existentialist understanding of human existence.

Bultmann's careful description of the religions of Hellenistic culture, to which the origins of the kerygma are closely bound, is continuous with his earlier work in the history-of-religions school. In *Primitive Christianity in its Contemporary Setting,* he specifies the characteristics of the religious movements contemporary with early Christianity and their common social-cultural context in the Hellenistic world. While this book was not published until 1949, its contents represent historical research on Hellenistic religions which occupied Bultmann throughout the 1920s.[17] In *Primitive Christianity in its Contemporary Setting* of 1949 and later works of the fifties, Bultmann still thinks and writes as the former student of Heitmüller, the avid reader of Reitzenstein and Bousset. His understanding of the historically conditioned form of the kerygma continues to reflect his indebtedness to the history of religions school (*Religionsgeschichtliche Schule*).

The importance of these historical readings for our understanding of Bultmann's theology cannot be overestimated. For Bultmann, it is a fundamental theological principle that God's word or revelation never appears in a pure or direct form. We can know such a word or revelation only through the mediation of human language, and that language, in turn, is always shaped by the thought forms and imagery of a particular culture. In reflecting upon those written forms of human speech, which are purported to be also the word of God, theology must pay careful attention to the existential conditions and cultural forms of expression dominant in their culture of origins. For purposes of understanding the kerygma, this has three very particular consequences.

First, all of the religions of the Hellenistic era — for example, Apocalyptic Judaism, Astral Worship, Mystery Cults, Gnosticism and Christianity — shared in common a particular form of thought which was as prominent in that culture as scientific thinking is in our own: namely, a mythological form of thought. In differing ways these several religions told how angels traveled down from heaven or demons up from hell to meet at the middle level of the earth, and there engage in cosmic battles. Such stories of the supernatural were sufficiently consistent with the thought-world of the first two centuries to be credible for the members of the religious movements noted above. Christianity was not unique in framing its story of redemption in such a mythological form; indeed, Bultmann spelled out in some detail the close parallels between the Gnostic story of the redeemer, who descended from the realm of God to reveal the way of salvation and then returned to the One from whom he came, and the Christian story of the Christ. In other writings, Bultmann focused upon the theological problem posed by these mythological forms of thought. For the moment, it is sufficient to note that the theological problem of mythology has its roots in Bultmann's historical studies of the origins of the kerygma.

Second, in *Primitive Christianity in its Contemporary Setting*, Bultmann not only describes the particularities of Hellenistic religions and their shared mythological form of thought but also depicts the existential situation of those who became the followers of these religious movements. In the first two centuries of the Common Era the Roman Empire was marked by sufficient political disorder and social disintegration to create a prevalent existential attitude of despair and hopelessness. People felt as if they were "helpless . . . a plaything of fate" and their world appeared as "a hostile, alien place (pp. 163-164). In such a situation, people looked to religions that offered some hope not contingent upon, or connected with, conditions in the real political-social order in which they lived. Perhaps they might align themselves with the power of the stars, the rulers of the heavens above, and probably also the earth below; at least, the stars were as good a choice as any amidst the continuing power struggles of Rome. Perhaps they might become Gnostics, knowers of hidden truth, especially the secret that their own true identity consisted essentially of a divine spark of light hidden deep within themselves. By following the way of the Gnostic heavenly redeemer, they might be saved from bondage to their body and this world, so that, at the end of their days, they would return to their true spiritual home, one with the One above. Perhaps they might become members of a mystery cult, whose secret rites of initiation promised an identification with one of the dying-rising gods. In these, and other ways, the religions of this period looked for a god who radically transcended this world, a god who was, in Bultmann's later language, "Wholly Other". There was "a close affinity between Christianity and Gnosticism . . . [in their depiction of] a great gulf between God and the world" (pp. 188,190). The existential attitude which Bultmann discerned in the Hellenistic era was not unlike the existential condition of humanity in his own time, as described by Martin Heidegger.[18]

Third, the similarities between Christianity and its contemporary religious movements did not extend to the theological core of the kerygma. That was the proclamation that God had chosen Jesus, who was crucified, as the one through whom humanity would be reconciled to himself. Like Paul, Bultmann claims the "scandalous fact of a crucified Lord" as the center of Christian proclamation (p. 197). The cross of Christ is central to the Christian story because it is, in Paul's words, such an "offense", such a "stumbling block" or "scandal". Gnosticism offered a sure escape route from the sufferings of this world; Christianity invited its believers to identify themselves with those who suffer, for in such persons they were one with their crucified Lord. The stars offered some hope of being a relatively secure center of power in the midst of a turbulent age; better to align oneself with any such centers of power than to have to confront one's own vulnerabilities in the story of Christ. For Bultmann, the self-understanding of Christian faith is as unique and different from the religions of its age as it is similar in its forms of expression. It does not appeal to our deepest wishes for a secure and happy life, to be won by our achievements and on our terms; rather, it judges such a self-understanding to be both an illusion, wholly unrealistic in its hope, and godless. Indeed, if left to ourselves, we would remain entrapped by the conspiracy of our own deepest wishes and the world's many temptations for power, all of which promise to give us what we long for.

Bultmann's 1930 essay on Paul expands upon this theology of the Cross. As in the earlier readings, Bultmann first locates Paul's thought in the context of Hellenistic culture, and only then goes on to explicate its distinctive Christian self-understanding. In this essay we hear the eschatological kerygma of the early church as interpreted consistently by the concepts of existentialism. Bultmann grants that Paul is sometimes confused in his own thought patterns. Occasionally, Paul writes as if God's saving deed were an objective event that happened in the lifetime of Jesus Christ, some sort of cosmic miracle. But most of the time, Paul understands God's saving deed to be accomplished through the preaching of the cross of Christ, not through some event of the past but through the preaching itself. For in the kerygma, as proclaimed, its hearers are confronted by the demand for a decision concerning their own self-understanding. Bultmann presents Paul's theology primarily in terms of the contrast between two existential possibilities: self-understanding as rooted in our natural inclinations; and self-understanding as given with the hearing of the kerygma in faith.

In "Man Prior to the Revelation of Faith", Bultmann portrays the beliefs towards which most people are, by instinct, disposed. Each of us

31

tends to believe that, if we try hard enough, we will be able, someday if not right away, to win a life secured against our known vulnerabilities. Sometimes, we feel as if we are on the right track, and we may regard others, doing less well in our eyes, from a superior vantage point, in a position of "boasting". Other times, God, or what we sometimes call the hard knocks of reality, intrudes upon our hard won gains, so that we lose our position of mastery and become ever more anxiously driven to regain what we have lost. In either case, we bet our futures on a particular belief: namely, that we are able to achieve our own authentic existence by a combination of our own powers and selected resources from the world around us. For Bultmann, as for Paul, the cost we pay for living according to these beliefs is too high. We become increasingly bound to our past, where our achievements lay, and closed to the always new future, which alone offers the possibility of authentic existence. We lose our freedom from others, and their significant institutional powers, as we make ourselves increasingly dependent upon them. In short, we become slaves to the transitory, to all that is dying, and ever more anxious about our own demise.

"Man under Faith" portrays the alternative self-understanding of faith. The beliefs about our self-sufficiency and future security are here exposed as both illusion and sin. In hearing the kerygma we find ourselves not only to be judged but enabled to accept that judgment, since God first accepts us. In Bultmann's language, "authentic existence" becomes, in faith, a real possibility just as for a person newly befriended, friendship becomes a real possibility. For, in faith, we have actually been freed from that oppressive and deceptive self-understanding which is so much a part of us that it sometimes seems to be all that we are. Faith, then, is not a new theoretical orientation, not a new set of beliefs about beings in the heavens above, but an actual enabling for a new pattern of living. Having come to question those beliefs given us by instinct, we trust ourselves instead to God's promise of new life in the message of the cross. In Paul's language, that new life is lived according to the Spirit, that is, out of a source of life which transcends the limits of our customary self-definition. At the core of this new life is its freedom: not the freedom to indulge our passions, not the freedom to oppress others, but freedom from our past and its burden of wrongs, freedom from anxious concern for the future and its terror of death, and freedom for others in relations of love.

The kerygma which makes such a new life possible cannot be confined to any sacred formulae from the past. Bultmann makes clear the open linguistic future of the kerygma in his brief essay, "The Relation between Theology and Proclamation". Even the most central and simple confession from the New Testament — that Jesus is Lord — cannot be taken as an adequate expression of the kerygma for all time. For the kerygma becomes God's liberating word only when it is *heard* as such, only when it confronts people, in the language of their situation, with the demand for a decision. The language of the kerygma can never be fixed, because its message is never complete; it is always being extended to new persons, and hence its language will always reflect the changing contexts of the people who hear it. Bultmann did not simply repeat the words of Paul, nor does this introduction simply repeat the words of Bultmann. Rather, to understand Bultmann is to think theologically with him, and that will always entail the use of a language closer to one's own concrete situation than Bultmann's language ever could be.

MODERNITY AND FAITH IN CONFLICT: SCIENTIFIC WORLD VIEW[19] AND THE SELF-UNDERSTANDING OF WORK*

In his theology, Bultmann speaks frequently of "modern man" or "modern culture". For him, modernity was not an accidental condition of our present, but defined the historical situation in which the church carried out its ministry. Theology, therefore, had to be clear in its understanding of modernity if it was to interpret the kerygma in the "modern" present so that its claim could be heard.

Fundamentally, Bultmann perceived faith and modernity to be in conflict with each other. Their opposition is not simply an expression of God's "Otherness", which would entail faith's conflict with any culture, modern or otherwise. Rather, considered by itself, modernity has certain specific characteristics which contribute to its opposition to faith. Two quite different expressions of modernity need to be distinguished.

First, modernity means modern culture, and that for Bultmann is a culture determined primarily by scientific thought. In our daily life we tend to take for granted a scientific world view. Obviously, human culture has not always been dominated by science; Bultmann sees this to be a specific characteristic of modern culture, one which creates certain

---

* For texts, see below pp. 240-287.

tensions with Christian faith. For the culture in which the Christian kerygma had its origins was not scientific, but mythological. Somehow, the difference between the scientific world view of modern culture and the mythological world view of the Christian kerygma has to be addressed.

Second, modernity also entails a particular self-understanding. While Bultmann would not describe it this way, in retrospect we can specify this self-understanding as characteristic of the middle-class. From a middle-class point of view, each person has responsibility for his or her own future. According to the mythos of the middle-class, society provides no barriers to the individual. Each person, no matter how humble his or her origins, can attain the highest position in government or business or education. If we do not succeed in our efforts to improve ourselves and secure our future, the assumption is that, individually, we have been at fault. If we would have tried harder, if we would only have applied ourselves more diligently, we would not have experienced failure.

Today we can recognize this self-understanding as class specific, and not a universal condition of humanity. To be sure, the anxious self-concern at the root of this self-understanding is not peculiar to the middle-class. However, the belief that one's own work will provide the means to meet the needs of self-concern is distinctive to the middle-class. The poor are not likely to be seduced by a promise of future security conditional upon their individual effort. They are more likely to recognize the origins of their condition in larger social structures and so perceive a better future (but hardly a secure one) as a result of collective efforts. Similarly, members of the aristocracy, insofar as they still exist, do not perceive their future as dependent upon their individual labor. Modern society, however, has been marked by an enormous expansion of the middle-class with the result that its self-understanding has become dominant, as characteristic of modernity as a scientific world view.

This middle-class self-understanding presumes a gross simplification and distortion of social reality. Regardless of our class-specific beliefs, we also know, from sociological studies, that the individual is not the sole agent in determining his or her destiny. The results of our work efforts are always conditioned by the particular social constraints of the society into which we were born. Many people today, regardless of class origins, would also recognize that their fulfillment as human beings depends more upon the quality of their relations with others than upon their work efforts. But we now live at a later moment of history, when the promise of the middle-class work ethos is as likely to evoke suspicion as belief. We can recognize the particularity of its class origins and its unrealistic hope.

At the time of Bultmann's writings, however, this middle-class self-understanding was sufficiently prevalent, and uncritically accepted, to become an object of concern in his theology. In his view, the belief that individuals could, by their own work efforts, determine their future security and fulfillment was destructive for individuals and dangerous for society as a whole. He therefore consistently sought to expose its illusory promise. Since modernity means both scientific world view and middle-class self-understanding, the nature of its conflict with faith needs to be described in each of these two quite different aspects.

Some preliminary clarification of "scientific world view" is required before addressing the issue posed by faith's relation to modern culture.

For Bultmann, a *Weltbild* (world view, picture of the world, or conception of the world) is a sense of order in the environment which people presuppose as they go about their daily tasks. Such a world view may be more or less conscious; in any case, it shows itself primarily in behavior. In one of Bultmann's well known examples, "using electric lights", "listening to the radio" or "going to a doctor when ill" are behaviors which presuppose the scientific world view of modern culture.[20] All people, in every period of history, have employed some world view in relating to their environs. Furthermore, none of us has a choice in selecting our world view; "it is given in our existence in the world" (p. 257). In terms of sociology, world views are a social construct, handed on to us by the particular societies into which we are born. In Bultmann's words, "No one can adopt a world view by his own volition — it is already determined for him by his place in history".[21]

By "scientific", Bultmann does not refer to either the theoretical constructs of science or the most recent results of laboratory experiments. Like "world view", "scientific" is used in the sense of a popular construct available for all participants of modern culture, not a few among the scientific elite. In this usage scientific has at least two meanings for Bultmann. First, a "scientific" world view is one in which any sequence of events, in nature or history, is understood to be determined by laws of cause-effect relations. Events do not happen randomly, according to this world view; rather, every event has a cause which can be stipulated, even if not known, because of the "universal validity of natural law" ("Wonder", p. 258). Second, a "scientific" world view understands all events to be interconnected in a single system of cause-effect relations.

The world is a unity, a closed system of cause-effect relations.[22] The unity of natural law does not allow for the introduction of causal agencies which are themselves not a part of the world as a whole. These are the two characteristics of the modern world view which defines it as scientific for Bultmann.

The Christian kerygma did not have its origins in a scientific world view. On the contrary, the kerygma was a product of the "mythological world view" of the Hellenistic era. Bultmann first began describing the contradiction between the mythological thought form of the kerygma and its expression in modern culture in 1930.[23] In contrast with the closed causal nexus of the modern world view, the kerygma presupposes a three-story universe in which some events may be explained by natural and historical causes of this world, while others seem to be the result of supernatural causes from heaven above or hell below.[24] Miracles, that is, acts of God which intrude into the otherwise closed web of the laws of nature, are a prime example of such mythological thinking. In his essay "The Question of Wonder", Bultmann affirms the category of "wonder" as an appropriate expression for an act of God, while rejecting its mythological counterpart, "miracle".

Later, we shall examine Bultmann's proposal to "demythologize" the New Testament. In part, this is Bultmann's resolution for the conflict of world views, modern and mythological. Bultmann argues that the mythological way of thinking, shared by New Testament authors with others of the Hellenistic era, is not distinctive to Christian faith, and hence need not be preserved in the modern period. No one should be obliged to believe in the mythological world view of the kerygma, or the specific stories that depend upon that world view. Indeed, because none of us can select the world view through which we perceive our environment and carry out our daily tasks, it is dishonest to ask people from the modern era to think in a mythological way. The fact that some people may be "superstitious", that is, think in terms of a mythological world view while living in the culture of a scientific world view, does not in any way alter Bultmann's contention. In our culture as a whole, the mythological way of thinking has been replaced by a scientific way of thinking and that is the only issue of concern.

In Bultmann's view the conflict between faith and modernity in their world views is not a substantive one. Faith, as a particular self-understanding, is no more bound to the mythological world view of Hellenistic culture than it is bound to the scientific world view of modern culture. World views are irrelevant for the actuality of faith. However, people who live in the modern era can be so put off by the obsolete world view of the kerygma that they never have a chance to hear its real claim, that is, its call for a decision in their own self-understanding. Hence, Bultmann advocates abandoning the mythological world view in which the kerygma first found expression. His proposal for demythologizing means, in part, stripping away its pre-scientific world view. Without such a correction in the language of the kerygma, modern people will be so distracted by the conflict of world views that they will never hear the word of God, only the strange and confusing beliefs of a pre-scientific culture.

While the faith-modernity conflict is almost irrelevant at the point of competing world views, at the point of self-understanding the conflict becomes decisive. The self-understanding of faith and the self-understanding of work are the combatants in the religious drama depicted in Bultmann's theology. In the readings of this section Bultmann devotes considerable attention to clarifying the characteristics of work, its roots in anxious self-concern and its expression in the scientific world view.

Before summarizing Bultmann's discussion of work, we must note that it is strongly biased in one direction. Almost always, work is described in pejorative terms. First, work is identified with the quest for knowledge and control, with the result that work is always manipulative in its purpose. In working, we presuppose that the whole of the world is amenable to our control (p. 253). Second, the motive for working in the present is a future goal of security; work, for Bultmann, seems to offer no intrinsic satisfaction in the present. Third, the driving power behind work is the anxious care which Heidegger identified as the core of human existence. Regardless of what our work might contribute to others, we ultimately work for our own individual good. Fourth, in the self-understanding of the work-world, we are most of all sinful and godless. Instead of trusting our future to serendipitous encounters with God, we seek, through work, to win that future for ourselves and on our own terms.

Bultmann develops these themes in his 1936 sermon on Matthew 6:25-33 ("do not be anxious"), his 1933 essay, "The Question of Wonder", and his 1931 essay, "The Crisis of Faith". The sermon illustrates the power of his synthetic imagination. Its message is simple, developed in continuing dialogue with the biblical text, and addressed to a congregation of believers, not an assembly of scholars. Yet, in this context, Bultmann weaves together Heidegger's philosophical understanding of human existence with middle-class perceptions of work, as both a means "to provide for our future" and a potential threat to our present, the "anxious consuming care" which would "become masters of our lives". In the essay on wonder, Bultmann links the scientific world view with the controlling intention of work. Wilhelm Herrmann had already pointed out how the scientific world view of modernity was rooted in our work-world: "The mere resolve to work includes the notion that the things on which we work will in their origin and activity obey laws which our thinking can comprehend" (p. 257). In Bultmann's own terms: "a working world in which we take for granted the regularity and the conformity to law of all that happens" (p. 263). The scientific world view, then, has its origins not in anything as recent as the modern laboratory, but in the most primitive and simple activity of working.

The self-understanding of faith, as previously described in Paul and in the essays of this section, always emerges in a relation of struggle with the self-understanding of work. In faith one acknowledges that one's own powers are limited and the future insecure. In faith one recognizes one's own vulnerabilities and limits, especially the limits set by other persons. In faith one finds the presumption to live according to one's own powers to be judged as godless, and exposed as an illusion. In faith one perceives anew the world process as a whole, not simply as an ordered chain of events (the scientific world view), but as an arena in which God acts. For this reason Bultmann describes "The Crisis of Faith" as constant; for the self-understanding of faith will always be in struggle with the self-will enshrined in work. To be sure, the dominant cultural role of science in the modern world can exacerbate the crisis of faith:

> The crisis of faith which is produced by natural science is only one form of the crisis in which faith as such always and everywhere stands, admittedly a form characteristic of a particular age. Hidden by the claim of natural science is actually the human claim to exist by oneself and to understand and shape one's life in terms of what one can control, what by thought and by application one can master, or intends to master. Faith in God, and not only Christian faith, demands abandonment of this claim and acknowledgment of the enigmatic powers which in reality shape life (p. 253).

Fundamentally, however, faith always arises in conflict with the self-understanding of work. Because that self-understanding has acquired a new prominence through its alliance with science in modernity, the existential issue may be more clear, but is still the same: How do I understand my future — as an unknown gift from God or as something earned by my own work?

In looking back at Bultmann's theological legacy, it seems appropriate to note that his understanding of work was shaped by a particular social class and historical context; it is not a universal or necessary condition of human life. However, that observation does not undermine Bultmann's focus on the self-understanding of work in the early decades of this century. As Bultmann always reminded us, God does not address humanity in general; his word always speaks to persons in their concrete existence. Reading Bultmann today, it is apparent that the middle-class work ethos and its corresponding self-understanding did, in fact, exercise extraordinary power on the lives of people in his social context. Furthermore, for many who read Bultmann today, that will be as true for their situation as it was for his. Insofar as we understand any theological issue from the past to be rooted in the social and cultural particularities of that time, we do not in any way diminish its existential significance. However, we do need to correct universal claims that only reflect the particularities of past social and cultural conditions. Otherwise we may fail to hear the word of God when we are confronted with decisions other than one involving our relationship to our work. By recognizing that Bultmann's struggle was not universal for all people at all times, we may become freed from past preoccupations to deal with existential struggles as decisive for our time as Bultmann's was for him.

DEMYTHOLOGIZING:
CONTROVERSIAL SLOGAN AND NEW FOCUS FOR
EXISTENTIALIST THEOLOGY*

Bultmann first proposed his project for demythologizing the New Testament in a 1941 lecture (published that same year as an essay), "New Testament and Mythology".[25] While the essay provoked an immediate controversy within Germany, even during some of the most devastating conditions of World War II, it was not generally known in the wider world until its 1948 publication in *Kerygma und Mythos*.[26] For the next fifteen years the subject of demythologizing stirred up a continuing controversy in the theological literature of several languages as

---

* For texts, see below pp. 288-328.

well as in the life of the church in both Germany and the United States.[27] In both countries, "heresy trials" and other church disciplinary actions were initiated by ecclesiastical authorities against clergy who were using Bultmann's theology in their preaching. Demythologizing was one theological proposal which did not pass unnoticed.

As indicated in prior sections of this introduction, demythologizing is new to Bultmann's theology only as a word. To be sure, it becomes a powerful word knitting together several themes developed separately in his earlier work. Its synthetic character as a concept consisting of several disparate elements becomes apparent through an analysis of the root concept of "mythology". The "de" only indicates removal, cutting off. The significant question is this: what is included in the "mythology" that is being cut off from the Christian kerygma?

First we need to remember that Bultmann's use of mythology grows out of his history-of-religions research from the 1920s. Early in *Jesus Christ and Mythology,* he writes:

It is evident that such conceptions [apocalyptic pictures of the end] are mythological, for they were widespread in the mythologies of the Jews and Gentiles, and then were transferred to the historical person of Jesus. Particularly the concept of the pre-existent Son of God who descended in human guise into the world to redeem mankind is part of the Gnostic doctrine of redemption, and nobody hesitates to call this doctrine mythological (p. 292).

Since the kerygma recounts the same sorts of stories, set in the same world view as these other religions, why should anyone be surprised to learn that Christianity was also mythological in its origins?

However, Bultmann's early historical research will not clarify his later concept of mythology. It establishes the similarities of early Christianity with the mythologies of other religious movements of that time, but does not specify what is being removed in demythologizing. Only later does Bultmann answer this question, and then in two distinct parts.

In the first place, Bultmann's concept of mythology designates a particular way of thinking about the world. Mythology offers pseudo-scientific explanations concerning the causes of worldly events, and in this way shares a purpose similar to that of science. But mythological thinking about the world is not subject to the discipline of rationality, with its laws governing a unified cause-effect nexus. Hence, mythology has become obsolete. The mythological world view has been replaced by a scientific one. To demythologize the kerygma, with this meaning of mythology, is to strip away its pre-scientific world view.

In the second place, Bultmann's concept of mythology also designates a particular way of thinking about God. Mythology employs objectifying concepts and images to understand that which is beyond the world, God. For example, mythology speaks of God in terms of space (heaven above) or time (the imminent future end of the world). Such categories as space and time are essential for our knowledge of the world, but can only distort the reality of God and faith. Existentialist interpretation, as described in prior sections, provides Bultmann with an alternative way of thinking about God. In this instance, demythologizing means simply "de-objectifying" or thinking of God in terms of existentialist concepts.

The synthetic character of Bultmann's concept, its union of two distinct issues of world view and of God-understanding, becomes apparent in those uses of the term which embrace only one or the other of these two meanings. For example, when Bultmann cites evidence for demythologizing in Paul and John, within the New Testament itself, he clearly does not intend to claim that either of them has abandoned the mythological world view. Rather, Bultmann sees both Paul and John as clarifying Christian proclamation, by turning away from any focus upon an objectified cosmic event in the future to the proclamation of the kerygma in the present. In differing ways, each has "de-objectified" a prior understanding of faith and God, but neither has a scientific world view. In a similar way, Bultmann will give examples from the eighteenth and nineteenth century of thinkers who have demythologized the Christian message by repudiating its pre-scientific world view, but they, however, have not gone on to a "de-objectified" (or existentialist) interpretation of faith. Usually, Bultmann's use of mythology embraces both meanings: a pre-scientific world explanation and an objectified understanding of God. But sometimes it is restricted to the one or the other, as is apparent by the context of its usage.

In *Jesus Christ and Mythology*, Bultmann goes out of his way to help his readers avoid confusion in understanding his proposal. For example, demythologizing does not mean the elimination of every mythological story from the New Testament. Bultmann does not intend to rewrite the kerygma so that it would be free from any taint of mythology. Rather, demythologizing is a method of interpretation. It is one step in an existentialist interpretation, the necessary critical judgment which dismisses both a pre-scientific view of the world and an objectifying understanding of God. But this moment of negation exists only for the sake of existentialist interpretation, so that the claim of the kerygma upon the self-understanding of modern people can be heard. Bultmann clearly intends to keep the stories of the New Testament for their meaning, without being tied to a mythological world view or understanding of God.

In concluding this introduction, I would especially call your attention to the beginning and the ending of *Jesus Christ and Mythology*. In the first few pages Bultmann writes about Johannes Weiss, his discovery of New Testament eschatology, and the theological problem which this posed for Christian faith. At the end of the book he reminds us that demythologizing stands in the tradition of justification by faith. Just as Luther sought to eliminate any tangible, visible merits or works which one could claim as an aid for faith, so demythologizing is clearing away all false props for faith, whether historical evidence for Jesus, rational foundations for faith, or miracles. Faith only has the word of God to which it can cling, and that word always appears only in the form of human language with all its ambiguities. Bracketed between Weiss' eschatology and Luther's justification by faith is set the whole argument for demythologizing.

Without wanting to simplify a complex story, this, in fact, is how it all came out. Demythologizing did provide the single theological focus which brought together in one proposal the multiple strands of Bultmann's theology. In the beginning, his early essays of the 1920s, his thought developed in response to the problem of New Testament eschatology and the Lutheran theological heritage of Wilhelm Herrmann. In the end, the book which knits together the multiple strands of almost thirty years of theological development still rests upon the same two pillars: New Testament eschatology and Herrmann's interpretation of Luther. While some might dismiss demythologizing as only a controversial slogan, others have found in this one proposal that single focus which Bultmann's theology, until that time, had been lacking.

At their best, introductions are rough guides, maps to the minds of others: in this case, a map for the mind of a major theologian of the twentieth century. An introduction like this one may fill in some of the edges of issues with which a theologian is grappling; it may help a reader find his or her way through some of the more difficult points; it may call attention to some of the deepest continuities in a long life of theological reflection. However, no introduction can ever be a substitute for encountering an original mind of the stature of Bultmann. Through reading his texts you can develop your own understanding of the formation of his theology; by pondering over his texts you can learn to think theologically with Bultmann, as well as about Bultmann. At this point, I can only recommend him highly to you. He is one from whom I have learned a great deal.

SELECTED TEXTS

1

GOD AS "WHOLLY OTHER"*

"CONCERNING THE HIDDEN AND REVEALED GOD"

The first selection in this volume is not an academic essay or research article, but a sermon. Bultmann preached this sermon on Pentecost Sunday 1917 and it was published that same year in the liberal Protestant journal Die Christliche Welt. *One of his earliest publications, it reminds us that Bultmann was, first of all, a theologian of the church. In this sermon, more than in most of his later writings, we sense the impact of World War I in destroying an older piety, which blended together God and the best of human endeavor in a happy, hopeful harmony. In this early sermon, before Bultmann had entered into the orbit of either Karl Barth or Martin Heidegger, we also discern distinctive patterns of his theology which will remain constant: God as "Wholly Other", the limits of human powers and the insecurity which constitutes the normal condition of human life. Schubert Ogden has translated this sermon which first appeared in English in his 1960 volume of Bultmann essays titled* Existence and Faith.

"What no eye has seen, nor ear heard, nor the heart of man conceived, what God has prepared for those who love him", God has revealed to us through the Spirit. For the Spirit searches everything, even the depths of God. For what person knows a man's thoughts except the spirit of the man that is in him? So also no one comprehends the thoughts of God except the Spirit of God. But we have not received the spirit of the world but rather the Spirit that comes from God, that we might know what God has given us in grace. (1 Cor. 2:9 ff.)

If I am to celebrate Pentecost this year, then there are two pictures that hover before my eyes and refuse to be suppressed. What the one presents is something that now lies many years in the past — the Pentecost that I once celebrated as a child in my home in the country. Spring-green birch boughs bedecked the house and filled it with their sweet, sharp fragrance, while yet others adorned the door, there to be played

---

* See also pp. 18-21.

44

upon by the light of the sun. Both household and village were clothed in bright festal garments and marched to the church when the bells exultantly sounded across the countryside. Over the whole day lay the brilliant light of the sun and the happy sound of the bells; and Pentecost was a festival of joy.

The other picture is of Pentecost just a year ago. On that day I stood in a military hospital in the midst of the wounded and could hardly bring myself to say that Pentecost should be a festival of joy. Pain and misery stared at me out of large, questioning eyes, and the spirits of strife and alarm, of blood and terror, hovered oppressively through the room. And my thoughts went out to those who still stood outside in the peril of battle and to those others for whom the boughs of spring have no fragrance and the rays of the sun cast no light.

These are the two pictures, the two inimical pictures, that refuse to be suppressed, though each would deny the other and suppress it. They are antagonistic pictures that both demand their rights and fill one's heart with pain.

I

And yet, this antagonism is really none other than the one that all of us now experience — and indeed fearfully experience, insofar as we have lived through the peacetime that is past with vigor and longing, excitement and joy, and now likewise experience wartime with the whole might of our heart — the heart that would let itself be permeated, filled, and sated by all the powers of ringing, roaring life. It is just then that we suddenly stop because we are filled with awe. We sense the frightful contrast of forces and powers that we call "life" and no longer know whether we should receive them into ourselves or whether we must rather close ourselves against them. Indeed, we become strangers to ourselves when we sense what inimical forces and currents we can receive into our lives. What is it that is still our self, our nature, when once it could enjoy itself gladly and unabashedly in the feeling that it was sustained by a power of serenity and goodness that controls the world? When we could and wanted to let ourselves be moved by a current that seemed to flow in harmony and life-emitting rhythm? Whereas now we look into powers of life which are cruel and harsh, which sometimes command and make demands on us with brassy voices, only at other times to stand dumb in pitiless silence, full of riddles and mystery! If this that we see now is the nature of life, then was what went before an illusion? Or is it that we at least did not understand

45

it so then and must now pass judgment against ourselves, must stifle whatever of the past is still alive in us and still constitutes a part of our self?

Yes, how many shadows have fallen over our past! How unreal so many of its hours now seem! Were there such hours once, hours of care-free joy with our friends who, having died the deaths of heroes, now rest in their graves? Those hours of pure, unalloyed joy in work and crea-tion, of devotion to the precious powers of spiritual life, of pure enjoy-ment in the ripe fruits of human creativity? Hours the worth and certainty of which now threaten to disappear? I do not speak of the hours of which we must be ashamed, though there were those hours also — hours of thoughtlessness and wasted time, hours that were petty and deplorable. They, too, lie behind us and ought to be behind us. With respect to them, we rightly sense that they have become strange to us, that we ought to have become more mature and serious. However, what now fills us with pain is that we have received into our inner lives powers of life that now belong to our present existence, that have rights in us that we cannot deny but must affirm — but that we still have not found the way to bring them into harmony, to view them in unity with the newer powers of life which have entered our lives with brutal force and have also demanded their rights, which we likewise must affirm. For here also I do not mean the powers of illusion, delusion, and falsehood. These are powers whose rights we deny, which we disavow by inwardly overcoming them in ourselves and working for their outward over-coming as well. Rather I mean the painfully great powers, the woefully oppressive and dreadfully humiliating powers, that demand recog-nition — like the thoughts of sacrificing everything precious and worthy of love, of tearing oneself away from a world full of light and warmth, which was our world, the steeling and stretching of oneself beyond the limits of human powers, the facing of a silent world in which pain and sorrow demand their due.

This split is not really a split between the past and the present, but rather runs through our lives here and now. For, as I have said, the old powers of life are still present in us — indeed, are alive in us not only as the background of our self, which has become second nature, or simply because they are present in memory, but also — and the longer the war lasts the more so — as actually making themselves felt in our present thinking and working. In fact, we have hours in which they alone rule and we can forget the others. But then come the hours of awakening in which this all once again becomes strange to us. We no longer under-

46

stand ourselves, and become strangers to ourselves. For we gaze into the abyss of our nature, and our self appears as a play of strange powers. We gaze into the abyss of life, and its opposing powers are incomprehensible to us. We look down into a depth of which we never dreamed.

And at this point we hear the strange word of Paul concerning the depths of God. The depths of God! We too gaze into a depth and are seized with horror. Do we want to say then that we gaze into the depths of God? Indeed, what is God, if not the infinite fullness of all the powers of life that rage around us and take our breath away, filling us with awe and wonder? What are these powers of life that sustain us and carry us away, that blend us together and separate us, that tear us apart and weld us together, if not the powers of the infinite God, who is full of creative might and joy, of endless forms and riddles? But do we dare to say this? There is also a word in the New Testament about those who say they have known the depths of Satan. And what about us? What kind of a depth are we looking into? Is it really the depth of the forces of *life*, of the forces of *God*? Or is it rather an abyss of *death*, a grappling of devilish powers that we see? Is it really the play of satanic forces that envelops our little, vain, fanciful self and mocks at it? Or is it the sway and movement of the great and infinitely creative power of God?

This is the question that gives us pain. And we will have neither rest nor security till we know that the powers really are forces of life and of God — till we not only see a confused and senseless strife of powers, but also hear in all of the enigmatic and abysmal darkness the sound of one great and deep tone, which hovers everywhere, giving to everything rest and security, and blending it all into one mighty harmony.

It frequently happens that in listening to a piece of music we at first do not hear the deep, fundamental tone, the sure stride of the melody, on which everything else is built, because we are deafened by the fullness of detail, the veritable sea of sounds and impressions which overwhelms us. It is only after we have accustomed our ear that we find law and order, and as with *one* magical stroke, a single unified world emerges from the confused welter of sounds. And when this happens, we suddenly realize with delight and amazement that the fundamental tone was also resounding before, that all along the melody had been giving order and unity. Could it be, then, that here, too, we need only accustom our eye and ear in order to see the harmony and to hear the great and mighty note of unity — to see *God* in this confusion of forces?

II

If we want to see God, then the first thing we should say to ourselves is that we may not see him as we have conceived him. We must remind ourselves that he may appear to be wholly other than the picture we have made of him; and we must be prepàred to accept his visage even if it terrifies us. Can we not see him in the present? Has our old picture of him fallen to pieces? If so, then we must first of all be grateful that we have lost our false conception; for the only way we can see him is as he actually is.

But were we not certain before that we had him and were experiencing him? Did he not so lay hold upon our heart that it trembled and rejoiced? None of us, of course, may dispute this. But what we nevertheless do see now is that we pictured him too small. He is greater; he is infinite. And if he at one time showed himself to us, i.e., allowed us to see a part of his infinite nature, he has also provided that we can never become complacent about this and imagine that we have known him completely. New sides of his infinity constantly emerge, strange and enigmatic; and as he himself is infinite, so also must our knowledge of him be infinite — never static and at rest, but constantly ready to yield anew, to allow itself to be raised anew.

And should it seem strange to us when we look into the depths, when we stand before riddle and mystery, as though God could not be found there? No! God *must* be a hidden and mysterious God, full of contradictions and riddles. Otherwise our inner life would become static, and we would lose the power to obtain experience from life's fullness. For what does "experience" mean? It means constantly to enrich oneself anew, to allow oneself to be given something anew. It means to perceive that miraculous forces hold sway in the world, which we cannot reckon with, cannot enlist as mere factors in our work. It means to know that over and above our knowledge, our work, yes, and even our moral duty, there is something else — a fullness of life that streams in upon us completely as a gift, completely as grace. Experience means to receive a destiny into oneself. Not simply to endure a destiny, like the grain of sand with which the wind and the waves play, or like the coin that wanders from hand to hand — both of which, to be sure, endure a destiny, but always without being influenced in their inmost being by any of the forces that drive them. Experience means to make your destiny truly your own. And this means always to be open for what is given to us, always to be ready to experience miracles. Not the miracles

48

in which an earlier age had its joy — miracles opposed to nature and to understanding — but rather the miracles of life, the miracles of destiny. To want to have experience means to be ready to take miracle and mystery into oneself — or, to express it somewhat differently, *it means to have reverence and humility in the presence of life.* For only when we approach life reverently and humbly can we hear God's voice in all its roar.

God has to be hidden and mysterious if we are to approach him in humility and reverence. Indeed, this is so even among men. We often feel with pain that we are mysteries to one another. "For there is no bridge that leads from man to man." And yet, when we rightly reflect on it, there is something precious in our being mysterious to ourselves, in our never being completely known to one another, in our being unable ever to see through even the person who is closest to our heart and to reckon with him as though he were a logical proposition or a problem in accounting. For if we were thus able to reckon with him, he would seem flat and empty to us and we would no longer be able to lavish our heart on him. Indeed, we want precisely from the person we love most that his riches be inexhaustible and that they bring forth every day some new miracle. We rejoice in hiddenness and mystery because it is a promise to us of the wonderful and undreamed-of powers that slumber in the heart of the other, awaiting only our readiness for their revelation. And this it is that throws across the bridge from one man to another — the acknowledgment of hiddenness and mystery, humility and reverence in the presence of the other's uniqueness, divine trust in the miracles that richly and ever more richly well up out of his inmost being, blessing and overwhelming us with grace.

And so God also has to be hidden and mysterious so that we may approach him in humility and reverence. But then he is also infinitely filled with contradictions and terrors. Scarcely is he known than he again disappears; and we once more stand in the presence of the unknown God, with whom we must wrestle anew till he gives himself to be known and speaks his name.

> I would know thee, thou Unknown One,
> Who dost lay hold of my soul in its depths,
> Moving through my life like a storm,
> Incomprehensible, and yet kin to me!
> I would know thee, and even serve thee![1]

God has to be hidden and mysterious, a God filled with contradictions; for what unfolds itself within such contradictions is the riches of an infinite creativity. And if we gaze down into undreamed-of depths and the contradictions of life threaten to break our hearts, we will still give thanks in humility and reverence that nothing has been spared us; and this we will do even now in this time of terror.

> Thou art a thicket of contradictions.
> I may rock thee like a child,
> And yet thy curses are accomplished,
> Which are frightful among the peoples.[2]

To be sure, it is wanton and shameful to proceed from some fixed concept of God and hastily locate the war and its suffering in the divine plan for the world, looking upon it as judgment and punishment and on this basis erecting sermons calling men to repentance. But it is just as wanton and undignified to say that God is not present in this war and its horrors. No, there is yet a far more profound view than the standpoint of the preacher of repentance who so quickly sees through God's intentions in ruling the world. This view has its beginning in humility and reverence. It knows that we will always see God as wholly other than we thought him to be. It expects of man the faith that, even with the most frightful destiny, God believes man capable of something grand and wants to make him completely free and noble. To be sure, it is our duty, the duty of mankind, to see to it that nothing as horrible as this war ever again falls over the earth. And yet, if the age of perpetual peace would come, would we not have to give thanks to God that our generation, that we, were permitted to experience this violence, which laid upon humanity such a burden as was never laid on it before? And would we not desire that no future generation ever forget what has been possible on earth? For never before has God expected something so grand from the race of men; never before have we experienced that everything became so strange to us and we stood in God's presence naked and alone; never before have we been so permitted to gaze into the depths of God!

III

But always we speak of the depths of *God!* May we do this? Is it *only* the depths, *only* hiddenness and mystery that constitute his being? Is there not always the temptation, then, that these depths are an abyss of death, that this riddle is the cunning of Satan? Indeed, mystery is *not* all there is to God; nor do we call that voice the voice of piety that is intoxicated with the terrible and the mysterious, that revels in the twilight zone of contradictions and in the motley of the enigmatic. That would be mere playing — indeed, would be sin. It would be the exact opposite of the humility and reverence that are the substance of piety. No, riddle and mystery lose their meaning if they are not loved for the sake of what lies behind them, if they do not awaken in us the presentiment of a rich and inexhaustible solution, if we are not brought to want a revelation and indeed to long for it with all our hearts. What makes riddle and mystery divine to us is precisely that we want an infinite revelation of God. And it is only because this revelation is *God's* revelation, is infinite, that it has to lead through riddle and mystery.

God the mysterious and hidden must at the same time be the God who is revealed. Not, of course, in a revelation that one can know, that could be grasped in words and propositions, that would be limited to formula and book and to space and time; but rather in a revelation that continually opens up new heights and depths and thus leads through darkness, from clarity to clarity.

The God who is revealed! One thing we must know, that through all the riddle and mystery there is a way, a sure direction. And how do we attain this certainty? "The Spirit searches everything, even the depths of God." What kind of being is this Spirit? Paul also tells us that we men are mysterious to one another and that only a man's own inmost being, his spirit, knows his thoughts; to the other person they remain hidden. And yet, we know that we have the power to reveal ourselves to one another. If we approach a man with humility and reverence for what lies within him, then his hidden being is unveiled and he gives to us of his inmost self; he permits us to gaze into his being. It is not that we see through him and compute him, but rather that he gives us a part of himself that opens up to us a view into his depths. And so it is also with God. It is not that we compute him and puzzle him out, but only that he gives us a part of his being, his Spirit, that opens our eyes. And this is the bridge that leads from man to God: reverence and humility, the readiness to yield oneself, to let oneself be given a gift. The heart that in the darkness humbles itself most deeply and implores the most vehemently, "O that thou wouldst rend the heavens and come down!" is the first to hear, "I will pour water upon him that is thirsty, and floods upon the dry ground."

If the split in our heart frightens us, we do not want to stifle it. If the contradiction between the powers of life frightens us, we ought not to close ourselves against them. And if we keep our heart from becoming closed and embittered and remain open in humble longing and reverent trust, then we will sense the power of the Spirit at work in our hearts. Paul tells us: "We have received the Spirit that comes from God, that we might know what God has given us in grace." Can we also say, when we pause to reflect on ourselves, that something in this confusion that has been given us is grace? This would be the test whether God's Spirit has begun his work in our hearts, to open our eyes.

Yes, I think we can say this. And even if it were only that the veil that hid the reality of life from us has been lifted, that an old and illusory concept of God has fallen to pieces, the whole process would not appear so senseless to us because there would still be something in it that brought us inner gain. We have learned to pose questions to destiny in a completely new and more profound sense. And do not answers also here and there flash before us? Have we not learned that there are forces in the heart of man of which we never dreamed? Have we not learned that there are duties that raise man high above everything commonplace, even, indeed, above everything that we once thought to be high and noble? Has not a reverence arisen in us for a greatness in mankind such as we never dreamed of, a greatness that reveals to us the forces of God in man? We have seen men and still see them on whose shoulders rests a superhuman responsibility, but who bear it without going to pieces. We see a sense of sacrifice and a heroism that wreathe even the humblest brow with a crown of glory. And one mystery has been revealed to us for which we had lost our sense; I mean the greatness of what we call "tragic". We have learned once again that even harshness and cruelty may be expected of a man for the sake of something higher without his thereby being defiled — and, indeed, in such a way that he may even be ennobled. We have learned that he, like God, can accept death and destruction into his work so that life may grow out of them. If we were to eliminate the tragic from human life, then we would eliminate the supreme test to which man's dignity can be put — namely, to make his destiny, even the most frightful destiny, entirely his own and to become lord of it. To be sure, in peacetime our poets found gripping words in which to express the melancholy in life, the pain and sorrow that encounter men in their struggle with nature and fate. But the power to understand the tragic was lost to us. What the war has once again given us is the crowning glory of the tragic.

But has the war not also revealed all of the dark, demonic forces of the human heart — all the passions of self-seeking and falsehood, of brutality and hate? Do we dare say here also that we gaze into the depths of God? Yes, we dare to say it even here! For this sight is a powerful reflection on ourselves and a perception of the miraculous riches of all the opposed forces and passions, all the heights and depths, that dwell in the soul of man — and in our souls also; for the human soul is still *one* great unity. And if in seeing this sight we are at first seized with horror, it still is a sight of indescribable grandeur:

> Yes, everything is in thee that only the cosmos offers,
> Heaven and hell, judgment and eternity.[3]

This is not to say that we want to leave men, to leave us ourselves, as we are. But precisely this sight with all its heights and depths, with all the fullness of the violent and the demonic, of the passionate and the uncanny, teaches us to put the goal of that which can and should become here all the higher. What creative possibilities for God's plans! But even more, what a mysterious wisdom of God is revealed here — a wisdom that compels even the demonic forces of sin and falsehood to merge in the harmony of the whole, so that even satanic power can only be a power that constantly wills evil, only constantly to create good. What a hidden wisdom of God that uses all the wild, unleashed passions only in order to put man's dignity to the supreme test, to give him the highest nobility of his being!

And do we not have a picture that concretely embodies all this and places before our very eyes all that we have been struggling so hard to say? Do we not have a picture in which God's hidden and revealed wisdom is embodied — the wisdom that is able to bring all of the demonic powers of darkness into its plan of salvation; that is able to create a noble life out of the agony of death and forsakenness; that swallows death up in victory and transforms a crown of thorns into the crown of a king? Indeed we do have such a picture of promise and redemption in the picture of the crucified Christ. And the picture of the crucified one as the embodiment of the hidden and revealed wisdom of God may help us also to understand the mysteries with which we are presently struggling.

"The Spirit of God searches everything, even the depths of God." Because it is knowledge of the Spirit, it is not a knowledge that rests on conclusions and proofs and that every man can understand. Each of us must learn to see for himself, i.e., each of us must be ready to bow before the hidden God in reverence and humility, so that his heart will be open for God's Spirit and his eyes will learn to see the God who is revealed — the God who endlessly reveals himself. To be sure, opposing powers abide in us and keep us in tension. But thus will it be and thus should it be as long as we are mortal men; for only so can we remain alive and become richer and more mature. We will never find the formula that solves all the riddles and enables us to see all the contradictions harmonized. We succeed in this only from level to level. The conflict in us will remain, but it will have lost its pain. We receive the good conscience to bear the contradictions in ourselves and to affirm the conflicting powers of life that lay claim to our heart. For we know that the depths into which we gaze are really the depths of God; that mysteries and riddles constantly emerge anew, that God is a God of contradictions because he always wants to reveal himself more powerfully in his infinity as the Creator. Clarity will be given to us from level to level, and as the riddles increase, so also will God's graces. As he is infinite as the source of terror, so also is he infinite as the source of grace; and the way must lead from every height through new depths to new heights. Thus there is law and order in God's working. If we have once acquired an ear for the divine melody, then it is always the same old theme endlessly proceeding in ever new ways, always blending itself into new harmonies, always more tempestuous, always more powerful. And if we kneel at first humbly and reverently before the hidden God of the riddle, we then kneel humbly and reverently before the revealed God of grace. And thus we may be permitted to see "What no eye has seen, nor ear heard, nor the heart of man conceived, what God has prepared for those who love him." *Existence and Faith*, pp. 23-34.

*

"KARL BARTH'S *EPISTLE TO THE ROMANS* IN ITS SECOND EDITION"

Karl Barth's Epistle to the Romans, *first edition (1919), did not awaken much interest or appreciation in Bultmann. In a 1920 article, he referred casually to Barth's book as an example of the recent tendency "to reinterpret history as myth" (*The Beginnings of Dialectic Theology, p. 230*). *Bultmann's response to Barth's totally rewritten* Epistle to the Romans, *second edition (1922), was longer and more positive. Indeed, his review essay was so long that the editor of the journal,* Die Christliche Welt, *gave him the choice of either drastically cutting his review or contributing 1700 marks to subsidize the cost of an extra half-sheet. Bultmann did neither, but did mail a copy of the review, with a note stating the editor's demands, to Karl Barth. Thus began a brief theological alliance but life-long correspondence between Bultmann and Barth [Karl Barth—Rudolf Bultmann*

Letters: 1922-1966, *ed. Bernd Jaspert (1981)]. The review was finally published, divided into four parts in successive issues of the journal, in May 1922. Barth devoted most of the Foreword to* Epistle to the Romans, *third edition, to a response to Bultmann's review. He there noted that "the most remarkable thing that has happened to the book* [Epistle to the Romans] *is surely the fact that Bultmann received it in its essentials in a friendly manner"* (Beginnings, *p. 126). New Testament specialists had responded to the book with such hostility that Bultmann's careful and appreciative response was all the more welcomed by Barth. The German original of this essay is available in* Anfänge der dialektischen Theologie, *Volume I (1962), ed. Jürgen Moltmann. Keith R. Crim translated this review for a 1968 volume,* The Beginnings of Dialectic Theology, *edited by James M. Robinson. Only limited portions from the original review will be included here.*

THE FRAMING OF THE QUESTION

Karl Barth's *Epistle to the Romans* may be characterized by one sentence, the phraseology of which he would disagree with, but which would still be valid in terms of the usage that has been prevalent in the present time: The book attempts to prove *the independence and the absolute nature of religion.* It thus takes its place, even though it is in the form of a commentary, in the same line with such works as Schleiermacher's *On Religion* and Otto's *The Idea of the Holy*, with modern attempts to demonstrate a religious a priori, and finally with the Letter to the Romans itself, which, with its radical contrast of works and faith, basically has no other intention than this. However different all these attempts may be in detail, they seek to give verbal expression to the consciousness of the uniqueness and absoluteness of religion.

It is natural that such an undertaking is always determined by the times to the extent that the front line of the battle is constantly determined by the intellectual situation of the time, and the undertaking basically demands the author's coming to grips with the situation. As Paul fought for faith against the law of works, so Schleiermacher fought against the "Enlightenment", and Otto against a rationalizing and ethicizing concept of religion that had held wide sway in the school of Ritschl. And on what front is Barth fighting? Against the psychologizing and historicizing concept of religion, which not only plays or has played a role in the historical (so-called liberal) theology, but in theology and modern intellectual life in general. He is fighting against all cults of "experience" (wherein experience is understood as a psychic factor or a psychic action), against every concept which sees in religion an interesting phenomenon of culture, which wishes to understand religion in the context of psychic historical life. He is fighting also against many other things, but that fight gives his book its distinctive character.

To be sure, Barth does not speak of "religion" in this sense, for this expression is for him only the designation of a psychic historical reality. But we should not be concerned with a quarrel about words, and in order to come to grips with Barth we are glad to concede to him the use of his own terminology. The question would then go like this: In what does the essence of faith consist?

FAITH AND "EXPERIENCE"

A religious a priori, a religious "drive", is always nothing but a part of the world, and has nothing to do with faith, if the latter really has to do with God. If this is not recognized, the theories arise in which "now the human or animal processes are elevated to experiences of God, now the being and work of God are 'experienced' as human or animal experience. That which is solid in this fog is the delusion that a unity or even the possibility of a compact between God and man could exist without the miracle (vertically from above), without the annulling of all that is given, apart from *the* truth which lies beyond birth and death. Religious experience, at whatever stage it takes place, insofar as it claims to be more than a vacuum, to be content, possession, and enjoyment of God, is the shameless and unsuccessful anticipation of that which can be and become true only from the side of the unknown God. It is in its historicalness, reality, and concreteness always betrayal of God" (p. 50).[4]

Thus far Barth is original (in the relative sense, which is all the word can have here) not in his thoughts, but in their clear and powerful formulation. Materially speaking, he stands throughout in the context of the modern polemic against "historicism" and "psychologism". I do not say this in order "to understand him historically", but in order to grasp the substance; much less do I say it to pass judgment on Barth, since the clarity and radicalism of Barth in each case reaches far beyond the usual polemics; much less since with him it is basically not a question of a modern fashionable trend, a reaction, a mere negation, but here speaks the self-confidence which has always belonged to living faith. No one in our time has proclaimed with this self-confidence the uniqueness and absoluteness of "religion" (of faith) with more clarity than Wilhelm Herrmann, with whom Barth is in complete agreement.[5]

FAITH AND CONSCIOUSNESS

It is clear that this radicalism, which does not shy away from paradox, or even from the appearance of blasphemy, is always seeking only to give expression to the fact that faith and justification are absolute miracles. But is not the paradox overdrawn? Is faith, when it is divorced from every psychic occurrence, when it is *beyond consciousness*, then anything at all real? Is not all talk of this faith only speculation and at that an absurd one? What is the meaning of the talk about my "ego" that is not my ego? What is the point of this faith of which I am not conscious and of which I can at most believe that I have it? Is not this alleged identity between my perceptible and imperceptible ego not in reality a speculation that is Gnostic or anthroposophic in nature? For these also talk of the relationship of my ego to higher worlds, relations that are really beyond my consciousness and in truth are matters of total indifference to me!

It seems to me — even though basically I believe I am one with Barth — that there is still some lack of clarity here. Certainly our justification is not an experience (in the Barthian meaning: as a psychic occurrence), not an occurrence in the consciousness. It is present with God, even without our knowing about it. And of *it* we can only say that we believe it. But that we can only believe that we *believe* is at least not the view of Paul, for whom faith is rather the conscious acceptance of the message of salvation, the conscious obedience under God's new saving ordinance. And that corresponds quite well with the subject matter. A faith beyond consciousness[6] is most certainly not the "impossible possibility", but in every sense an absurdity. Surely the proper dynamic of faith does not lie in its perceptibility as a conscious occurrence. But does it follow from this that faith is not the perception of that identity of the perceptible with the imperceptible subject?

As strongly as Barth (with full right!) has separated faith from every psychic process, as much as he (with full right!) stresses its nature as creation, its constantly "being at the beginning", so clearly must faith still be distinguished from the object of any speculation. Perhaps I possess all sorts of astral or other bodies of which I know nothing. They are to me a matter of total indifference, and a speculation which asserts the identity of my "perceptible" ego with such astral bodies either leaves me completely cold, or seems comic. My justification and my faith, however, are not some sort of pseudo other-wordly factors, but my faith is something definite and precise in my consciousness. And this then means that faith cannot be without confession, but what faith is as confession seems to me to be treated too briefly by Barth.

THE WAY TO FAITH

At another point, however, Barth marks progress beyond Herrmann, that is, in the question: How do I come to faith? In an address, Heitmüller once made clear accurately and relevantly wherein Luther's progress over Paul consists, namely, in the question: How do *I* get a gracious God? Paul demands obedience for the message of faith, and the question of how I can be obedient does not come into view for him. Obedience consists in the acknowledgment of the proclaimed facts of salvation as the new saving ordinance of God. For Luther, as a true son of the church, this acknowledgment was self-evident, but he saw that obedience did not really consist in *that*, and that such obedience was dead if it were not at the same time the personal appropriation of the message, the inner submission to the revelation. Following Ritschl, Herrmann consistently advocated this view with great emphasis. Obedience remains a "work" as long as it does not signify the inner conviction of revelation. It is not genuine as long as the reality of God does not show itself to be reality in my life. Obedience as an act of the will would be a "work"; real obedience can only be "free self-commitment" under the compelling and transforming (creative) impression of revelation. And for this reason, the question of how I come to faith, that is, how I succeed in subjecting myself to the revelation with inner veracity, assumes decisive significance.

Now, to be sure, Herrmann — not exclusively, but yet with strong emphasis — answered this question by reference to a psychologically understandable "experience", to a process, a psychic historical procedure, and in this he was not free from a trace of pietism. His answer consists in the well-known theory of rationally grounded obedience under the moral law, of the despair which is the end of this road, of the intervention of the forgiving grace of God, revealed in Jesus, for which this is the preparation. To ask and to answer the question of the way to faith in this sense is false — Barth was right here. Even Herrmann's students were often not fully satisfied with this schema, which does not fit Paul at all. And indeed this schema dulls the edge of the miracle of faith, or at least endangers it. In another sense, however, the question of how I come to faith has its necessary significance if faith is to be honorable, true obedience.

It is only evading the question to speak — as is now so popular — of subjugation to the "objective". For as surely as God is not the symbolization of subjective "experiences", but the objective, so surely can the "objective" be the reality before which I bow only when it becomes reality *for me*. It becomes this only when it destroys, kills my old self — the perceptible man. By wanting to use the talk about the "objective" to gain support for dogmas of old or new provenience, one makes faith into a work and God into an idol, and in truth, empties the objective of its character. And how many messages calling upon us to believe in them offer us the "objective"! How many messiahs are preached! Where is the objective to which I should bow? Thus there remains the question of how I come to faith. And to answer *here* — as is now often done — with the secret of predestination, is dodging the issue, not really a serious answer. For at this point the concept of predestination can be only speculation which is intended to explain something. The concept of predestination takes on meaning only in the moment of faith.

The question "Where is the objective to which I must bow?" must rather be stated as "Where is the objective to which I *can* bow?" And with this insight the question of how I come to faith gains its simple and clear meaning. It can only be answered by showing what faith *means*. For in that the meaning of that which is called faith is made clear; faith is protected from every misinterpretation as a psychic process and is severed from every "method". It becomes clear that the possibility of bowing becomes the necessity of bowing, and that the man who is confronted with the question "How do I come to faith?" can find his answer only by taking thought whether and where in his life he meets the reality which he can absolutely bow to and must bow to. Inner veracity is the only "way" to faith, veracity which does not avoid the ultimate question of the meaning of human existence, veracity which is ready to sacrifice its own self, which is ready for the path to the "King of the dark chamber". That veracity can never be made "perceptible", and the decision must be made by every man for himself. Others can only help him in that they try to say what faith means.

THE CHRIST

Or is there nonetheless a bit of reality which can enter the life of every man, and which is "perceptible" as the *revelation of God*? Herrmann would answer, Jesus! The inner life of Jesus, that which perceived from the Gospel tradition grasps the observer as reality, as the living embodiment of holiness and love, overcomes, transforms, redeems him. Barth rejects this answer, not only because he knows that New Testament research has generally led to the concession that we can know little, or almost nothing of the inner life of Jesus, but because Jesus as a man belongs to the psychic historical reality, to the "world", and we cannot be helped by such psychic historical perceptibleness. Barth's answer rather runs, "The Christ is the revelation of God." And here I confess that I simply do not understand him. Here I can discover only contradictions.

According to Barth there is a line at which the two planes of God and the world intersect. (Can this be spoken of in earnest, when the contrast between God and the world is a purely dialectic one? But let us first hear Barth further!) "The point of the line of intersection, where it is to be seen and is seen, is Jesus, Jesus of Nazareth, the 'historical' Jesus, 'descended from David according to the flesh'. 'Jesus' as a historical designation signifies the point of the break between the world which is known to us and an unknown one. At this point of the world that is known to us, time, things, and men are not superior to other times, things, and men, but yet they are superior insofar as they delimit that point which lets the hidden line of intersection between time and eternity, things and origin, man and God, become visible. Therefore the years 1 to 30 are a time of revelation, a time of discovery" (p. 29). To be sure, every other time can also become a time of revelation and discovery, but that is a possibility which is given only by that basic time of revelation (p. 29). For here we really meet, at *one* point of time, the truth of another order, of a divine answer (p. 96).

And to what extent does the divine world now become perceptible in Jesus? "The life of Jesus . . . is complete obedience to the will of the true God. As a sinner he joins the sinful. He places himself totally under the judgment under which the world stands. He places himself where God can be present only as the question about God. He takes the form of a servant. He goes to the cross, to death. . . . 'Therefore God has highly exalted him'," etc. (p. 97). We see here a paraphrase of Philippians 2:6ff., the Pauline Christ myth, and nothing of the life of Jesus, of the historical Jesus. These sentences take on meaning only if one already has a definite opinion of their subject (of this "he"); this, however, cannot be gained from psychic historical perceptibleness, for it is interpreted by the latter. To what extent therefore is revelation contained in the life of Jesus? Other statements of Barth may be compared here (e.g., pp. 105ff., 178, 202f., 276ff., 327f.). They all come to the same thing.

Alongside this are statements such as that in the life and death of Jesus as an act of obedience, it is not an individual, a personality, one person, that is illustrated, but the individual, the personality, the person (p. 182). "Neither the personality of Jesus nor the Christ concept, neither his Sermon on the Mount nor his healing of the sick, neither his trust in God nor his brotherly love, neither his call to repentance nor his message of forgiveness, neither his struggle against traditional religion nor his exhortation to follow him in poverty, neither the social nor the individual, neither the indirect nor the eschatological side of his gospel" constitutes the meaning of the "Christ", but only his death on the cross, in the light of which all those possibilities appear as merely human; the death in which the "imperceptible" life becomes "perceptible"; his death, which means dying *for us,* "insofar as in this death the imperceptible God becomes perceptible for us" (pp. 159f.; cf. 202f.). So in the Son of God we recognize ourselves again, and see in him the existential nature of the new man who is alive in God (p. 282), and are ourselves "sons of God" (p. 296). As "I myself am the one crucified, who appears to me in the mirror image of the death of Christ" (p. 198), so "we believe in our identity with the imperceptible new man who appears beyond the death of the cross" (p. 202). Thus also, Jesus' resurrection is "no event of historical extent *beside* the other events of his life and death, but the 'unhistoric' relationship of his *whole* historic life to its origin in God" (p. 195). If the resurrection were itself in any sense a fact of history, then no assertion however strong, and no deliberation however refined, would be able to prevent it from appearing to be drawn into that see-saw of Yes *and* No, of life *and* death, of God *and* man, which is characteristic of the historical superficiality" (p. 204).

Good. But cannot this also be said of the "life of Jesus" in general? And what meaning would it then have to speak of the years 1 to 30 as the time of revelation? Is not the "historical Jesus" in truth completely ignored? "Jesus Christ, however, is the new man beyond the humanly possible man, especially the pious man. He is the abrogation of *this* man in his totality. He is the man who has come from death into life. He is — not I, my existential I, I as I am in God, in the freedom of God" (p. 269). I can understand all this only to mean that *the historical Jesus has become a symbol.* This does not mean he has become an idea (Barth rightly rejects this, p. 160), and neither does it mean an illuminating or aesthetically fascinating illustration of a general truth (of reason), but a symbol as living, present power — not the power of any sort of magic, but simply as *verbum visibile* (cf. Barth, p. 529; Jesus Christ authentically "interprets"

God to us as he meets us in the reality of our life!). The Word speaks and is heard, and is therefore a living, present reality in connection with which it is completely unimportant how the historical Jesus of Nazareth is to be included in the context of psychic historical occurrences. The Christ speaks through Grünewald's painting of the crucifixion, of which Barth likes so much to speak, just as much as through the Synoptic Gospels. And what does he say? He is, as the crucified and risen one, the most powerful sermon of God concerning God's judgment, in which his No becomes his Yes, and embodies "God's existentiality, illuminated by his uniqueness" (p. 276). "God is personality, unique, alone, peerless, and as such the eternal and almighty, and nothing else. The proof of this is Jesus, the human, historical Jesus. But Jesus is the *Christ*. This is God's uniqueness illumined by his existentiality. Therefore despite all believing and unbelieving historicism and psychologism, the *skandalon* of an eternal revelation in Jesus, a revelation of that which truly Abraham and Plato also had already seen" (pp. 276f.; cf. 381ff.).

I do not know if I understand Barth correctly, but I can interpret his statements only thus: that Jesus is a symbol for the truth (preaching of the truth), that God's revelation is neither a psychic historical fact or form as such, so that it would be possible to read off directly the divine reality in the methodically conceived, "perceptible" history — perhaps in its "high points" — nor something that would be at all immanent for all "perceptible" occurrences. As a result, the attempts of a certain liberalism to have revelation immediately in the historical person of Jesus are just as false as all pantheistic talk of the revelation of the "God-nature" in the All. Therefore he is a symbol for the fact that God's revelation is present always unhistorically and supra-historically, always unnaturally and supra-naturally, always only in a definite now, in a definite man. The symbol for this is the "Christ", and that not as an idea (all rational considerations are eliminated), but as *verbum visibile*, as living, present power.

How I can get beyond this, I do not see, even though I exert myself to follow the Barthian thought patterns and reflect on the meaning of faith and revelation. "Christ" is thus just as much a "sign" as baptism "in its paradoxical uniqueness" is for Barth (p. 192), or as Adam, in whom the imperceptible No of God becomes perceptible; in this connection Barth expressly declares the historicity of Adam a matter of indifference (p. 171). In reality, Barth makes Adam and Jesus parallel in this sense: "In the one man Adam the imperceptible becomes perceptible, that

God says No to us. . . . In the one Jesus Christ the imperceptible becomes perceptible, that God does not cease to say Yes to us" (p. 178).

THE RELATIONSHIP TO THE TEXT

With my references and critical comments I have not exhausted this book, which despite all its one-sidedness is a rich one. I also intentionally declined to go into the relationship of the new edition to the first one, and hope that someone else will undertake this task. I must confess, however, that the new edition made a much deeper impression on me than the first did. I have also refrained from regarding the book as a commentary on the Letter to the Romans, for the sake of the clarity of the issue with which it basically deals. But precisely because of the issue it seems to me that in conclusion a word is necessary about the relationship of Barth to the text. In the understanding of the task of explaining the text as Barth develops it in the Foreword, I am quite in agreement with him. As it is self-evident for him that the philological historical explanation of the text is a necessary side of exegesis, it is self-evident for me that a text can be explained only when one has an inner relationship to the matter with which the text deals. And I agree also when Barth formulates the high point of exegetical understanding as follows: "As one who would understand, I must press forward to the point where insofar as possible I confront the riddle of the *subject matter* and no longer merely the riddle of the *document* as such, where I can almost forget that I am not the author, where I have almost understood him so well that I let him speak in my name, and can myself speak in his name." In other words, a paraphrase, truly the greatest art of exegesis, is the best commentary.

But I must reproach Barth for having let this ideal become a schema by means of which he does violence to the Letter to the Romans and to Paul. Before I go into the matter, I would like to confess once again that Barth has grasped Paul's view of faith in its depths, and likewise that through his exegesis many details have become more alive for me. But I must express the verdict that his "commentary" does violence to the individual life of the Letter to the Romans and to the richness of Paul. It is not at all a matter of a more or less correct or complete presentation of psychic historical perceptibleness, but of the understanding of the subject matter.[7] The measuring "by the subject matter of all words and phrases contained" in the document to be explained, which Barth justifiably demands in the Foreword, cannot, if one is in earnest, occur without criticism. And this criticism is much more radical than philological historical criticism; nor is it criticism from a standpoint taken outside the text and its subject matter, which Barth correctly rejects for exegesis (p. 10), even though it may be justified in other contexts. Rather it is the consistent carrying out of the basic principle, which it is agreed is correct, of understanding the text on the basis of the subject matter. One must measure by the subject matter to what extent in all the words and sentences of the text the subject matter has really found adequate expression, for what else can be meant by "measuring"? In Barth, however, I find nothing of such measuring and of the radical criticism based on it. It is impossible to assume that everywhere in the Letter to the Romans the subject matter must have found adequate expression, unless one intends to establish a modern dogma of inspiration, and something like this seems to stand behind Barth's exegesis — to the detriment of the clarity of the subject matter itself.

It would not be doing Barth a favor to leave the book uncriticized; for example, to ignore to what degree Neo-Kantian (Cohenian) terminology often has influenced the words and concepts, or not to consider that many antitheses are based on the origin of the author in the land of psychoanalysis, that many formulations are obviously determined by the works he happened to be reading at the moment (and in a new edition will probably share the fate of corresponding expressions in the first edition, that is, to disappear) — in short, to forget that the subject matter is greater than the word which interprets it. And I believe it is from no lack of respect when I say that the same is true of Paul and his Letter to the Romans. When I discover in my exegesis of Romans tensions and contradictions, heights and depths, when I endeavor to show where Paul is dependent on Jewish theology or on popular Christianity, on Hellenistic enlightenment or Hellenistic sacramental beliefs, then I am thereby practicing not only philological historical criticism (at least not if I do not consider my task as an exegete mechanical), but I am doing it from the point of view of showing where and how the subject matter is expressed, in order to grasp the subject matter, which is greater even than Paul. I believe that such criticism can only serve to clarify the subject matter, for the more strongly I feel that in this matter it is a question of saying the unsayable (and Barth knows this very well), the more clearly I perceive also the relativity of the word and as an exegete stress it. It is not merely a question of the relativity of the word, but also of the fact that no man — not even Paul — can always speak only from the subject matter itself. In him there are other spirits speaking besides the *pneuma Christou*. And therefore criticism can never be radical enough. Such criticism therefore is — it follows from Barth's own basic premise of "measuring by the subject matter" — inseparable from exegesis and real history. Only in such criticism can the historical work attain its final goal, in which it meets the systematic theology which has traveled on another road — reflection on the motives and forces, on the bases of our life.

The Beginnings of Dialectic Theology, ed. James M. Robinson, pp. 100-120 *passim*.

*

"LIBERAL THEOLOGY AND THE LATEST THEOLOGICAL MOVEMENT"

Bultmann first gave this essay as a public lecture, with the same title, for the Theological Society at Marburg University on 6 February 1924. On 9 January of that year he wrote to Karl Barth about this coming lecture, with the result that Barth and twelve of his students from Göttingen University traveled to Marburg for the event. While others expected strong disagreements to erupt between Barth and Bultmann, their meeting together at this occasion was particularly comfortable. Reading the text suggests the reasons for their agreement. Bultmann concentrates here on a critique of those forms of Liberal Theology which confuse the "Wholly Other" God and any form of human endeavor: e.g., moralism, psychologism, church social work, or a theology of the "historical Jesus". Barth and Bultmann were most often able to agree in their objections to other positions, even if they seldom agreed concerning their own affirmations. The revised lecture was first published in the journal, Theologische Blätter *(1924). The German original, "Die liberale Theologie und die jüngste theologische Bewegung", is available in* Glauben und Verstehen, Volume I *(1933). Louise Pettibone Smith translated this essay for the English edition of that first volume,* Faith and Understanding *(1969). Only selections from the original article are included in this reading.*

In the polemic of the latest theological movement — a movement which is particularly associated with the names of Barth and Gogarten — the attack against the so-called liberal theology is not to be understood as a repudiation of its own past, but as a discussion with that past. The new movement is not a revival of orthodoxy, but rather a carefully reasoned consideration of the consequences which have resulted from the situation brought about by liberal theology.

It is no accident that the latest movement originated not from within

65

orthodoxy but out of liberal theology. Barth was a student at Marburg, Gogarten at Heidelburg, Thurneysen at both.[8]

It is essential to understand also that the issue raised by the new movement is not a debate with individual theologians but a protest against a specific theological trend. That trend is, of course, supported by individual theologians, but it is not to be identified with all their incidental pronouncements. Liberal theology therefore cannot evade criticism by showing that this or that liberal theologian has now and then said something quite different and is not responsible for what some other theologian has said. Moreover, it can be readily granted that themes can be seen in the work of some liberal theologians which would lead to the defeat of their own position. As examples, I would mention W. Herrmann and the great proponent of liberal theology, E. Troeltsch.

The subject of theology is *God*, and the chief charge to be brought against liberal theology is that it has dealt not with God but with man. God represents the radical negation and sublimation of man. Theology whose subject is God can therefore have as its content only the "word of the cross" ($λόγος\ τοῦ σταυροῦ$). But that word is a "stumbling-block" ($σκάνδαλον$) to men. Hence the charge against liberal theology is that it has sought to remove this stumbling-block or to minimize it.

Here I shall seek to demonstrate conclusively what kind of conception of God and man serves as the basis of liberal theology and to make clear the objections raised against it.

I

Liberal theology owed its distinctive character chiefly to the primacy of *historical interest*, and in that field it made its greatest contributions. These contributions were not limited to the clarification of the historical picture. They were especially important for the development *of the critical sense*, that is, for freedom and veracity. We who have come from a background of liberal theology could never have become theologians nor remained such had we not encountered in that liberal theology the earnest search for radical truth. We felt in the work of orthodox university theology of all shades an urge towards compromise within which our intellectual and spiritual life would necessarily be fragmented. We can never forget our debt of gratitude to G. Krüger for that often cited article of his on "unchurchly theology". For he saw the task of theology to be to imperil souls, to lead men into doubt, to shatter all naïve credulity. Here, we felt, was the atmosphere of truth in which alone we could breathe.

But to what result has the course of historical criticism actually led? If it was at first directed by a confidence that such critical research would free men from the burden of dogmatics and lead to a comprehension of the real figure of Jesus on which faith could be based, this confidence soon proved to be delusion. Historical research can never lead to any result which could serve as a basis for faith, for *all its results have only relative validity.* How widely the pictures of Jesus presented by liberal theologians differ from one another! How uncertain is all knowledge of "the historical Jesus"! Is he really within the scope of our knowledge? Here research ends with a large question mark — and here it *ought* to end.

The error is not that men did this historical work and obtained results which are more or less radical; rather, it is that they did not understand the significance of such work nor the meaning of the inquiry. The real question was evaded even when it was put as precisely as Troeltsch stated it in his work, "The Meaning of the Historical Jesus for Faith" (1911).[9] For Troeltsch a picture of the historical Jesus is necessary for the faith of the church, and, "Accordingly there remains an actual dependence (if one likes to put it that way) on scholars and professors, or — better expressed — on the general sense of historical reliability which results from the impact of scientific research." Nicely put — but "better"?

The very character which is the special "gift" ($\chi\acute{\alpha}\varrho\iota\sigma\mu\alpha$) of liberal theology is denied if at the end of the road stands a sign: The situation is not yet really very bad; the results of historico-critical theology are still usable for faith. The position of liberal theology becomes frighteningly clear in the fourteenth question which von Harnack addressed to Barth. "If the *person of Jesus Christ* stands at the centre of the Gospel, how can the foundation for a reliable and generally accepted knowledge of that person be gained except through *historico-critical research?* Is not such research essential to prevent the substitution of an *imagined* Christ for the real Christ? And who can carry on this research unless he pursues it as a scientific theology?" Barth answers rightly: "Historico-critical research represents the deserved and necessary end of *the* 'foundations' of this understanding (i.e. the understanding of *faith*). Such foundations do not exist except when they are laid by God himself. Anyone who does not yet know (and in truth all of us do not know *yet*) that we *cannot* any longer know Christ after the flesh should let himself be taught by critico-biblical research that the more radically he is horrified, the better it is for him and for the cause. This may well be the service which 'historical science' can perform in the real task of theology."

Thus there can be no question of discarding historical criticism. But we must understand its true significance. It is needed to train us for freedom and veracity — not only by freeing us from a specific traditional conception of history, but because it frees us from bondage to every historical construction which is within the scope of historical science, and brings us to the realization that the world which faith wills to grasp is absolutely unattainable by means of scientific research.

This truth becomes even clearer when a second error in the historical understanding of liberal theology is recognized. It forgets not only that all the results it presents within its overall picture of reality have merely a relative validity, but also that all historical phenomena which are subject to this kind of historical investigation are only relative entities, *entities which exist only within an immense inter-related complex.* Nothing which stands within this inter-relationship can claim absolute value. Even the historical Jesus is a phenomenon among other phenomena, not an absolute entity. Liberal theology has indeed recognized this conclusion up to a certain point. It speaks of the historical Jesus with great assurance, but in terms which do not ascribe an absolute value to him. Again it is Troeltsch who speaks most unambiguously. In the work already cited, we read the plain statement that there cannot be a *necessary* binding of the Christian faith to the person of Jesus. Faith in God leads to acknowledgment of the person of Jesus not vice versa.

But here again the final result is compromise. We are told that, almost as by a law of social psychology, the Christian church, like every religious organization, requires a cult with a concrete centre. The figure of Christ is such a centre. "The linking of the Christian *idea* to the central position of Jesus in cult and teaching is not a conceptual necessity derived logically from the idea of salvation. But in terms of social psychology it is indispensable for the cult, for action, for proselytizing. That indispensability is sufficient justification for the assertion of the link. (Troeltsch)"

A statement of that kind makes it entirely clear that *Christianity* is understood as *a phenomenon of this world, subject to the laws of social psychology.* It is equally clear that such a conception runs exactly counter to the Christian view. Although Troeltsch's view may to some extent be justified — only orthodoxy would dispute that — certainly it is not *theology*, not if *God* is the subject of theology and the theologian is speaking as a *Christian.*

That such a conception could be offered and accepted as theology was possible partly because no objection was made to the inclusion of the person of Jesus in the complex of general historical inter-relations. Indeed, it was acceptable as theology because of the belief that *the revelation of God in history could be perceived precisely within this nexus of relations.* Therefore it is possible to speak of a "pantheism of *history*" in liberal theology, analogous to a pantheism of nature. This pantheism depends on the assumption of a similarity between nature and history; that is, the concepts which are valid for nature are accepted as equally valid for history. And man, in so far as he acts in this history, is similarly regarded, as it were from outside, as an object, rather than under the categories which are drawn from man himself.

W. Herrmann was always pointing out that "the laws of nature hide God as much as they reveal him". And although different terms are used, that statement is the equivalent of the constantly repeated assertion of Barth and Gogarten: "There is no direct knowledge of God. God is not a given entity."

The same objection holds against *the view of history held in liberal theology.* Indubitably, in primitive or ancient religions man saw the act of deity in historical events; but he saw it in particular events: in the misery or the prosperity of a people, in a battle, in a war, in servitude or liberation (for example, the Exodus from Egypt!), or in individual historical persons: Moses, the prophets, men of God of every kind. But here also occurs the shift to a recognition of inter-connection, to the concept of historical forces and laws, to the understanding of history as a unity. The views of individual adherents of liberal theology differ in detail, but on the whole a vague, idealistic, psychological concept of history prevails. Historical forces are viewed as spiritual powers which are nonetheless conceived entirely on the analogy of the forces of nature. Through the action of such forces, it appears, mankind develops from a state of nature to civilization and culture. History is a struggle in which the powers of the true, the good and the beautiful are victorious, and it is a struggle in which man participates, in that he is supported by these powers and thus emerges from his bondage to nature to become a free personality with all its riches.

In these powers of truth, goodness and beauty lies the meaning of history, its divine character. God reveals himself in human personalities who are the bearers of these powers. And Jesus, so far as he is also in this sense a personality, is the bearer of revelation. Such a doctrine is certainly a pantheism of history. The old "history of salvation" is wholly divested of its character. By the demonstration of the inter-relatedness of historical phenomena, man thinks he has attained to the comprehension of divine powers. Proof of the historical necessity of the phenomenon of Christendom serves as its best apologetic.

The same concept serves for the interpretation of the "fullness of the time" (Gal. 4.4) and replaces the recognition of the truth that history has come to a dead end, that its meaninglessness has become plain. At the very least, the liberal view of history is assumed to serve Christian faith by demonstrating that such powers as are manifested in Christianity, the powers of love, of self-sacrifice and the like, are the forces actually operative in history. The essence of Christianity seems so easily understood when it is viewed in its place along with other forces and ideas which appear in principle in other spiritual movements.[10]

Along with such statements often appears — with a certain inconsistency of viewpoint — the attempt to prove that some ideas or impulses entered history for the first time in Christianity. Apart from the doubtful nature of the proof in specific instances, *newness* is not a category which is determinative for the divine. That category is eternity. Newness can be claimed equally for this or that imbecility. Newness is never a guarantee of the *value* of what claims to be new.

Neither by one road nor by the other can a way be found out of the *unending inter-relatedness* in which no single epoch and no single person can claim absolute significance. It is no more possible to see divine forces or the revelation of the divine in the inter-related complex of history and in historical forces than it is in the inter-relatedness of nature and natural forces. Truly, here, too, it is only man that is deified; for the human powers are alleged to be divine. Here again is to be seen merely the attempt to win direct knowledge of God. Here, too, is the concept of God as a given object.

And here, too, appears the reaction — especially among the young. There is the realization that such inter-relatedness connotes fatalism, that the "riches" which the personality wins are a curse, because the distinctively human characteristic, the creative in man, has been destroyed or imprisoned. They feel that history so understood "puts man in question", leaves him at a loss and makes him a ghost. At every point — against both pantheism of nature and pantheism of history — the polemic of Barth and Gogarten is valid. For that polemic is aimed directly against the temptation to deify man; it is a protest against every kind of direct knowledge of God.

In so far as the Word of God is judgment upon the whole nature and condition of man, it is the "stumbling block" for every kind of pantheism of history. But *only* in so far! It is not so easy to deal with the stumbling block as it seemed to be in the view of history commonly accepted by orthodox theology; that is, by asserting the occurrence of supernatural phenomena and powers within history. We are not required to make *that* sacrifice of reason (*sacrificium intellectus*), which would involve the repudiation of all effort to gain a rational view of history. The meaning of history can be found only by relating visible history to an invisible origin — not by setting up a second, alien history alongside the other (Barth, *Der Römerbrief*, 3rd ed., München, 1923, p. 90; ET, *The Epistle to the Romans*, London and New York, 1933, p. 140). "The judgment of God is the *end* of history, not the beginning of a new, a second, epoch" (*ibid.*, p. 51; *ibid.*, p. 77).

The same objection holds against similar formulations, for example, that found in Heitmüller's *Jesus* (Tübingen, 1913).[11] He affirms that we have religious experiences even without Jesus. But those experiences "acquire content and convincing force and certainty, they become revelation, *only* and *first* when they are conjoined with a powerful experience of the divine *outside ourselves*, only through contact with the streams of religious life which flow around us and encompass us". Further, "For the individual, the road to the Father does not necessarily lead by way of Jesus Christ. But the more sure and independent we wish to become in our faith, so much the less can we refuse to go by that way. . . . No faith escapes periods of uncertainty, of wavering, of trepidation — chiefly as consequence of our own sins. In such times we find a basis and support for our faith in the historical fact, Jesus of Nazareth, in whom we encounter a faith full of power and strength, independent of our desires, as a sure victorious reality." A reality? What if Jesus' faith were also illusion? Are not illusions which were characterized by convictions of power and victory found elsewhere in history? What is the criterion by which we can determine that we are not allowing our illusions to be strengthened by the stream of life which encompasses us?

The pantheism of history which marks such statements appears especially clear in this excerpt: "The consideration of this figure, bringing him vividly before us, provides us with a means of edification, exaltation and inspiration. All of the religious forces, experiences,

71

moods, impulses, and demands which are active in Christianity are visible, embodied in the figure of Jesus. His figure is the symbol and the bearer of all religious and ethical goods and verities. It becomes ever richer, ever fuller of content. For into this figure are woven all that later Christians have experienced. . . ." But what if all that were illusion? Also, could the statement not apply equally to the Roman Catholic cult of the Virgin Mary?

In all these varied formulations the "stumbling block" (σχάνδαλον) has been removed from Christianity. All of them totally lack the insight that God is other than the world, he is beyond the world, and that this means the complete abrogation of the whole man, of his whole history. Their common aim is to give faith the kind of basis which destroys the very essence of faith, because what they seek is a basis here in this world.

II

Deeply rooted in modern Protestantism, including Protestant liberal theology, is the view based on Luther that our *secular daily work* in the place assigned to us in history is service to God. A man is not required to do some specific kind of work in order to serve God. Whatever work the labourer and artisan, the farmer and the merchant, the scholar and the official, perform in their own calling can be and ought to be performed as service to God. So far the view really is Luther's. But it becomes un-Lutheran when it is assumed that labour in every kind of occupation is in itself direct service to God; when it is forgotten that my activity in my own occupation can separate me from God and can become service to idols. My secular work, since it serves the purposes and forces which determine and promote human cultural life, can be the service of God only indirectly — never directly. Only when I recognize that the work *in itself* does not serve God, only if I undertake it in *obedience* and maintain an inner detachment from it, only if I do it as if I did not, can it be the service of God.

Here, also, God's Word can act only as a "stumbling block". "My kingdom is not of this world" holds true here, too. However conscientiously we do the work of our calling, that work as such can never make it possible for us to know ourselves as co-workers in the service of God. God is wholly "Beyond". He calls in question both ourselves and our faithfulness in our calling. The idea that our regular work is a service of God can, if it is carried consistently to its conclusion, confront us again with the precariousness of our whole self. We are forced to admit honestly that if we *are seeking* God we do not find him in our daily occupation, that we cannot of ourselves prove a right to call our work the service of God.

But the identification of daily labour with the service of God is perhaps not an especially significant facet of liberal theology. Its attitude towards practical life may be more revealing in another aspect. Liberal theology betrays its true character in so far as it commits itself to the view that specific ideals for the activity of life in the world are to be derived from faith. That is to say, that Christian concepts of the kingdom of God, of love, *et al.*, can determine man's life within the world, that they can provide the norm, setting the goal and showing the road to it. The consequences of this view are clear in such slogans as "the work of God's kingdom", "the vineyard of God on earth", "Christian Socialism", "Christianity and Pacifism".

If anyone supposes that social work — i.e. work concerned with the creation of proper social conditions which are suitable for human beings, whether the work is officially "welfare work" or not — is as such the work of God's kingdom, that it is "Christian action", then he is unaware of the "stumbling block" of the Word of God. The "stumbling block" is very much bigger, very much more obvious when that Word speaks the stern judgment, "That is not a Christian act", against actions which in themselves are a duty, worthy of honor, and terribly necessary.

No act exists which can relate itself directly to God and his kingdom. All forms of community life, the worst and the most ideal alike, stand equally under the judgment of God. We except ourselves from that judgment, we refuse to take it seriously, when we suppose that in social work or in total abstinence from alcohol or the like (just because the duty to perform such acts is recognized) it is possible to produce in this world some sort of situation which is more pleasing to God. Therefore, for example, the *general* question of whether a *Christian* must be a pacifist is to be rejected. *Each man* must answer the question for himself in his specific historical situation. If pacifism is an ideal of human society, then even if its realization lies in the infinite future, in which lie the realization of all ideals, pacifism would be a *human* possibility. But God's Word demands the impossible from man, impossible in every sense. It demands that man live a sinless life. And we fail to recognize the "stumbling block" when we ignore the sinfulness of our whole life and activity, when we think we can fulfil God's demands in the historical course of human life.

All attempts to derive ideals of possible human conduct from the Christian faith deny the "stumbling block". *In Christian faith*, man is without sin and the fellowship of Christian believers is a fellowship without sin. Both, therefore, are impossibilities on earth. On earth there is no direct service of God. "We cannot be blind to the warning which is raised against the whole, to the final all-encompassing provision which applies not only to forbidden actions, but with especial force to all permitted, even to all commanded actions."[12]

There is service of God only when man surrenders himself to God's judgment and then obediently under God takes up the work in the world to which God has set him, when he never averts his eyes from the sin of the world — especially not from his own sins — and never dreams that any sort of approximation to God's world can be realized in this world. "A system of ethics for this world, based on the Gospel, would have this singular character: its action would be without any immediate relation to God and the Eternal."[13] Certainly the behavior of the man of faith (if the existence of men of faith may be assumed) will appear different from that of the unbeliever. But in what respects it will differ cannot be deduced from his faith. He will learn the difference through his obedience when he takes upon himself service in this world with the responsibilities and the duties which are realities in this world and for this world.

The Word of God is a "stumbling block" for this world and primarily a "stumbling block" for an earnest mind, for the moral consciousness. Here again Barth and Gogarten state the conclusions which are actually inherent in liberal theology. For who has emphasized more forcibly than W. Herrmann that there is no specifically Christian ethic? And who has shown more convincingly than Troeltsch[14] the problematic character of the relation of the Christian to the world?

III

What conception of *God and man* forms the basis for this criticism of liberal theology?

God is not a given entity. The question of the adequacy of our knowledge of God must be rejected completely. For that question conceives of God as a given entity of which direct knowledge is possible, as an object which we can recognize in more or less the same way as other objects. Such knowledge could be a possession and could produce effects within our life. It could progress and grow like other segments of knowledge. But it could still not take us to God, who can never be something given, something which is, so to speak, crystallized in knowledge. God, on the contrary, is known only when he reveals himself. His revelation comes only contingently; it is *act*, act directed towards *men*. God's revelation does not make him something known in the sense of intellectual knowledge.

God is not a given entity. This truth is equally valid against a religion of experience, which supposes it possible to achieve contact with the divine object by substituting spiritual states for intellectual knowledge. God becomes equally a directly accessible object, whether he is conceived as creative life forces, or as the irrational, or as anything else of the sort.

Nor, however, is God "self-actualizing" or "unactualized" in the sense of idealistic philosophy, so that God may actualize himself to man's intellect by the process of revelation or may be actualized in the Logos, which lies at the roots of rational human life. That would involve the deification of man. *God represents the total annulment of man, his negation, calling him in question, indeed judging him.* Whether God is known adequately or inadequately, whether or not God is to be spoken of in anthropomorphic terms is irrelevant.[15] The one essential question is: What does God represent for men? And wherever the idea of God is really grasped, the result is the radical calling of man in question.

Now this result — this "minus sign before the bracket" — does not mean *scepticism.* No doubt of man's intellectual capacity is involved, no degradation of his reason, no passive resignation. On the contrary, it becomes impossible to speak of God so cheaply as to call him "the irrational". Indeed it is impossible to think highly enough of reason. Precisely when reason has followed its road to the end, the point of crisis is reached and man is brought to the great question mark over his own existence.

"Calling in question" is *not pessimism;* it is not despair of the world under the impact of its evil or its suffering. All pessimism makes man its criterion — man's moral judgment or his claim to happiness. And for exactly that reason, such pessimism is sin before God, because it implies both man's claim to happiness and his claim to his own righteousness.

Man as such, the whole man, is called in question by God. Man stands under that question mark, whether he knows it or not. His moral transgressions are not his fundamental sin. "It is not a matter of a few steps more or less on this road."[16] *Man's fundamental sin is his will to justify himself as man,* for thereby he makes himself God. When man becomes aware of this, the whole world is taken off its hinges; for man then puts himself under the judgment of God. The whole world — which was *man's* world — is annihilated; nothing in it any longer has meaning and value, for everything had received this from man. But to know this judgment is also to know it as grace, since it is really liberation. Man becomes free from himself. And for man to become free from himself is redemption. Man then knows that the question is also the answer; for it is only God who can *so* question him. And he knows that the answer is primary. A question so radical cannot originate from man, from the world. But if the question is asked by God, then it originates from the claim of *God* on man. Man is called.

The knowledge of this truth is called faith. *Faith* cannot generate itself in man; it can only arise as man's answer to the Word of God in which God's judgment and God's grace are preached to him. Indeed, faith can be in man only as God's creation. So far as faith is real in man, it manifests itself in him as obedience to God's Word. The man who has faith is therefore the man whom God has transformed, the man whom God has put to death and made alive again; he is never the natural man. Faith is never self-evident, natural; it is always miraculous. The belief that God is the Father and man is the child of God is not an insight which can be gained directly — it is not an insight at all. On the contrary, it must be believed, ever and again, as the miraculous act of God. But it must be *believed,* truly, in faith.

It is not surprising that such disregard of what is essentially Christian has not remained unopposed within liberal theology. It is not only research into the history of religion with its attention focused on what is characteristic in historical phenomena which has registered opposition to the unrestrained rationalization and moralization of Christian ideas. Rudolf Otto's book *The Idea of the Holy,* in particular, resulted from the theological situation very much as did the protest of Barth, Gogarten and their circle. Otto's designation of God as the "Wholly Other" and his emphasis on "creature feeling" as the essential element of religious piety are characteristic of that protest. Just as the purpose underlying his concept of "the Holy" was to define the nature of the divine as beyond the sphere of the rational and ethical, so equally his emphasis on the inner relatedness of the moments of dread (*tremendum*) and fascination (*fascinans*) in the numinous has an analogy, which is more basic than the obvious parallelism, to the assertion of the inner conjunction of the knowledge of judgment and of grace. But certainly the theological solution which Otto proposed for this paradoxical situation leads in the opposite direction.

Barth's divergence is shown most plainly in his consistent emphasis on the truth that *faith is not a state of consciousness*. No doubt, along with faith there is also a state of consciousness — at least there can be. But as long as it is a state of consciousness it cannot be faith. To speak of the faith of men is to accept the full paradox of asserting something which cannot be affirmed of any visible man, something which is completely unverifiable as a spiritual situation and which must never be identified with any such situation. From this concept of faith arises the polemic against all "religion of experience", against piety, sense of sin, and inspiration. Hence comes the utter scepticism of religion as such, since religion claims to be a particular area of human spiritual life in which inheres the relation of man to God. On the contrary, the real truth is that what is confessed in faith is the calling in question of the *whole* man by God. The justified man, the new man, is believed in faith.

Whatever belongs to religion is something present with man and in man. It can be, indeed it must be, doubted time and again. I can never so relate myself to my experience that I can put my trust in it. I can trust only the promises of God. Even if the revelation of God is understood as the revelation of judgment and grace, the meaning is not that the two are successive experiences. The despair is not conceived as a sort of overwhelming preliminary stage which must be surmounted so that it may be followed by the consciousness of redemption. The despair, radically conceived, is the realization that the natural man is trying to flee from before God and that he cannot flee because he was trying to flee before *God*. That despair, therefore, comes only when there is awareness of God. But when there is awareness of God as God, flight has ended and a turning to God has begun. There are not two acts. *Faith is not an act which can be performed once for all*, an act by which justification is achieved. Nor is it an act which is repeatable, so that judgment and grace, sin and forgiveness alternate in human life.

Only the man who knows *himself* to be a sinner can know what grace is. He knows himself as a sinner only in so far as he stands before *God*; therefore he can only know of sin when he also knows of grace. The sight of God's judgment and God's grace *together* belongs to the nature of faith. There is no grace except grace for sinners, no grace except grace in judgment. And as man can only speak of sin with real meaning if he sees himself before God, so also he can speak of grace only as grace for sinners. There is no possible standing ground on some achieved insight; there is no position which can be permanently won. For man *always* remains a sinner and he is always under condemnation and justified. Here it is truly necessary to speak of "walking on a knife edge". Even that metaphor is a very inadequate expression of the paradoxical character of faith. The grace of God is never a general truth; it is always real only in the act of God directed to a specific man. The judgment of God is never universal. Anyone who thinks it can be so conceived does not yet stand under that judgment.

Justification is not a qualitative change in men of this world; it is never present except in the "Beyond", in God's judgment. The "new man" is always the man of the "Beyond", whose identity with the man of this world can only be believed in faith. So Barth can repeat Luther's paradoxical dictum: "We only believe that we believe."

Faith so comprehended is distinct from every kind of *mysticism*. Mysticism, too, wills to seek God beyond the given, not only beyond the natural world but also beyond intellectual and spiritual life. Mysticism follows its path methodically, calling upon us to silence everything in us, even all intellectual and spiritual activity. In pure passivity, in the emptying of the self, the mystic is prepared for the revelation of God. God enters the soul so prepared and fills it with joy unutterable.

The first objection to such mysticism is the necessity of rejecting the possibility of any method of reaching God. Even silence as a method is human activity. In this falsity ($\psi\varepsilon\tilde{v}\delta o\varsigma$) is revealed the primary falsity ($\pi\rho\tilde{\omega}\tau ov\ \psi\varepsilon\tilde{v}\delta o\varsigma$), the delusion that an escape from the given is possible — as if man could escape from himself, as if he were not obliged to put up with himself just as he is.[17] We cannot suppose that the annulment of men and world is an act within the power of man to perform by abstraction, by averting his eyes or closing them — while all the time it is *I* myself who am practicing the annulment.

No! The annulment can come from God alone and it is always dialectical — that is, this world is always sublimated by a "Beyond" and never replaced by it. In the latter case, the Beyond would always itself become this world, just as it does become a very real this world in that "joy unutterable". Since the Beyond can never become this world, just as my justification can always be only justification in the Beyond in which I have faith, clearly this justification is not any kind of supernatural quality in me. Yet *I* am the justified person. This means that man does not need to escape from himself, as the mystic assumes. Only the *sinner* is justified. Hence the justified person is an individual man who accepts the whole burden of his past, present and future. With that burden he stands under God's judgment. To desire to escape the burden means to desire to flee from God's judgment and to know nothing of grace.

In view of the whole situation presented here, we can understand why Barth refuses to assume a definite theological position. Naturally when he is engaged in a theological argument, he cannot avoid adopting a position. Yet there are good grounds for his refusal. One reason is that the refusal is an expression of the truth that faith, the exposition of which is theology, is not an actual position which a man, even if he is a theologian, *can* take. In practice faith always happens as an act of God; and seen from the human point of view it is the abandonment of every position. Faith is the supremely paradoxical cry: "I believe, Lord help my unbelief." But then it follows that because theology can be nothing other than the exposition of faith, no concepts of knowledge which have meaning can be gained from it apart from the miraculous actualization of faith. The subject of theology is God. Theology speaks of God because it speaks of man as he stands before God. That is, theology speaks out of faith. *Faith and Understanding*, pp. 28-52 *passim*.

*

"WHAT DOES IT MEAN TO SPEAK OF GOD?"

In this 1925 essay, "What Does it Mean to Speak of God?", Bultmann first introduces that existentialist point of view which later became so prominent in his theology. In 1923 Martin Heidegger began teaching philosophy at Marburg University where Bultmann was Professor of New Testament. From 1923 to 1928, when Heidegger left Marburg for Freiburg University, he and Bultmann frequently taught together in joint seminars. Two years after the appearance of this essay, Heidegger published his major work in existentialist philosophy, Being and Time (1927). After 1925, Bultmann's writings, including the 1926 Jesus, consistently expressed, with increasing clarity and explicitness, an existentialist understanding of faith. This early essay presents us with some of these existentialist themes. To exist is to be responsible for one's self in a situation which is wholly insecure and which we can never make secure. To attempt to speak about God as some sort of universal principle is to deny the truth of our own existential condition and God's claim upon us. Older themes, concerning God as "Wholly Other" and the critique of religious experience, link this essay with the previous readings. First published in Theologische Blätter *(1925) with the title, "Welchen Sinn has es, von Gott zu reden?" the German original was later printed in* Glauben und Verstehen, I *(1933). Franklin Littell provided the first English translation in the journal* Christian Scholar *(1960). The English translation used in this volume is by Louise Pettibone Smith from* Faith and Understanding *(1969).*

I

If "speaking of God" is understood as *"speaking about God"*, then such speaking has no meaning whatever, for its subject, God, is lost in the very moment it takes place. Whenever the idea, God, comes to mind, it connotes that God is the Almighty; in other words, God is the reality determining all else. But this idea is not recognized at all when I speak *about* God, i.e. when I regard God as an object of thought, about which I can inform myself if I take a standpoint where I can be neutral on the question of God and can formulate propositions dealing with the reality and nature of God, which I can reject or, if they are enlightening, accept.

Anyone who is persuaded by arguments to believe the *reality* of God can be certain that he has no comprehension whatever of the reality of *God.* And anyone who supposes that he can offer evidence for God's reality by proofs of the existence of God is arguing over a phantom. For every "speaking *about*" presupposes a standpoint external to that which is being talked about. But there cannot be any standpoint which is external to God. Therefore it is not legitimate to speak about God in general statements, in universal truths which are valid without references to the concrete, existential position of the speaker.

It is as impossible to speak meaningfully about God as it is about *love.* Actually, one cannot speak *about* love at all unless the speaking about it is itself an act of love. Any other talk about love does not speak about *love,* for it stands outside love.

Therefore a psychology of love would in every case treat something other than love. Love is not something external in respect of which it is possible either to act and speak or to refrain from acting and speaking. Love exists only as a determining element of life itself. Love *is* there only when I love or am loved; it has no existence alongside me or behind me.

The same is true of the relation of fatherhood and sonship. When that relation is viewed as a natural phenomenon — so that it can be spoken about — the essential character of the relation is not discoverable, for the relation then appears as a special case of a natural process which operates between individuals of the same species. Where the relationship really exists, it cannot be viewed from outside. That is, it is not something in respect of which, for example, the son can claim for himself or permit to himself this or that, or feel himself obligated to this or that because of it. The essential relation is destroyed when any thought of this "in respect of which" enters. It *is* there only where in his life the father *lives* truly as father and the son as son.

If the preceding statements are correct, then, for example, the *atheistic position* taken by any particular science would not consist in a denial of the reality of God. It would be equally atheistic if, as science, it affirmed that reality. For speaking of God in scientific propositions, that is, in general truths, means speaking in propositions the significance of which is their universal validity — a validity which is not related to the concrete situation of the speaker. But just because the speaker speaks in this manner, he puts himself outside the actual reality of his own existence, and therefore at the same time outside God. He therefore can speak only of what is not God.

To speak of God in this sense is not only error and without meaning — it is *sin*. In his interpretation of Genesis, Luther made it very clear that Adam's sin was not really the act of eating the forbidden fruit by which he disobeyed the command. His sin was that he raised the question, "Ought God to have said?" He began to "argue about God" (*disputare de deo*) and so set himself outside God and made God's claim upon men a debatable question.

If we try to evade this condemnation by saying: such discussion may not have intended any ill; it could on the contrary arise from intellectual honesty, from the longing for God, then we should merely have demonstrated once more that we have not comprehended the concept of God. We should have fallen into the old error and should again have represented the omnipotence of God and the determination of ourselves by it as a fact to be accepted as a universal truth, like the dependence of every earthly object on the law of causality. But then we should have wholly failed to comprehend what the determination of our existence by God means. For that determination also involves the *claim* of God on us. Consequently, every setting of ourselves outside God would be a denial of God's claim on us; it would therefore be atheism and would be sin.

A different conclusion would be possible only if neutrality in relation to God were a possibility. But to assume such a position of neutrality is to abandon the idea of God. Adam thought he could flee from before God; but God's claim is not annulled by flight. Consequently, speaking about God becomes sin. And *sin* it remains — even when it arises from a sincere quest for God.

It is therefore evident that if we are in a situation which requires that we honestly argue about God, we are sinners and of ourselves can do nothing to escape from sin. It would not help us at all if, because of a correct understanding of the idea of God, we determined to stop "argument about God" (*disputare de deo*). For to speak otherwise of God — and that would mean to speak "from God" — is obviously nothing we can undertake of ourselves. As *our* undertaking, that would again be sin, because it would be merely an undertaking *of ours* in which the thought of *God's* omnipotent rule would be abandoned. Speaking of God as *from* God can evidently be only the gift of God himself.

II

It is therefore clear that if a man will speak of God, he must evidently *speak of himself*. But how? For if I speak of myself am I not speaking of man? And is it not essential to the concept of God that God is the "Wholly Other", the annulment of man? Are we not then confronted by two negatives which make no position possible for us except resignation to silence? On the one side is the specific certainty: no speaking in which we detach ourselves from our own concrete existence is a speaking of God. It can only be a speaking about our own existence. On the other side is the equally specific certainty: no speaking of ourselves can ever be a speaking of God, because it speaks only of man.

Actually, every confession of faith, all talk of experience and of the inner life would be a man's speech. And however enthusiastic the confession of faith which another man makes to me, his confession would be of no help to me in my situation of doubt unless I were willing to deceive myself. Indeed, even my own experiences, if I tried to put my trust in them or to depend on them for support in the situation of doubt, would dissolve in my hands. For who can assure me that the experience was not an illusion? That it is not something I should leave behind? That I do not now see reality more clearly?

Or ought the claim nonetheless to be made that we are speaking directly *from* God when we confess our faith, when our inner life speaks, when our experience finds expression? That unquestionably can happen. But *at the very moment* when we set before ourselves *our* creed, *our* inner life, *our* experience *on the basis of which* we trust in God, or when we recommend them to others as something *on the basis of which* they can be certain of God — in that moment we are speaking *about* our existence and have detached ourselves from it.

The situation is the same when we go looking for experiences and coveting them for ourselves. We are seeking after ourselves, not after God. If, looking backward or forward, I rely on myself, then I split my personality. The relying self is my existential self; the other self on which I rely, taking it as something objective, is a phantom without existential reality. And the existential self, who looks around, who questions, is proved by this very questioning, this looking around, to be godless. So if we wish to speak of God, evidently we cannot begin by speaking of our experiences and our inner life, for both of these lose their existential character as soon as we objectify them. It is in opposition to this human nature seen as something objectively given that the statement that *"God is the Wholly Other"* is valid.

But that statement has meaning only in such a context. That is, its meaning is understood only in relation to the primary statement that God is the reality that determines our existence. Detached from the first statement, the second can only mean that God is *something* wholly different from man, a metaphysical being, a kind of an immaterial world, perhaps of a complex of mysterious forces, a creative source (at this point any assertion that the terms are used figuratively is itself misunderstanding, because God here is really being thought of in purely naturalistic terms), or finally, *the Irrational.*

A piety which desired to base itself upon this conception of God would be flight from before God, because man would be trying to flee from the very reality in which he exists. What he desires to escape is precisely his own concrete existence; yet only in that existence can he grasp the reality of God. This kind of modern piety strikingly demonstrates how right Luther was in saying that the natural man flees from before God and hates God. For man in seeking to escape from the reality of his own existence is endeavoring to escape from that wherein alone he can find God.

It is quite understandable that the pseudo-god of "the Creative" or "the Irrational" can bewitch and seduce the human hunger for God, for this pseudo-god promises man freedom from himself. But this promise is a misconception and a fraud. When man tries in this fashion to be freed from himself, he runs away from God — since God is the power determining his concrete existence — and runs into his own arms, since such concepts as the creative force and the irrational are human abstractions, and the experiences on which man relies in such relations are the most human of transactions. The idea of the "Wholly Other" can never be utilized in any such way. Moreover, a man does not really escape from God. For since his relation to God is that of hatred (*aversio*), his existence determined by God is the existence of a sinner.

When speaking of God the Almighty, therefore, the concept of God as the "Wholly Other" cannot mean that God is something apart from me for which I must search, and that in order to find God I must first escape from myself. The statement that the God who determines my existence is nevertheless the "Wholly Other" can only have the meaning that as *the* "Wholly Other" he confronts me who am a sinner. Further-more, in so far as I am *world*, he confronts me as *the* "Wholly Other". To speak of God as the "Wholly Other" has meaning, then, only if I have understood that the actual situation of man is the situation of the sinner who wants to speak of God and cannot; who wants to speak of his own existence and cannot do that either. He must speak of it as an existence determined by God; but he can only speak of it as sinful, as an existence such that *he* cannot see God in it, an existence in which God confronts him as the "Wholly Other".

III

We thus find ourselves in the same astonishing predicament in relation to our existence as in relation to God. We cannot really talk about either; we have no power over either. What is involved here?

Reality, as we commonly use the term, reflects a view of the world (*Weltbild*) which has dominated our thinking since the Renaissance and the Enlightenment, both of which were under the influence of the world-view of Greek philosophy. We consider something to be *real* if we can understand it in relation to the unified complex of this world. The relation may be thought of as determined causally or teleologically, its components and forces may be conceived as material or spiritual. The antithesis between idealism and materialism is irrelevant for the question with which we are concerned.

In both views, the picture of the world (*Weltbild*) is conceived without reference to our own existence. We ourselves are observed as an object among other objects and are put in our proper place in the structure of this picture of the world which has been fabricated without reference to the question of our own existence. When this picture of the world is completed by the inclusion of man, it is customary to call it a [general] world-view (*Weltanschauung*). We strive to acquire such a world-view or, if it supposedly has been attained, to propagate it.

It is not surprising that such [general] world-views are very highly valued even though they present an estimate of man which is not very flattering, describing him as the accidental result of a combination of atoms, as the highest vertebrate, related to the apes, or as an interesting phenomenon of psychological complexes. Such explanations do man the great service of freeing him from himself. They relieve him of the problem of his concrete existence, of anxiety about it and responsibility for it. That is, of course, the reason why man desires a so-called world-view. He can turn to it when he is confronted by the riddle of destiny and death. He can dismiss the problem of his existence from his mind when his existence becomes shattered and precarious. He need not take the moment of crisis seriously, for he can understand it simply as a special case of a general class, fit it into a context, objectify it, and so find a way out of it.

But that very view is the primary falsity ($\pi\rho\tilde{\omega}\tau o\nu\ \psi\epsilon\tilde{\upsilon}\delta o\varsigma$) and it leads necessarily to mistaking the truth of our own existence, since we are viewing ourselves from outside as an object of scientific investigation. Nor is there any gain if we label ourselves "subject" in distinction to the other objects with which we see ourselves in interaction. For man is seen from outside even when he is designated "subject". Therefore the distinction between subject and object must be kept separate from the question of our own existence.

Nor will there be any improvement if we take a theistic or a Christian *"Weltanschauung"*, accepting some idea of the dependence of our existence upon God, and then assume that the incorporation of such assertions in our world-view will satisfy all claims and comprehend our existence. For here again God is seen from outside as an object, just as men are.

Anyone who holds the modern view of the world (*Weltbild*) as a world governed by law has a godless conception of the world, even though he may think of the laws governing the world as forces and forms of divine activity, or look upon God as the origin of this rule of law. The work of God cannot be seen as a universal process, as an activity which we can observe (as we observe the workings of the laws of nature), apart from our own existence. Nor can it be conceived as a process into which we can subsequently insert our own existence in order to make it comprehensible to ourselves. In that case, we should have abandoned the primary concept of God as the reality determining our existence. This we admit unintentionally and unconsciously whenever we clearly differentiate ourselves in our essential being from the working of the laws governing the world. Nobody considers the living relationships by which he is bound to others in love, gratitude, and reverence to be functions of law — at least not when he is truly living in them.

Clearly, then, it is not feasible to think of God as the world-principle on the basis of which the world and our own existence along with the world becomes comprehensible. For then God would be seen from outside and the affirmation of his existence would be a general truth with its place in a system of cognitions (universal truths), in a self-supporting system that was also meant to support our existence — instead of being an expression of our existence. For God would be objectively given; and knowledge of that *given object* would be accessible to us and could be achieved at will. God or his existence would be something *in respect of which* we could establish an attitude of one kind or another. But this is again the primary falsity. For if the idea of God is taken seriously, God is nothing *in respect of which* anything at all can be undertaken. For then he would be seen from outside and we should equally have been looking at ourselves from outside.

We cannot say, for example, that because God rules reality, he is also my Lord. Only when a man knows himself in his own existence to be claimed by God, has he reason to speak of God as the Lord of reality. For all talk of reality which ignores the element in which alone we can have reality — that is, talk which ignores our own existence — is self-deceit. God can never be seen from without, can never be something at our disposal, can never be a "something in respect of which".

Since it is a fact that the world seen from outside is godless and that we, since we see ourselves as a part of the world, are godless, it is again clear that God is the "Wholly Other", not because he is somewhere outside the world but because this world, being godless, is sinful. This world seen from outside, the world in which we move around as subjects, is our world. We take it seriously and thereby we declare it sinful.

Only one double truth of our existence is clear: (1) We do worry about our existence and must exercise responsibility for it: "It is *your* business" (*Tua res agitur*). (2) Our existence is wholly insecure and we cannot make it secure — to do that we should have to stand outside it and ourselves be God. We cannot talk about our existence since we cannot talk about God. And we cannot talk about God since we cannot talk about our existence. We could do the one only along with the other. If we could talk of God from *God*, then we could talk of our existence, or vice versa. In any case, talking of God, *if* it were possible, would necessarily be talking at the same time of ourselves. Therefore the truth holds that when the question is raised of how any speaking of God can be possible, the answer must be, it is only possible as talk of ourselves.

IV

But does it not follow from the situation just depicted, from the recognition that we are sinners and therefore wholly other than God, that we ought not to speak at all? That would necessarily also mean that we ought not to act at all! Does not the belief that God is the "Wholly Other", that he is the annulment of men, lead to *Quietism?* Anyone who thought this would be making the old mistake — that is, he would be regarding the idea of God as something *in respect of which* a specific attitude is possible or appropriate. This would be the mistaken assumption that the concept of God can be entered on the credit side of a ledger, that we have it as something objectively given which we can utilize.

If the ideas of God as the Almighty and the "Wholly Other" are taken seriously in their strict relation to each other, they clearly show that we are not given authorization to investigate for ourselves or to decide on intellectual grounds whether we ought to speak or be silent, act or be quiet. The decision is God's. And his decision is simply a question of *must* for us. We *must* speak or we *must* keep silent. We *must* act or we *must* not act. The only true answer to the question of whether and when we can speak of God is: if we *must.*

But we shall do well to consider the true meaning of that "must". For according to our established pattern of thought, we still see this "must" from outside. We see ourselves, who *must,* as the object which lies under the causal compulsion of a subject; here specifically we see God who gives the command as the subject. This means that we see men's being determined by God, of whom they *must* speak, as a natural process observable from outside. But the only *must* which can be meant here is a free act. For only a free act springs from our essential being; it is only in a free act that we are ourselves and are completely whole. Such a free act is obedience. For obedience means freely to put one's self under a "must". This does not mean a work which we must decide to undertake as the will of God. For in that case God would really be seen from outside and we should not be really ourselves in the work which we accomplish and present to God; we should be standing outside it. Obedience means complete dependence — not as a religious emotion but as a free *act,* since only in act are we ourselves. Therefore this *must* means obedience.

Consequently, one can never ask in general when such a *must* may confront us. Nor can one have beforehand any knowledge of this *must*. For such knowledge would require a position outside the compulsion, and hence outside the self of those who *must*. The meaning of this existential *must* would then be completely misunderstood. The act which is done because a compulsion preceded it cannot be done as a free act. The act can be free only if it is *simultaneous* with the *must*.

It need hardly be said that this does not mean that the act arises from a compulsive enthusiasm or any other emotion, or out of a secret depth in our inner self. In that case the *must* would signify a natural necessity. A greater or lesser degree of enthusiasm has as little to do with a free act as has greater or lesser resistance, greater or lesser self-mastery, which may make an act appear to be a greater or a lesser sacrifice in human eyes. We are not discussing psychological compulsions. The *must* is a word spoken by God and is wholly outside our control. Only the free act is ours.

We are, of course, speaking hypothetically when we say that there is the possibility for us to speak and act from within God *if* that possibility is a *must*. We cannot know beforehand whether such a *must* may become a reality for us. We can only make clear to ourselves the meaning of such a *must*. We have to understand that on our part it can be only a free act, because otherwise it would not involve our existential being. We can only *believe in faith* that the *must* is a reality.

V

This and nothing else is the meaning of *faith*. But belief in the *must* does not exhaust the meaning of faith. For when we say that only the free act is ours, that statement — or rather the conviction that some specific deed is our free act — is itself only faith. For the free act which is truly the expression of our existence (in the proper sense we exist only in such action and not otherwise and such action is really nothing other than our existence itself), the truly free act can never be known in the sense of being objectively proven. It cannot be offered for investigation as something "to be proved' (*probandum*). For in that case we should be objectifying it and putting ourselves outside it. A free act can only be *done* and in so far as we *speak* of such doing, the possibility of it can only be believed.

Thus we find ourselves led to the conclusion that our own existence, since it depends on our free act, can never be known by us. Is this existence illusion? Unreality? Certainly it is nothing about which we

88

have knowledge, about which we can speak. And yet it is only our existence which can, if it is really present in our speaking and acting, give reality to that speaking and acting. *We* can only believe it in faith. And does this faith lie within our powers so that we can decide to adhere to it? Obviously faith must also be a free act, the primary act in which we become certain of our existence. But this basic act is not an optional affirmation which we decide to make. It is obedience, a *must* — it is, in truth, faith.

The question of how to attain such faith is insoluble if it is understood as a question about a process which takes place while we look at ourselves from outside. It makes no difference whether the process is conceived rationalistically or psychologically, dogmatically or pietistically. The question has meaning only when it asks what faith means — and in this sense it is unavoidable.

Faith can be only the affirmation of God's action upon us, the answer to his Word directed to us. For if the realization of our own existence is involved in faith and if our existence is grounded in God and is non-existent outside God, then to apprehend our existence means to apprehend God. But if God is not universal law, nor a principle, nor anything objectively given, obviously we can know his reality only because he speaks to us, only because he acts upon us. We can speak of him only in so far as we are speaking of his Word spoken to us, of his act done to us. "Of God we can only tell what he does to us."[18]

The meaning of this Word of God to us, this act of God upon us, would then clearly be that God, granting us existence, makes righteous men of us sinners, that he, forgiving our sins, justifies us. This would not mean that he overlooks this or that trivial or serious misdeed, but that he gives us freedom to speak and act from God. For only in action as the free expression of a person — or rather in the free act in which alone a person really exists — can persons come into a relationship with persons. Such relationship is totally destroyed if the action is brought under the category of conformity to law.

But this statement cannot be interpreted to mean that God inspires us, making us into ecstatics or miracle workers. It means that he accepts us as justified even while we are separated from him and can only talk *about* him or ask questions about him. It is not that some special, demonstrable change happens in our lives, that we are imbued with special qualities and can do special things or speak special words which are of a non-human kind. What could we ever do or say that would *not* be human! But *this* has happened: all our acts and words are freed from the curse of dividing us from God. Our speech or action always remains sinful, since it is always something undertaken by us. But as *sinful* it is justified; that is, justified *by grace.* We never possess *certain knowledge* of God; neither do we *know* our own reality. We have both certainties only in our faith in God's grace.

Could faith then be the Archimedean point from which the world is moved off its axis and is transformed from the world of sin into the world of God? Yes! That is the message of faith. But anyone who wanted to question further on the necessity of faith, on its correctness, on its basis, would get only an answer referring him to the message of faith which comes to him with the claim to be believed. He would receive no answer which would demonstrate the rightness of faith before any authority. If there were such an answer, the Word would not be *God's* Word. God would be made answerable to man's judgment. Faith would not be obedience.

Wholly fortuitously, wholly contingently, wholly as specific event, the Word enters our world. No guarantee comes with it by virtue of which it is to be believed. No appeal to authority can have a preferential claim on the belief of others, whether it be made for Paul or for Luther. Even for ourselves, our own faith can never be a standing ground on which we can establish ourselves. Faith is continually a fresh act, a new obedience. It always becomes uncertain again as soon as we observe ourselves from outside as men and begin to question ourselves. It is always uncertain as soon as we reason about it, as soon as we talk about it. Only in act is it sure. It is always sure as faith in the grace of God who forgives sin and who, if he pleases, justifies me who cannot speak from God but can only undertake to speak about God. All our action and speech has meaning only under the grace of the forgiveness of sins. And that is not within our control. We can only have faith in it.

Even this lecture is a speaking about God and as such, if God is, it is sin, and if God is not, it is meaningless. Whether it has meaning and whether it is justified — none of us can judge. *Faith and Undertaking,* pp. 53-65.

2

JESUS AND THE ESCHATOLOGICAL KINGDOM*

"JESUS AND THE WORD"

Bultmann's 1926 Jesus integrated the results of recent historical research, his own literary analysis of the first three (synoptic) gospels, and his newly won existentialist understanding of faith. Albert Schweitzer's The Quest of the Historical Jesus *(1906) had already called attention to the strangeness of Jesus' eschatological message, with its expectation of an imminent end of world history, and the false efforts of nineteenth century liberal theologians to portray Jesus as consistent with modern ideals. Like Schweitzer, Bultmann dismisses previous "lives of Jesus" as nothing but projections from the nineteenth century on to a vague, little known figure of the first century. From the point of view of historical research, Bultmann is clear that "We can now know almost nothing concerning the life and personality of Jesus." What we do know is only that he was crucified and that he proclaimed the imminent breakthrough of God's Reign or Kingdom. In a prior publication,* The History of the Synoptic Tradition *(1921), Bultmann had delineated a method (Form Criticism) for distinguishing between the several layers of oral tradition in the three synoptic gospels (Mark, Matthew, and Luke).* Jesus *presupposes the results of this literary analysis. As early as 1920, Bultmann had already summarized the negative implications of his literary analysis for historical knowledge of Jesus: "The analysis of the synoptic gospels has shown more and more clearly how little we know for certain about Jesus" (Beginnings, p. 223). In this reading, Bultmann will identify the "Jesus" of which he writes simply in terms of "the oldest layer of the synoptic tradition". Finally,* Jesus *is one of his earliest publications to utilize his newly formulated existentialist understanding of faith. Terms like "encounter", "crisis of decision", and "interpreting our own existence" (later expressed as "self-understanding"), introduced in this book on Jesus, will appear with increasing frequency in later writings. Louise Pettibone Smith and Erminie Huntress translated Jesus under the English title,* Jesus and the Word. *Published in 1934, the same year as Frederick Grant's translation of "The Study of the Synoptic Gospels", it anticipated all of Bultmann's other English language books by almost twenty years. Professor Smith's early appreciation of Bultmann was not widely shared by English language New Testament specialists of her era; the book was noticed by few reviews, and most were negative.*

---

* See also pp. 10-17 above.

INTRODUCTION
VIEW-POINT AND METHOD

In strict accuracy, I should not write *"view-point"*; for a fundamental presupposition of this book is that the essence of *history* cannot be grasped by "viewing" it, as we view our natural environment in order to orient ourselves in it. Our relationship to history is wholly different from our relationship to nature. Man, if he rightly understands himself, differentiates himself from nature. When he observes nature, he perceives there something objective which is not himself. When he turns his attention to history, however, he must admit himself to be a part of history; he is considering a living complex of events in which he is essentially involved. He cannot observe this complex objectively as he can observe natural phenomena; for in every word which he says about history he is saying at the same time something about himself. Hence there cannot be impersonal observation of history in the same sense that there can be impersonal observation of nature. Therefore, if this book is to be anything more than information on interesting occurrences in the past, more than a walk through a museum of antiquities, if it is really to lead to our seeing Jesus as a part of the history in which we have our being, or in which by critical conflict we achieve being, then this book must be in the nature of a continuous *dialogue with history*.

Further, it should be understood that the dialogue does not come as a conclusion, as a kind of evaluation of history after one has first learned the objective facts. On the contrary, the actual encounter with history takes place only in the dialogue. We do not stand outside historical forces as neutral observers; we are ourselves moved by them; and only when we are ready to listen to the *demand* which history makes on us do we understand at all what history is about. This dialogue is no clever exercise of subjectivity on the observer's part, but a real *interrogating* of history, in the course of which the historian puts this subjectivity of his in question, and is ready to listen to history as an authority. Further, such an interrogation of history does not end in complete relativism, as if history were a spectacle wholly dependent on the individual standpoint of the observer. Precisely the contrary is true: whatever is relative to the observer — namely all the presuppositions which he brings with him out of his own epoch and training and his individual position within them — must be given up, that history may actually speak. History, however, does not speak when a man stops his ears, that is, when he assumes neutrality, but speaks only when he comes seeking answers to the questions which agitate him. Only by this attitude can we discover whether an objective element is really present in history and whether history has something to say to us.

There is an approach to history which seeks by its *method* to achieve objectivity; that is, it sees history only in a perspective determined by the particular epoch or school to which the student belongs. It succeeds indeed, at its best, in escaping the subjectivity of the individual investigator, but still remains completely bound by the subjectivity of the method and is thus highly relative. Such an approach is extremely successful in dealing with that part of history which can be grasped by objective method, for example in determining the correct chronological sequence of events, and in so far forth is always indispensable. But an approach so limited misses the true significance of history. It must always question history solely on the basis of particular presuppositions, of its own method, and thus quantitatively it collects many new facts *out* of history, but learns nothing genuinely new *about* history and man. It sees in history only as little or as much of man and of humanity as it already explicitly or implicitly knows; the correctness or incorrectness of vision is always dependent on this previous knowledge.

An example may make this clear. A historian sets himself the aim of making a historical phenomenon or personality *"psychologically comprehensible"*. Now this expression implies that such a writer has at his disposal complete knowledge of the psychological possibilities of life. He is therefore concerned with reducing every component of the event or of the personality to such possibilities. For that is what making anything "comprehensible" means: the reduction of it to what our previous knowledge includes. All individual facts are understood as specific cases of general laws, and these laws are assumed to be already known. On this assumption the criticism of the tradition is based, so that everything which cannot be understood on that basis is eliminated as unhistorical.

So far as purely psychological facts of the past are the objects of investigation, such a method is (for the psychological expert) quite correct. There remains, however, the question whether such a method reveals the essential of history, really brings us face to face with history. Whoever is of the belief that only through history can he find enlightenment on the contingencies of his own existence will necessarily reject the psychological approach, however justified that method is in its own sphere. He must reject it if he is in earnest in his attempt to understand history. In such a belief this book is written. Hence no attempt is here made to render Jesus as a historical phenomenon psychologically explicable, and nothing really biographical, apart from a brief introductory section, is included.

Thus I would lead the reader not to any *"view"* of history, but to a highly personal *encounter* with history. But because the book cannot in itself be for the reader *his* encounter with history, but only information about *my* encounter with history, it does of course as a whole appear to him as a *view*, and I must define for him the point of observation. Whether he afterward remains a mere spectator is his affair.

If the following presentation cannot in the ordinary sense claim objectivity, in another sense it is all the more objective; for it refrains from *pronouncing value judgments.* The "objective" historians are often very lavish with such pronouncements, and they thus introduce a subjective element which seems to me unjustified. Purely formal evaluations of the meaning of an event or a person in the immediate historical sequence are of course necessary; but a *judgment of value* depends upon a point of view which the writer imports into the history and by which he measures the historical phenomena. Obviously the criticisms which many historians deliver, favorable or unfavorable, are given from a standpoint beyond history. As against this I have especially aimed to avoid everything beyond history and to find a position for myself *within* history. Therefore evaluations which depend on the distinction between the historical and the super-historical find no place here.

Indeed, if one understands by the historical process only phenomena and incidents determinable in time — "what happened" — then he has occasion to look for something beyond the historical fact which can motivate the interest in history. But then the suspicion becomes most insistent that the essential of history has been missed; for the essential of history is in reality nothing *super*-historical, but is event in time. Accordingly this book lacks all the phraseology which speaks of Jesus as great man, genius, or hero; he appears neither as inspired nor as inspiring,[19] his sayings are not called profound, nor his faith mighty, nor his nature child-like. There is also no consideration of the eternal values of his message, of his discovery of the infinite depths of the human soul, or the like. Attention is entirely limited to what he *purposed*, and hence to what in his purpose as a part of history makes a present demand on us.

For the same reason, *interest in the personality of Jesus* is excluded — and not merely because, in the absence of information, I am making a virtue of necessity. I do indeed think that we can now know almost nothing concerning the life and personality of Jesus, since the early Christian sources show no interest in either, are moreover fragmentary and often legendary; and other sources about Jesus do not exist. Except for the purely critical research, what has been written in the last hundred and fifty years on the life of Jesus, his personality and the development of his inner life, is fantastic and romantic. Whoever reads Albert Schweitzer's brilliantly written *Quest of the Historical Jesus* must vividly realize this. The same impression is made by a survey of the differing contemporary judgments on the question of the Messianic consciousness of Jesus, the varying opinions as to whether Jesus believed himself to be the Messiah or not, and if so, in what sense, and at what point in his life. Considering that it was really no trifle to believe oneself Messiah, that, further, whoever so believed must have regulated his whole life in accordance with this belief, we must admit that if this point is obscure we can, strictly speaking, know nothing of the personality of Jesus. I am personally of the opinion that Jesus did not believe himself to be the Messiah, but I do not imagine that this opinion gives me a clearer picture of his personality. I have in this book not dealt with the question at all — not so much because nothing can be said about it with certainty as because I consider it of secondary importance.

However good the reasons for being interested in the personalities of significant historical figures, Plato or Jesus, Dante or Luther, Napoleon or Goethe, it still remains true that this interest does not touch that which such men had at heart; for *their* interest was not in their personality but in their *work*. And their work was to them not the expression of their personality, nor something through which their personality achieved its "form", but the cause to which they surrendered their lives. Moreover, their work does not mean the sum of the historical effects of their acts; for to this their view could not be directed. Rather, the "work" from *their* standpoint is the end they really sought, and it is in connection with their purpose that they are the proper objects of historical investigation. This is certainly true if the examination of history is no neutral orientation about objectively determined past events, but is motivated by the question how we ourselves, standing in the current of history, can succeed in comprehending our own existence, can gain clear insight into the contingencies and necessities of our own life purpose.

In the case of those who like Jesus have worked through the medium of *word*, what they purposed can be reproduced only as a group of sayings, of ideas — as *teaching*. Whoever tries, according to the modern fashion, to penetrate behind the teaching to the psychology or to the personality of Jesus, inevitably, for the reasons already given, misses what Jesus purposed. For his purpose can be comprehended only as teaching.

But in studying the teaching there is again danger of misunderstanding, of supposing such teaching to be a system of general truths, a system of propositions which have validity apart from the concrete life situation of the speaker. In that case it would follow that the truth of such statements would necessarily be measured by an ideal universal system of truths, of eternally valid propositions. In so far as the thought of Jesus agreed with this ideal system, one could speak of the super-historical element in his message. But here it would again become clear that one has missed the essential of history, has not met with anything really new in history. For this ideal system would not be learned from history, it implies rather a standard beyond history by which the particular historical phenomena are measured. The study of history would then at best consist in bringing this pre-existent ideal system to clearer recognition through the observation of concrete "cases". Historical research would be a work of "recollection" in the Platonic sense, a clarifying of knowledge which man already possesses. Such a view would be essentially rationalistic; history as event in time would be excluded.

Therefore, when I speak of the teaching or thought of Jesus, I base the discussion on no underlying conception of a universally valid system of thought which through this study can be made enlightening to all. Rather the ideas are understood in the light of the concrete situation of a man living in time; as his interpretation of his own existence in the midst of change, uncertainty, decision; as the expression of a possibility of comprehending this life; as the effort to gain clear insight into the contingencies and necessities of his own existence. When we encounter the words of Jesus in history, *we* do not judge *them* by a philosophical system with reference to their rational validity; *they* meet *us* with the question of how we are to interpret our own existence. That we be ourselves deeply disturbed by the problem of our own life is therefore the indispensable condition of our inquiry. Then the examination of history will lead not to the enrichment of timeless wisdom, but to an encounter with history which itself is an event in time. This is dialogue with history.

There is little more to say in introduction. The subject of this book is, as I have said, not the life or the personality of Jesus, but only his teaching, his message. Little as we know of his life and personality, we know enough of his *message* to make for ourselves a consistent picture. Here, too, great caution is demanded by the nature of our sources. What the sources offer us is first of all the message of the early Christian community, which for the most part the church freely attributed to Jesus. This naturally gives no proof that all the words which are put into his mouth were actually spoken by him. As can be easily proved, many sayings originated in the church itself; others were modified by the church.

Critical investigation shows that the whole tradition about Jesus which appears in the three synoptic gospels is composed of a series of layers which can on the whole be clearly distinguished, although the separation at some points is difficult and doubtful. (The Gospel of John cannot be taken into account at all as a source for the teaching of Jesus, and it is not referred to in this book.) The separating of these layers in the synoptic gospels depends on the knowledge that these gospels were composed in Greek within the Hellenistic Christian community, while Jesus and the oldest Christian group lived in Palestine and spoke Aramaic. Hence everything in the synoptics which for reasons of language or content can have originated only in Hellenistic Christianity must be excluded as a source for the teaching of Jesus. The critical analysis shows, however, that the essential content of these three gospels was taken over from the Aramaic tradition of the oldest Palestinian community. Within this Palestinian material again different layers can be distinguished, in which whatever betrays the specific interests of the church or reveals characteristics of later development must be rejected as secondary. By means of this critical analysis an oldest layer is determined, though it can be marked off with only relative exactness. Naturally we have no absolute assurance that the exact words of this oldest layer were really spoken by Jesus. There is a possibility that the contents of this oldest layer are also the result of a complicated historical process which we can no longer trace.

Of course the doubt as to whether Jesus really existed is unfounded and not worth refutation. No sane person can doubt that Jesus stands as founder behind the historical movement whose first distinct stage is represented by the oldest Palestinian community. But how far that community preserved an objectively true picture of him and his message is another question. For those whose interest is in the personality of Jesus, this situation is depressing or destructive; for our purpose it has no particular significance. It is precisely this complex of ideas in the oldest layer of the synoptic tradition which is the object of our consideration. It meets us as a fragment of tradition coming to us from the past, and in the examination of it we seek the encounter with history. By the tradition Jesus is named as bearer of the message; according to overwhelming probability he really was. Should it prove otherwise, that does not change in any way what is said in the record. I see then no objection to naming Jesus throughout as the speaker. Whoever prefers to put the name of "Jesus" always in quotation marks and let it stand as an abbreviation for the historical phenomenon with which we are concerned is free to do so. Further I need say only that I have in what follows seldom given the critical considerations; they can be found in their context in my book *The History of the Synoptic Tradition* in connection with my own critical analysis.

After a historical introduction, this presentation of the message of Jesus is developed in three concentric circles of thought. In each circle we are concerned with the same question; but this common center can first be clearly recognized only in the smallest circle. The smallest circle is, however, comprehensible only when one has passed through the two outer circles.

Finally I wish to say that this book does not deal with especially complicated or difficult matters, but with extremely simple ones, so far as theoretical understanding is concerned. Of course the understanding of simple things can be difficult, but such difficulty is due not to the nature of the things but to the fact that we have forgotten how to see directly, being too much burdened with presuppositions. This is so characteristic of our contemporary situation that the following discussion may appear difficult simply because it is trying to gain for the author as well as for the reader the right method of seeing. If I am wrong in anticipating difficulty, so much the better; but the reader should realize that no end is gained by making the matter seem easier than it really is, in relation to the intellectual attitude of the present day. The essential difficulty in this book, however, lies not in the theoretical understanding nor in the acceptance of it as a "point of view", but in the actual encounter with reality which it demands. Now for a great end one must be ready to pay the price, and I would rather frighten a reader away than attract one who wants something for nothing.

THE COMING OF THE KINGDOM OF GOD:
THE NECESSITY OF DECISION

The future Kingdom of God, then, is not something which is to come in the course of time, so that to advance its coming one can do something in particular, perhaps through penitential prayers and good works, which become superfluous in the moment of its coming. Rather, the Kingdom of God is a power *which, although it is entirely future, wholly determines the present.* It determines the present because it now compels man to decision; he is determined thereby either in this direction or in that, as chosen or as rejected, in his entire present existence. Future and present are not related in the sense that the Kingdom begins as a historical fact in the present and achieves its fulfillment in the future; nor in the sense that an inner, spiritual possession of personal attributes or qualities of soul constitutes a present hold on the Kingdom, to which only the future consummation is lacking. Rather the Kingdom of God is genuinely future, because it is not a metaphysical entity or condition, but the future action of God, which can be in no sense something given in the present. Nonetheless this future determines man in his present, and exactly for that reason is true future — not merely something to come "somewhere, sometime", but destined for man and constraining him to decision.

The coming of the Kingdom of God is therefore not really an event in the course of time, which is due to occur sometime and toward which man can either take a definite attitude or hold himself neutral. Before he takes any attitude he is already constrained to make his choice, and therefore he must understand that just this necessity of decision constitutes the essential part of his human nature. Because Jesus sees man thus in a crisis of decision before God, it is understandable that in his thought the Jewish Messianic hope becomes the absolute certainty that in this hour the Kingdom of God is coming. If men are standing in the crisis of decision, and if precisely this crisis is the essential characteristic of their humanity, then every hour is the last hour, and we can understand that for Jesus the whole contemporary mythology is pressed into the service of this conception of human existence. Thus he understood and proclaimed his hour as the last hour.

This message of the Kingdom of God is absolutely alien to the present-day conception of humanity. We are accustomed to regard a man as an individual of the species "man", a being endowed with definite capacities, the development of which brings the human ideal to him to realization — of course with variations in each individual. As "character" or as "personality", man achieves his end. Harmonious development of all human faculties, according to the individual endowment of each man, is the way to this ideal. Perhaps no man can travel this road to the end, but progress along the road, bringing the ideal nearer to realization, justifies human existence. We are accustomed to distinguish between the physical or sensuous and the mental or spiritual life. And even if at the same time the connection between them is assumed, and symmetrical development is the shining goal, still the spirit is the guiding principle, and the life of the spirit is the true meaning of human existence.

All this is completely alien to the teaching of Jesus. Jesus expresses no conception of a human ideal, no thought of a development of human capacities, no idea of something valuable in man as such, no conception of the spirit in the modern sense. Of the spirit in our sense and of its life or experience, Jesus does not speak at all. The word which in the English Biblical translations is generally rendered "soul" or "spirit" usually means simply "life", as in the well-known saying: "What shall it profit a man if he gains the whole world and loses his soul?" (Mark 8:36.) The meaning is simply: Of what use are all the possessions of the world to a man who must die? The greed of man for property and profit is here shown to be as absurd as in the story of the rich farmer.

"There was a rich man whose land had yielded well. And he thought to himself, What shall I do? I have no place to put my grain. And he said, This is what I will do; I will pull down my barns and build greater ones, and there I will put all my grain. And then I will say to my soul [*i.e.*, simply 'to myself'], Soul, you have much wealth stored up for many years; rest, eat, drink, and be merry. But God said to him, Fool, tonight your soul [*i.e.*, your life] will be taken, and who then will own your possessions?" (Luke 12:16-20.)

The modern conception differs fundamentally from that of Jesus, because the former assumes the *intrinsic worth of humanity*, at least of the highest and noblest in it. The highest in man, indeed, is often designated without qualification as divine. By way of contrast, the worth of a man for Jesus is not determined by his human quality or the character of his spiritual life, but simply by the decision the man makes in the here-and-now of his present life. Jesus sees man as standing here and now under the necessity of decision, with the possibility of decision through his own free act. Only what a man now does gives him his value. And this crisis of decision arises for the man because he is face to face with the coming of the Kingdom of God. Somewhat similarly one might see the essential quality of human life defined by the fact that death awaits men and by the way they allow themselves to be determined thereby. And indeed the Kingdom of God and death are alike in this — that both the Kingdom and death imply the end of earthly human existence as we know it, with its possibilities and interests. Moreover it may be said that death, like the Kingdom, is not to be considered by man as an accidental event, which sometime will bring to an end the everyday course of life, but as the true future which confronts man and limits him in the present and puts him under the necessity of decision. Thus in either case the judgment is pronounced upon man not from the human standpoint, as if man's value were somehow immanent and securely possessed by him, but from without — according to Jesus, of course, God is the only Judge.

However, the coming of the Kingdom of God differs from the coming of death, because death is darkness, silence, while the Kingdom is a positive promise to man. Evidently when a man is constrained by the inevitable coming of death to make the decision, this decision can have only a negative sense, that is, to live his present life as a dying man, as an alien. On the contrary the decision which is forced upon him because of the coming of the Kingdom is positive — that is, to act in his present life in accordance with the will of God. What positive meaning "to do the will of God" has for men has yet to be determined from the teaching of Jesus.

First, it must again be stressed that the eschatological message of Jesus, the preaching of the coming of the Kingdom and of the call to repentance, can be understood only when one considers the *conception of man which in the last analysis underlies it,* and when one remembers that it can have meaning only for him who is ready to question the habitual human self-interpretation and to measure it by this opposed interpretation of human existence. Then it becomes obvious that the attention is not to be turned to the contemporary mythology in terms of which the real meaning in Jesus' teaching finds its outward expression. This mythology ends by abandoning the fundamental insight which gave it birth, the conception of man as forced to decision through a future act of God. To this mythology belongs the expectation of the end of the world as occurring in time, the expectation which in the contemporary situation of Jesus is the natural expression of his conviction that even in the present man stands in the crisis of decision, that the present is for him the last hour. To this mythology belongs also the figure of Satan who now fights against the hosts of the Lord. If it is true that to Jesus the world can be called bad only in so far as men are bad, that is, are of evil will, then it is clear how little the figure of Satan really meant to him.

Finally, it is also clear why Jesus cannot give a description of the Kingdom of God. Any such description would be possible only by projecting the demands and ideals of man or his spiritual experiences into the other world; and thereby the essential character of the beyond would be taken away. The Kingdom would be a creation of human desire and imagination; it would not be the Kingdom of *God.* But the Kingdom of God is not something dark, silent, and unknown, so that the idea of its relation to man is based wholly on speculation; rather the will of God is a comprehensible concept for men.

Jesus and the Word, pp. 3-15, 51-56.

*

"THE MESSAGE OF JESUS"

While "The Message of Jesus" was published fourteen years after Jesus, *it is remarkably consistent with the earlier work. Jesus' proclamation of the Kingdom and God's demand for radical obedience are portrayed here in much the same terms as in* Jesus. *Because of its brevity, it is a particularly useful summary of Bultmann's position concerning the figure of Jesus. The distinctive contribution of this essay appears primarily through its location in a larger work. It is the first chapter of Bultmann's 1948* Theology of the New Testament, Vol. I. *In the opening line of this volume, Bultmann establishes a clear boundary between the Kingdom message of Jesus and the church's proclamation of faith in the crucified and risen Christ (*kerygma*). For Bultmann, the life and message of Jesus are presuppositions for the* kerygma *of the early church, but are quite distinct from it. Christian faith does not appear until the early church announces God's saving act in Christ and this* kerygma *(proclamation) is thus the historical successor to the Kingdom message of Jesus. The concluding section of this introduction makes explicit the distinction between Jesus' message of the Kingdom and the church's proclamation of the Christ: in Bultmann's view, Jesus came to be regarded as Messiah or Christ, not in his own eyes or during the period of his own ministry, but only in the later church proclamation. Kendrick Grobel translated into English Bultmann's* Theology of the New Testament *(Scribners); Volume I appeared in 1951 and Volume II in 1955.*

PRELIMINARY REMARKS

1. *The message of Jesus* is a presupposition for the theology of the New Testament rather than a part of that theology itself. For New Testament

theology consists in the unfolding of those ideas by means of which Christian faith makes sure of its own object, basis, and consequences. But Christian faith did not exist until there was a Christian kerygma; i.e., a kerygma proclaiming Jesus Christ — specifically Jesus Christ the Crucified and Risen One — to be God's eschatological act of salvation. He was first so proclaimed in the kerygma of the earliest Church, not in the message of the historical Jesus, even though that Church frequently introduced into its account of Jesus' message motifs of its own proclamation. Thus, theological thinking — the theology of the New Testament — begins with the *kerygma* of the earliest Church and not before. But the fact that Jesus had appeared and the message which he had proclaimed were, of course, among its historical presuppositons; and for this reason Jesus' message cannot be omitted from the delineation of New Testament theology.

2. The synoptic gospels are the *source for Jesus' message*. Their use as history is governed by the so-called two source theory: i.e. Mark (which we know, however, only in a later redaction) is one source of Matthew and Luke; the other is a collection of Jesus' sayings (Q). Furthermore, throughout the synoptics three strands must be distinguished: old tradition, ideas produced in and by the Church, and editorial work of the evangelists. The critical analysis of these strands cannot be presented here; it is available in my book, *The History of the Synoptic Tradition.* Throughout this book, passages from Mark are cited without the addition of "par." wherever the Matthew and Luke parallels offer no independent tradition; "par." is added to a passage from Matthew or Luke wherever a tradition taken from Q is involved. That is what "par." is intended to indicate.[20]

1. THE ESCHATOLOGICAL MESSAGE

1. The dominant concept of Jesus' message is the *Reign of God.* Jesus proclaims its immediately impending irruption, now already making itself felt. Reign of God is an eschatological concept. It means the regime of God which will destroy the present course of the world, wipe out all the contra-divine, Satanic power under which the present world groans — and thereby, terminating all pain and sorrow, bring in salvation for the People of God which awaits the fulfillment of the prophets' promises. The coming of God's Reign is a miraculous event, which will be brought about by God alone without the help of men.

With such a message, Jesus stands *in the historical context of Jewish expectations about the end of the world and God's new future.* And it is clear that his thought is not determined by the *national* hope then still alive in certain circles of the Jewish people, in which the time of salvation to be brought in by God was thought of as the restitution of the idealized ancient kingdom of David. No saying of Jesus mentions the Messiah-king who is to crush the enemies of the People, nor the lordship of Israel over the earth, nor the gathering of the twelve tribes, nor the joy that will be in the bounteous peace-blessed Land. Rather, Jesus' message is connected with the hope of other circles which is primarily documented by the *apocalyptic* literature, a hope which awaits salvation not from a miraculous change in historical (i.e. political and social) conditions, but from a cosmic catastrophe which will do away with all conditions of the present world as it is. The presupposition of this hope is the pessimistic-dualistic view of the Satanic corruption of the total world-complex, which is expressed in the special doctrine of the *two aeons* into which the world's career is divided: The old aeon is approaching its end, and the new aeon will dawn with terror and tribulation. The old world with its periods has an end determined by God, and when the day he has determined is here, the judgment of the world will be held by him or by his representative, the Son of Man, who will come on the clouds of heaven; the dead will arise, and men's deeds, good or bad, will receive their reward. But the salvation of the faithful will consist not in national prosperity and splendor, but in the glory of paradise. In the context of these expectations stands the message of Jesus. However, it is free from all the learned and fanciful speculation of the apocalyptic writers. Jesus does not look back as they did upon past periods, casting up calculations when the end is coming; he does not bid men to peer after signs in nature and the affairs of nations by which they might recognize the nearness of the end. And he completely refrains from painting in the details of the judgment, the resurrection, and the glory to come. Everything is swallowed up in the single thought that then God will rule; and only very few details of the apocalyptic picture of the future recur in his words.

The contrast between this aeon and that is barely mentioned. The passages which speak of the "sons of this age" (Lk. 16:8; 20:34f.) and of the reward in the age to come for having followed him (Mk. 10:30) are secondary. The expression "close of the age" (Mt. 13:49) may be genuine tradition, though it is secondary in the parable interpretations (Mt. 13:39f. and 24:3). "The present time", Καιρὸς οὗτος, meaning the remnant of time before the eschatological end, at

JESUS AND THE ESCHATOLOGICAL KINGDOM

Lk. 12:56 is probably original, but at Mk. 10:30, as the opposite of "the age to come", is secondary.

But it is evident that Jesus has this conviction: This age has run out. The summary of his preaching in the saying, "The time is fulfilled, and the Reign of God is at hand" (Mk. 1:15), is appropriate. Jesus is convinced that the world's present course is under the sway of Satan and his demons, whose time is now expired (Lk. 10:18). He expects the coming of the "Son of Man" as judge and savior (Mk. 8:38; Mt. 24:27 par. 37 par. 44 par.; [Mt. 10:23; 19:28]; Lk. 12:8f.; [Mt. 10:32f.]; Lk. 17:30).[21] He expects the resurrection of the dead (Mk. 12:18-27) and the judgment (Lk. 11:31f. par., etc.). He shares the idea of a fiery Hell into which the damned are to be cast (Mk. 9:43-48; Mt. 10:28). For the blessedness of the righteous he uses the simple term "Life" Ζωή (Mk. 9:43, 45, etc.). While he can indeed speak of the heavenly banquet at which they will recline at table with Abraham, Isaac, and Jacob (Mt. 8:11) and also of his hope of drinking wine anew in the Reign of God (Mk. 14:25), he nevertheless also says, "When they rise from the dead, they neither marry nor are given in marriage, but are like angels in heaven" (Mk. 12:25).

2. Thus Jesus does take over the apocalyptic picture of the future, but he does so with significant reduction of detail. What is new and really his own about it all is the certainty with which he says, *"Now the time is come! God's Reign is breaking in! The end is here!"* That is what the following words mean:

"Blessed are the eyes which see what you see!
For I tell you:
Many prophets and kings desired to see what you see and did not see it,
And to hear what you hear, and did not hear it!"
(Lk. 10:23f. par.)

Now is no time to mourn and fast; this is a time of joy like that of a wedding (Mk. 2:18f.). So he now cries his "Blessed are you!" to the waiting, expectant ones:

"Blessed are you poor, for yours is the Reign of God!
Blessed are you that hunger now, for you shall be satisfied!
Blessed are you that weep now, for you shall laugh!" (Lk. 6:20f Blt.).

Satan's reign is now collapsing, for "I saw Satan fall like lightning from heaven" (Lk. 10:18).

Signs of the time there are, indeed; but not such as those after which

105

apocalyptic fantasy peers. For "God's Reign comes not so that it can be calculated; and none can say, 'Lo, here or there!' For lo, God's Reign is (all at once) in your midst!" (Lk. 17:21 Blt.). "And if you are told: lo here! lo there! do not go, do not follow them. For as the lightning flashes and lights up the sky from one side to the other, so will it be with the Son of Man in his day" (Lk. 17:23f. Blt.).

The people, it is true, are blind to the true signs of the time; they can well enough interpret the signs of the heavens (clouds and wind) and know when it is going to rain or be hot — why can they not discern the signs of the present? (Lk. 12:54-56). When the fig tree sprouts and gets green men know summer is near; so from the signs of the time they should know that the End is at hand (Mk. 13:28f.).

But what are the signs of the time? He himself! *His presence, his deeds, his message!*

"The blind see, and the lame walk,
 Lepers are cleansed and the deaf hear,
 The dead arise and the poor have the message of salvation pro-
  claimed to them" (Mt. 11:5 par. Blt.).

It can be asked whether these words only express the certainty that the prophetic predictions of salvation (Is. 35:5f.; 29:18f.; 61:1) will presently be fulfilled, or whether Jesus means that their fulfillment is already beginning in his own miracles. Probably the latter. For though he refuses the demand made of him to legitimate himself by a "sign from heaven" (Mk. 8:11f.), he nevertheless sees God's Reign already breaking in in the fact that by the divine power that fills him he is already beginning to drive out the demons, to whom he, like his contemporaries, attributes many diseases: "If I by the finger of God drive out demons, then God's Reign has come upon you!" (Lk. 11:20 par. Blt.). "No one can enter a strong man's house and plunder his goods, unless he first binds the strong man" (Mk. 3:27), hence, since he is robbing Satan of his plunder, it is apparent that Satan has been attacked by one stronger than himself.

All that does not mean that God's Reign is already here; but it does mean that it is dawning. Man cannot hasten the divinely determined course of events, either by strict observance of the commandments and by penance — as the Pharisees supposed — or by driving out the Romans by force of arms — as the Zealots fancied. For "with the Reign of God it is as if a man should scatter seed upon the ground and should sleep and rise night and day, and the seed should sprout and grow, he knows not how. The earth produces of itself, first the blade, then the ear, then the full grain in the ear. But when the grain is ripe, at once he sends the harvesters, because the harvest has come" (Mk. 4:26-29 Blt.).

From this *parable of the seed growing of itself,* in which "of itself" is the point, one must not draw the conclusion that God's Reign (or Kingdom) is an entity growing in history; rather it assumes that its coming is a miracle independent of every human act — as miraculous as the growth and ripening of seed, which proceeds without human help or comprehension. It is far from Jesus and the world he moved in to regard the growth of seed as a natural process of development. The meaning of the parable can be clarified by placing beside it a similar one, handed down to us in 1 Clem. 23, which is intended to picture how certainly the judgment of God will come: "O fools, compare yourselves with a tree, for instance a grapevine! First it casts off its old leaves, then young shoots arise, then leaves, then blossoms, then the tiny clusters, then the full bunch is there. You see how quickly fruit gets ripe. Verily, quickly and suddenly shall God's decree be accomplished. . . ."

Neither do the *parables of the mustard-seed and of the leaven* (Mk. 4:30-32 or Mt. 13:31f. par.) tell of a gradual development of the "Kingdom of God" in history. Their point is the contrast between the minuteness of its beginning and the magnitude of its completion; they do not intend to give instruction about the process which leads from beginning to completion. Both beginning and completion of God's Reign are miraculous, and miraculous is the happening which brings its fulfillment. Then Jesus' presence and activity are understood to be its beginning — that is, if these parables really have for their subject the beginning and completion of God's Reign. That is admittedly uncertain; the related parables in the Shepherd of Hermas (Mand. V 1, 5f.; XI 20f.) about the drop of wormwood which makes a whole jug of honey bitter, and about the hailstone which can cause great pain, have an entirely different meaning. The former intends to illustrate how practice in patience is brought to nought by an attack of wrath; the latter illustrates the power of the Holy Spirit. So it might be that the parables of the mustard-seed and of the leaven originally dealt with the individual and were intended to instruct him either as a warning or as a consolation, how great a result may grow out of small beginnings.

The introductory formula, "The Kingdom is like" (ὁμοία ἐστιν) or "is likened" (ὁμοιώθη) in these parables and in Matthew's so-called *Kingdom-of-Heaven parables* (Mt. 13:44, 45; 18:23; 20:1; 22:2; 25:1) does not mean that what is named in the parable is to be directly compared with the Reign of God, but does mean that the parable teaches a truth that in some way applies to the Reign of God — for example, that God's Reign requires sacrifice of men; for when it is said (Mt. 13:45), "The Reign of God is like a merchant," it is clear that the merchant is not a portrait of God's Reign, but that his conduct portrays the attitude required by it. Besides, the introductory formula, frequently at least, is due to the editing of the evangelist; it is missing in the Lucan parallel (14:16) to Mt. 22:2 as well as in all the parables peculiar to Luke. On the interpretation of the parables in general *cf.* Ad. Jülicher *Die Gleichnisreden Jesus* I 2nd ed. (1899), II 2nd ed. (1910); R. Bultmann, *The History of the Synoptic Tradition.*

3. All that man can do in the face of the Reign of God now breaking in is this: Keep ready or get ready for it. Now is the *time of decision,* and Jesus' call is the *call to decision.* The "Queen of the South" once came to hear the wisdom of Solomon; the Ninevites repented at the preaching of Jonah — "behold, something greater than Solomon is here! behold, something greater than Jonah is here!" (Lk. 11:31f. par.). "Blessed is he who takes no offense at me!" (Mt. 11:6 par.).

Basically, therefore, *he in his own person is the "sign of the time".* Yet the historical Jesus of the synoptics does not, like the Johannine Jesus, summon men to acknowledge or "believe in" his person. He does not proclaim himself as the Messiah, i.e. the king of the time of salvation, but he points ahead to the Son of Man as another than himself. *He in his own person signifies the demand for decision,* insofar as his cry, as God's last word before the End, calls men to decision. Now is the last hour; now it can be only: either — or! Now the question is whether a man really desires God and his Reign or the world and its goods; and the decision must be drastically made. "No one who puts his hand to the plow and looks back is fit for the Reign of God!" (Lk. 9:62 Blt.). "Follow me, and leave the dead to bury their own dead!" (Mt. 8:22 par.). "Whoever comes to me and does not hate his father and mother, wife and children, brothers and sisters, yes, and even himself, he cannot be my disciple" (Lk. 14:26 par. Blt.). "Whoever does not bear his own cross and follow me, he cannot be my disciple" (Lk. 14:27 par. Blt. or Mk. 8:34).

He himself renounced his relatives; "whoever does God's will, he is brother and sister and mother to me" (Mk. 3:35 Blt.). And evidently he also uprooted by his word a band of men out of their homes and occupations to accompany him in his wandering life as his "disciples" — i.e. his pupils (Mk. 1:16-20; 2:14). Still he did not found an order or a sect, far less a "Church", nor did he expect that everyone should or could forsake house and family.

The saying about the building of the "Church" (ἐκκλησία) Mt. 16:18 is, like the whole of Mt. 16:17-19, a later product of the Church; cf. *The History of the Synoptic Tradition.*

But everyone is confronted with deciding what he will set his heart upon — on God or on worldly goods. "Do not lay up for yourselves treasures on earth. . . . For where your treasure is, there will your heart be also!" (Mt. 6:19-21 par.). "No one can serve two masters!" (Mt. 6:24 par.). How dangerous wealth is! "It is easier for a camel to go through the eye of a needle than for a rich man to enter the Reign of God!" (Mk. 10:25 Blt.). Most men cling to earthly goods and cares; and when the time for decision comes, they fail — as the parable of the banquet shows (Lk. 14:15-24 par.). A man must make up his mind what he wants, what degree of effort he is capable of, just as the means for building a tower or waging a war must first be estimated (Lk. 14:28-32). But for the Reign of God one must be ready for any sacrifice — like the farmer who finds a treasure and gives all he has to get possession of it, or like the merchant who sells everything in order to acquire the one precious pearl (Mt. 13:44-46).

"If your hand causes you to sin, cut it off! It is better for you to enter life maimed than with two hands to go to hell. . . ."

"If your eye causes you to sin, pluck it out! It is better for you to enter the Reign of God with one eye, than with two eyes to be thrown into hell" (Mk. 9:43, 47 Blt. or Mt. 5:29f.).

But this renunciation toward the world, this "unworldliness", is not to be thought of as asceticism, but as simple readiness for God's demand. For the positive thing that corresponds to this renunciation, the thing, that is, which constitutes readiness for God's Reign, is the fulfillment of God's will, as Jesus makes evident in combating Jewish legalism.

2. JESUS' INTERPRETATION OF THE DEMAND OF GOD

1. As interpretation of the will, the demand of God, Jesus' message is a great *protest against Jewish legalism* — i.e. against a form of piety which regards the will of God as expressed in the written Law and in the Tradition which interprets it, a piety which endeavors to win God's favor by the toil of minutely fulfilling the Law's stipulations. Here there is no dif-

ferentiation between religion and morality, nor are laws about worship and ethics separated from statutes of everyday law. This state of affairs is typified by the fact that the "scribes" are theologians, teachers, and lawyers all at the same time. What religion and morality require is prescribed by the Law, but civil and criminal law are also regarded as divine Law. The result is not merely that a mass of ordinances which have lost the meaning they once had under earlier conditions remain in force and so have to be twisted by artificial interpretation into relevance for today; not merely that regulations appropriate to the present have to be wrung out of the ancient Law by artificial deduction to meet new conditions of life. Nor is the result merely that a plethora of cultic and ritual laws are regarded as God's demand, or as ethical demand, and thus frequently overshadowed the really ethical demands. The real result is that motivation to ethical conduct is vitiated. That is the result not only in the wide extent to which the idea of reward and punishment becomes the motiviation, but also — and this is the characteristic thing for Judaism — that the obedience man owes to God and to his demand for good is understood as a purely formal one; i.e. as an obedience which fulfills the letter of the law, obeying a law simply because it is commanded without asking the reason, the meaning, of its demand. And though many a scribe protests against the prevalence of reward and punishment as the motive for obedience, demanding instead an obedience from the heart which would fulfill the commandment not out of fear but out of love to God, nevertheless obedience cannot be radical, genuine obedience so long as man obeys only because it is commanded — so long, that is, as he would do something else if something else were commanded, or, rather, would not do the thing in question if it did not stand in the commandment. Radical obedience is only possible where a man understands the demand and affirms it from within himself. And only of such obedience is it meaningful to say that in fulfilling the ethical demand it fulfills God's demand, for God requires radical obedience. The error of Jewish legalism reveals itself finally in the following. A statute, unlike an ethical demand, can never embrace every specific situation of life, instead there inevitably remain many cases unprovided for, cases for which there is no command or prohibition; that leaves room not only for every desire and passion that may arise but also — and that again is characteristic of Judaism — for works of supererogation. In principle, when a man's duties are conceived of as the committing or omitting of specific acts under legal requirement, he can completely discharge them and have room left over for extra deeds of merit. So there developed in Judaism the notion of "good works" that go beyond the required fulfillment of the Law (such as almsgiving, various acts of charity, voluntary fasting, and the like), establishing literal merits and hence also capable of atoning for transgressions of the Law. This indicates that here the idea of obedience is not taken radically.

2. Seen against this background *Jesus' proclamation of the will of God appears as a great protest.* In it the protest of the great prophets of the Old Testament against the cultic worship of God in their time is renewed under altered circumstances. Whereas they had upheld justice and uprightness as God's demand in opposition to the cultic piety of the people, Jesus demanded radical obedience in opposition to that merely formal obedience which to a large extent regarded the fulfillment of the ritual prescriptions as the essential thing. He does not, as the prophets did, raise the demand for justice and right; for the preaching of these things, once decisive for Israelitic national life, has lost its meaning now that there is scarcely any national life left. What Judaism has left as the product of the prophets' work is codified law, which now, however, no longer serves primarily to regulate national life but governs the relation of the individual to God. And that is just what Jesus protests against — that man's relation to God is regarded as a legal one. God requires radical obedience. He claims man whole — and wholly. Within this insight Jesus takes for granted that God requires of man the doing of the good and that ethical demands are the demands of God; to that extent religion and ethics constitute a unity for him, too. But excluded from the demands of God are all cultic and ritual regulations, so that along with ethics Jesus sets free the purely religious relation to God in which man stands only as one who asks and receives, hopes and trusts.

The antitheses (Mt. 5:21-48) *in the Sermon on the Mount* throw legalism and the will of God into sharp contrast: "You have heard that it was said to the men of old . . ., But I say to you . . .!" The meaning is this: God does not lay claim to man only so far as conduct can be determined by formulated laws (the only way open to legalism), leaving man's own will free from that point on. What God forbids is not simply the overt acts of murder, adultery, and perjury, with which law can deal, but their antecedents: anger and name-calling, evil desire and insincerity (Mt. 5:21f., 27f., 33-37). What counts before God is not simply the substantial, verifiable deed that is done, but how a man is disposed, what his intent is. As the laws concerning murder, adultery and perjury are thus radicalized, so others which were once meant to restrict arbitrary action but now are conceived as concessions defining an area of leeway for per-

111

missive acts, are from the point of view of God's intention altogether abolished: the provision for divorce, the law of retaliation, the limitation of the duty of love to one's neighbor alone (Mt. 5:31f., 38-41, 43-48). *God demands the whole will of man* and knows no abatement in His demand.

Are grapes gathered from thorns,
    or figs from thistles?
Each tree is known by its own fruit;
    a good tree cannot bear evil fruit.

(Mt. 7:16, 18 combined with Lk. 6:43f. Blt.)

The eye is the lamp of the body.
So, if your eye is sound,
Your whole body will be full of light.
But if your eye is not sound,
Your whole body will be full of darkness.   (Mt. 6:22f. par.)

Man, upon whose whole self God's demand is made, has no freedom toward God; he is accountable for his life as a whole — as the parable of the talents teaches (Mt. 25:14-30 par.). *He may not, must not, cannot raise any claim before God*, but is like the slave who only has his duty to do and can do no more (Lk. 17:7-10).

This parable is paralleled in the saying of a pre-Christian rabbi, Antigonus of Socho: "Be not like servants who serve their lord on condition of receiving reward; but rather be like servants who serve their lord under no condition of receiving reward" (Pirqe Aboth 1, 3). In demanding unconditional obedience Jesus and the rabbi agree. That the idea of obedience is taken radically by Jesus follows from the whole context of his ethical utterances.

Man must become like a child, who, knowing no such thing as appeal to any rights or merits of his own, is willing simply to be given a gift (Mk. 10:15). Those who proudly brag of their merits are an abomination to God (Lk. 16:15), and the virtue-proud Pharisee has to take a lower place than the guilt-conscious publican (Lk. 18:9-14). So Jesus rejects all this counting up of merit and reward: The worker who went to work in the last hour of the day is rewarded just as much as the one who had worked all day long (Mt. 20:1-15). And Jesus also refuses to regard the misfortune that befalls individuals as punishment for their special sins; no man is better than another (Lk. 13:1-5).

One must, of course, admit that for Jesus it is certain that God does reward faithful obedience; back of the demand stands the promise; and in view of his battle against the motive of retribution his position must be so described: He promises reward precisely to those who obey not for the sake of reward. Even so, his words are not without self-contradiction, since he does occasionally use the *idea of recompense* as motivation for a demand — either by referring to heavenly reward (Mt. 6:19f. par. Mk. 10:21 and elsewhere) or by threatening with hell-fire (Mt. 10:28 par. Mk. 9:43, 47 and elsewhere). Still the contradiction can probably be resolved in this way: The motive of reward is only a primitive expression for the idea that in what a man does his own real being is at stake — that self which he not already is, but is to become. To achieve that self is the legitimate motive of his ethical dealing and of his true obedience, in which he becomes aware of the paradoxical truth that in order to arrive at himself he must surrender to the demand of God — or, in other words, that in such surrender he wins himself. This paradoxical truth is taught in the following saying:

> "Whoever seeks to gain his life will lose it,
> But whoever loses his life will preserve it."   (Lk. 17:33).

Both Mark and Q hand down this saying. At Mk. 8:35 "whoever loses it" has the addition: "for my sake and the gospel's". The parallels to this passage, Mt. 16:25 and Lk. 9:24, read only "for my sake", and that is probably all they had found in their Marcan text. To accord with it Mt. 10:39 also added "for my sake" in the Q-parallel to Lk. 17:33. John also knew the saying, and knew it without the addition, so that he corroborates the form of Lk. 17:33 as the original one when he says "He who loves his life loses it, and he who hates his life in this world will keep it for eternal life" (12:25), though he, on his part, has added "in this world" and "for eternal life".

3. From the standpoint of this radical attitude of Jesus toward the will of God, what is to be said of *his position toward the Old Testament?* Without contesting its authority he makes critical distinctions among the demands of the Old Testament. Yes, Moses did permit divorce, but only "in consideration of your hard-heartedness". By no means is that the actual intention of God; rather he intends marriage to be inseparable (Mk. 10:2-9).

"Woe to you, scribes and Pharisees, hypocrites! For you tithe mint and dill and cummin, and have neglected the weightiest in the Law: justice and mercy and good faith; these things ought to be done and the others not neglected. You blind guides, straining out a gnat and swallowing a camel!" (Mt. 23:23f. Blt.). If the words "These things ought to be done and the others not neglected" are really an original component of this "woe" (they are missing in the Luke-parallel 11:42 in Codex D), they indicate that a reformer's polemic against the Old Testament legislation is far from Jesus' intention. In any case these verses indicate a sovereign attitude assumed by Jesus toward the Old Testament, an attitude which critically distinguishes the important from the unimportant, the essential from the indifferent. This is in harmony with the rest of Jesus' words concerning the Old Testament.

God did indeed declare his will in the Old Testament. Whoever inquires about the will of God is referred to the ethical demands of the Old Testament — for instance, the rich man with his question: "What must I do to inherit eternal life?" or the "lawyer"-scribe with his query about the highest commandment (Mk. 10:17-19, 12:28-34). But the rich man straight away has to accept the accusation that his previous fulfillment of the commandments has been an illusion, since he is incapable of giving up everything — he cannot radically obey.

That Jesus did not polemically contest the authority of the Old Testament is proven by the course later taken by his Church; it clung faithfully to the Old Testament Law and thereby came into conflict with Paul. The Church formulated its standpoint — no matter whether against Paul or against other Hellenistic missionaries — in the words placed on Jesus' lips about the imperishability of even the tiniest letter in the Law and expressly declaring that Jesus did not come to abolish the Law, but to fulfill it (Mt. 5:17-19) — a saying that in view of other sayings of Jesus and of his actual practice cannot possibly be genuine; rather it is a product of the Church coming out of the later period of conflict over the Law. Yet clearly this conservative attitude of the Church would not have been possible if Jesus had called into question the validity of the Old Testament. Its authority stands just as fast for him as for the scribes, and he feels himself in opposition to them only in the way he understands and applies the Old Testament. Neither did he oppose *the pious practices of Judaism* — almsgiving, prayer, and fasting — though he did protest against their being put into the service of personal vanity and so becoming a lie (Mt. 6:1-4, 5-8, 16-18).

His answer to the question about fasting, Mk. 2:19, does not reject fasting on principle, but means that in the dawning of messianic joy the mourning custom of fasting (which in itself is not opposed) does not make sense. The original meaning of the sayings about the new patch on an old garment and new wine in old skins (Mk. 2:21f.) is no longer clearly discernible. It may have intended some such meaning as this, that in the messianic period the old mourning customs have become meaningless.

Polemic against the temple cult is completely absent from the words of Jesus. As a matter of fact it, too, had essentially lost its original meaning in his time; for Judaism was no longer a cultic religion, but had become a religion of observance. The temple cult was faithfully carried out, and at the great festivals really cultic piety probably revived. But in general the temple cult with its sacrifices was carried out as an act of obedience — for was it not commanded in the Law? The synagogue with its interpretation of the regulation of daily life by the Law had pushed the temple service into the background; for the people, the scribes had replaced the priests as the seat of authority. So Judaism, borne up by the synagogue and the scribes, survived the fall of the temple without disaster. In Mt. 5:23f. participation in the temple cult is taken for granted without misgiving. It may well be a genuine saying of Jesus, whereas Mt. 17:24-27 is a later legend, but one that proves, nevertheless, that the Christian Church paid the temple tax. In the same way accounts contained in Acts also show that the Church held gatherings within the temple area.

Actually the Old Testament legislation, so far as it consists of cultic and ritual prescriptions, has been lifted off its hinges by Jesus. As he rises above the Sabbath law, so he attacks *legalistic ritualism* which strives for an external correctness which can go hand in hand with an impure will. Thus he quotes the prophet (Is. 29:13):

"This people honors me with their lips
  But their heart is far from me.
  In vain do they worship me,
  Teaching as doctrines the precepts of men." (Mk. 7:6f.)
"Woe to you, scribes and Pharisees, hypocrites!
  For you cleanse the outside of the cup and of the plate,
  But inside you (*cf.* Lk. 11:39) are full of extortion and rapacity!". . .
"Woe to you, scribes and Pharisees, hypocrites!
  For you are like whitewashed tombs, which outwardly appear beautiful,
  But within they are full of dead men's bones and all uncleanness.
  So you also outwardly appear righteous to men,
  But within you are full of hypocrisy and iniquity." (Mt. 23:25-28 par. Blt.).

How alms, prayer, and fasting can be misused to impress others (Mt. 6:1-4, 5f., 16-18)! Unless fasting expresses real grief, it has no meaning (Mk. 2:18f.). How God's command to honor one's parents can be set aside by declaring a cultic command to be more important (Mk. 7:9-13)! The laws of cleanliness are meaningless, for "there is nothing outside a man which by going into him can defile him; but the things which come out of a man are what defile him" (Mk. 7:15). "The sabbath was made for man, not man for the sabbath" (Mk. 2:27). And though it is true that the same insight flashes up now and then among the scribes, still Jesus is the first to draw the consequence of it with his question:

"Is it lawful on the sabbath to do good or to do harm,
    To save a life or to kill?" (Mk. 3:4 Blt.)

that is, there is no third choice, no holy indolence. To do nothing where an act of love is required would be to do evil. So Jesus is "a friend of publicans and sinners" (Mt. 11:19 par., Mk. 2:15-17); he cannot avoid being slandered as "glutton and drunkard" (Mt. 11:19), and he can actually use a Samaritan as a good example (Lk. 10:30-36).

4. What, positively, is the will of God? *The demand for love.* "You shall love your neighbor as yourself!" as the second greatest commandment belongs together with the first: "You shall love the Lord your God with all your heart and with all your soul and with all your mind and with all your strength" (Mk. 12:28-34). There is no obedience to God which does not have to prove itself in the concrete situation of meeting one's neighbor, as Luke (10:29-37), probably unhistorically but with the right of correct understanding of the subject-matter, makes clear by combining the illustrative narrative of the Good Samaritan with Jesus' discussion of the greatest commandment.

The demand for love surpasses every legal demand; it knows no boundary or limit; it holds even in regard to one's enemy (Mt. 5:43-48). The question, "How often must I forgive my brother when he sins against me? Is seven times enough?" is answered: "I tell you: not seven times, but seventy times seven" (Mt. 18:21f. par. Blt.).

The demand for love needs no formulated stipulations; the example of the merciful Samaritan shows that a man can know and must know what he has to do when he sees his neighbor in need of his help. The little words "as yourself" in the love-commandment pre-indicate both the boundlessness and the direction of loving conduct.

Jesus completely refrained from making the love-commandment concrete in specific prescriptions. That fact shows that his proclamation of the will of God is not an ethic of world-reform. Rather, it must be described as an eschatological ethic. For it does not envisage a future to be molded within this world by plans and sketches for the ordering of human life. It only directs man into the Now of his meeting with his neighbor. It is an ethic that, by demanding more than the law that regulates human society does and requiring of the individual the waiver of his own rights, makes the individual immediately responsible to God.

5. At this point it begins to be clear how *Jesus' eschatological message and his ethical message constitute a unity* — in other words, how the same Jesus can be both the prophet who proclaims the irruption of God's Reign and the rabbi who expounds God's Law.

There is such a unity, but it is a false unity if it is reached by conceiving God's Reign as the triumph of the Demand for Good either in the human mind or in historical human affairs. This misconception may say: God's Reign is a reigning of God in the mind which occurs when the divine Demand prevails there and takes shape in ethical character. Or it may say: It is a reigning of God in human affairs which occurs when the divine Demand prevails there and takes shape in an ethical social order. Both forms not only distort the concept Reign of God but also misunderstand the intent of God's demand — it aims neither at the formation of "character" nor at the molding of human society.

Neither is it feasible, recognizing the rivalry between the eschatological and the ethical message of Jesus, to deny one of the two to belong to the historical Jesus and pronounce it a later product of the Church. It cannot be maintained that Jesus was only a teacher of ethics who taught a "superior righteousness" and that it was the Church that first put into his mouth the eschatological message of the irruption of God's Reign. For we can readily see that the origin of the Church lies in the certainty of that imminent End, but not that that certainty itself could have been a later community product. The tradition shows, on the contrary, that alarmed anxiety arose in the Church at the delay of the expected Reign of God. This alarm is expressed in words put into the mouth of Jesus (Lk. 12:35-38, Mk. 13:31, 33-37). But above all, the movement which Jesus evoked among the people and his crucifixion by the Roman procurator show that it was in the role of a messianic prophet that he appeared. On the other hand, it is just as impossible to regard only his eschatological message as historically genuine and his ethical preaching as a secondary product of the Church. For, aside from the fact that it would not be intelligible how the Church should have come to make a rabbi of him whom they regarded as

Messiah, the scrupulous observance of the Law by the earliest Church indicates that the radical sayings about the Law and its observance cannot have originated in it.

The unity of the eschatological and the ethical message of Jesus may be so stated: Fulfillment of God's will is the condition for participation in the salvation of his Reign. Only "condition" in that statement must not be taken in the external sense of an arbitrarily set task, in place of which some other could have been set — a condition, that is, without inner relation to the gift for whose receipt it constitutes the presupposition — as it is taken to mean, for instance, when Jesus' interpretation of the divine demand is held to be no more than an "interim ethic" and its imperatives are therefore regarded as exceptional commands which only held for the last short interval until the end of the world. Rather, these imperatives are clearly meant radically as absolute demand with a validity independent of the temporal situation. Neither the demands of the Sermon on the Mount nor Jesus' attacks against legalistic morality are motivated by reference to the impending end of the world. But precisely Jesus' knowledge of the absolute validity of the divine demand is the basis of his radical verdict over "this evil and adulterous generation" ripe for divine judgment (Mt. 12:39 par., Mk. 8:38) — the same verdict, that is, that comes to expression in the eschatological proclamation. Then this is clear: The fulfillment of God's will is the condition for participation in the salvation of God's Reign in *this* sense, that it means nothing else but true readiness for it, genuine and earnest desire for it. The Reign of God, demanding of man decision for God against every earthly tie, is the salvation to come. Hence, only he is ready for this salvation who in the concrete moment decides for that demand of God which confronts him in the person of his neighbor. They who, conscious of their poverty, wait weeping and hungering for salvation, are identical with those who are merciful, pure of heart, and peace-makers (Mt. 5:3-9). Whoever has his will set upon God's Reign also wills to fulfill the commandment of love. It is not that he fulfills the commandment of love as an irksome requirement while his real will is directed at something else (viz. God's Reign), for the sake of which alone he obeys the commandment of God. Rather there is an inner connection: Both things, the eschatological proclamation and the ethical demand, direct man to the fact that he is thereby brought before God, that God stands before him; both direct him into his Now as the hour of decision for God.

6. Thus it happens that at the sight of the actual state of the leaders of

118

the people and of the great mass of the people itself — at the sight of religion frozen into ritualism, at the sight of superficiality and love of self and the world — Jesus' message becomes *a cry of woe and repentance*.

"Woe to you, scribes and Pharisees! . . ."
(Mt. 23:1ff. par.; Mk. 12:38ff.)
"Woe to you that are rich, for you have received your consolation!
Woe to you that are full now, for you shall hunger!
Woe to you that laugh now, for you shall mourn and weep!"
(Lk. 6:24-26)

"The time is fulfilled, the Reign of God is at hand! Repent!" (Mk. 1:15) — this is the condensed summary of Jesus' cry. But this contemporary "generation" is "adulterous and sinful" (Mk. 8:38; Mt. 12:39). Men say "yes" to God's demand and then do not do what he requires (Mt. 21:28-31). They refuse to "repent", to turn about from their perverted way (Lk. 11:31f. par.), and so the judgment will break in upon sinners (Lk. 13:1-5), and all predictions of woe will come to pass (Mt. 23:34-36 par.), especially upon Jerusalem (Mt. 23:37-39 par.) and its temple: not a stone that will not be thrown down! (Mk. 13:2). Only in the despised — the publicans, sinners, and harlots — is there readiness to repent; to them and not to the "righteous", Jesus considers himself sent (Mk. 2:17); these who first said "no" repent (Mt. 21:28-31), and God has more joy over one sinner who repents than over ninety-nine "righteous" (Lk. 15:1-10). They who await God's Reign aright, hungering and sorrowing, knowing how poor they are — to them pertains the promise of salvation (Lk. 6:20f. or Mt. 5:3-6).

3. JESUS' IDEA OF GOD

1. Once one has understood the unity of the eschatological and the ethical preaching of Jesus, one also has the answer to the real meaning of the eschatological message, namely: the answer to the question, what *idea of God* is at work in it. For, in view of the fact that the proclamation of the irruption of God's Reign was not fulfilled — that is, that Jesus' expectation of the near end of the world turned out to be an illusion — the question arises whether his idea of God was not also illusory. This question is frequently avoided, it is true, by the escape-reasoning that Jesus saw the presence of God's Reign in his own person and in the followers who gathered about him. But such a view cannot be substantiated by a single saying of Jesus,[22] and it contradicts the meaning of "God's Reign". On

119

the contrary, Jesus clearly expected the irruption of God's Reign as a miraculous, world-transforming event — as Judaism, and later also his own Church, did. Nowhere to be found in his words is there polemic against this view, so taken for granted by his time, or any correction of it.

But it is a fact that *prophetic consciousness* always expects the judgment of God, and likewise the time of salvation to be brought in by God, in the immediate future, as may be clearly seen in the great prophets of the Old Testament. And the reason this is so is that to the prophetic consciousness the sovereignty of God, the absoluteness of his will, is so overpowering that before it the world sinks away and seems to be at its end. The consciousness that man's relation toward God decides his fate and that the hour of decision is of limited duration clothes itself in the consciousness that the hour of decision is here for the world, too. The word which the prophet is conscious of having to speak by God's commission takes the form of the final word by which God summons men to definitive decision.

So also with Jesus. He is certain that he is acquainted with the unswerving will of God, who sternly demands the good from man and, through the message by which he is preached, thrusts man into the alternative of salvation or condemnation. It is this certainty which gives Jesus the consciousness of standing at the end of time. His message grows neither out of weariness with the world and longing for the world beyond nor out of fanciful speculation, but out of knowing the world's futility and man's corruption in God's eyes and out of knowing the will of God. The essential thing about the eschatological message is the idea of God that operates in it and the idea of human existence that it contains — not the belief that the end of the world is just ahead.

2. God, in keeping with Old Testament tradition, is, for Jesus, *the Creator* who governs the world with his care, feeds the beasts and adorns the flowers, without whose will not a sparrow falls dead to earth, and who has counted every hair of our heads (Mt. 6:25-34 par., 10:29f. par.). All anxious care, all haste to get goods to insure life, is therefore senseless — yes, wicked. Man is at the mercy of the Creator's will; he can neither add a cubit to his height nor make a single hair of his head white or black (Mt. 6:27 par., 5:36). If he imagines himself self-insured by the wealth he has amassed and able now to take his ease, he has forgotten that he still can die this very night (Lk. 12:16-20). Trust in God and consciousness of dependence are both alike demanded of man.

In the above, Jesus' idea of God does not essentially differ from that of the Old Testament and of Judaism, though it is true that in the common piety of Judaism faith in God the Creator had weakened even while it was strictly preserved in its official theology and confession. God had retreated far off into the distance as the transcendent heavenly King, and his sway over the present could barely still be made out. For Jesus, God again became *a God at hand.* He is the power, here and now, who as Lord and Father enfolds every man — limiting and commanding him. This contrast finds expression in the respective forms of address used in prayer. Compare the ornate, emotional, often liturgically beautiful, but often over-loaded, forms of address in Jewish prayer with the stark simplicity of "Father!" The "Prayer of Eighteen Petitions", for instance, which the devout Jew is expected to say three times daily, begins, "Lord God of Abraham, God of Isaac, God of Jacob! God Most High, Creator of heaven and earth! Our Shield and the Shield of our fathers!"[23] The "Lord's Prayer" stands out above Jewish prayers not only in its simple address but in its direct simplicity throughout (Mt. 6:9-13, or Lk. 11:2-4). God is near; he hears and understands the requests which come thronging to him, as a father understands the requests of his own child (Mt. 7:7-11 par.; *cf.* Lk. 11:5-8; 18:1-5).

But God has also come near as the "Demand-er" whose will need not wait to be found in the letter of the Law or its scribal exegesis. The remoteness interposed by Law and Tradition between God and man is closed up, and man's uncertain searching for what is forbidden and what allowed is over. A man learns what God wants of him immediately out of his own situation in the encounter with his neighbor. And so God also stands before every man as the Judge to whom he owes accounting. "I tell you, on the day of judgment men will render account for every careless word they utter" (Mt. 12:36). "Do not fear those who kill the body but cannot kill the soul! Rather fear him who can destroy both soul and body in hell!" (Mt. 10:28 par.).

But the demanding God of judgment is also the merciful *God of forgiveness*; and whoever turns back to him in repentance can be certain of his forgiving kindness. The scribes shut the Kingdom of heaven in men's faces with their legalism (Mt. 23:13 par.); Jesus' very call to repentance opens the way to it and they have no need of the long penitential prayers that are characteristic of Judaism. The publican who dares not raise his eyes to heaven, but strikes his breast and says, "God be merciful to me, a sinner!" is accounted righteous (Lk. 18:9-14). The "prodigal son" says only, "Father, I have sinned against heaven and before you; I am no longer worthy to be called your son" — and then fatherly kindness embraces him (Lk. 15:11-32). The proud and self-righteous are an abomination to God (Lk. 16:15; 18:9-14); but over the sinner who contritely repents, God rejoices (Lk. 15:1-10). But forgiveness has been truly received only when it makes the heart forgiving, as the parable of the wicked servant teaches (Mt. 18:23-35; *cf.* Lk. 7:47), and only he who is willing to forgive can honestly ask for God's forgiveness (Mt. 6:12, 14f.). God's forgiveness makes a man new; and whoever is willing to become new receives it.

3. Jesus no longer speaks, as the ancient prophets did, of the revelations of God in the history of the Nation and the nations. And when he refers to the coming judgment of God, unlike them he is no more thinking of catastrophes in the affairs of nations than he expects God's Reign to be fulfilled in the erection of a mighty and glorious Israelite kingdom. Unlike the prophets' preaching, his preaching is directed not primarily to the people as a whole, but *to individuals.* The judgment is coming not on nations but on individuals who must give account of themselves before God; and it is individuals whom coming salvation will bless. Judgment and salvation are eschatological events in the strict sense; i.e. events in which the present world and all history cease to be.

Thus, *Jesus in his thought of God* — and of man in the light of this thought — "de-historized" God and man; that is, released the relation between God and man from its previous ties to history (history considered as the affairs of nations). While this was already more or less the case in Judaism (but not in the religion of the Old Testament prophets), Jesus' thought, in contrast to that of Judaism, also *radically "historized"* God in a different sense of "history". In Judaism God is de-historized by having become a distant God enthroned in heaven; his governance of the world is carried out by angels, and his relation to man is mediated by the book of the Law. And man in Judaism is de-historized by being marked off from the world by ritual and by finding his security within the ritually pure congregation. The Jewish congregation artificially accomplishes its de-secularization (*Entweltlichung*) by means of its legalism. For Jesus, however, man is de-secularized by God's direct pronouncement to him, which tears him out of all security of any kind and places him at the brink of the End. And God is "de-secularized" by understanding his dealing eschatologically: he lifts man out of his worldly ties and places him directly before his own eyes. Hence, the "de-historization" or "de-secularization" both of God and of man is to be understood as a paradox (*dialektisch*): precisely that God, who stands aloof from the history of nations, meets each man in his own little history, his everyday life with its daily gift and demand; de-historized man (i.e. naked of his supposed security within his historical group) is guided into his concrete encounter with his neighbor, in which he finds his true history.

4. THE QUESTION OF THE MESSIANIC CONSCIOUSNESS OF JESUS

1. The Church of Jesus' disciples understood his claim that men's destiny is determined by their attitude to him in such a way that they regarded Jesus himself as the Messiah they had been expecting, or else still awaited Jesus himself as the coming Son of Man. The common opinion is that this belief of the earliest Church rests upon the self-consciousness of Jesus; i.e. that he actually did consider himself to be the Messiah, or the Son of Man. But this opinion is burdened with serious difficulties. It does agree with the evangelists' point of view, but the question is whether they themselves have not superimposed upon the traditional material their own belief in the messiahship of Jesus. In discussing this question it is important to bear in mind that if the fact should be established that Jesus was conscious of being the Messiah, or the Son of Man, that would only establish a historical fact, not prove an article of faith. Rather, the acknowledgment of Jesus as the one in whom God's word decisively encounters man, whatever title be given him — "Messiah (Christ)", "Son of Man", "Lord" — is a pure act of faith independent of the answer to the historical question whether or not Jesus considered himself the Messiah. Only the historian can answer this question — as far as it can be answered at all — and faith, being personal decision, cannot be dependent upon a historian's labor.

Some advance the following reasoning as an argument from history: The Church's belief in the messiahship of Jesus[24] is comprehensible only if Jesus was conscious of being the Messiah and actually represents himself as such — at least to the "disciples". But is this argument valid? For it is just as possible that belief in the messiahship of Jesus arose with and out of belief in his resurrection. The scene of *Peter's Confession* (Mk. 8:27-30) is no counter-evidence — on the contrary! For it is an Easter-story projected backward into Jesus' life-time, just like the story of the Transfiguration (Mk. 9:2.8). The account of Jesus' baptism (Mk. 1:9-11) is legend, certain though it is that the legend started from the historical fact of Jesus' baptism by John. It is told in the interest not of biography but of faith, and it reports Jesus' consecration as Messiah. It originated in the time when Jesus' life was already regarded as having been messianic, whereas the transfiguration story, originally a resurrection-account, dates his messiahship from the resurrection onward. The Temptation story (Mk. 1:12f. or Mt. 4:1-11 par.), which involves reflection about what kind of messiah Jesus was or what kind of messiah the Christian believes in, is legend. The story of Jesus' entry into Jerusalem has been colored by legend, and the passion-narrative is also to a considerable degree overspread with legend; for to the Church that venerated the Crucified as the Messiah it was soon perfectly certain that it was as Messiah that he had been crucified.

Moreover the synoptic tradition leaves no doubt about it that *Jesus' life and work* measured by traditional messianic ideas *was not messianic*. And Paul, like others, also did not understand it as messianic, as the Christ-hymn quoted by him at Phil. 2:6-11 indicates. It conceives Jesus' life as that of a mere man, without messianic glory. Likewise Acts 2:36 and Rom. 1:4, where Paul is evidently using a traditional formulation, show that in the earliest Church, Jesus' messiahship was dated from the resurrection. Actually, "Messiah" was the term for the eschatological ruler; the word means "the Anointed" and came to mean simply "king".[25] But it was not as a king, but as a prophet and a rabbi that Jesus appeared — and, one may add, as an exorcist. Nothing of the might and glory, which according to Jewish supposition would characterize the Messiah, was realized in Jesus' life — not in his exorcisms, for example, nor in his other mighty works. For though miracles were indeed a characteristic of the messianic period in Jewish belief, still the Messiah himself was not thought of as a miracle-worker. And even if it be said, in view of Jesus' words about the Son of Man, that Jesus thought of the Messiah not so much, or not at all, as the Davidic king, but rather as that other figure, the heavenly judge and salvation-bringer (viz. the apocalyptic Son of Man), that does not change the situation, for it was not as judge of the world and supernatural bringer of salvation that Jesus appeared.

2. Well, then, it has often been asked, did Jesus *reinterpret the traditional Messiah-concept*? Did he "spiritualize" it by exercising his sovereign office through the effect of his word? Only the tradition could inform us as to that. But where in it is such a thing indicated? Where, in the words of Jesus, is there polemic against the conventional Messiah-concept? It is no more to be found than is any criticism of the Jewish conception of the Reign of God!

At the most, the question about the Son of David (Mk. 12:35-37) might be cited; it seems to contain a criticism of the conception of the

Messiah as the Son of David: The Messiah is not a descendant of David since David himself called him his lord. In any case, that does not constitute a re-interpretation of the Messiah-concept of such sort that a prophet-and-teacher's life and activity are to be regarded as messianic, and there is no thought here of "spiritualization". What it does say is that when the Messiah is called Son of David, his rank and dignity are given too humble a name. What, then, is the implied but unexpressed Messiah-concept out of which the title "Son of David" is criticized? It could be the apocalyptic concept of the heavenly Son of Man, and it is not impossible that criticism of this sort might go back to Jesus or to the Church. In that case, however, it would be hard to understand how the view came to prevail in the Church that Jesus was a Son of David (*cf.* the lineages of Jesus — Mt. 1:1ff.; Lk. 3:23ff.; Rom. 1-3, and the unretouched report that Jesus was addressed as Son of David — Mk. 10:47; Mt. 9:27, etc.). Or is the title "Son of God" implied as the counter-concept? If so, this could only be meant as Hellenistic Christianity meant it: as a term for supernatural origin; for in Jewish-Christian use, this term, like Messiah, is only a designation of the king (*cf.* W. Staerk, *Soter* 1:89 and e.g. Mk. 14:61; Lk. 1:32, 4:41, etc.). But in that case the passage had its origin in the Hellenistic Church. But if the meaning of Mk. 12:35-37 is held to be that the Messiah is both Son of David and Son of Man, then this passage is all the more meaningless for deciding whether Jesus' life had messianic character.

3. Since alleged re-interpretation and spiritualization of the Messiah-concept to mean anything but the king of the time of salvation has now been ruled out, there remains only the frequently chosen escape of saying that Jesus was conscious of being the one *destined to be the future Messiah*, that his idea of the Messiah was "futuristic". Nothing could be cited in favor of this idea except those words of Jesus in which he speaks of the coming Son of Man (Mk. 8:38 or Lk. 12:8f. par.; Mt. 24:27, 37, 44 par.; Lk. 11:30). But it must be admitted that in them he speaks of the Son of Man in the third person without identifying himself with him. There is no question but that the evangelists — and likewise the Church which had handed down these sayings — make this identification, but can that be asserted of Jesus himself?

At any rate, the synoptic tradition contains no sayings in which Jesus says he will sometime (or soon) return. Neither was the word παρουσία, which denotes the "coming" of the Son of Man, ever understood in the earliest period of Christianity as "return", but correctly as "arrival, advent". The apologete Justin in the second century was the first to speak of the "first" πρώτη and "second coming" δευτέρα παρουσία (Dial. 14:8, 40:4) and of the "coming back" πάλιν παρουσία (Dial. 118:2). And how would Jesus have conceived *the relation of his return as Son of Man to his present historical activity*? He would have had to count upon being removed from the earth and raised to heaven before the final End, the irruption of God's Reign, in order to come from there on the clouds of heaven to perform his real office. But how would he have conceived his removal from the earth? As a miraculous translation? Among his sayings there is no trace of any such fantastic idea. As departure by natural death, then? Of that, too, his words say nothing. By a violent death, then? But if so, could he count on that as an absolute certainty — as the consciousness of being raised to the dignity of the coming Son of Man would presuppose? To be sure, *the predictions of the passion* (Mk. 8:31, 9:31, 10:33f.; *cf.* Mk. 10:45, 14:21, 41) foretell his execution as divinely foreordained. But can there be any doubt that they are all *vaticinia ex eventu*? Besides, they do not speak of his parousia! And the predictions of the parousia (Mk. 8:38, 13:26f., 14:62; Mt. 24:27, 37, 39, 44 par.) on their part, do not speak of the death and resurrection of the Son of Man. Clearly the predictions of the parousia originally had nothing to do with the predictions of death and resurrection; i.e. in the sayings that speak of the coming of the Son of Man there is no idea that this Son of Man is already here in person and must first be removed by death before he can return from heaven.

Observe in what unassimilated fashion the prediction of the parousia Mk. 8:38 follows upon the prediction of the passion and resurrection 8:31. In Mk. 9:1, 11-13 only the parousia is assumed (v 12b is an interpolation modeled after Mt. 17:12b), while the transfiguration 9:2-10, which the evangelist inserted between these originally connected verses, contains only the idea of resurrection. Later Mt. 17:12b connects the motif of the suffering Son of Man with the sayings that involve reflection about the parousia, and Lk. 17:23-25 likewise combines the passion-motif with prediction of the parousia (*cf.* Lk. 17:23-25 with Mt. 24:26-27) — an altogether secondary combination.

Furthermore, it is not to be doubted that the predictions of the parousia are older than those of the passion and resurrection; Q knows only the former and not yet the latter. The latter are probably later products of the Hellenistic Church, in which the title "Son of Man" was no longer understood in its original sense, while the predictions of the parousia are old and are probably original words of Jesus.

The synoptic Son-of-Man sayings fall into three groups, which speak of the Son of Man (1) as coming, (2) as suffering death and rising again, and (3) as now at work. This third group (Mk. 2:10, 28; Mt. 8:20 par., 11:19 par., 12:32 par.) owes its origin to a mere misunderstanding of the translation into Greek. In Aramaic, the son of man in these sayings was not a messianic title at all, but meant "man" or "I". So this group drops out of the present discussion. The second group contains the *vaticinia ex eventu* which are not yet present in Q; the first group alone contains very old tradition. The sayings belonging to it speak of the Son of Man in the third person. — The secondary material peculiar to Matthew or Luke does not need to be taken into account here; it is significant that for these later evangelists the original meaning of the title is lost and Son of Man has become so completely a self-designation of Jesus that Matthew can substitute either "I" for a traditional Son of Man (Mt. 10:32f. against Lk. 12:8f.; *cf.* Mk. 8:38; *cf.* Mt. 16:21 with Mk. 9:31; Mt. 5:11 with Lk. 6:22), or, vice versa, Son of Man for an "I" (Mt. 16:13 against Mk. 8:27).

Now it is true that in the predictions of the passion the Jewish concept Messiah-Son-of-Man is re-interpreted — or better, singularly enriched — insofar as the idea of a suffering, dying, rising Messiah or Son of Man was unknown to Judaism. But this re-interpretation of the concept was done not by Jesus himself but by the Church *ex eventu*. Of course, the attempt is made to carry the idea of the suffering Son of Man back into Jesus' own outlook by assuming that Jesus regarded himself as Deutero-Isaiah's Servant of God who suffers and dies for the sinner, and fused together the two ideas Son of Man and Servant of God into the single figure of the suffering, dying, and rising Son of Man. At the very outset, the misgivings which must be raised as to the historicity of the predictions of the passion speak against this attempt. In addition, the tradition of Jesus' sayings reveals no trace of a consciousness on his part of being the Servant of God of Is. 53.[26]

The messianic interpretation of Is. 53 was discovered in the Christian Church, and even in it evidently not immediately. The passion story, whose telling is colored by proof of predictions, reveals the influence especially of Ps. 21 (22) and 68 (69), but not before Lk. 22:37 is there any influence from Is. 53; and in Mt. 8:17, even Is. 53:54, so easily applied to vicarious suffering, serves as a prediction not of the suffering but of the healing Messiah. The earliest passages in which the Suffering Servant of God of Is. 53 clearly and certainly appears in the *interpretatio christiana* are: Acts 8:32f., I Pet.

2:22-25, Heb. 9:28; such interpretation may be older than Paul and perhaps is behind Rom. 4:25, probably a saying quoted by Paul. Whether Is. 53 is thought of in "according to the scriptures", I Cor. 15:3, cannot be said. It is significant that Paul himself nowhere adduces the figure of the Servant of God. The synoptic predictions of the passion obviously do not have Is. 53 in mind; otherwise why is it nowhere referred to? Only later do such specific references as I Clem. 16:3-14 and Barn. 5:2 come along. So far as it understood Is. 53 messianically, the synagogue applied precisely the suffering and death of the Servant not to the Messiah, but to the People (or to something else).

4. It was soon no longer conceivable that Jesus' life was unmessianic — at least in the circles of Hellenistic Christianity in which the synoptics took form. That Jesus Christ, the Son of God, should have legitimated himself as such even in his earthly activity seemed self-evident, and so the gospel account of his ministry was cast in the light of messianic faith. The contradiction between this point of view and the traditional material finds expression in the theory of the Messiah-secret, which gives the Gospel of Mark its peculiar character: Jesus functioned as the Messiah, but his messiah-ship was to remain hidden until the resurrection (Mk. 9:9). The demons, who recognize him, are commanded to be quiet; silence is also commanded after Peter's Confession (8:30), after the Transfiguration (9:9), and after some of the miracles. The motif of the disciples' incomprehension likewise serves the secrecy-theory: though the disciples receive secret revelation, they fail to understand it. Of course, this secrecy-theory, whose existence and importance W. Wrede pointed out, was incapable of being consistently carried through; hence the Gospel of Mark has been rightly characterized by the paradoxical term, book of "secret epiphanies".

The attempt to understand the Messiah-secret not as a theory of the evangelist but as historical fact, falls to pieces against the fact that its literary location is in the editorial sentences of the evangelist, not in the body of the traditional units. This understanding would further assume that Jesus had on the one hand spiritualized the conception of the Messiah's activity (for this was the case if his activity on earth was to be regarded as already secretly messianic) and on the other hand that Jesus regarded himself as the Son of Man whose secret would someday come out at his return. But against this assumption arise the already named difficulties of attributing to Jesus the supposition that he was himself the future Son of Man.   *Theology of the New Testament*, I, pp. 3-32.

3

EXISTENTIALIST INTERPRETATION*

"THE PROBLEM OF A THEOLOGICAL EXEGESIS OF THE NEW TESTAMENT"

This essay was first presented as a public lecture at Marburg on 1 February, 1925. It was subsequently revised and given as a lecture on 6 February at Göttingen University, where Karl Barth was then teaching. Because of Barth's delicate situation at Göttingen, Bultmann had been asked to avoid "any open rift that might weaken Barth's position" in public discussion after the lecture. He agreed, but with the request for substantive discussion the next day. Martin Heidegger, the existentialist philosopher, accompanied Bultmann and several Marburg students to Göttingen for this event. The essay still displays the intersection of Dialectical Theology, as represented by Barth, and the philosophical existentialism of Heidegger. "Das Problem einer theologischen Exegese des Neuen Testament" first appeared in the journal of Dialectical Theology, Zwischen den Zeiten (1925). Louis De Grazia and Keith R. Crim translated the essay for The Beginnings of Dialectic Theology edited by James M. Robinson and published in 1968. The following selections from that essay are taken from their translation.

Orthodox Lutheran exegesis regards the Bible as a book of doctrines, directly related to me, the reader. They are not designed to enrich my theoretical knowledge, but to offer illumination about my true nature and to determine the course of my life. Insofar as these authoritative doctrines are regarded as general truths, earlier Rationalism was only drawing the conclusion of this concept of Scripture when it took the teachings of Scripture seriously as general truths. For if they are, they are rational truths, since reason is the court of appeal in deciding the universal validity of statements. What appears non-rational in Scripture is then re-interpreted or explained as accommodation to or limitation of the times in which it was written. But the study of the elements that are unique, or determined by the times, became an end in itself, because it permitted a differentiation among the separate writings and groups of writers, and thus gave rise to a historical presentation. The transition then occurred within Rationalism which produced the mod-

---

* See also pp. 21-28 above.

ern interpretation in terms of historical conditioning. This resulted in the loss of the original contrast between those things limited by the times and the eternal rational truths. The individual elements came to be understood as expressions of the general regularity which establishes the unity of history.

This regularity can be variously conceived. In the Idealist, specifically the Hegelian, concept of history, which attained a lasting domination of New Testament exegesis through the Tübingen school, it is teleologically determined. The forces which move history are ideas, which constitute the moments of the unfolding of absolute spirit, but which have their reality only in the concrete process occurring in individual manifestations, the process in which absolute spirit comes to self-realization.

Into the place of, or parallel to, the Idealist concept of man which underlies this view of history, there came gradually a different concept of man, the naturalistic. In this concept, man is the product of circumstances, and the regularity of history, accordingly, is conceived of as causally determined. The ideas, ideals, and institutions of an epoch or an individual are explained completely as the results of a developmental process. Even though the factor of personality (the irrational aspect) is taken into account, its underlying concept is still explained naturalistically. The irrational element taken into accout here is no different from that of historical geology, which is unable to explain why certain rock types were formed one way rather than another. And the irrational element, the x, is basically the admission that the being of persons cannot be seen in that which determines the essence of history.

The causal factors which determine history can be variously conceived. Man can be viewed biologically, as invested with varying capacities of thinking and feeling, moral will, etc. — history then consists of the development of these capacities. Since this view does not lead to chronological history, but only to a natural history of mankind, the drives which lie in economic, social, and political necessities are claimed for the realization of historical movement. Indeed, these drives alone may dominate the picture, and the history of Christianity then is turned into sociology. On the other hand, the biological view of man may be carried over from the individual to humanity as a species, and the entire movement of history be presented as a biologically understood morphology.

Similarly, since man is viewed more or less psychologically, the psychological point of view may become dominant, with the danger that our ability to understand historical movement is lost again in the process and our interpretation becomes a psychological analysis of individuals and groups. As a rule the danger is not recognized, since in the absence of fundamental clarity all other interpretations of man and history are included under psychology. In essence, however, the psychological point of view dominates the exegesis of the so-called history of religion school; it gives itself away immediately when it allows the "doctrines" of Scripture to be obscured by and reduced to experiences and moods, and turns "piety" into a theme for the historian. Cult and myth receive particular attention; institutions are explained, as far as possible, through their genesis in primitive conditions (psychologically understood). The conclusions are drawn from an approach characterized (unjustly, in my opinion) as phenomenological; it is an approach which consciously rejects the viewpoint of historical causality and passes off a refurbished psychology as phenomenology.

In all these cases the original position, in which the text lays its claim upon the reader, is surrendered — the view that it is there not to be inspected, but to determine the existence of the reader. In all the cases mentioned, the text is viewed at a distance, in the desire to see "what is there", with the presupposition that what can be perceived is perceived *only* without reference to one's own position and that it is possible to interpret the text without, at the same time, interpreting its subject matter. From texts so interpreted, the attempt is made to understand history without asking whether there are perhaps fundamental realities in history which may be grasped only by giving up a detached position, only by being ready to take a stand. To be sure, New Testament exegesis does not say that what is there is of no ultimate concern to a person. However, exegesis itself is not determined by this *tua res agitur* (your interest is at stake), but proceeds on the basis of the expectant, neutral attitude of the exegete. Historical and psychological exegesis establish primarily that this or that has been thought, said, or done at a particular time and under such and such historical circumstances and psychological conditions, without reflecting on the meaning and demands of what is said. For these views, to the extent that a particular aspect has a significance beyond the moment, that significance is only from the viewpoint of the regularity (mostly causal) of events, and thus history becomes a great relational connection in which every particular manifestation is only relative. This may result in the enterprise of reconstructing lost history. If it is correctly reconstructed, such history has equal footing for the viewer with history based on available sources.

131

It does not help here or elsewhere to demand a return to the Idealist writing of history. History only appears to be different in Idealism; that is, it only appears that the Idealist reads the text from the viewpoint of *tua res agitur*. This impression is created through the fact that individual historical manifestations are understood as objectifications of spirit in its historical movement, in which, indeed, the interpreting subject participates. In this process the interpreter achieves clarity concerning the nature of spirit and thus of himself. Here the interpreting subject is coordinated with history, whereas in the other case they stand alongside each other. Nevertheless, even here the distance of the viewer from history is not overcome, for the exegete sees himself from the same perspective that he sees history; that is, he views himself only as a particular case of man in general and thinks of everything individual as an expression of the laws of development. That means that the connection of the existing *[existentiell]* subject with history does not take place at all — or only if the existence of man does not lie in the sphere of the universal or rational, but in the individual, in the concrete moment of the here and now.[27] For the Idealist, there is nothing in history which places demands on the individual in the sense that something new is said which is not already potentially his, which is not at his disposal by virtue of his participation in universal reason. He finds nothing which encounters him as authoritative; he finds only himself in history; this he does by reducing the content of history to the movement of the ideas impressed on man's reason. He thus controls all possible historical occurrences from the outset. Here also, then, the enterprise of reconstructing lost history may appear meaningful.

But the decisive question is whether we confront history in such a way that we acknowledge its claim upon us, its claim to say something new to us. When we give up a neutral attitude toward the text, the question of truth can dominate the exegesis. In the final analysis then the exegete is not interested in the question "What was the meaning of what is said (purely as something said) in its contemporary situation, its contemporary context?" He asks instead: "What is the content of what is said, and to what kind of reality does it lead?" Since this question is concerned not with explaining nature but with understanding history, to which we ourselves belong, it implies: What does it mean for me and how am I to understand it on its objective ground? Thus, at this stage the context in which the above two questions form the task of the exegete remains a problem. Can one be answered without the other, and if so, to what extent? The intent of such reflection is not at all to dispose of all the

132

old methods in favor of a new one, but only to ask how far the old methods can carry us in our concern for the reality of history.

Provisionally it may be put in this way: Historical exegesis asks: "What is said?" We ask: "What is meant?" In a certain sense, of course, historical exegesis also asks about meaning, but in such a way that all history is sketched on one plane, one map; and then, a certain field or point on this map is identified by means of the most comprehensive knowledge possible of the surrounding area. All the light shed by the history of the period is concentrated on the point to be identified. Objective exegesis, on the other hand, considers this map of history as transparent and seeks to perceive the light which shines through from beyond the surface, believing that this is the only way to understand what is meant.

But if one has taken the question this far, he suddenly sees that the initial distinction of a neutral exegesis from one that takes a position — a contemplative exegesis over against one that grasps the demand of the text — is only rough and inadequate. It was occasioned by the false understanding modern exegetes have of their task. Actually, there is no neutral exegesis. There is no bare interpretation of "what is there", but in some way (a specific way, in fact, for each case) the interpretation of the text always goes hand in hand with the exegete's interpretation of himself. We do not encounter history in the same way that we do nature; we can assume a distance from nature; but we stand in history and are a part of it. Therefore, every word we utter about history is necessarily a word about ourselves; that is, it discloses how we interpret our own existence; it shows what sort of openness we have to the possibilities of our existence as humans.

If we again take up the question of where the meaning of the text lies and of its accessibility for the exegete, then it is clear that we are asking about the possibilities for our existence which arise from our encounter with history. But it is also clear that we may not expect an answer to this question, which will become a presupposition from which the text may be questioned. Then we would have control in advance over the possibilities of our existence, about which the text should inform us. We reject every exegesis which regards the possibilities of human existence as either closed or foreseeable, and we maintain that the only possible attitude is to be conscious of the problematic character of our existence. The attitude underlying the interpretation of a text may perhaps be formulated in this way: We attempt to understand the way in which the text shows its writer's interpretation of his concept of existence as the real possibility of existing. In this approach we attempt an elucidation of our own existential possibility, and thereby confront the text just as we confront other men to whom we stand in living relationship and with whom we first achieve any existence at all, that is, in the relation of I and Thou. Then it is clear that there can be no reconstruction of actual history, any more than of the relation of I to Thou, friend to friend, husband to wife, or father to child. Nevertheless, our own existence occurs precisely in these relations; in them we *are*. And just as these relations are temporal events for us, events which bear the character of decision, so then the existential encounter of history takes place in temporal moments which demand our decision.

And this event — insofar as in our activity our existence unfolds as our own possibility for living — would be a free act. Naturally, this does not mean one feels induced to act on the basis of his understanding of the text; rather, the understanding itself is the act. As a free act it stands beyond my control and occurs only in decision, so that I cannot stand alongside it and control it at the same time. Therefore, it cannot become a methodological principle, but arises as a decision evoked by the question posed in the text; and to the extent that the decision is demanded by history, it is obedience to the authority of history.

The presupposition of every exegesis should be recognition of the uncertainty of our existence, the knowledge that our existence is occasioned in our free act of decision; add to that an attitude toward history which acknowledges it as authoritative and thus sees it not with the detachment of the spectator but in the light of present decision. However, before inquiring into the distinctive aspect of New Testament exegesis or theological exegesis, we must emphasize again that no new method is being put forward. The question of how far methods are really adequate for the understanding of a text, how far every concrete task of exegesis must always be methodical, is expressly set aside. The answer depends first on realizing that we do not really grasp history by a method, since the method comprehends only that which we have at our disposal. This becomes much clearer when we consider that interpretation as a rule ought to mediate the text to a third person, who, in his existential being, is also not at our disposal. As already pointed out, therefore, definitive results are not obtained by a postulated exegesis; such results, in fact, would only serve to kill history, because they lose the character of temporality and block the way to an existential encounter with history for the third person. The results of an existentially inspired exegesis therefore cannot be justified and established in the same manner as those of a methodological exegesis. The possibilities of textual comprehension can no more be limited after exegesis than before, but are inexhaustible as the possibilities which grow out of the encounter of I and Thou.

The distinctive characteristic of New Testament exegesis is that although it remains in the realm of secular exegesis it is still confronted by the New Testament contention that man does not have his own existence at his disposal in such a way that he can pose the question of existence for himself and possess the possibility of free action — all this is found only in the experience of faith. The decisive question for understanding the New Testament would then be whether or not the demand of faith is acknowledged. True, but in the face of all these considerations, the situation of the exegete would be completely impossible. For not only is the possibility of this decision of faith refused him; the New Testament even asserts that in himself man cannot know what faith is, since this knowing results only from a believing exegesis. And if he desires to pose his questions correctly, even this questioning must be a believing questioning!

Must this readiness for believing questioning be a prerequisite for the exegete? Obviously that would be as senseless as requiring him to leap over his own shadow. It shows that reflection cannot be carried out in its entirety on the basis of a principle, that is, when the exegete is viewed as standing in the unreal, abstract situation which the secular exegete seeks; when, that is, in reflection his concrete situation is disregarded. The concrete situation is precisely that New Testament exegesis becomes the task of the man who stands in the tradition of the church of the word. There can be such a readiness for believing questioning only if I stand in my existence under the tradition of the word, not if I view myself externally as an individual conditioned by time.

An exegesis for which faith is the presupposition would be a theological exegesis, but it can be carried on only as a conscious risk; it cannot be established and justified, since the presupposition is not at our disposal. That settles the question, then, of whether Augustine, Luther, Schleiermacher, or even the Bhagavad-Gita must be interpreted in the same way as the New Testament. Insofar as I reflect theoretically, and put myself in an abstract, traditionless situation, there will be no difference. But whether in such an interpretation we will see the text with the eyes of faith is a question that we cannot answer theoretically.

Insofar as the New Testament is the Word of God only indirectly and not directly for the conceptual thinking of exegetical theology, it is completely valid for us to draw on theological tradition to formulate its main theme as "New Testament theology". This is merely to take seriously the fact that God's Word is a hidden word spoken to man, that the revelation present in Scripture is a veiled revelation. We are confronted in Scripture, therefore, by a kind of speech which is primarily a speaking *about* God and *about* man, for it is uttered in the human sphere. Just as there is no direct encounter between I and Thou, but only the encounter concealed in the word by its being an expression of something, so there is no direct revelation, but only revelation concealed in human words. Just as this fact makes it necessary for exegetical theology to transform the statement of the text into present concepts, so objective criticism is necessary for all exegesis. For in transforming the textual assertion into present-day concepts, it must be shown to what extent the concern of the text receives equivalent expression in what is said. Barth is certainly right in saying that criticism must avoid the misunderstanding that it thinks the Spirit of Christ is found in competition with other spirits in the text.[28] But one must not overlook the fact that the human statements of the text cannot be regarded as direct statements of the Spirit of Christ. Furthermore, insofar as Paul speaks of the "subject", he represents a human standpoint, which not only may be compared with other standpoints, but which Paul himself may not always have accepted so firmly. If one wishes to do theological exegesis scientifically, he should not be shocked by the question: "At which particular place can one assert that the Spirit of Christ comes to expression?" One must in fact be concerned with such a distinction; the question is reminiscent of the peculiar situation of the exegete who is moved by the question of existence and knows therefore that he has no criterion at his disposal with which to grasp decisively the reality of history. However, he cannot for this reason refuse to make definite statements, but neither can he make the nature of the text as the Word of God into a controllable presupposition of exegesis. To undertake the responsibility of objective criticism is surely no occasion for arrogance on the part of the exegete, but a constant reminder of the obligation to undertake self-criticism, self-criticism in an existential sense.

Since there is no direct encounter with God, but his revelation is hidden in the word, there can be no appeal to an inner light for exegesis, no "pneumatic" exegesis which counts on the pneuma as a possession previously bestowed on the exegete. We have at our disposal no pneuma which is not bound to the word. Exegesis can proceed only from the interpretation of the word. Since exegetical work is work with concepts, and since the word of the text is never the subject matter itself, but its expression, this subject matter becomes available to the exegete only if he understands the word. The understanding of the word is certainly loaded with all sorts of ambiguity, because words are not only the unique expression of the concrete here and now, but also have their own history; in fact, they can be the former only to the extent that they are the latter. The exegete must be thoroughly familiar with the entire history of the words of the text without imagining he has thereby grasped the meaning of a passage in the concrete here and now. Therefore all the philological historical work on the New Testament is valid, in fact, obligatory, and has its special character because the New Testament is written in Greek. In the actual process of exegesis, the relationship of historical and theological exegesis cannot really be analyzed, since genuine historical exegesis rests on the existential encounter with history and therefore coincides with theological exegesis, provided that the validation of theological exegesis rests on precisely the same basis. And that existential encounter is not something that could be undertaken like anything else and as such find its place within or behind methodical, philological, and historical interpretation.

The Beginnings of Dialectic Theology, pp. 236-256 *passim.*

*

"THE PROBLEM OF HERMENEUTICS"

"Hermeneutics", or the science of interpreting written texts, was a life-long concern of Bultmann. "The Problem of Hermeneutics" (1950) offers the most comprehensive statement of his position. In part, the essay was occasioned by criticism of his 1941 proposal for demythologizing as a part of existentialist interpretation. In part, the essay offers a clarification of Bultmann's early thinking on this subject. In particular, Bultmann here repudiates an existential (existentiell) understanding of exegesis, oriented solely toward the attitude of the individual interpreter, as he had proposed in his 1925 essay. In contrast he now advocates an existentialist (existential) model of exegesis, which systematically uses the conceptuality derived from Heidegger's philosophy as a means to clarify the meaning of faith. "Das Problem der Hermeneutik" first appeared in Zeitschrift für Theologie und Kirche *(1950) and was then included in* Glauben und Verstehen, II *(1952). James C. G. Greig prepared the earliest English version of this essay for the 1955* Essays: Philosophical and Theological. *The following*

translation is by Schubert Ogden from his 1984 collection of Bultmann essays, New Testament and Mythology.

I

According to Wilhelm Dilthey, hermeneutics as the "art of understanding expressions of life fixed in writing" always draws attention to itself only "during a great historical movement". Such a movement makes "understanding unique historical existence", or "scientific knowledge of individual persons, in fact, of the great forms of unique human existence in general", an urgent concern of science.[29] If we today are in the midst of "a great historical movement", there is reason to consider the problem of hermeneutics. And in point of fact, discussion with the historical tradition forms an essential part of contemporary self-reflection, which is simultaneously reflection on "the great forms of unique human existence".

The problem with which hermeneutics is concerned, according to Dilthey, arises from the question, "Is such a knowledge [namely, of the great forms of unique human existence] possible, and what means do we have for attaining it?" More specifically it is the question "whether understanding the unique can be raised to the level of general validity". "How can one individual come to an objective, generally valid understanding of another individual's expression of life as given through the senses?"[30] Thus, it is the question of the possibility of achieving objectivity in understanding unique historical existence of the past. In principle, it is a question of the possibility of understanding historical phenomena in general insofar as they are witnesses to unique human existence, in which case hermeneutics would be the science of understanding history in general. In fact, Dilthey restricts hermeneutics to the interpretation of "expressions of life that are enduringly fixed", namely, monuments of culture, and so primarily literary documents, although works of art, also, are of essential importance.[31]

II

Ever since Aristotle hermeneutical rules have been developed for the interpretation of literary texts, and these rules have become traditional and are usually followed as a matter of course.[32] As Aristotle himself saw, the first requirement is for a formal analysis of a literary work with respect to its structure and style.[33] Interpretation has to analyze the composition of the work, understanding the parts in light of the whole and the whole in light of the parts. This yields the insight that any interpretation moves in a "hermeneutical circle". As soon as one undertakes to interpret texts in an ancient or foreign language, one becomes aware of the further requirement that the interpretation must be done in accordance with the rules of grammar. Already with the Alexandrians this demand for a grammatical knowledge of the language was supplemented by the demand for a knowledge of the individual author's usage, so that, for example, a criterion was acquired by means of which to decide questions of authenticity in the interpretation of Homer. With the development of historical work during the Enlightenment, the question about the individual author's usage was expanded into the question about the use of language in the particular period in which the text was written. But hand in hand with insight into the historical development of language went knowledge of historical development in general, and hence of the fact that all literary documents are historically conditioned by circumstances of time and place, which henceforth must be known if there is to be any appropriate interpretation.

The science that has as its object the interpretation of literary texts and that makes use of hermeneutics to this end is philology. In the course of its development, however, it becomes clear that hermeneutics as the art of scientific understanding is by no means adequately defined by these traditional hermeneutical rules. Harald Patzer has shown how philology, which began by using the science of history for the purpose of interpretation, gradually came to be used by history, or itself became the branch of history for which texts are only "witnesses" or "sources" for projecting a historical picture by reconstructing some past time.[34] This is certainly an understandable development, since there is also naturally a circle between philological and historical knowledge. But the upshot was that philology lost its real object in the interpretation of texts for the sake of understanding them. The deeper reason for this development, however, is that the task of understanding was not understood profoundly enough and thus seemed to have already been accomplished simply by following the hermeneutical rules. In other words, the insight into the process of understanding for which Friedrich Schleiermacher had once striven had been lost.

Schleiermacher had already seen that a genuine understanding cannot be achieved simply by following the hermeneutical rules. In addition to the interpretation that they serve to guide, which in his terminology is called "grammatical", there must also be "psychological" interpretation. Schleiermacher recognized that the composition and unity of a work cannot be grasped solely by the categories of a formal logical and stylistic analysis. Rather, the work must be understood as a moment in the life of a certain human being. In addition to grasping the "outer form", one must grasp the "inner form", which is a matter not of objective but of subjective, "divinatory" interpretation.[35] Thus, interpretation is a matter of "reproduction" or "reconstruction" that takes place in living relation to the process of literary production itself. Understanding becomes "one's own recreation of the living nexus of thoughts".[36] Such "recreation" is possible because "the individuality of the interpreter and that of the author do not stand over against one another as two incomparable facts." Rather, "both have been formed on the basis of universal human nature, whereby the community of human beings with one another in speech and understanding is made possible."[37] Dilthey appropriates these ideas of Schleiermacher and seeks to explain them further. "All distinctions between individuals are ultimately conditioned not by qualitative differences between one person and another but by differences of degree between their psychical processes. If as interpreters, then, we transpose our own life experimentally, as it were, into another historical milieu, we are able for the time being to stress or strengthen one psychical process, even while allowing another to recede, and thus to reproduce another alien life in ourselves." The condition of understanding "lies in the fact that nothing can appear in the expression of another individual that is not also contained in the life of the interpreter". Thus, it can be said that "interpretation is a work of personal art whose consummate exercise is conditioned by the genius of the interpreter; it rests on congeniality, intensified by living closely with the author by constant study."[38]

Schleiermacher's view of understanding is naturally connected historically with J. J. Winckelmann's "interpretation of works of art" and with J. G. von Herder's "congenial empathy with the souls of epochs and races".[39] It is oriented to the interpretation of philosophical and poetic texts. But is it also valid for other texts? Does the interpretation of a text in mathematics or medicine, say, grow out of reenacting the psychical processes that took place in the author? Or what about the inscriptions of Egyptian kings reporting their deeds in war, or the historical and chronological texts of ancient Babylonia and Assyria, or the grave inscription of Antiochus of Commagene, or the *Res Gestae Divi Augusti?* Are they, too, understandable only insofar as one transposes oneself into the inner creative process out of which they emerged?

No, it would not appear so. And in point of fact, it is not in this way that they must be understood insofar as the interpretation has to do with what they directly communicate — thus, for example, their mathematical or medical knowledge or their report of the facts and processes of world history. But this, of course, is the primary interest of those who read such texts. To be sure, even they may be read with another interest, as is shown, for example, by Georg Misch's interpretation of the inscriptions in question as "expressions of life" or "forms of unique human existence", whether of individual persons or as expressing the "feeling for life", or understanding of existence, of certain epochs.[40] It thus becomes clear that the view of Schleiermacher and Dilthey is one-sided insofar as it is guided by a certain way of asking questions.

The upshot, then, is that any understanding or interpretation is always oriented to a certain way of asking questions or to a certain objective. This means that it is never without presuppositions; more exactly, it is always guided by a preunderstanding of the subject matter about which it questions the text. Only on the basis of such a preunderstanding is a way of asking questions and an interpretation at all possible.[41]

The subject matter about which Dilthey questions text is "life", namely, the personal, historical life that has taken shape in the texts as "expressions of life that are enduringly fixed"; it is the "psychical life" that is to be objectively known by interpretation of "expressions that are given and perceptible through the senses". But this is not the only subject matter with which interpretation can have to do; therefore, the process of understanding characterized by this interest is not the only such process that can be enacted in an interpretation. Rather, in each case the process of understanding will be different, depending on how the objective of interpretation is determined.

It is evidently not enough to say "depending on the kind of text", that is, on the subject matter that is directly expressed in the text or the interest by which it itself is guided. For all texts can in fact be interpreted in the way in which Dilthey asks questions, that is, as documents of personal, historical life. Of course, in the first instance questioning of the text is oriented to the subject matter that is talked about in the text and mediated by it. Thus, I interpret a text in the history of music by asking what it contributes to my understanding of music and its history, and so on.

141

III

A way of asking questions, however, grows out of an interest that is grounded in the life of the questioner; and the presupposition of all understanding interpretation is that this interest is also alive in some way in the text to be interpreted and establishes communication between the text and the interpreter. Insofar as Dilthey designates kinship between the author and the interpreter as the condition of the possibility of understanding, he does in fact discover the presupposition of all understanding interpretation. For this condition holds good not only for the special way of asking questions distinctive of Schleiermacher and Dilthey but also for any other interpretation that can never be accomplished simply by following the traditional "hermeneutical rules". All that is necessary is that this presupposition be more exactly defined. What is required instead of reflection on the individuality of the author and of the interpreter, on their psychical processes, and on the interpreter's genius or congeniality is reflection on the simple fact that the presupposition of understanding is the life relation of the interpreter to the subject matter that is — directly or indirectly — expressed in the text.[42]

Interpretation does not come about simply because "the individuality of the interpreter and that of the author do not stand over against one another as two incomparable facts" but because or insofar as both have the same life relation to the subject matter under discussion or in question. And this they have because or insofar as they both stand in the same context of life. This relation to the subject matter with which the text is concerned, or about which it is questioned, is the presupposition of understanding.[43] For this reason it is also understandable that every interpretation is guided by a certain objective, for a question that is oriented somehow is possible only because of the conditions of a context of life. It is likewise understandable for the same reason that every interpretation includes a certain preunderstanding, namely, the one growing out of the context of life to which the subject matter belongs.

The fact that underlying any interpretation there is a life relation to the subject matter with which the text is concerned, or about which it is questioned, can be readily illustrated by reflecting on the process of translating from a foreign language. The nature of this process is as a rule obscured because knowledge of ancient languages in our cultural sphere is mediated to us by tradition and does not have to be acquired anew. Knowledge of a foreign language can be acquired anew (provided there are no texts in more than one language) only when the subject matters designated by the words (things, modes of conduct, etc.) are familiar from use and association in life. An object or a way of acting that is simply meaningless in my context of life, in my environment, or in my way of living is also unintelligible and untranslatable when it is designated in language, unless a word is chosen for it that describes its outer appearance — as, for example, when the *churunga* of the Australian aborigines is rendered in German by *Schwirrholz* (literally, whirring wood).[44] Observing use, insofar as it is understandable, can lead to further descriptions, so that a *churunga* can be described as a "powerful instrument of magic", assuming that the idea of instruments of magic is intelligible to me in my own context of life. In principle, the same process is involved whenever texts are given in or with pictorial presentations that for their part can be understood in terms of my life context. In fact, a child's understanding language and learning how to speak take place together with its becoming familiar with the environment and with human associations, in short, with the context of life.

Therefore, interpretation always presupposes a life relation to the different subject matters that — directly or indirectly — come to expression in texts. I understand a text that treats of music only if and insofar as I have a relation to music, which explains why many parts of Thomas Mann's *Doktor Faustus* are unintelligible to many readers. Likewise, I understand a mathematical text only if I have a relation to mathematics or a historical account only insofar as I am familiar with life in history and know from my own living what a state is and what possibilities there are for living in a state. Finally, I understand a novel only because I know from my own life what is involved, for example, in love and friendship, family and vocation, and so on. It is for just this reason that many pieces of literature are closed to many persons, depending on their age or education.

Naturally, my life relation to the subject matter can be utterly naive and unreflective, and in the process of understanding, in the interpretation, it can be raised to the level of consciousness and clarified. It can also be superficial and ordinary, and through understanding of the text it can be deepened and enriched, modified and corrected. In any case, a life relation to the subject matter in question is presupposed, and recognizing this eliminates certain false problems right from the outset — like, for example, the question about the possibility of understanding an "alien soul". The possibility of such understanding is given simply in the common relation of author and interpreter alike to the particular subject matter. If Dilthey affirms that the condition of the possibility of understanding is a "basis of universal human nature", or the fact that "nothing can appear in the expression of another individual that is not also contained in the life of the interpreter", this can be put more precisely by saying that the condition of interpretation is the fact that interpreter and author are human beings who live in the same historical world in which human existence takes place as existence in an environment in understanding association with objects and other persons. Naturally, it belongs to such understanding association that it should also include questions and problems, struggle and suffering, joy as well as resigned withdrawal.

IV

Interest in the subject matter motivates interpretation and provides a way of asking questions, an objective. The orientation of the interpretation is not problematic when it is guided by a question concerning the subject matter that the text itself intends to communicate — as, for example, when I seek to acquire knowledge of mathematics from a mathematical text or of music from a text in musicology. The same is true of the interpretation of a narrative text when all I want to learn is what it narrates — as, for instance, in the interpretation of chronicles or even of Herodotus or Thucydides, when I want to know nothing more than the historical relations and processes that they recount. The same holds good even of a Hellenistic novel, which narrates fictitious happenings but which I read as an entertaining story. In the one case, the objective of understanding is historical instruction, in the other, entertainment. But in both cases the way of asking questions is quite naive, as becomes clear when the text to be understood is a poetic text of distinction such as Homer, which, however, is not read as poetry but, as is often the case to begin with, simply as narration, very much in the way in which works of graphic and plastic art are viewed by naive observers, especially children, by asking what they are about. In part, of course, the fine arts themselves have just such a meaning as illustration, as in "illuminated" manuscripts of the Bible or in cycles of mosaics such as those in the cathedral of Monreale. It is in principle the same kind of thing when in the modern world a Goethe album is published with illustrations of Goethe's life.

But the whole business soon becomes more complicated, for a naive way of questioning the text does not last beyond the stage of childhood even if it never ceases to be justified as a way of asking about what the text directly intends to communicate. The naive way of questioning retains its place especially in the case of scientific texts that seek to mediate knowledge directly. Even when the questioning proceeds to the point of understanding the texts as sources for the history of the science concerned, there is no excluding a prior understanding of what they directly transmit by way of knowledge. Thus, even an interest in the history of mathematics normally remains oriented to mathematical knowledge itself, and thus to the subject matter intended by the texts in question, as distinct from subordinating its interpretation to some other interest, say, in the history of culture. This is illustrated, for example, by the fact that the historian of culture, from the other side, can ignore the history of mathematics, as Jacob Burckhardt actually does in his *Kultur der Renaissance*. Even so, the objective has become different when scientific texts are read simply as so many witnesses for the history of science.

A similar modification occurs in a twofold way in the interpretation of narrative, particularly historical, texts. In the first place, they are not read primarily as witnesses to what they report but rather as witnesses to their own time, out of which they do their reporting. This can still be done in keeping with the intention of the reporter insofar as historical knowledge of the reporter provides a critical standard for understanding his or her report. But in the second place, historical texts can be interpreted as witnesses to the history of historiography, or the science of history. In this case the intention of the text is completely disregarded, for it does not intend to communicate the science of history but intends, rather, to recount history itself. Nevertheless, it is now put in its own place in history and no longer interpreted as the mediator of historical knowledge but rather as the object thereof.

What about a novel? Even the naive reader does not read merely with a curious interest in what is happening; in straining to learn what is yet to happen, the reader is moved by more than curiosity, namely, by inner participation in the fate of the hero with whom the reader has identified. The reader not only comes to know something but rather shares in the experience of something, being "gripped", with his or her affections touched and passions aroused. And is it not this that alone fulfills the author's intention?

This way of understanding is indeed appropriate in the case of genuine works of literature. They disclose themselves to participatory understanding, as Aristotle in his way already pointed out by his teaching that pity and terror are the effect of tragedy. And what they disclose to such participatory understanding is human existence and its possibilities as also the possibilities of anyone who understands them.

Of such a kind, however, is not only the appropriate understanding of literature and of the effect that it makes possible but the appropriate understanding of art in general. If one may describe the beautiful as "the true expressed in what is visible",[45] and if one understands "the true" in a radical sense as the disclosure of human existence, which is disclosed by art as the power of displaying the true in the beautiful, then interpretation should understand the possibilities of human existence that are expressed in art as well as in literature.

"The true" is made visible in literature and in art, and it is to be appropriated there by participatory understanding. But it is also the object of reflective and investigative thinking insofar as it becomes the object of philosophy. Therefore, if the interpretation of philosophical texts is really to be understanding, it itself has to be motivated by the question of truth, that is, it can take place only as a discussion with the author. One understands Plato only if one philosophizes with him. Interpretation fails of real understanding when it questions the statements of the text as so many results of research, and when, as a consequence, it takes a particular text as a "source" for a certain stage in the history of philosophy, viewing this history as a happening in the past instead of raising it to the level of the present. There is indeed no need to abandon real philosophical understanding in order to describe the history of philosophy. But this description must be done in such a way that understanding philosophy's history becomes an understanding of philosophy itself, in that through this history the problem of understanding being and therewith of understanding oneself becomes clear.

V

The right way of asking questions in interpreting the texts and monuments of literature and art, philosophy and religion, had to be acquired anew after it had been suppressed by the prevailing way of asking questions during the period of so-called historicism. This is the interest served by Dilthey's efforts and by his recourse to Schleiermacher. Under the hegemony of historicism, texts and monuments had been understood in different ways as "sources", for the most part as sources for reconstructing a picture of some past age or period of time. They were interpreted as witnesses to some historical epoch or as the parts or phases of some historical process, in which case it made no difference in principle how the historical process was understood, whether as political or social history, as intellectual history, or as the history of culture in the broadest sense.

It is not as though texts and monuments cannot also be understood as "sources". There are, in fact, texts whose contents are such that they deserve to be treated only as sources; they are to be distinguished from "classic" texts and monuments even if the boundaries cannot be sharply drawn. If such documents are to be interpreted as sources, however, they must always already be understood in the sense of their own intention — at least provisionally — and they often are so understood in an unreflective, superficial way. If Plato, for example, is to be used as a source for the culture of fifth century Athens, the contents of his work already have to be understood somehow, else he could not serve as a source at all. Nevertheless, to question his work as a document of the history of culture bypasses his own real intention and hardly even catches sight of it in its real scope and depth. The way of asking questions that takes the text to be a source has its proper place in the service of genuine interpretation. For any interpretation necessarily moves in a circle: on the one hand, the individual phenomenon is understandable in terms of its time and place; on the other hand, it itself first makes its time and place understandable. Understanding Plato in terms of his own time stands in service of a genuine interpretation of Plato and belongs to the sphere of the traditional hermeneutical rules previously discussed.

By analogy, other ways of asking questions that were developed during the period of historicism have a legitimate place in the service of genuine understanding. This is true, say, of Heinrich Wölfflins's interpretation of works of art in the context of the history of style or of the countless studies in the history of types and motifs both in literature and in the fine arts. To be sure, all such studies could also obscure the real question of interpretation. And the same is true of formal analysis of works of literature and art undertaken from the aesthetic standpoint: to carry out such analysis is not to achieve real understanding, even though it can be prepared for by such analysis, as, for example, in Karl Reinhardt's book on Sophocles or in Paul Friedländer's work on Plato.[46] How different an interpretation of the same work of art can be, depending on whether it is guided by interest in the form or by interest in the content, becomes clear when one compares the interpretations of Michelangelo's Last Judgment by Jacob Burckhardt and Graf Yorck von Wartenburg, which Karl Löwith has set alongside one another.[47] Erich Auerbach displays complete mastery in his book *Mimesis* in making the formal analysis of works of literature fruitful for the interpretation of their content.[48]

As we have seen, Dilthey takes genuine understanding of literature and art as well as of works in philosophy and religion to be oriented to the question of understanding unique historical existence; and, as has also become clear, all historical documents whatever can be subjected to this way of asking questions. Can this mode of interpretation be understood any more aptly and precisely? It has already been modified by saying that it involves exhibiting the possibilities of human existence that are disclosed in literature and in art as well as in philosophical and religious texts. I now want to try to make this somewhat clear.

In an essay on J. J. Winckelmann's picture of the Greeks, Fritz Blättner has very instructively contrasted the *intentio recta* and the *intentio obliqua* in the reception of religious works of art.[49] The first presupposes the faith of the observer, who sees the divine that he or she believes in presented as something objective in the work of art; thus it does not at all look upon the work as a work of art, and for its purposes an oleograph of the Madonna would perform the same service as a painting by Raphael or a Pietà by Michelangelo. By contrast, the *intentio obliqua* does not ask about the objective meaning of the work of art, and it is indifferent "whether it sees an Apollo or a St. Sebastian, whether what was objectively meant was a Christ or a Moses or a slave"; it asks about the "humanity" or about the "spirit out of which the work of art arose and of which it was a witness".

This change came about with Winckelmann, who "looked behind what is objectively said and meant to the spirit or genius of the creator and of his or her people and perceived it to be the essential thing in the work" (Blättner). So, too, did the great philologists Friedrich Ast and August Boeckh ask about the "spirit" of antiquity as the whole in the light of which the individual work has to be understood.[50] This is the mode of understanding that was developed by J. G. von Herder and came to dominance with romanticism. Naturally, this way of looking at things can also be combined with historicism, even as Winckelmann discovered the epochs of the history of Greek art; because he held the sequence of these epochs to be regular, he could even be regarded as a precursor of Oswald Spengler. During the time of National Socialism, this way of asking questions — qualified, to be sure, by biologism — was reduced to absurdity, although in its basic idea it is also present in the essays in the history of art by Hermann Grimm, whose aim was to write a history of the national artistic imagination.[51]

Naturally, this way of looking at things has a certain justification; and the relativism that belongs to it (which can have its background in a pantheistic faith in the divinity present in everything human) need not become dominant (or conscious). Thus, in the case of Winckelmann, the spirit that he saw acquiring form in Greek art was the exemplary representation of the human spirit as such, on which human beings in every age have to model themselves.

Dilthey's effort, obviously, is to get beyond this ultimately aestheticizing way of looking at things that was typical of romanticism. He remains caught in it, to be sure, when he takes "sympathy with other psychical states" to be grounded in the happiness to which it gives rise and speaks of the "enchantment" that one "enjoys" when one looks beyond the limits of one's own time to the cultures of the past. Nevertheless, one not only enjoys the enchantment but "also takes the strength of the past into oneself". Because through understanding we "find the history of the soul in all history", we thereby "complete" our own individuality and learn "to come to ourselves understandingly".[52] Sentences such as these make clear that genuine understanding does not have to do with happily viewing other individuality as such but is basically directed to the possibilities of human existence that manifest themselves therein, possibilities that are also possibilities for anyone who understands and that are brought to consciousness precisely through understanding. Thus, genuine understanding is a matter of hearing the question raised in the work or the claim encountered in it, and the "completion" of one's own individuality consists in the richer and deeper disclosure of one's own possibilities, in being called beyond oneself by the work (that is, one's incomplete, inertial self, which is constantly in danger of simply continuing as it is).[53]

Yorck sees more clearly even than Dilthey when he says, in defining himself over against Ranke's writing of history, "If anywhere, it is in history that heaven and earth are one." Lying behind this statement is the view that understanding history does not consist in regarding it aesthetically but is a religious process because the reality of history is not even visible to the spectator who is personally uninvolved. "Ranke is a great eyepiece for which what has disappeared cannot become a reality."[54] Yorck's words make clear how historical understanding is hearing the claim of history and critically reflecting on oneself: "Michelangelo preached the renaissance of morality with the most forceful one-sidedness in the Sistine Chapel. The mute, simple crosses scratched by Christians in the stones of the Mamertine prison came to expression through Luther. If anything is more forceful than Michelangelo's Last Judgment, it is those crosses, points of light in a subterranean heaven, signs of the transcendence of consciousness."[55]

The problem of understanding has been decisively clarified by Martin Heidegger's demonstration that understanding is an "existential", by his analysis of interpretation as the development of understanding, and, above all, by his analysis of the problem of history and his interpretation of the historicity of human existence.[56] Following Heidegger's ideas, Fritz Kaufmann has provided a critical survey of contemporary philosophy of history, from which the meaning of interpreting historical documents understandingly clearly emerges.[57]

VI

Let us now summarize the preceding discussion.

The presupposition of any understanding interpretation is a prior life relation to the subject matter that is directly or indirectly expressed in the text and that provides the objective in questioning it. Without such a life relation in which text and interpreter are bound together, questioning the text and understanding it are impossible, and questioning it is not even motivated. This is also to say that any interpretation is necessarily sustained by a certain preunderstanding of the subject matter that is expressed or asked about.

It is out of interest in the subject matter that there emerges some way of asking questions, some objective in questioning the text, some particular hermeneutical principle. The objective of questioning can be identical with the intention of the text, in which case the text mediates the subject matter asked about directly. But the objective can also grow out of interest in matters that appear in any possible phenomena of human life and, accordingly, in any possible text. In this case, the objective of questioning does not coincide with the intention of the text, and the text mediates the subject matter asked about indirectly.

Thus, for example, the objective of interpretation can be given by an interest in reconstructing the continuum of past history — whether political history, the history of the forms and problems of social life, intellectual history, or the history of culture in the broadest sense. In this case the interpretation will always be determined by the understanding that the interpreter has of history in general.

The objective of interpretation can also be given by a psychological interest, which subjects the texts to some way of asking about psychology, whether individual, social, or religious — for instance, by asking about the psychology of literature or of technology, and so on. In all such cases the interpretation is guided by some presupposed preunderstanding of psychological phenomena.

Or again the objective can be given by an aesthetic interest which subjects the text to a formal analysis and questions a work of art about its structure, its "outer" and "inner" form. This aesthetic interest may be combined with a romantic-religious interest, or it may remain simply in the sphere of stylistic analysis.

Finally, the objective of interpretation can be given by an interest in history as the sphere of life in which human existence takes place, in which we acquire and develop our possibilities, and in which, by reflecting on these possibilities, we each come to an understanding of ourselves and of our own possibilities. In other words, the objective can be given by the question about human existence as one's own existence. The texts that most nearly lend themselves to such questioning are the texts of philosophy and religion and literature. But in principle all texts (like history in general) can be subjected to it. Such questioning is always guided by some prior understanding, some particular understanding of human existence, which can be quite naive, but out of which the categories first emerge that alone make the questioning possible — as when one asks, for example, about "salvation", or about the "meaning" of one's personal life or of history, or about the norms of moral action and of order in human community, and the like. Without such a preunderstanding and the questions guided by it, the texts are dumb. The point, then, is not to eliminate the preunderstanding but to risk it, to raise it to the level of consciousness, and to test it critically in understanding the text. In short, in questioning the text one must allow oneself to be questioned by the text and to give heed to its claim.

With this insight we also find the answer to the sceptical question whether we can achieve objectivity in interpretation and in the knowledge of historical phenomena. If the concept of objective knowledge is taken over from natural science (where, by the way, its traditional meaning has also become problematic today), it is not valid for the understanding of historical phenomena, which are of a different kind from the phenomena of nature. As historical phenomena they do not exist at all without a historical subject who understands them. For facts of the past become historical phenomena only when they become meaningful for a subject who exists in history and participates in it. They become historical phenomena only when they speak, and this they do only for the subject who understands them. This is not to say, of course, that the subject simply attaches a meaning to them by arbitrary preference; it is to say, rather, that they acquire a meaning for anyone who is bound together with them in historical life. Thus, in a certain sense, it belongs to a historical phenomenon that it should have its own future in which it alone shows itself for what it is.

It would be misleading to express this by saying that every historical phenomenon is ambiguous. For even if it is indeed vulnerable to arbitrary interpretation according to preference, it is nevertheless in principle unambiguous for scientific understanding. On the other hand, every historical phenomenon is complex and many-sided; it is open to different ways of asking questions, whether the way of intellectual history, psychology, sociology, or what have you, provided only that it arise out of the historical bond between the interpreter and the phenomenon. Any such way of asking questions leads to objective, unambiguous understanding if the interpretation is carried through in a methodical way. And, naturally, there is no reason to object that real understanding is developed only by discussion and the conflict of opinions; the simple fact that every interpreter is limited in his or her subjective capacity is in principle irrelevant.

Knowledge acquired in a methodical way is "objective", which can only mean "appropriate to the object once it comes within a certain way of asking questions". To call the way of asking questions as such "subjective" is pointless. It may indeed be so called if one considers that it naturally has to be chosen in each case by some subject. But what does "choosing" mean here?[58] The way of asking questions as such does not grow out of individual preference but out of history itself, in which every phenomenon, in keeping with its complex nature, offers different aspects, that is, acquires — or, better, claims — significance in different directions. And it is in the same history that every interpreter, in keeping with the motives present in the variety of historical life, acquires the way of asking questions within which the phenomenon begins to speak.

Thus, the demand that the interpreter has to silence his or her subjectivity and quench any individuality in order to achieve objective knowledge could not be more absurd. It makes sense and is justified only insofar as it means that the interpreter must silence his or her personal wishes with respect to the results of interpretation — such as a wish, say, that the text should confirm a certain (dogmatic) opinion or provide useful guidelines for praxis. Often enough, such wishes have been present in exegesis past and present; and, of course, being without presuppositions with respect to results is as unalterably required in the case of interpretation as in any other scientific research. For the rest, however, this demand completely misjudges the nature of genuine understanding, which presupposes the utmost liveliness of the understanding subject and the richest possible unfolding of his or her individuality. Just as we can succeed in interpreting a work of art or literature only by allowing it to grip us, so we can understand a political or sociological text only insofar as we ourselves are concerned with the problems of political and social life. The same holds good, finally, of the kind of understanding to which Schleiermacher and Dilthey orient their hermeneutical theory and which can be said to be understanding of historical phenomena in the ultimate and highest sense, namely, the interpretation that questions texts about the possibilities of human existence as one's own. Here the "most subjective" interpretation is the "most objective", because the only person who is able to hear the claim of the text is the person who is moved by the question of his or her own existence. The monuments of history "speak to us out of the depth of reality that has produced them only when we ourselves, out of our own readiness for experience, are aware of the problem, the finally insurmountable need and threat, that constitute the ground and the abyss of our being-in-the-world."[59]

VII

Interpretation of the biblical writings is not subject to different conditions of understanding from those applying to any other literature. Beyond question, it is subject first of all to the old hermeneutical rules of grammatical interpretation, formal analysis, and explanation in terms of contemporary conditions. But then it is clear that here, also, the presupposition of understanding is the bond between the text and the interpreter, which is established by the interpreter's prior relation to the subject matter mediated by the text. Here, too, the presupposition of understanding is a preunderstanding of the subject matter.

This assertion is contested today by the claim that the subject matter of holy scripture, especially of the New Testament, is the act of God. Of this act there simply cannot be any preunderstanding because we human beings do not naturally have any prior relation to God but rather can know of God only through God's revelation, and thus through God's act.

This counterclaim is only apparently right. It is indeed true that one can no more have a preunderstanding of God's act as a real event than one can have of other events as events. Before I learn from tradition about the death of Socrates I can know nothing about it, anymore than I can know about the assassination of Julius Caesar or Martin Luther's posting of his Ninety-Five Theses. But in order to understand these events as historical events and not merely as arbitrary happenings, I have to have a preunderstanding of the historical possibilities within which they acquire their significance and therewith their character as historical events. I have to know what it means to lead a life of philosophical inquiry, what makes happenings into political events, or what Catholic and Protestant self-understandings are as possibilities open to human beings who must decide who they are to be. (It is hardly necessary to observe that such knowledge naturally need not be explicit.)

Likewise, understanding reports of events as the act of God presupposes a preunderstanding of what in general can be called God's act — as distinct, say, from the acts of human beings or from natural events. And if it is objected that we human beings cannot know who God is and hence also cannot know what God's act means prior to God's revelation, the proper reply is that we can very well know who God is in the question about God. Unless our existence were moved (consciously or unconsciously) by the question about God in the sense of Augustine's "Thou has made us for thyself, and our heart is restless until it rests in thee", we would not be able to recognize God as God in any revelation. There is an existential knowledge of God present and alive in human existence in the question about "happiness" or "salvation" or about the meaning of the world and of history, insofar as this is the question about the authenticity of our own existence. If the right to describe this question as the question about God is first acquired by faith in God's revelation, still the phenomenon as such is a relation to the subject matter of revelation.

This existential knowledge of God is always somehow interpreted wherever it is consciously present. If it becomes conscious, for example, in the question, "What must I do to be saved?" (Acts 16:30), some idea of "salvation" is necessarily presupposed. Any question directed to the New Testament must be prepared to have the idea that it brings with it corrected by hearing the word of the New Testament itself, and yet it can receive such correction only if the basic intention of the question interpreted by the concept of "salvation" concurs with the intention of the answer given in the New Testament.

So far at least as the scientific exegesis of theology is concerned, everything turns on the appropriate interpretation of the question, and this means at the same time the appropriate interpretation of what it means to be a human being. To work this out is a matter of human reflection, and concretely it is the task of a philosophical, existentialist analysis of human existence. Of course, this kind of work is not a presupposition of a simple hearing of the word of the New Testament, which is addressed directly to existential self-understanding and not to existentialist knowledge. But it is otherwise in the case of a scientific interpretation of scripture. It finds its objective by asking about the understanding of human existence that scripture brings to expression. Consequently, it has to concern itself with the appropriate concepts for talking about human existence.

These are grounded in the exegete's life relation to the subject matter expressed in scripture and include a preunderstanding of it. It is an illusion to think that one can do without such a preunderstanding, and the concepts flowing from it, and understand a single word of the New Testament as word of God. The interpreter is in need of critical reflection on the appropriate concepts precisely when he or she seeks to let scripture itself speak to the present as a power addressing our own existence, and thus does not treat the biblical writings as a compendium of dogmatic statements, or as "sources" for reconstructing a bit of past history, or for studying some particular religious phenomenon or the essence of religion in general, or for learning about the psychological development and objectification of religious experiences. If the objective of interpretation is said to be the question about God, or about God's revelation, this means that it is the question about the truth of human existence. But then interpretation has to concern itself with the conceptuality of an existentialist understanding of existence.

VIII

Karl Barth rejects the opinion that a theological statement can be valid only if it can be shown to be a genuine element in the Christian understanding of human existence.[60] This is relevant to the present discussion only insofar as theological statements are interpretations of the assertions of scripture, and thus only insofar as Barth disputes my existentialist interpretation of scripture. This he does in the following passage (which in context has to do with the chief statements of the Christian confession): "They [sc. these statements] are indeed all related to human existence. They ground and make possible a Christian under-standing of it, and so — inflected — also become determinations of human existence. But this is not what they are to begin with. To begin with, they determine the being and action of the God who is other than us human beings and who encounters us: Father, Son, and Holy Spirit. For this reason they are not to be reduced to statements about the inner life of a human being."

The last sentence betrays a complete misunderstanding of existen-tialist interpretation and of what it means by human existence. This is in no way "the inner life of a human being", which can be understood apart from all that is other than it and encounters it (whether the environ-ment, fellow human beings, or God). This may indeed be how psychol-ogy of religion, say, considers human existence, but it is not the way of existentialist analysis. For such analysis seeks to grasp and understand the actual (historical) existence of human beings, who exist only in a context of life with "others", and thus in encounters. Existentialist anal-ysis endeavors to develop an appropriate conceptuality for just such an understanding. But Barth evidently orients his notion of it to a concept of anthropology derived from Ludwig Feuerbach, which he even attrib-utes to Wilhelm Herrmann, instead of seeing that Herrmann was struggling to understand human existence as historical (even if in an inadequate conceptuality).

The demand to make of Barth is that he gives an account of his own conceptuality. He grants my claim, for example, that the resurrection of Jesus is not a historical fact that could be established as such by means of the science of history. But it does not follow from this, he thinks, that the resurrection did not occur: "Is it not possible for a story to have really happened and for an acknowledgment of the story to be legitimate even in a case where, simply for reasons of good taste, one would not speak of 'historical fact' and where the 'historian' may very well prefer to speak of 'saga' or 'legend' because the story does indeed elude the means and methods, together with the tacit presuppositions, of this historian?"[61]

I ask, What does Barth understand here by "story" and "happened"? What kind of an event is it of which one can say that "it far more certainly really happened in time than all the things that the historians as such can establish"?[62] It is perfectly clear that Barth interprets the statements of scripture by means of a conceptuality that he brings with him. But what is the source and meaning of this conceptuality?

Furthermore, what way of "believing" is it if credence is to be given to the assertion of events that are supposed to have happened in time and history and yet cannot be established by the means and methods of historical science? How do such events come within the purview of the believer? And how is such faith to be distinguished from a blind acceptance by means of a *sacrificium intellectus*? In what sense does Barth appeal to a demand for honesty that is of another or higher kind than the demand for honesty that requires me to hold nothing to be true that contradicts the truths which are the factual presuppositions of the understanding of the world that guides everything I do?[63] What elements are contained in the mythical world picture to which we do not have to commit ourselves as a whole, but from which we can appropriate certain things eclectically?[64] To ask about a valid meaning of the mythical world picture is precisely the intention of my existentialist interpretation of myth, in which I attempt to proceed methodically, even while all I can find in Barth are arbitrary assertions. What is *his* principle of selection?

It is clearly in Barth's sense that Walter Klaas confronts me with the statement: "One interprets scripture who allows it alone to be the rule and guide of proclamation [where do I dispute this?], who knows the word of prophets and apostles to be foreordained and repeats it as one has responsibly heard it."[65] Such a statement shows only that the person making it still does not see the problem of interpreting scripture. The exegete is supposed to "interpret" scripture after he or she has responsibly "heard" its word. But how is one to hear without understanding? The problem of interpretation is precisely the problem of understanding.   *New Testament and Mythology,* pp. 69-93.

4

KERYGMA[*]

"PRIMITIVE CHRISTIANITY IN ITS CONTEMPORARY SETTING"

While Primitive Christianity in its Contemporary Setting *is one of Bult-mann's later works (1949), its subject matter grows out of his research and publications from the 1920s. During this period Bultmann was actively engaged in the work of the history-of-religions school* (Religionsge-schichtliche Schule). *Bultmann was particularly involved with the work of those scholars who came to a new understanding of Christianity by com-paring its teachings with those of other religious movements from the first two centuries of the Common Era. In particular, Bultmann acknowledged his indebtedness to the writings of Wilhelm Heitmüller, Richard Reitzen-stein and Wilhelm Bousset. While the essays of the twenties were very technical, and often limited to research issues of interest only in that decade, Bultmann later provided a more general introduction to the reli-gious milieu of early Christianity in* Primitive Christianity in its Contem-porary Setting. *The German text,* Das Urchristentum im Rahmen der antiken Religionen, *was published in 1949. Our readings are taken from Reginald Fuller's English translation published in 1957.*

CONCEPTUAL RESOURCES FOR THE KERYGMA

Jewish Apocalyptic

The most important development in this period was the growth of apocalyptic writings, where, under Babylonian and Persian influence, there was worked out a cosmic eschatology. Under the impact of pres-ent disasters as well as through Babylonian and Persian mythology, the Jewish world view was modified along the lines of a pessimistic dualism, though without abandoning the doctrine of creation. This earth, the scene of so much distress and misery, sickness and death, sin and vio-lence, is the habitat of evil spirits with Satan at their head, opposing the sovereignty of God.[66] The power of darkness makes war on the power of light. But the power of darkness is not eternal and static, so that the way

[*] See also pp. 28-33 above.

to regain freedom from it would be by sacraments and asceticism, which enable the soul to rise to the realm of light, where it will ascend one day after death. As in Iranian religion the present state of affairs will come to an end, and God will vindicate his kingly rule.

> Then shall his kingdom appear throughout all his creation,
> And then Satan shall be no more,
> And sorrow shall depart with him.[67]

The course of the world is divided into two ages, this age and the age to come. "The Most High has not made one age, but two" (IV Ezra 7.50). It is the conviction of the apocalyptic writers that the turning point between the two ages is near at hand. "Creation is already grown old, and is already past the strength of youth" (IV Ezra 5.55; cf. 4.26). The epochs of world history are predetermined, one succeeding another in such a way that the apocalyptists can calculate the point which history has reached at the present moment by looking back on the past. The course of history is depicted in poetical imagery or mythological allegory. Nebuchadnezzar dreams that he sees the world empires succeeding one another in the form of different metals (Dan. 2), while in the vision of the seer in Daniel 4 there appear fantastic, gruesome beasts, which are succeeded by the Reign of Israel as 'the saints of the most High' (Dan. 7).

It is supremely important to recognize the signs of the approaching end. It will be heralded by the "Messianic woes", when Satanic evil reaches its climax in the coming of Antichrist. There is confusion among men and nations, friends and relations, fighting on opposite sides. The whole of nature is out of course: there are unnatural births, cosmic disturbances, the sun shining by night and the moon by day, fountains running blood, the stars running out of course, fire bursting forth from the bowels of the earth, trees dripping blood, stones crying out, and so forth (IV Ezra 5.4-12).

Finally, the end will be there, with the resurrection of the dead and the judgment. The resurrection of the dead, a doctrine still foreign to the Old Testament was clearly taken over by Judaism from Iranian sources. By the time of Jesus it was widely accepted, though not by the Sadducees. There was no need to fear that only those who were alive at its coming would share in the age of redemption. "I will liken my judgment to a ring; just as there is no retardation of them that are last, even so there is no hastening of those that are first" (IV Ezra 5.42).[68]

> The earth shall restore those that are asleep in her,
>> and the dust those that are at rest therein,
> and the chambers shall restore those that were committed unto
>> them (IX Ezra 7.32).

The judgment is a great forensic act. The earliest description we have of it is to be found in Daniel 7. God comes forth to judgment in white hair as the Ancient of Days. He takes his seat on his throne, surrounded by his court of angels. The books are brought in, in which all the deeds of men are recorded. Then the judgment itself takes place (Dan. 7.9-12).

> The Most High shall be revealed upon the throne of judgments
>> and then cometh the end,
>> and compassion shall pass away,
>> and pity be far off,
>> and longsuffering withdrawn;
> But judgment alone shall remain,
>> truth shall stand,
>> and faithfulness triumph.
> And recompense shall follow,
>> and the reward be made manifest:
> Deeds of righteousness shall awake,
>> and deeds of iniquity shall not sleep.
> And then shall the pit of torment appear,
>> and over against it the place of refreshment;
> The furnace of Gehenna shall be made manifest,
>> and over against it the paradise of delight (IV Ezra 7.33-7).

Then the new age begins:

> Then shall the heart of the inhabitants of the world be changed,
> and be converted to a different spirit.
>> For evil shall be blotted out,
>>> and deceit extinguished;
>> Faithfulness shall flourish,
>>> and corruption be vanquished;
>> And truth . . . shall be made manifest (IV Ezra 6:26-8).

> Corruption is passed away,
>> weakness is abolished,
>> infidelity is cut off;

while righteousness is grown,
and faithfulness is sprung up (V Ezra 7.113f.).

For the righteous the new age brings eternal life. When they rise they shall be changed into radiant glory (Syr. Bar. 49-51), and arrayed in celestial robes and crowns on their heads, like angels. "In the age to come there is no eating or drinking, no begetting of children, or multiplying, but the righteous sit with crowns on their heads, and rejoice in the radiance of the Godhead" — so runs a Rabbinic saying [Bab. Berakoth 17a, Trans.]. It should, however, be added that there are other sayings which speak of women in the age to come giving birth daily. By and large, fantasy has free scope to elaborate the details of life in the age to come. A typical expectation is the return of Paradise and the heavenly Jerusalem coming down to earth. All the blessings of salvation have been predetermined by God from of old, indeed they are often regarded as being actually pre-existent in heaven.

For you
    is opened Paradise,
        planted the tree of life:
    the future age prepared,
        plentiousness made ready;
    a city builded,
        a Rest appointed;
    Good works established,
        wisdom preconstituted;
The evil root is sealed up from you,
        infirmity from your path extinguished;
And death is hidden.
        Hades fled away;
Corruption forgotten,
        sorrows passed away;
and in the end the treasures of immortality are made manifest
    (IV Ezra 8.52-4).

For everything that is corruptible shall pass away,
And everything that dies shall depart,
And all the present time shall be forgotten . . .
And the hour comes which abides forever.
And the new world . . . (Syr. Bar. 44.9, 12).

But the fate of the ungodly is destruction or eternal torment in hell fire.

The idea of hell as a place of torment was still foreign to the Old Testament, and was adopted only much later from Iranian sources. It is called "Gehenna", after the Valley of Hinnom, where children were sacrificed to Moloch in olden times.

Nationalistic and cosmic hopes are in some places combined unsystematically by an interchange of imagery. The rabbis achieve this more systematically by making the Messianic age a prelude to the new age. Hence the doctrine of the intermediate kingdom, which is expected to last four hundred or a thousand years. In the new age proper there is no place for the Messiah as the national king. Instead of him, there emerges a new figure, the supernatural agent of redemption who is to appear at the end of the days to inaugurate the new age. This figure bears the enigmatic title "Man". He is a figure of cosmic eschatology, the archetypal man as the head of a new humanity, entering first into Judaism from the East, and thence penetrating westwards until he is found eventually in the Fourth (Messianic) Eclogue of Vergil. It is possible that the same conception underlies the picture of the Man coming on the clouds of heaven in Daniel 7.13, though here it is transformed into the embodiment of the people of Israel. In later Jewish apocalyptic writings the "Man" combined the functions of Judge and agent of redemption, thus becoming a rival to God himself. Hence we may easily understand how the figures of the Messiah and the "Man" coalesced in the Synoptic Gospels.[69]   *Primitive Christianity in its Contemporary Setting;* pp. 82-86.

*

Star Worship, Fatalism and Astrology

The Greeks had always believed that the stars were supernatural beings, but they had never actually worshiped them during classical times.[70] In the Hellenistic age, however, star worship penetrated into the Mediterranean lands from the Near East and gradually conquered the Roman world. And although the Greek gods proved intractable to any attempt to convert them into astral deities, popular Hellenistic philosophy was influenced by ideas picked up from star worship in a number of different ways. It was the Syrian Baals ("Lords") which lent themselves most readily to this process. Originally gods of vegetation, they became astral deities under Chaldean influence. Syrian merchants, slaves and mercenaries introduced them into the West, e.g. as Jupiter of Doliche or Jupiter of Heliopolis, and even before the end of the Republic such cults had found their way into Italy. In the age of the Empire their influence grew apace, especially under the Severi. Julia Domna (= Martha), the wife of Septimius Severus (193-211), was the daughter of the high priest of Baal of Emesa. Heliogabalus, who became Emperor in 218, was himself a priest of this same deity. Aurelian (270-5) promoted the Syrian sun god, whose picture he had stolen from Palmyra, to the status of an imperial deity with the title, *Sol Invictus.* Mithraism, a cult which was particularly popular with the army, contributed greatly to the propagation and development of the worship of *Sol Invictus.*

More important, however, than the worship of these Syrian deities was the theology which came along with it. The Oriental deities of the sky and sun naturally offered a congenial soil for the development of a belief in a supreme God. The tendency towards monotheism already existing within philosophical enlightenment, particularly among the Stoics, was thus reinforced by this sacerdotalist theology from the Orient, where the sun had become an omnipotent deity pervading the world with its vital force. So it came about that solar pantheism conquered the entire Roman world during the age of the Empire.

The last formula reached by the religion of the pagan Semites, and in consequence by that of the Romans, was a divinity unique, almighty, eternal, universal and ineffable, that revealed itself throughout nature, but whose most splendid and most energetic revelation was the sun.[71]

The historical significance of this influx of Oriental star worship was not however exhausted in this development of a solar pantheism. Along with it there came a development of a belief in the transcendence of the deity combined with fatalism, the symptom of which is astrology. This was one of the consequences of the invasion of the Oriental religions, though it was by no means exclusively a result of them. For in the Hellenistic world the Greek view of life was in any case undergoing a profound change, making it receptive to Oriental ideas. The latter simply added fuel to the fire.

This sense that man was simply the plaything of fate became very prevalent among many classes of society, particularly in the ever increasing population of the great cities. The political upheavals which had destroyed the ancient city states as well as the Roman Republic left the individual utterly bewildered and helpless. Everything was now on such a large scale that he could no longer understand what it was all about or see any law at work behind it. He could no longer, as in the old days of the city state, with its much smaller scale, contribute effectively to politics, and thus to his own personal destiny. He had become simply the plaything of fate. The continuous upheavals, the triumphal processions, the foundation and collapse of one empire after another, party strife and civil war at home — all of these left the individual with a sense of utter helplessness. In great men, men of daring and action unhampered by inhibitions or scruples, generals and despots, and even adventurers, this feeling takes the form of a proud conviction of being the instruments of fate. The capricious goddess Tyche ($\tau\acute{v}\chi\eta$, "chance"; Latin, *fortuna*), who governs world events, is for them a propitious deity who brings good luck. But for the countless myriads who feel themselves to be the slaves of fate, she is stern necessity ($\grave{a}\nu\acute{a}\gamma\kappa\eta$), ineluctable fate ($\epsilon\acute{\iota}\mu\alpha\varrho\mu\acute{\epsilon}\nu\eta$).

Everywhere in the whole world at every hour by all men's voices Fortune alone is invoked and named, alone accused, alone impeached, alone pondered, alone applauded, alone rebuked and visited with reproaches; deemed volatile and indeed by most men blind as well, wayward, inconsistent, uncertain, fickle in her favors and favoring the unworthy. To her is indebted all that is spent and credited, all that is received, she alone fills both pages in the whole of mortals' account; and we are so much all at the mercy of chance that Chance herself, by whom God is proved uncertain, takes the place of God.

So wrote the elder Pliny.[72] But can fate, with her caprice, still be conceived as a deity? We can understand how she acquired the name of "Spontaneity" ($\tau\grave{o}$ $\alpha\grave{v}\tau\acute{o}\mu\alpha\tau o\nu$). "Spontaneity seems to be a god", runs a saying of Menander and to Spontaneity there is dedicated an inscription from Pergamum in the age of the Empire.

This sense of helplessness in the hands of fate, of living in a world where it is impossible to plan their future, makes men wonder whether it is possible to be at home in the world at all. The world becomes a hostile, alien place. It was just this mood that led men to turn to star worship, where they found just what they wanted. For that worship implied that the universe was not a harmonious unity, but that it was split into two spheres, the lower, sublunary world, and the world of the stars. Moreover, the lower world was not centered in itself, but was under the control of the stars. Everything that happened in this lower world was determined by what went on in the world of the stars. Hence, in the last resort all activity here is trivial and meaningless, and if it seems to be independent, that is a mere illusion.

But the consequence of radical dualism was not invariably drawn. The late Stoics endeavored to combine their fatalism and star worship with the traditional Greek conception of the cosmos. They maintained the discredited feeling for the world with a kind of defiance. Man must, they contended, make no attempt to resist fate, but accept it. Fate is also providence, and can be traditionally understood. Thus the unity of the cosmos was preserved. Epictetus calmly asserts his conviction to this effect. Seneca's attempt to maintain it is more of a *tour de force*.

Fate [*fata*] guides us, and it was settled at the first hour of birth what length of time remains for each. Cause is linked with cause.... Therefore everything should be endured with fortitude, since things do not, as we suppose, simply happen — they all come [*non, ut putamus, incidunt cuncta, sed veniunt*]. Long ago it was determined what would make you rejoice, what would make you weep, and although the lives of individuals seem to be marked by great dissimilarity, yet is the end one — we receive what is perishable, and shall ourselves perish [*accipimus peritura perituri*]. Why, therefore, do we chafe? Why complain? For this were we born [*ad hoc parti sumus*]. Let Nature deal with matter, which is her own, as she pleases: let us be cheerful and brave in face of everything, reflecting that it is nothing of our own that perishes. What then is the part of the good man? To offer himself to fate [*praebere se fato*]. It is a great consolation that it is together with the universe we are swept along [*cum universo rapi*]; whatever it is that has ordained us so to live, so to die, by the same necessity it binds us also to the gods. One unchangeable course [*cursus*] bears along the affairs of men and gods alike. Although the great creator and ruler of the universe himself wrote the decrees of fate, yet he follows them. He obeys for ever, he decreed but once.[73]

But this kind of fatalism can just as easily degenerate into superstition. The world of the stars, in whose law and order the divine government of the universe is more clearly manifest than in the sublunary world, becomes the object of veneration. The wise man — and not only the Stoic — strives frantically to attain the vision of this world. He turns his back on this life with its wild ambitions and lusts. "The contemplation of the sky has become a communion." By contemplating the harmonious movements of the stars the devotee himself "participates in their immortality, and already, before his appointed hour, converses with the gods". Thus Vettius Valens, an astrologer of the second century A.D. But this kind of absorption in the contemplation of the world of the stars is already to be found in Seneca. Writing to his mother Helvia, he says:

Inside the world there can be found no place of exile; for nothing that is inside the world is foreign to mankind. No matter where you lift your gaze from earth the heaven, the realm of God, and man are sep-arated by an unalterable distance. Accordingly, so long as my eyes are not deprived of that spectacle with which they are never sated, so long as I may behold the sun, and the moon, so long as I may fix my gaze upon the other planets, so long as I may trace out their risings and set-tings, their periods, and the reason for the swiftness or the slowness of their wanderings . . . so long as I may be with these, and in so far as it is permitted to a man, to commune with celestial beings, so long as I may keep my mind directed over to the sight of kindred things on high, what difference does it make to me what soil I tread upon.[74]

Similarly, in his letter of consolation to Marcia he describes the vision which the soul will some day enjoy when it ascends to heaven after death:

You will see the gleaming of countless stars, you will see one star flooding everything with his light and the sun that marks off the spaces of day and night in his daily course, and in his annual course distributes even more equably the periods of summer and winter. You will see the moon taking his place by night, who as she meets her brother borrows from him a pale, reflected light, now quite hidden, now overchanging the earth with her white face exposed, ever chang-ing as she waxes and wanes, ever different from her last appearance. You will see the five planets pursuing their different courses and sparkling down to earth from opposite directions; on even the slight-est motions of these hang the fortunes of nations, and the greatest and smallest happenings are shaped to accord with the progress of a kindly or unkindly star.[75]

Finally, in his correspondence with Lucilius, Seneca portrays the day of a man's death, the "birthday of eternity", when the spirit leaves its earthly body and returns to the gods. Then:

the secrets of nature shall be disclosed to you, the haze will be shaken from your eyes, and the bright light will stream in upon you from all sides. Picture to yourself how great is the glow when all the stars mingle their fires: no shadows will disturb the clear sky. The whole expanse of heaven will shine evenly; for day and night are inter-changed only in the lowest atmosphere. Then you will say that you have lived in darkness, after you have seen, in your perfect state, the perfect light — that light which now you behold darkly in a vision that is cramped to the last degree. And yet, far off as it is, you already look upon it in wonder; what do you think the heavenly light will be when you have seen it in its proper sphere?[76]

In such visions or fantasies men still cling to the old idea of the unity of the cosmos. This was possible so long as the Stoic attitude of the freedom of the wise man from everything that happens in the outside world and the idea of the independence of the inner Ego and its relationship to the divine, universal law are not allowed to go by the board. Once that happens, however, the law which prevails in the world of the stars is seen in a different light. It is no longer the law whose writ runs throughout the universe, and which even the stars themselves obey. It is the law which is defined by the stars, which are now regarded as the omnipotent despots of the universe. That is just how they appear in Oriental astrology. Here the astral deities have lost their personal nature and have become cosmic powers of an abstract kind. They operate on strictly causal lines, and are susceptible of mathematical calculation. This kind of science, which can predict the future from the movement of the planets, is astrology.

It penetrated from the East, and gained a powerful hold on all classes of society, no matter whether it was practised by pundits or by charlatans. It became fashionable to have one's horoscope read, and to consult the Chaldeans about the favorable moment for any undertaking, whether great or small. Augustus had his horoscope published, and coins were minted inscribed with the sign of his birth — Capricorn. Astrology also played a fateful role in the life of Tiberius. Manilus wrote an astrological poem of a didactic nature in Rome and dedicated it to Tiberius. It was intended as a Stoic refutation of Lucretius. In the second century A.D. Vettius Valens wrote a book on the interpretation of the stars, while his Alexandrian contemporary, Claudius Ptolemaeus, sought to combine astrological superstition with scientific astronomy in his *Tetrabiblos*. Firmicus Maternus (fourth century A.D.) was an astrologer before his conversion to Christianity, when he became a doughty opponent of pagan religion.

An essential feature in the view of life of which these developments are symptomatic is, first, that as a result of the depreciation of the sublunary world at the expense of the world of the stars the idea of transcendence was modified in a sense foreign to Greek thought. God's transcendence is no longer his spirituality, which man, since he participates in it, can understand by rational thought as the power in the universe which imparts form to matter. A new dualism replaces the old dualism of form and matter, of spirit and sensuality. It is the dualism of the two worlds, the sublunary, and the world of the stars. It is symptomatic that whereas the classical Greeks regarded light as the light of

167

day, articulating the universe in its fullness, and enabling man to find his way in it, it now becomes the object of direct vision for those who have turned their backs on the sublunary world. A symptom of this is that the deity is now characterized by attributes foreign to the classical mind. Thus God becomes the "Most High" (ὕψιστος) and the "Almighty" (παντοκράτωρ), a term which eventually found its way into the Christian creed. Theology develops the concept of omnipotence and eternity.

Further, it is of the utmost significance that astrology produced a wholly new attitude to time. The stars are the world rulers because they are the lords of time. World events move with their motion, in periods. History is not governed by its own immanent laws, proceeding automatically at every moment of time, as a harmonious process. It is subjected to the changes of time governed by the motions of the stars. It runs in periods, each of which — days, weeks or epochs — is under the control of a particular planet. Another symptom is the spread from the East during the age of the Empire of the idea of planet weeks. The division of time into periods provides a congenial soil for the development of an eschatology. Men begin to look for an age of redemption which will follow the confusions and disasters of the present. This kind of belief offers a clue to the understanding of the political upheavals which are going on in the world. The end of the civil wars and the reign of Augustus can be hailed as the dawn of a new era, as the Golden Age, the age of redemption, ushered in by the appearance of a new star, which Virgil in his fourth Eclogue, celebrating the birth of the Savior of the World, identifies with Apollo. The conception of omnipotent time finds its symbol in the Aeon, a figure of Iranian mythology, further developed by Chaldean theology.

Finally, star worship introduces an eschatology of the individual. The soul of man, which derives from the star world, will, after death, reascend to its native world, a belief which originally applied to the souls of kings, but which was later made "democratic" — that is, it was applied to all human souls. Heaven is the home of the souls, and they long to return thither all through their sojourn in their earthly prison.

Of course, at the outset this belief was far from being universally accepted. It was only a comfortable promise preached by a few sects to the myriads who felt themselves to be the slaves of fate. Sometimes it competed with other redemptive religions, sometimes it was combined with them. For there were many religions which offered deliverance from fate and from the tyranny of the stars.

Among these were the mysteries. In them the initiate becomes the master of his own destiny.

Let fortune go and fume with fury in another place [cries the priest of Isis, pointing to Lucius, whom the goddess has summoned]. For fortune (*casus infestus*) hath no puissance against them which have devoted their lives to serve and honor the majesty of our goddess. . . . Let such, which be not devout (*inreligiosi*) to the goddess, see and acknowledge their error: "Behold, there is Lucius that is delivered from his former so great miseries by the providence of the goddess Isis, and rejoiceth therefore and triumpheth of victory over his fortune."[77]

Among these too, was Gnosticism. Those who have "knowledge" are not only secure from the attacks of demons, but are no longer prisoners of fate (*fatum*). For of the Gnostic it may be said:

In truth, Mind (νοῦς), the soul belonging to God (ἡ τοῦ θεοῦ ψυχή), is Lord over all things, over fate (εἱμαρμένη), over the law and over all else. And nothing is impossible to it, whether it be to lift the human soul above fate, or to subject it to fate, indifferent as it is towards whatever happens.

The pneumatic man, who has attained to the knowledge of himself, has no need to resort to magic for the sake of advantage, though magic in itself is a good thing. Nor need he make any attempt to get Ananke into his power. He lets everything take its natural or determined course. He goes his own way, seeking himself alone. And when he comes to know God, he holds fast to the ineffable [divine] triad, and lets fate (εἱμαρμένη) do what it will with his mortal clay — that is to say, his body.

Among these finally, is the Christian gospel. Paul takes for granted that this is what the gospel promises when he writes to the Galatians:

Even so we, when we were children, were in bondage under the elements of the world (τὰ στοιχεῖα τοῦ κόσμου). But when the fulness of time was come, God sent forth his Son . . . to redeem them that were under the law, that we might receive the adoption of sons. . . . But now, after that ye have known God, or rather are known of God, how turn ye again to the weak and beggarly elements, whereunto ye desire again to be in bondage? (Gal. 4.3f., 9).

Christian Gnosticism provides us with the statement:

But both the stars and the powers (οἱ ἀστέρες καὶ αἱ δυνάμεις) are of different kinds: some are beneficent, some maleficent, some right, some left. . . . From this strife and battle of the powers the

169

Lord rescues us and supplies peace from the array of powers and angels, in which some are arrayed for us and others against us.[78]

Primitive Christianity in its Contemporary Setting, pp. 146-155.

*

The Mystery Religions

With the Oriental cults and the world of thought which went with them, there was also a simultaneous influx of demonology into the West. Of course, the Greeks and Romans had long believed in ghosts and evil spirits, though such things had played only a minor role. Now, however, they acquired a new popularity and influence, being enriched by Oriental motives. In addition to Egyptian and Chaldean influences, others derived from Iranian dualism played a particularly important part. Thus, there was the figure of the devil, at the head of a host of evil spirits, battening on the flesh and smoke of burnt sacrifices, and seeking to creep into men's bodies and bring sickness and all manner of evil. Such ideas not only became popular among the uneducated masses, but, what was more important, were taken up by the Neoplatonists.

Like astrology before it, demonology brought in its train all kinds of practices connected with exorcism and necromancy. Magic also became very popular. There is no need for us to describe these tendencies in detail. They are symptoms of the age, and contributed to the recovery of the sense of the mysteriousness and even hostility of the universe, which reason and science seemed to have gone so far to understand and control. Reason and action — so at least many thought — were futile. They could not help man to become master of his fate. Rather, man felt himself to be the victim of elusive, malicious powers which lay in wait for him. Hence he looked for superhuman powers to deliver him. He was ready to listen not only to professional exorcists and magicians, who were able to subdue the spirits and reduce them to servitude, but also to the propaganda of religions which offered supernatural powers and even promised him divinity. These were the so-called mystery religions.

When we speak of mystery religions we mean a series of new cults coming in from the Near East and acquiring a new form in the Greco-Roman world. Originally tribal religions, they were introduced into the West by slaves, merchants and soldiers, and the natives increasingly joined the congregations thus founded. Thus there arose worshiping communities whose religion was quite distinct from the city state cults, and which represented in essentials a homogeneous type of piety. The most important of these new cults were those which came from Asia Minor and Phrygia, especially the cult of Attis, then the Egyptian cult of Isis and Osiris, and the Syrian religion with its cult of Adonis. Mithraism should also be included among the mystery religions though it differs from the others in that only men were admitted to it. This religion, whose austerity made it alien to the Greek world, is the typical soldier's religion. It does not, like the other mystery religions, offer redemption, but aims at promoting the ethical and military efficiency of its devotees by a process of education. There is no need to go into any further detail about it here.

The mystery religions were originally national or tribal cults. By the time they had become mystery religions they were completely divorced from their native soil. They produced worshiping communities constituted by the voluntary adherence of their devotees. In these communities the class distinctions of the secular world, difference of nationality and race, of economic and social position, were abolished. Free men and slaves, the important and insignificant were all brethren there, and women associated freely with men (except of course, in Mithraism). The community was organized on a hierarchical pattern, the priest or mystagogue being the father of the community.

Thus far the mystery communities form a parallel to the Christian congregation. At the same time, however, there are important differences. In the first place, they were not exclusive. True, their rites and ceremonies were, partly at least, held in secret, a fact which tended to make them secret societies. But membership of a particular community did not prevent its adherents from joining in the official cultus of the city state, or even from seeking initiation in other mysteries. Moreover, the mystery societies were not, like the Jewish or Christian congregations, united in a single Church.

The following features are common to all the mysteries (including, in the first instance, Mithraism as well). Admission to the community was by a rite of initiation, taking the form of a solemn consecration ($\tau \varepsilon \lambda \varepsilon \tau \acute{\eta}$). This was, of course, held in secret, which explains why they were called mysteries. The consecrated were joined together by the mystery, which separated them from the unconsecrated, and they were bound by an oath to keep it secret. The actual initiation was preceded by numerous rites of purification. There were fastings, lustrations and baptisms, and occasionally (in Mithraism at least) castigation. After these preliminaries, there followed the delivery ($\pi \alpha \rho \acute{\alpha} \delta o \sigma \iota \varsigma$) of the sacred formula (σύνθημα, σύμβολον), culminating in the vision of the deity (ἐπό-πτεια), in which the appearance of lights played a part. In this vision union with the deity was attained, the initiate being thus endowed with immortality. In many of the mysteries this union was symbolically effected by sexual intercourse (συνουσία). Other symbolic rites, regarded as possessing sacramental efficacy, are the vesting with the robe of the deity, in which the initiate "put on" the deity, and sacred banquets which effected or sealed his communion with the deity.

The general sense of the mysteries may be defined as the imparting of "salvation" (σωτηρία). Hence the deities are called "saviors" (σωτήρ, e.g. Serapis, or σώτειρα, e.g. Isis). This salvation includes all the blessings it is possible to desire; deliverance from all the perils of life, such as storm and shipwreck, protection from sickness and misfortune. But above all it includes the salvation of the soul and immortality (ἀθανασία, ἀφθαρσία).

As we might expect, the central figure in the cultus is, with the exception of Mithraism, the youthful god who dies and rises again. For these deities were originally vegetation deities which had lost their former associations. The cultic union with them identifies the initiate with their fate. He shares the death of the god as his rising again to immortal life. The mystic utterance preserved by Firmicus Maximus provides a good illustration of this:

Take courage, ye initiates! As the god was saved,
So too for us comes salvation from suffering.

Hence also — in many of the mysteries at any rate — the rite in which the initiate dies and rises again from death. This process is also described as rebirth. The initiate is "born again", "changed", "deified", and "enlightened". He now possesses the "medicine of immortality" in his soul. To make things sure, the consecration may be repeated. It is difficult to be sure to what extent a deeper spiritual experience was associated with the consecration. But at least it is clear that, given certain conditions, it could establish a real personal union with the deity. The Isis cult in particular seems to have produced a really living and spiritual type of deity. Isis becomes the sum of all deity, the Queen of Heaven. She is also the Mother goddess, who, like the Christian Madonna in later times, nurses the holy child in her bosom. The initiate's prayer of thanksgiving recorded by Apuleius may serve as an illustration of the devotion to Isis:

O holy and blessed dame, the perpetual comfort of human kind, who by thy bounty and grace nourishest all the world, and bearest a great affection to the adversities of the miserable as a loving mother, thou takest no rest night or day, neither art thou idle at any time in giving benefits and succoring all men as well on land as sea; thou art she that puttest away all storms and dangers from men's life by stretching forth thy right hand, whereby likewise thou dost unweave even the inextricable and tangled web of fate, and appeasest the great tempests of fortune, and keepest back the harmful course of the stars. The god's supernal do honor thee; the gods infernal have thee in reverence; thou dost make all the earth to turn. Thou givest light to the sun, thou governest the world, thou treadest down the power of hell. By thy mean the stars give answer, the seasons return, the gods rejoice, the elements serve: at thy commandment the winds do blow, the clouds nourish the earth, the seeds prosper, and the fruits do grow. The birds of the air, the beasts of the hill, the serpents of the den, and the fishes of the sea do tremble at thy majesty: but my spirit is not able to give thee sufficient praise, my patrimony is unable to satisfy thy sacrifices; my voice hath no power to utter that which I think of thy majesty, no, not if I had a thousand mouths and so many tongues and were able to continue for ever. Howbeit as a good religious person, and according to my poor estate, I will do what I may: I will always keep thy divine appearance in remembrance, and close the imagination of thy most holy godhead within my breast.

Clearly, among the mystery religions, especially in those which hailed from Egypt, there grew up a form of worship and devotion hitherto unparalleled in Greco-Roman antiquity. They also provided a fertile soil for a type of mysticism in which the rites and ceremonies were interpreted as mere outward symbols of psychical appearances achieved in meditation and ecstasy.

In view of the varieties of religious experience offered, it is impossible to say that the mystery religions represent any one type of theology. Those who took part in them did so from varying motives. It is therefore difficult to discern in them any one type of philosophy of life. Yet it would be true to say that the spread of the mystery religions is symptomatic of the change in the general view of life which had come over the Greco-Roman world. They show how uncertain men had become about their relation to the world in which they lived. It could no longer give them what they wanted if they were to be really themselves, if they were to live a life in which they could understand the world and their place in it. The performance of civic duty offered no real satisfaction, nor, except that a general attitude of Stoic self-sufficiency was possible, did it help to retreat to the inner recesses of the spirit, to indulge in intellectual contemplation of the world and its unity, or to appreciate man's oneness with the universal Logos. For the average man the only possible explanation of the universe is in terms of fate. He knows he is the slave of fate. It makes no difference whether he turns to astrology, or if, in a naive and primitive fashion he regards himself as the plaything of chance (Tyche). He knows that he is exposed to the vicissitudes of good and evil. He knows finally, that he is subject to the gloomy prospect of death, and that enemy he can never hope to conquer. If any god can help him, it is not the patron deity of the city state and its constitution, nor even the Logos, the rational law of nature which makes the world a unity and shows the individual his rightful place within it. It must be a deity above the world, on whose caprice or grace he is utterly dependent. He knows he is in the hands of a power beyond his control. His experience of fate does not suggest that it is a divine power to which he can surrender as a power in whose hands his salvation rests. From this predicament he is delivered by the grace of the deity which comes to him in the mystery.

However, one cannot speak of an explicit dualism as the underlying assumption of the mysteries. For the majority of their devotees clearly do not regard the world in itself as evil, or as the devil's handiwork. Religion here does not mean a thoroughgoing renunciation of the world. The mystery worshipers would fain find their security *in* the world and its blessings. And if the principle function of the mysteries is to enable men to acquire immortality, they are also expected to provide protection and salvation in *this* life. But there is a strong sense that the world is a very untoward place with hostile demonic powers at work in it. The presuppositions for a dualistic interpretation of the world are present here, and the logical conclusion is drawn in mysticism, which grows up out of the mystery religions. Where that conclusion is drawn, we are already in the presence of Gnosticism.

Primitive Christianity in its Contemporary Setting, pp. 156-161.

*

Gnosticism

Gnosticism is the name given to a phenomenon which appears in a variety of forms, but always with the same fundamental structure.[79] It first appeared and attracted the attention of scholars as a movement within the Christian religion, and for a long time it was regarded as a purely Christian movement, a perversion of the Christian faith into a speculative theology, the "acute Hellenization of Christianity". Further research has, however, made it abundantly clear that it was really a religious movement of pre-Christian origin, invading the West from the Orient as a competitor of Christianity. Since it appropriated all sorts of mythological and philosophical traditions for its expression, we may call it a synthetic phenomenon. Yet it would be wrong to regard it only as such. All its forms, its mythology and theology, arise from "a definite attitude to life and an interpretation of human existence derived therefrom".[80] In general, we may call it a redemptive religion based on dualism. This is what gives it an affinity to Christianity, an affinity of which even its adherents were aware. Consequently, Gnosticism and Christianity have affected each other in a number of different directions from the earliest days of the Christian movement. True, Christianity gradually came to draw a line of demarcation in its struggle against Gnosticism, and although certain features in the Gnostic imagery claimed a rightful place within the Church, other Gnostic ideas were not only ignored, but bitterly resisted.

We shall make no attempt to describe the various Gnostic images which developed on Oriental and Greek soil, both within and outside the Christian movement, or its very scanty literature. Gnostic sects, building up their rites and doctrines under various influences, including, in the Greek world, the philosophical tradition, arose partly in the form of "baptist" movements in the region of the Jordan. Elsewhere they assumed the form of mystery cults, where, by a process of syncretism, the Gnostic motives took on concrete form in one of the mysteries. Sometimes, for instance, the Gnostic redeemer is identified with the Phrygian Attis. But Gnosticism as a tendency was not confined to the religious sects. It even penetrated to religious philosophical literature of Hellenism, and is also found in Philo, the Jewish philosopher of religion, while it influenced Neoplatonism, despite Plotinus' polemic against it.

The Gnostic myth recounts — with manifold variations — the fate of the soul. It tells of its origin in the world of light, of its tragic fall and its life as an alien on earth, its imprisonment in the body, its deliverance and final ascent and return to the world of light. The soul — or, more accurately in the language of Gnosticism itself, man's true, inner self — is a part, splinter, or spark of a heavenly figure of light, the original man. Before all time this figure was conquered by the demonic powers of darkness, though how that came to pass is a point on which the various mythologies differ. These powers tore the figure of light into shreds and divided it up, and the elements of light thus produced were used by the demons as cohesive magnetic powers which were needed in order to create a world out of the chaos of darkness as a counterpart of the world of light, of which they were jealous. If these elements of light were removed, this artifical world of ours, the cosmos, would return to its primordial state of chaos. Therefore the demons jealously watch over the sparks of light which they stole. Naturally, interest is concentrated on these sparks of light which are enclosed in man and represent his innermost self. The demons endeavor to stupefy them and make them drunk, sending them to sleep and making them forget their heavenly home. Sometimes their attempt succeeds, but in other cases the consciousness of their heavenly origin remains awake. They know they are in an alien world, and that this world is their prison, and hence their yearning for deliverance. The supreme deity takes pity on the imprisoned sparks of light, and sends down the heavenly figure of light, his Son, to redeem them. This Son arrays himself in the garment of the earthly body, lest the demons should recognize him. He invites his own to join him, awakens them from their sleep, reminds them of their heavenly home, and teaches them about the way to return. His chief task is to pass on the sacred passwords which are needed on the journey back. For the souls must pass the different spheres of the planets, the watch-posts of the demonic cosmic powers. The Gnostic redeemer delivers discourses in which he reveals himself as God's emissary: "I am the shepherd," "I am the truth," and so forth. After accomplishing his work, he ascends and returns to heaven again to prepare for his own to follow him. This they will do when they die and the spark of light is severed from the prison of the body. His work is to assemble all the sparks of light. That is the work he has inaugurated, and it will be completed when all the sparks of light have been set free and have ascended to heaven to rejoin the one body of the figure of light who in primordial times fell, was imprisoned and torn to shreds. When the process is complete, this world will come to an end and return to its original chaos. The darkness is left to itself, and that is the judgment.

This myth testifies to a definite philosophy of life. It represents a discovery of the radical difference between man and the world in which he lives. Thus it is the exact opposite of the Greek understanding of human nature. It has a sense of the radical otherness of man, of his loneliness in the world. The world, for man, is not only an alien abode, but a prison, a dark, noisome cave. He has been flung into this cave without any fault of his own, and before he was capable of any conscious choice. It is this view of life which the doctrine of the pre-existence of the soul is intended to secure.

Who flung me into Tibil? (= the earthly world)
Into Tibil who flung me?
Who sealed up in the walls,
Who hurled me into the stocks
Which this world resembles?
Who bound me with this chain,
So intolerable to bear?
Why arrayed me in this robe,
Of many a varied hue and shape?

. . .

Who has cast me into the abode of darkness?

. . .

Why have ye snatched me away from my home, and brought me into this prison, and incarcerated me in this stinking body?

. . .

How far are the frontiers of this world of darkness?

. . .

The way we have to go is far and never-ending!

Such lamentations are constantly repeated. In the *Song of the Naassenes* the human Self — here actually called the soul — is depicted as a stag in flight, seeking in vain the way to freedom from earthly fate:

Now she wears the crown and beholds the light,
now she is cast down into the depths of misery;
now she weeps, now she recovers her joy;
now she weeps and laughs at the same time;
now she is judged and passes away in death;
now she is born anew;
and without hope of escape, the hapless, wandering soul is shut up in
a labyrinth of woe.

177

Man is the lonely victim of a dreadful fear — fear of infinite space and time, fear of the turmoil and hostility of the world, or rather, fear of the demonic powers at work in it, seeking to lead him astray and alienate him from his true self. He is also afraid of himself, for he feels he is in the clutches of the demonic powers. He is no longer his own master, but the playground of the demons. He is estranged from his own spiritual life, the impulses of his desire and will. Gone is the old idea of education, of the development of personality towards an ideal. Physical and sensual life is not matter needing the mind to give it form. Nor is it merely something $\dot{a}\lambda\lambda\acute{o}\tau\rho\iota o\nu$, alien, as the Stoics held, something the wise man can turn his back on and retreat from to his inmost being, his reason, the organ of thought and knowledge. No, it is the enemy of his Self, and even his soul can be his enemy, insofar as it subdues and overpowers him. "The abyss of the Self conceals within its own darkness the forces which rise up from it and oppose it." It is impossible to abandon the vital faculties of desire and will and seek refuge in the rational life of the mind. Every step we take is infected with the poison of the demonic. Man's true Self is differentiated not only from the body and its senses, but also from his soul. The anthropology of Gnosticism is therefore trichotomous. It distinguishes body, soul and Self. The designation for the Self may vary. Greek-speaking Gnosticism calls it $\pi\nu\epsilon\hat{v}\mu a$, "spirit", though in a sense which must be distinguished from the classical idea of the spirit. The adjective $\psi\nu\chi\iota\kappa\acute{o}\varsigma$, "of or belonging to the soul", thus acquires the pejorative significance which it bears in the New Testament.[81] But it is impossible to state in positive terms what the true self really is. It can be defined only in negative terms. Since it is a pre-existent spark of heavenly light, it is an entity of absolute transcendence. It is as it were the postulate behind all yearning and faith. Gnosticism is incapable of defining transcendence in positive terms. Having abandoned the Greek idea of the spirit (and the conception of transcendence which goes with it), it cannot get rid of the notion that the Self must be placed in the category of substance (as a spark of light), or cease to place the fate of the Self in the category of natural events. A comparison with the Christian understanding of the Self will make this clear. For Christianity abandons not only the Greek conception of the spirit, but also its accompanying doctrine of transcendence. Consequently it is able to do justice to the radical distinction between human personality and its objective environment, while its transcendence is conceived in terms of pure futurity. My real Self is always a future possibility. It is realized ever anew in each successive decision, whether active or receptive.

The Self is no longer an instance of the universal which finds its peace by turning away from the particular and contemplating the universal. Thus man's philosophy of the universe has undergone a complete change since classical times. In Greek Gnosticism, it is true, the outward form of the Greek view of the universe is retained. It is still thought of as a harmonious structure, as unity of law and order. But it is just the cosmos so conceived which undergoes a radical depreciation. Its very law and order are now the source of its terror. This harmony is a prison.[82] The stars, whose brilliant lustre and orderly movement were once contemplated as symbols of the divine nature, now become satanic powers, in whose prisons the sparks of light are bound. The separation between God and the world has become complete. God's transcendence is conceived in radical terms, and therefore eludes all definition.[83] His transcendence is purely negative. He is *not* the world (the world being deprived of all divinity). This view of the world, so typical for the decay of antiquity, is developed to an extreme which will prove of decisive significance for the future. After the decay of the mythological view of the world, the world will now be left in its "pure, indifferent objectivity", thus offering free scope for a purely secular scientific observation, whereas for the ancient world theology and physics had never been divorced from one another.

If transcendence is simply the negation of everything in this world, how can it have any relevance for human life? What more can it be than a criterion by which to judge this life, or an object of yearning? What about the God who can only be defined as "Not-world"? How can he be made relevant to real life? How can the true Self, if it be the bare negation of the empirical, psychic Self, get to grips with itself and come into its own? In mythological language, how can the imprisoned spark of light be liberated?

This liberation can only come in the form of redemption. It must be a redemption which frees man from his prison by freeing him from himself. It is out of the question that man should redeem himself, e.g. by reforming himself or undergoing an inner change. Redemption cannot be conceived as a real event in this world at all. For in this world the only visible events are physical or psychological. Hence redemption must be an absolutely eschatological event, a breach, a dissolution or separation of the real Self from the body and soul. It can only be realized mythologically as the separation of the constituent elements in the human personality which ensues upon death. On leaving the body and soul, the real Self, the pre-existent spark of light, ascends to its home, the heavenly world of light. Both the real Self and its redemption are objects of faith. Such redemption can only be secured by the preaching of a word which comes as a message from the other world, by a message brought by the emissary from the world of light. In the last resort, this is the only way in which the transcendent can become a present experience. It is the only possible way of realizing the other world in this. In mythological language this also means that when the Self becomes aware of its otherworldliness, it is at the same time conscious of its absolute superiority over the world. It interprets the discovery of its true Self as a revelation from the other side. Thus awakened, the Self becomes conscious of its "calling".

This faith in the reality of the calling which comes to the individual through the medium of the tradition is thus the true Gnostic existence. It is belief in a message which combines cosmological information with a summons to repentance or a call to awake and detach oneself from this world. It is a faith which at the same time includes the hope of an eschatological deliverance and the ascent of the soul.

"O ye peoples, earth-born men who have abandoned yourselves to drunkenness and sleep and to ignorance of God, be sober, and bring your carousals to an end — ye who are bewitched by unspiritual sleep." Thus exhorts the prophet, and continues:

Why, ye earth-born men, do ye abandon yourselves to death, ye who have the power to become partakers of immortality? Change your minds, ye consorts of illusion and comrades of ignorance. Free yourselves from the light that is darkness, claim your share in immortality, and leave corruption behind.

Whither are ye fleeing, O men, ye drunken ones, who have drunk to the full the wine of ignorance . . .? Stand still, be sober, look up with the eyes of your hearts. And if all is not possible to you, at least do what ye can. . . . Seek the Leader, who guideth you to the gates of knowledge, thither, where the radiant light shineth, there, where none is drunk, but all are sober, and in your hearts look upon him who will grant you the vision of himself. For he cannot be heard or named, nor seen with the eyes, but only with the mind and the heart. But first thou must rend the garment that now thou wearest, the attire of ignorance, the bulwark of evil, the bond of corruption, the dark prison, the living death, the sense-endowed corpse, the grave thou bearest about with thee, the grave, which thou carriest around with thee, the thievish companion who hateth thee in loving thee, and envieth thee in hating thee . . . that thou mightest not hear what thou must hear, and see what thou must see.[84]

In practice, the Gnostics were organized as mystery communities. In them the traditional formulae were handed on which were needed by the Self for its ascent. There were also sacraments, baptisms and sacred meals, for the purifying and strengthening of the Self. In the life of the community the transcendent destiny of the soul was manifested (in a way which was fundamentally illogical) by ascetic practices (rites of purification). Of course, it is impossible to be sure at this distance how far in any given case their basic ideas were carried through to their logical conclusion. Sometimes, no doubt, Gnosticism was little better than magic, while at other times miracles were regarded as a proof of mastery over the world. Sometimes this superiority was displayed in the miraculous odors or radiant light which exuded from their persons, symptoms which became very important later on in monastic mysticism. In another direction the same superiority over the world might be shown in a libertinism emancipated from all moral obligations.

The assurances of the Gnostic are typical. In the first place his true self is invisible. It is not the self which is visible to others, or which the painter can portray. No less typical are the statements assuring the Gnostic that this present world has ceased to be of any importance. It is just this which gives rise to libertinism. Once he has attained to liberty, the Gnostic cannot be affected by anything from the outside. Any kind of abstinence is out of the question, and indeed would be meaningless. There is no point in doing any work, no point in trying to make the world a better place, no point in training the soul for bliss. Such activity as there is is purely negative in character: abstinence from certain kinds of food, purifications, giving up sleep, and so forth. Yet even these things, except in so far as they spring from primitive fears of defilement, are only meant as exhibitions of the pneumatic's detachment from the world. Such Gnostic virtues ($\dot{\alpha}\varrho\varepsilon\tau\alpha\iota$) as there are have ceased to be capabilities for an $\ddot{\varepsilon}\varrho\gamma o\nu$; they are simply ascetic or cathartic modes of behavior.

The Gnostic feels himself to belong not to the nation or the city state, or even the world. He is no cosmopolitan. True, the unity of the human race is taken for granted. All men are fundamentally endowed with the divine spark. The preaching of conversion is directed to all. Yet in practice, mankind is divided into two classes, the pneumatic and the "hylic" (sometimes we find a middle class, the "psychic"), according as to whether they have the pneuma or spark of light alive in them or not, or whether they do not have it at all. The fellowship realized among the pneumatics is not like that of a natural, human or political society. It is based exclusively on a common detachment from the world. All earthly distinctions and all earthly ties are disregarded. Fundamentally, there is an invisible community which can only be seen by faith. Social life is not encouraged, as in any earthly society. The aim is simply to help men to achieve otherworldliness or redemption.

Despite this, however, in the last resort the Gnostic has no real need for cultus or community. It is significant that Gnosticism tends to produce an individualistic type of mysticism, in which the redemption, the ascent of the Self, is anticipated in meditation and ecstasy.[85] Gnosis, which in its initial stages stood for the knowledge of man's predicament, ends with the vision of God. The purpose of all spiritual endeavor is to achieve the experience of the true Self, and that can be defined only in negative terms. This is illogical and contradictory, for all experience must take place in this world.

There is a hymn of thanksgiving which provides a good illustration of Gnostic spirituality:

> I was delivered from my bonds,
>   and am escaped to thee, my God.
> For thou didst stand by to champion my cause,
>   didst redeem me and succor me.
> Thou didst keep back mine adversaries
>   that they showed their faces no more.
> For thy Person was with me,
>   and It saved me in thy grace.
> I was despised and rejected of many
>   and was in their eyes as base metal.
>
> But I received strength and succor from thee.
> Thou didst set lights on my right and my left,
>   that there might be no darkness round about me.
> I was bedecked with the covering of thy Spirit
>   and stripped off the garments of hide.
> For thy right hand hath exalted me,
>   thou hast removed sickness from me.
>
> I became whole in thy truth
>   and holy in thy righteousness.
> All mine adversaries yielded before my face;
>   I became the Lord's in the name of the Lord.

I was justified by his loving kindness,
and his peace endureth for ever and ever. Amen.[86]

Primitive Christianity in its Contemporary Setting, pp. 162-171.

*

PRIMITIVE CHRISTIANITY AS A SYNCRETISTIC PHENOMENON

Primitive Christianity arose from the band of Jesus' disciples, who, after their Master had been put to death by Pontius Pilate on the Cross, had seen him as one risen from the dead. Their belief that God had raised him from the dead gave them at the same time the assurance that Jesus had been exalted to heavenly glory and raised to the dignity of the "Man" who would very shortly come on the clouds of heaven to set up the Reign of God. The growing company of those who awaited his coming was conscious of itself as the Church of the last age, as the community of the "saints" and "elect", as the true people of God, for whom the promises were now being fulfilled, as the goal and end of the redemptive history of Israel.

The eschatological community did not split off from Judaism as though it were conscious of itself as a new religious society. In the eyes of their contemporaries they must have looked like a Jewish sect, and for the historian they appear in that light too. For the resources they possessed — their traditions about Jesus, which were carefully preserved, and the latent resources of their own faith, led only gradually to a new form of organization and new philosophy of human life, the world and history.

The decisive step was taken when the good news of Jesus, crucified and risen, the coming Judge and agent of redemption, was carried beyond the confines of Palestinian Judaism, and Christian congregations sprang up in the Greco-Roman world. These congregations consisted partly of Hellenistic Jewish Christians, partly of Gentiles, wherever the Christian mission sought its point of contact in the Hellenistic synagogues. For here, without going farther afield, it was possible to reach many of the Gentiles, who had joined the Jewish community, sometimes closely, sometimes more loosely. On other occasions the Christian missionaries went direct to the Gentile population, and then, in the first instance, to the lower classes in the cities. There were probably churches of Gentiles only, but few, if any, of the churches could have been purely Jewish. In any case Christianity found itself in a new spiritual environment: The Gospel had to be preached in terms intelligible to Hellenistic audiences and their mental outlook, while at the same time the audience themselves were bound to interpret the gospel message in their own way, in the light of their own spiritual needs. Hence the growth of divers types of Christianity.

By and large, the chief difference between Hellenistic Christianity and the original Palestinian version was that the former ceased to be dominated by the eschatological expectation and the philosophy of life which that implied. Instead, there was developed a new pattern of piety centered in the cultus. The Hellenistic Christians, it is true, continued to expect an imminent end of the world, the coming of the Judge and Savior from heaven and the resurrection of the dead and the last judgment. But there were also Christians who became sceptical of the primitive Jewish Christian eschatology and rejected it. Indeed, some tried to get rid of it altogether. Above all, the Gentile Christians found the idea of a redemptive history foreign to them, and as a result they lost the sense of belonging to the community of the last days. They could no longer feel that they were standing at the culmination of redemptive history directed by the providence of God. This was the case wherever the tradition of the Synagogue and Christian catechetical instruction had failed to implant the idea of redemptive history. The speedy disappearance of the apocalyptic title "Man" is symptomatic; even Paul himself refrains from using it. It was no longer understood that "Christos" was a translation of "Messiah", and meant that Jesus was the Lord of the age of redemption: the title simply became a proper name. Other titles took its place, such as "Son of God" and "Savior", titles which were already current in the Gentile world to designate agents of redemption. It was however the title "Kyrios" which became the most popular designation of Jesus. It characterizes him as the cult deity who works supernaturally in the worship of the Church as a cultic body. Hellenistic pneumatology, with ecstasy and speaking with tongues, find their way into the churches. The Kyrios Jesus Christos is conceived as a mystery deity, in whose death and Resurrection the faithful participate through the sacraments. Parallel with this sacramental cultus piety we very soon find Gnostic ideas of wisdom affecting the churches. Ideas originating from the Gnostic redemption myths are used to describe the person and work of Jesus Christ and the nature of the Church, and, accompanying these, ascetic and even libertinist tendencies.

At the same time, however, the Hellenistic Christians received the gospel tradition of the Palestinian churches. Admittedly, the importance attached to this tradition varied from place to place. Paul himself seldom refers to it. Yet almost everywhere the Old Testament asserts itself, being accepted as canonical scripture by all except extreme gnosticizing circles. This adoption of the Old Testament followed as a matter of course in those congregations which grew out of the Synagogue. The latter was also the medium by which Hellenistic Christianity adopted conceptions emanating from philosophical enlightenment, conceptions which the Synagogue itself had assimilated at an earlier stage. Christian missionary preaching was not only the proclamation of Christ, but, when addressed to a Gentile audience, a preaching of monotheism as well. For this, not only arguments derived from the Old Testament, but the natural theology of Stoicism was pressed into service. Quite early on the Christian churches adopted a system of morality, with its pattern of catechetical instruction derived in equal proportions from the Old Testament Jewish tradition and from the ethics of popular philosophical pedagogic, shortly to be enriched by the moral ideals of the Hellenistic bourgeoisie.

Thus Hellenistic Christianity is no unitary phenomenon, but, taken by and large, a remarkable product of syncretism.[87] It is full of tendencies and contradictions, some of which were to be condemned later on by orthodox Christianity as heretical. Hence also the struggles between the various tendencies, of which the Pauline Epistles give such a vivid impression.

Yes, at first sight we are bound to agree that Hellenistic Christianity is the outcome of syncretism. The world is the creation of God, who cares for the birds and decks the grass of the field with its beauty (Matt. 6.26, 30). Yet at the same time it is the realm of Satan, the "god of this world" (II Cor. 4-4), the "prince of this world" (John 12:31). The earth is the Lord's and all the fullness thereof (I Cor. 10.26). Yet creation is subject to vanity and corruption ($\mu\alpha\tau\alpha\iota\acute{o}\tau\eta\varsigma$ and $\varphi\theta\omega\varrho\acute{\alpha}$), yearning for the day of its deliverance (Rom. 8.19-22). The terms in which this deliverance is conceived are derived partly, and indeed mainly, from the Jewish tradition. The old age is already coming to an end, and the new age is about to dawn soon with the coming of the "Man", the resurrection of the dead and the judgment. But side by side with these conceptions we get the eschatology of the Fourth Gospel, which uses not the Jewish dualism of the two ages but the Gnostic dualism of the two realms of light and darkness, truth and falsehood, above and below, and which asserts that the judgment and resurrection have already been realized, or at least have been inaugurated because "the light is come into the world" (John 3.19).[88] Now that Jesus has come, those who believe in him

185

have already passed from death unto life (John 5.24f.). The person of Jesus is sometimes defined in terms of Jewish and apocalyptic categories, sometimes as the "Lord" of the cultus, as a mystery deity, sometimes again as the Gnostic redeemer, the pre-existent being from the heavenly world, whose earthly body is only an outward garb. This explains why the "rulers of this world" failed to recognize him, as only "his own" can. The Christian community is sometimes described in Old Testament categories as the people of God, the true seed of Abraham, sometimes in Gnostic categories as the "body of Christ", in which individuals are incorporated by means of the sacraments of baptism and the Lord's Supper. Of course, some of these concepts are confined to particular writings or groups of writings in the New Testament (which varies a great deal in its language and thought). But they are also to be found side by side or in combination in the same author, especially in Paul and the Epistle to the Hebrews.

Is Christianity then really a syncretistic religion? Or is there a fundamental unity behind all this diversity? A comparison of primitive Christianity with the various traditions and religious movements in which it was cradled and which influenced its growth should help us to answer this question. Does primitive Christianity contain a single, new and unique doctrine of human existence? The comparison may best be conducted by selecting certain main subjects as test cases. In doing this, we shall rely chiefly on the Pauline and Johannine writings, because they provide the clearest evidence for the Christian attitude to existence.

Primitive Christianity in its Contemporary Setting, pp. 175-179.

*

THE DISTINCTIVENESS OF NEW TESTAMENT CHRISTIANITY

The Situation of Man in the World

Freedom from the past, openness for the future — that is the essence of human existence. But it is the conviction of the New Testament that man needs first to be restored to his true nature through the event of redemption accomplished in Christ. Until this event has taken place, until man has appropriated the grace of God manifested in that event, he is alienated from his own true nature, aliented from life, enslaved under hostile powers and in bondage to death.

The situation of natural man in the world appears to Christian eyes very much as it does to Gnosticism. In fact, Christianity may employ Gnostic ideas and terminology to describe it. Impotence and fear mark the life of pre-Christian man. When he assures the Roman Christians, "Ye have not received the spirit of bondage again to fear; but ye have received the Spirit of adoption," Paul is taking for granted that the Romans, as Gentiles, had lived in the bondage of fear. The same idea of man's enslavement is presumed by the Jesus of the Fourth Gospel, when he says: "If ye continue in my word, then are ye disciples indeed; And ye shall know the truth, and the truth shall make you free" (John 8.31f.), though his audience cannot make head or tail of what he is saying, as the ensuing dialogue shows. For this is the worst feature of man's plight. He is totally unconscious of his enslavement. He has not the least notion what he is doing when he strives to attain life by himself, by his own efforts. The Jew imagines he can do this by his observance of the law. But his zeal in the service of God is futile: it only leads him into death (Rom. 7.14-24, 10.2). When the law is read in the synagogue, there is a veil over their hearts. They are hardened in thought and action, just as the "god of this world" has blinded the thought and action of those who do not believe (II Cor. 3.14, 4.4). Thus the constant misunderstandings to which the sayings of Jesus are exposed in the Fourth Gospel show that men are in darkness and love the darkness rather than the light (John 3.19).

The powers under which man is enslaved are, as in Gnosticism, the cosmic powers. They are the elements of the world, the astral spirits (τὰ στοιχεῖα τοῦ κόσμου, Gal. 4.3, 9), the "dominions, principalities and powers" (Rom. 8.38; Col. 1.16, etc.). They are the "rulers of this world" or even the "god of this world" or the "prince of this world" (I Cor. 2.6; II Cor. 4.4; John 12.31, etc.). All these terms are mythological, and are derived from Gnosticism. There is no reason to doubt that the early Christians regarded these powers as real demonic beings. Paul is using mythological concepts derived from Gnosticism when he states that the Old Testament law does not come from God, but was given by angelic powers. If the Gentile Christians adopt the Jewish law, they will be turning again to the "weak and beggarly elements" (Gal. 3.19f., 4.9). He is equally using the language of mythology when he says that the "rulers" (ἄρχοντες), deceived by the secret wisdom of God, crucified Christ, the "Lord of glory", because they did not know him. This was because he was disguised in the form of a servant (I Cor. 2.9; Phil. 2.6ff.).

Primitive Christianity never adopted the Gnostic doctrine of the pre-existence of the soul. Paul did indeed make use of the Gnostic myth of the archetypal man in order to make man's situation in the world intelligible. The fall of the archetypal man (which Paul naturally identifies with the fall of Adam as related in Genesis 3) has determined the fate of all men since. Adam brought sin and death into the world, and until Christ their sway has been unquestioned (Rom. 5.12ff.). Paul is drawing even more heavily on Gnostic mythology when he attributes the burden of man's sinful past to the nature of Adam:

> The first man is of the earth, earthy; the second man is the Lord from heaven. As is the earthy, such are they also that are earthy: and as is the heavenly, such are they also that are heavenly. And as we have borne the image of the earthy, we shall also bear the image of the heavenly (I Cor. 15.47f.).

And in describing the nature of Adam as "psychic" and that of Christ as "pneumatic" (I Cor. 15.44-6) he is again using the language of Gnosticism. Neither classical Greek nor the language of the Old Testament furnishes any precedent for the pejorative sense in which the adjective "psychic" is used here. Like the Gnostics, Paul distinguishes between "psychic" and "pneumatic", the latter meaning those who have "gnosis", which enables them to fathom the "deep things of God" (I Cor. 2.10-16).

In this conception of man's situation in the world as a bondage to the hostile cosmic powers, as a fate brought upon him by the fall of the archetypal man, there is a close affinity between Christianity and Gnosticism. But there is also a crucial difference. Both systems agree that empirical man is not what he ought to be. He is deprived of authentic life, true existence. Nor can he ever achieve that existence by his own strength. But according to the Gnostics, this is due to fate or destiny, whereas for primitive Christianity it is due not only to fate, but to man's guilt as well. This is at once apparent from the way Christianity dropped the doctrine of the pre-existence of the soul. It is further apparent in the refusal to abandon the Old Testament doctrine of creation (or the identity of the Creator and Redeemer) and of man's responsibility before God. Now it is true that the exact connexion between fate and guilt is never submitted in the New Testament to theological analysis. Man's enslavement to the cosmic powers and his personal responsibility, his impotence and his guilt are allowed to stand side by side without any attempt to reconcile them. In Romans 5.12ff. sin and death are attributed to the fall of Adam. They are a malignant destiny which has come upon man. In Romans 1.18ff., on the other hand, mankind incurred guilt and continues to incur it by its refusal to perceive God in the works of his creation. Romans 2.1ff. takes it for granted that man is responsible for his plight, for it speaks of judgment hanging as a threat over him —

over Gentile as well as Jew. Indeed, Paul feels obliged to give an explicit proof of the responsibility of the Gentiles: although they did not have the Mosaic law, they had the conscience, and the conscience taught them the law of God (Rom. 2.14f.).

The solution of this contradiction is that man's guilt has become his fate. It is essential to see how Paul (and John likewise) conceives the way in which these cosmic powers in actual practice work in the historical existence of man. They make themselves felt in practice as the powers of the flesh, the law, sin and death.

By "flesh" Paul means in the first instance the whole realm of concrete, tangible reality. It denotes not merely the sphere of the material or sensual, but equally life under the law, with its tangible achievements in keeping the letter of the commandment. This whole realm becomes a demonic power when man makes himself dependent upon it and lives "after the flesh". This may take the form of frivolity and licentiousness (Gal. 5.19ff.), which are thought to offer true life. Or it can be quite serious — scrupulous observance of the law (Gal. 3.3; Phil. 3.6), which again is thought to offer true life. In either case the thing man supposes he can control, whether it be pleasure or serious moral effort, becomes a power which controls him and drags him into the clutches of death. For by supposing that he can attain life from transitory things he makes himself dependent upon them, thus becoming himself a victim of transitory reality. Thus sin results in death, for sin is just this attempt of man to attain life through his own efforts. Sin does not, however, become explicit until man is confronted by the law. This awakens man's desire. This may happen either by his transgressing the law through his lustful impulses, or by his misusing the law in order to be able to "boast" before God — that is to say, in order to attain life by his own strength (Rom. 5.20, 7.7-11). Thus the law, which is intrinsically holy, righteous and good, and comes from God, becomes a lethal power. That is why at times Paul can speak of it in quite a Gnostic way. Thus the rule is: "The sting of death is sin, and the strength of sin is the law" (I Cor. 15.56). Once man has set out on this road, there is no turning back. He does now know what he is doing. While fondly supposing he is attaining life, he is on the road to death. Flesh, law, sin and death have become ineluctable powers. Man's guilt has become his fate.

The same truth is expressed in the dominant sense in which the term "world" is used in the New Testament, often in a typically depreciating manner called "this world". Of course, the world, as in the Old Testament and in Judaism, is the creation of God. Yet at the same time it is an alien place for man. Only Christians, it is true, know that they are "strangers and pilgrims" (I Pet. 2.11; cf. 1.1, 17), that their "citizenship" is in heaven (Phil. 3.20), that here they have "no continuing city, but seek one to come" (Heb. 13.14). But they are only realizing what is true of all men. That is what the gospel summons men to realize. It bids them awaken out of sleep, to stop being "drunk" and to become sober, just as in the preaching of the Gnostics. For this world lies under the thrall of the "rulers" (ἄρχοντες). Its god is Satan. Hence "the whole world lieth in the evil one" (I John 5.19). Further, hence, "the world passeth away, and the lust thereof" (I John 2.17; I Cor. 7.31). The world, like the law, drags the man who has surrendered to it into the clutches of death. It, too, is a demonic power, embodied in Satan, who inspires the world with a spirit opposing the Spirit of God (I Cor. 2.12). Yet the world is not a mythical entity; in the last resort it is an historical one. This is shown by the way in which the world is generally an all-inclusive term for the environment in which men live, and is sometimes used in an even more restricted sense, meaning human society, with its aspirations and judgments, its wisdom, its joys and its sufferings. Thus every man makes his contribution to the "world". It is the world in just this sense which becomes a power tyrannizing over the individual, the fate he has created for himself. There is therefore no ultimate cosmological dualism such, as we find in the Gnostics. This is proved by the way in which, for those who have been freed by Christ, the world recovers its character as creation, although even now it is not their home; "The earth is the Lord's, and the fullness thereof." "Every creature of God is good, and nothing to be refused, if it be received with thanksgiving." Thus the Christian is lord of the world (I Cor. 10:26; I Tim. 4.4; cf. Tit. 1.15; Rom. 14.14, 20; I Cor. 3.21f.).

Finally both the affinity between Christianity and Gnosticism and the difference between them are illustrated by the Christian conception of God's transcendence. In both systems that transcendence is conceived radically. There is nothing to suggest the classical view that God is immanent in the world, no suggestion that the orderly, law-abiding process of nature and course of history are proofs of the divine immanence. The New Testament knows nothing of the Stoic conception of providence. There is a great gulf between God and the world. The world is the "lower region"; the place of darkness. God is "above". He is the light and the truth. "No man hath seen God at any time" (John 1.18). He "dwelleth in the light which no man can approach unto" (I Tim. 6.16). The admonition "Love not the world, neither the things that are

in the world" is justified by the assertion that "all that is in the world . . .
is not of the Father, but is of the world" (I John 2.15f.). The Christian
receives the Spirit of truth, whom the world cannot receive, because it
does not see him or know him (John 14.17).

But this transcendence is not conceived ontologically as in Gnosticism. The gulf between God and man is not metaphysical. Light and
darkness are not cosmic forces of a material kind. Nor is the transcendence of God confined to the pure negativity of the "not worldly". In the
first place, it is his glorious sovereignty, which refuses to tolerate the
pride of man or his forgetfulness of his creaturely status. "God resisteth
the proud, but giveth grace to the humble" (Jas. 4.6; I Pet. 5.5, after Prov.
3.34). All human planning must be qualified by the proviso "If the Lord
will, and we live" (Jas. 4.13-15). God treats man as a potter treats his
clay: he has mercy on whom he will, and whom he will he hardens (Rom.
9.18, 20f.). It is "a fearful thing to fall into the hands of the living God"
(Heb. 10.31).

> Let no man deceive himself. If any man among you seemeth to be wise
> in this world, let him become a fool, that he may be wise. For the wis-
> dom of this world is foolishness with God. For it is written, He taketh
> the wise in their own craftiness. And again, The Lord knoweth the
> thoughts of the wise, that they are vain (I Cor. 3.18-20).

No flesh may glory before God: "He that glorieth, let him glory in the
Lord" (I Cor. 1.29, 31; II Cor. 10.17).

Up to this point we are still moving within the orbit of the Old Testament tradition. But at this point it acquires an entirely new sense
through the New Testament recognition that God, precisely by shatter-
ing all human boasting, reveals himself as the God of grace. The transcendence of God and his grace are one and the same thing. The Cross
of Christ, which is God's judgment over the world and the means by
which he makes the wisdom of this world foolishness, is the revelation
of his grace. The man who accepts the Cross as God's judgment upon
himself is delivered from the world. "God forbid that I should glory save
in the cross of our Lord Jesus Christ by whom the world is crucified unto
me, and I unto the world" (Gal. 6.14). As God's judgment is his grace, so
is his grace his judgment. For to be judged is simply to shut our hearts to
grace (John 3.18).

The grace of God is not visible like worldly entities. His treasures are
hidden in earthly vessels (II Cor. 4.7). The resurrection life is manifested in the world in the guise of death (II Cor. 12.9). Only in human
weakness is the power of God made known. Once again, this means that

the grace of God is never an assured possession. It is always ahead of man, always a future possibility. As grace, the transcendence of God is always his futurity, his constant being ahead of us, his always being where we would like to be. He is always there already as the gracious God for those who are open to the future, but as the judge for those who shut their hearts against the future.

Primitive Christianity in its Contemporary Setting, pp. 190-195.

*

Redemption

Man is incapable of redeeming himself from the world and the powers which hold sway in it. Of these powers, the most important are the flesh, sin, the law and death. Man's redemption — and at this point Primitive Christianity and Gnosticism are in agreement — can only come from the divine world as an event. It is something that must happen to man from outside. Now Christian faith claims that this is precisely what has happened in Jesus of Nazareth, in his death and resurrection. The significance of his person may be expressed in terms derived from many different sources, though it is not long before one particular interpretation of his person and work becomes the accepted norm. For the original Palestinian Church Jesus is the "Man" exalted by God, whose impending advent is the subject matter of eager expectation. Through his past activity on earth, Jesus had gathered around him the community of the last times. Apparently, a redemptive significance was attached to his death. It was regarded as an atoning sacrifice for sin, perhaps also as the sacrifice by which God inaugurated the new covenant with his people. In the Hellenistic churches terms derived from the mysteries had to be used to describe the redemptive significance of Jesus. He is the Lord worshiped in the cultus. The initiated participate in his death and resurrection through the sacraments of baptism and the Lord's Supper. The most important development, however, was the interpretation of the person of Jesus in terms of the Gnostic redemption myth. He is a divine figure sent down from the celestial world of light, the Son of the Most High coming forth from the Father, veiled in earthly form and inaugurating the redemption through his work.

Even before Paul this interpretation of the person of Jesus had found its way into the churches. For Paul is quite obviously quoting a traditional Christological hymn in Philippians 2.6-11, when he relates how Christ, a pre-existent divine being, left the celestial world and appeared on earth in the form of a servant, and after his death was exalted as Lord.[89] The same Gnostic myth lies behind the allusions of Paul to the mysterious divine wisdom, which the "rulers of this world" did not recognize; for had they done so they would not have crucified the Lord of glory. In his earthly disguise he was invisible to them, and as a consequence, by crucifying him they brought about their own destruction (I Cor. 2.8f.). With these Gnostic concepts Paul combines quite naively the already traditional interpretation of the death of Jesus as an atoning sacrifice, which came partly from the Jewish cultus, partly from the juridical notions prevalent in Judaism (Rom. 3.25, etc.). He can just as easily interpret the death and Resurrection of Jesus in terms of the mysteries and their sacramentalism (Rom. 6.2ff.). But the dominant interpretation of the death and Resurrection of Jesus is the Gnostic conception of it as a cosmic event through which the "old things" have been done away and the "new" inaugurated (II Cor. 5.17). For Paul, Christ has lost his identity as an individual human person. He knows him no longer "after the flesh" (II Cor. 5.16). Instead, Jesus has become a cosmic figure, a body to which all belong who have been joined to him through faith and baptism (I Cor. 12.12f.; Gal. 3.27f.). For it is "into him" that men are baptized (Gal. 3.27), and "in Christ" that the Christian lives henceforth. The Pauline "in Christ" is often wrongly interpreted in a mystical sense, whereas it is a Gnostic cosmic conception. It may also be called an *ecclesiological* formula, since the "body" of Christ is the Church, or an *eschatological* formula, since with the establishment of the body of Christ the eschatological event has been inaugurated.

The most thorough-going attempt to restate the redemptive work of Jesus in Gnostic terms is to be found in the Fourth Gospel. Here Jesus is the pre-existent Son of God, the Word who exists with him from all eternity. He is sent from God, sent into the world, as its light, to give sight to the blind, and to blind those who see (John 9.39). He is not only the light, but also the life and the truth. As the agent of revelation, he brings all these blessings and calls to his side his "own", those who are "of the truth". After accomplishing his Father's mission, he is exalted from the earth and returns to heaven to prepare a way for his own, that they may join him in the heavenly mansions. Indeed, he is himself the "way" (14.6). "I, if I be lifted up, from the earth, will draw all men unto me" (12.32).

It is easy to see why the Christian Church took over these ideas from the Gnostic redemption myth. That myth offered a terminology in which the redemption wrought in the person and work of Jesus could be made intelligible as a present reality. The eschatological event was already being realized in the present. This sense of being the eschatological community, of being already raised from this world by the grace of God, of deliverance from its powers, could not be adequately conveyed to the Hellenistic world in terms of the Jewish eschatological hope, which looked for redemption in the future. Indeed, a thinker of Paul's caliber was already sensitive to the difficulty. The eschatological event must be understood as a process already inaugurated with the coming of Jesus, or with his death and Resurrection, and the Gnostic redemption myth lay ready to hand as a vehicle for its expression.

In Paul the Gnostic ideas are still combined with the Jewish apocalyptic element. He still uses the apocalyptic conception of the two ages thus: "When the fullness of time came, God sent forth his Son" (Gal. 4.4). But the real point is that the coming of Christ is thus designated as the inauguration of the eschatological event. Isaiah's prediction of the day of redemption is now being fulfilled: "Behold, now is the accepted time; behold, now is the day of salvation" (II Cor. 6.2).

The man in Christ is already a "new creature", for "old things are passed away; behold, all things are become new" (II Cor. 5.17). Hence the triumphant cry:

Death is swallowed up in victory.
O death, where is thy sting?
O death, where is thy victory? . . .
Thanks be to God, who giveth us the victory through our Lord Jesus
    Christ (I Cor. 15.54-7).

The cosmic powers have already been dethroned:
When we were in the flesh, the motions of sins, which were by the law, did work in our members to bring forth fruit unto death. But now we are delivered from the law, being dead [with Christ] to [the power] wherein we were held: that we should serve in newness of spirit, and not in the oldness of the letter (Rom. 7.5f.).
Or:
But before faith came, we were kept under the law, shut up unto the faith which should afterwards be revealed. . . . But after that faith is come, we are no longer under a schoolmaster. For ye are all the children of God by faith in Christ Jesus. For as many of you as have been baptized into Christ have put on Christ . . . for ye are all one in Christ Jesus (Gal. 3.23-8).
When we were children, [we] were in bondage under the elements

of the world; but when the time was fulfilled, God sent forth his Son ... to redeem them that were under the law, that we might receive the adoption of sons (Gal. 4.3ff.).

With all this, Paul still combines the apocalyptic picture of the parousia, the resurrection of the dead and the judgment. But for the Fourth Gospel, the redemption is exclusively a present process.

And this is the condemnation, that light is come into the world. . . . (John 3.19).

Verily, verily, I say unto you. He that heareth my word, and believeth on him that sent me, hath everlasting life, and shall not come into condemnation; but is passed from death unto life. Verily, verily, I say unto you, The hour is coming, and now is, when the dead shall hear the voice of the Son of God: and they that hear shall live (John 5.24f.).

I am the resurrection, and the life: he that believeth in me, though he were dead, yet shall he live: And whosoever liveth and believeth in me shall never die (John 11.25f.).

Now is the judgment of this world: now shall the prince of this world be cast out (John 12.31).[90]

Christianity thus agrees with Gnosticism in placing the eschatological event in the present. It is inaugurated by the appearance of the redeemer on earth. Hence it follows that for Christianity, as well as for Gnosticism, the present salvation is not visible like an event in history. Indeed, some of the sayings which express this have quite a Gnostic ring. "Ye are dead, and your life is hid with Christ in God" (Col. 3.3). Or: "Now are we the sons of God, and it doth not yet appear what we shall be" (I John 3.2). The believers are, in principle, no longer "in the flesh",[91] though, of course, in practice they are still in it (II Cor. 10.3; Gal. 2.20). The outward man is decaying while the inner man is being renewed, but this process is no more visible to the outward eye than the glory of Christ which far outshines the glory which once covered Moses' face (II Cor. 3.7ff.), or the transformation of the believers into this same glory as they behold it (II Cor. 3.18). We live by faith, not by sight (II Cor. 5.7), and the knowledge we have at present is as problematical as an image reflected in a mirror. We shall not see face to face until the end (I Cor. 13.12).

Yet as in Gnosticism, the event of redemption is exhibited in certain phenomena, which somehow or other represent it. Indeed, at first sight it would seem that this is truer of Christianity than it is of Gnosticism. For in Gnosticism the mission and advent of the redeemer and the inauguration of the eschatological event were relegated to a mythical age before history began, while in Christianity these things are events of the recent past. It is the appearance of Jesus of Nazareth and his crucifixion, events whose historicity is vouched for by eye witnesses and by the tradition of which they are the source. All the same, it would be wrong to lay too much stress on this. For to begin with the historical person of Jesus was very soon turned into a myth in primitive Christianity. Furthermore, the Gnostics also believed that the advent of the redeemer was a real event, and the source of the tradition enshrined in their worship and doctrine.

The really important point is that for both Christianity and Gnosticism the tradition is itself the presence of the spiritual world in this world. Or, to put it more precisely, the redeemer is present in the word of preaching, the message from above. In the proclamation the eschatological event is bodied forth into the present. According to Paul, when God inaugurated the event of redemption in the death and Resurrection of Christ, he simultaneously established the word of preaching, the ministry of reconciliation. Where this word is heard, the eschatological redemption becomes a present reality (II Cor. 5.18f., 6.2). Similarly, the Fourth Gospel ascribes to Jesus the title of Logos or Word. Originally, this had been a mythological term. According to John Jesus is the Word because he has received from the Father the commission to proclaim the message with which he has been entrusted to the world, and is fulfilling it (8.26, etc.). His words are "spirit and life" (6.63). They bring both purification and judgment.

In conjunction with the word there are also the sacraments, as in the Gnostic systems. Christian sacramental theology differs little from that of Gnosticism, if at all. But its conception of the word is different, and that is decisive. It is true that in both systems the word is a call to awake, a summons to repentance and a challenge to decision. But in Gnosticism this call could only be a summons to become conscious of one's alienation from the world and to detach oneself from it. That it also meant something positive, a real turning to the grace of God, was something that Gnosticism could only make clear by cosmological instruction, by the myth of the archetypal man and the fate of the spark of light, which was man's true Self. Such mystagogic instruction could hardly have the urgency of a call to decision. Primitive Christian preaching had no use for cosmological instruction or for the doctrine of the pre-existence of the soul. And although it presents the Cross and Resurrection of Jesus in mythological terms, the preaching of the Cross is nevertheless a decisive summons to repentance. This is because the redemptive significance of the Cross (and therefore of the Resurrection also) can only become apparent to those who submit to being crucified with Christ, who accept him as Lord in their daily lives. Adherence to the gospel message is called "faith", and faith involves a new existential understanding of Self. In it man realizes his creatureliness and guilt. It is an act of obedience,[92] in which man surrenders all his "boasting", all desire to live on his own resources, all adherence to tangible realities, and assents to the scandalous fact of a crucified Lord. Thus he is freed from the world by being freed from himself. It is true that both primitive Christianity and Gnosticism agree in attributing man's liberation to the act of God. But in Gnosticism what was freed was the true self, the spark of light in man, whereas for Christian faith man is freed *for* his authentic self by being freed from himself — from the self which man, qualified as he is by his guilty past, brings along with him into the present. The Gnostic is one "saved by nature" ($\varphi\acute{\upsilon}\sigma\epsilon\iota\ \sigma\omega\zeta\acute{o}\mu\epsilon\nu o\varsigma$), the Christian through his faith. Hence the typical designation for the Christian religion is not knowledge ($\gamma\nu\tilde{\omega}\sigma\iota\varsigma$), but faith ($\pi\acute{\iota}\sigma\tau\iota\varsigma$).

This shows that the New Testament understands human existence as an historical existence. The Gnostics, on the other hand, attribute everything to fate, and therefore they understand human existence in the categories of natural Being. This is made abundantly clear in the doctrine of the pre-existence of the soul. For an existence which lies behind me, but must nevertheless be accepted as my own, despite the fact that it lies outside the range of my experience, and I can never be responsible for it, belongs not to history, but to nature. The discovery of the absolute distinction between humanity and its objective environment, the discovery made in the experience of the blows of fate, is nullified when that distinction is interpreted in ontological terms, as can be seen by the use of the phrase "being saved by nature".

There is a similar difference when we compare the Gnostic conception of the body of the redeemer with the Pauline doctrine of the body of Christ. Paul, of course, makes use of cosmological categories when he expounds the doctrine of the body of Christ. But in practice he always transposes it into an historical key. For although he does not reject the view that the sacraments of baptism and the Lord's Supper are the means by which men are grafted into the body of Christ, the decisive point is that membership of the body of Christ is acquired by faith. And faith after all is genuine historical decision. Hence Paul can use the Gnostic conception of the body of Christ in combination with the metaphor, common in Greco-Roman literature, of the body as the social organism of the state in order to describe the solidarity of the Christian community (I Cor. 12.14ff.). The body of Christ thus acquires shape in an historical context founded on preaching and faith, in which the individual members belonging to it are bound together in mutual care for one another, sharing each other's sufferings and joys.

Finally, the affinity and difference between Gnosticism and Christianity are illustrated from their conception of the pneuma or Spirit. The Gnostics identified the pneuma with the spark of light which has its abode in the inward man. When the agent of revelation came, he quickened the divine spark to newness of life, or if it was dead, restored it. This is similar to the Christian idea that the Spirit is imparted to the baptized and that it operates in them as a divine vital power. In popular Christianity, the Spirit was naïvely regarded as the source of miraculous phenomena. As in Gnosticism, such phenomena were, in an illogical manner, accepted as visible demonstrations of the supernatural otherworldly character of the baptized. We are referring, of course, to prophecy; ecstasy and speaking with tongues. But neither for Paul nor for the author of the Fourth Gospel, nor even for the New Testament as a whole is ecstasy the high water mark of the Christian life, or the visible manifestation of the transcendent. This is all the more remarkable in the case of Paul, for he knows all about such things as ecstasy, and if he wanted to could boast about ecstatic experiences of his own. But that is just what he refuses to do. He prefers to glory in his "infirmities". It is here that he sees the divine power at work in himself (II Cor. 12.1-10). But while Paul does not reject the popular view, he gives it a new turn. He finds real evidence of the Spirit's working in Christian moral behavior, in victory over lust and passion, and in simple, everyday acts of love. Here of course the operation of the pneuma loses its evidential value. This is shown by the way the Gnosticizing Corinthians criticize Paul for not displaying visible evidence of his pneumatic endowments. It is against such criticism that Paul is directing his polemic in II Cor. 10-13.

According to Paul, the pneuma — and here he determines the line of all future development — is not a magic power working in the hearts of the believers, but the norm of practical behavior. Whereas in the past Christians had lived after the flesh — that is to say, they had centered their lives on visible tangible realities — they must now orientate their lives on the Spirit. But since the Spirit is already enjoyed as a gift, it is in the last resort equivalent to the new possibility of life opened up by the grace of God, the life of freedom. Just because it is a gift, freedom is power (δύναμις). It is man's own capacity freed from the cosmic powers. And this power is at the same time the norm of behavior, because freedom means openness for the future — openness, that is, for every fresh claim of God both to action and to the acceptance of his fate. To possess the pneuma does not mean therefore that once a man has made the decision of faith and has been baptized he is now perfect, and need make no further decisions. On the contrary, he is now free as never before for each successive genuine decision in life. His life has become historical in the true sense of the word. Hence the Pauline paradox: "Work out your own salvation with fear and trembling. *For* it is God which worketh in you both to will and to do of his good pleasure" (Phil. 2.12f.).

Every decision in life involves a renewal of the decision of faith. It means a determination to live "after the Spirit". To be "led by the Spirit" (πνεύματι ἄγεσθαι) is something realized in the accomplishment of such decisions. It is obedience to the imperative, "walk in the Spirit" (Rom. 8.12-14; Gal. 5.16f.). So far from being abrogated, the divine imperative is now grounded on the indicative of freedom; "If we live by the Spirit, let us also walk in the Spirit" (Gal. 5.25; cf. Rom. 5.12-23; I Cor. 5.7, 6.11). The fulfillment of the law is now no longer the way to salvation, for salvation has already been granted as a gift. Rather, it is the outcome of that gift. The law as the way to salvation has been abrogated. But in so far as it is an expression of the good and holy will of God (Rom. 7.12), it is fulfilled as never before "in us, who walk not after the flesh, but after the Spirit" (Rom. 8.4), and that means the commandment of love, which comprehends all the precepts of the law. Paul is, of course, thinking here only of the ethical precepts of the law. "For all the law is fulfilled in one word, even in this; Thou shalt love thy neighbour as thyself" (Gal. 5.14). "For he that loveth another hath fulfilled the law. Love worketh no ill to his neighbor, therefore love is the fulfilling of the law" (Rom. 13.8-10). If there is any demonstration of faith to the world, any proof of the new life, it is love. "By this shall all men know that ye are my disciples, if ye have love one to another" (John 13.35). Love is the only criterion by which the believer can know that he has ceased to belong to the old world. "We know that we have passed from death unto life, because we love the brethren" (I John 3.14).

It is those who share the Spirit and are bound in mutual love who make up the body of Christ, the Church. Since it is a fellowship of the Spirit, it is essentially invisible to the world. In one sense, of course, it is visible, like the Gnostic communities. It consists of real men and women, who still live "in the flesh". But here we are faced with a paradox. This conglomeration of believers is also the eschatological community, the "body of Christ", whose existence is not subject to objective proof. Those who are united in the Church are not bound together by any worldly interests or motives. They are not joined by a common nationality, or even by an Idea, but by the Spirit which dwells in each of them. And just because of this, just because the Church depends for its existence, not on worldly motives or resources, but on the power available through the grace of God, Paul can describe it as that cosmic entity, the "body of Christ".

The practical behavior of the Church and its members in the world resembles that of the Gnostics in that it rests upon a sense of superiority over the world, in an awareness that "neither death, nor life, nor angels, nor principalities, nor powers, nor things present, nor things to come . . . shall be able to separate us from the love of God, which is in Christ Jesus" (Rom. 8.38f.). This absolute independence from the world, however, produces a certain detachment from all worldly interests and responsibilities. Primitive Christianity is quite uninterested in making the world a better place, it has no proposals for political or social reform. All must do their duty to the State. But they have no direct political responsibilities. After all, the Christian is a "citizen of heaven" (Phil. 3.20). The slave who is "in the Lord" has become free from the world, but he must not therefore suppose that he ought to seek sociological freedom: "Let every man, wherein he is called, therein abide with God" (I Cor. 7.17-24). Freedom might in itself breed license, but against that the Old Testament, the Jewish tradition and the words of the Lord are a surety. Where such tendencies appear, they are vigorously resisted (I Cor. 6.12-20). Instead, this negative attitude to the world tends to find its outlet in asceticism. Such tendencies appear very early in Christian history, even in Paul himself, when he allows marriage as a necessary evil, and regards celibacy as a special charisma. Ritualistic asceticism, which appears here and there, he tolerates as an infirmity (Rom. 14; I Cor. 8; 10), but he knows that "there is nothing unclean of itself: but to him that esteemeth anything to be unclean, to him it is unclean" (Rom. 14.14). "All things are pure; but it is evil for that man who eateth with offense" (Rom. 14.20). The fundamental principle behind such questions is: "Whatsoever is not of faith is sin" (Rom. 14.23). Paul's own standpoint is not one of legalistic asceticism, but a dialectic of participation and inward detachment:

It remaineth that both
they that have wives be as though they had none;
And they that weep, as though they wept not;
and they that rejoice, as though they rejoiced not;
And they that use this world, as though they had no dealings with it
   (I Cor. 7.29-31).

This interior detachment is described in that saying of Paul about his knowing how to be filled and to be hungry, to abound and to be in want (Phil. 4.11-13). And when he exhorts his readers to "Rejoice with them that do rejoice, and weep with them that weep" (Rom. 12.15), he is, of course, taking it for granted that the faithful share in the ordinary experiences of life.

Yes, in a certain sense action and experience in this world is not a matter of indifference, but vital and essential. It is the action and experience of the free man borne along by love. True, the Spirit is not a principle which can be applied to the improvement of the world. In this respect, it is the Christian's duty to be indifferent to the world. But just because he has no definite program, the Christian must be always discovering new duties. He is a new man, and by "the reviewing of his mind" he has been given the capacity to "prove what is that good, and acceptable, and perfect, will of God" (Rom. 12.2). Hence it was possible for the early Church to develop a pattern of catechetical instruction, in which it adopted many ethical concepts of Hellenism (Phil. 4.8), the lists of duties formulated in the "household codes", and finally, in the Pastoral Epistles, the ideals of the Hellenistic *petit bourgeoisie*.

It would therefore be true to say — and without questioning its fundamentally dialectic attitude to the world — that Christian detachment from civic duty and from political and social responsibility is not one of principle, but only a temporary exigency forced upon the Church by its historical situation. It was due partly to the expectation of an imminent end of the world, partly to the social composition of the earliest Christian communities. It would never have occurred to their members that they might assume social, still less political responsibilities.

In their experience of the Spirit and their knowledge that the grace of God makes men free to love, the problem which was so fatal for Gnosticism, i.e. the problem of the unworldliness of the Self, finds its solution. In Gnosticism the unworldly self could only be described in negatives. It could only be a matter of faith. It was a point from which every possible human action and experience was denied. In primitive Christianity, on the other hand, that same problem found a positive solution. It was still an object of faith, for it always lay in the future. It could never be present as an objective datum. Yet in the moment of action it was a present reality. For in the moment of action man is always grasping at the future, always being translated anew into the future. In the love which is grounded on faith (Gal. 5.6) the unworldly always becomes a present, objective reality, while in hope it is still in the future. Every act of love, though performed in the objective world, is paradoxically an eschatological event.

In the last analysis, however, the future can never, as in Gnosticism, be conceived in fantastic cosmic terms, despite all the apocalyptic imagery which has found its way into the New Testament. It can only be understood in the light of God's grace as the permanent futurity of God which is always there before man arrives, wherever it be, even in the darkness of death. Paul can certainly speak of a glory which is ready to be revealed for us (Rom. 8.18), of the eternal "weight of glory" which awaits us (II Cor. 4.17). But at the same time he speaks of faith, hope and love as things which will not cease, even when that which is perfect is come (I Cor. 13.13). In other words he can conceive no state of perfection in which the unworldly is a mere possession. The openness of Christian existence is never-ending.

Primitive Christianity in its Contemporary Setting, pp. 196-208.

*

"PAUL"

Like Luther before him, Bultmann understood the writings of Paul to occupy a privileged position within the New Testament canon. In Bultmann's view, Paul was the founder of Christian theology; in his writings Christian faith first found expression in an adequate understanding of itself. Not surprisingly, Bultmann devoted almost half of volume I, Theology of the New Testament *(1948), to an exposition of Paul. This selection is much briefer and from an earlier period of his writings. For the 1930 second edition of the German encyclopedia,* Die Religion in Geschichte und Gegenwart, *Bultmann wrote this article titled simply "Paulus". This essay presents not only Paul's theology but also Bultmann's, as the bond between the two has grown increasingly close. Schubert Ogden translated the essay for inclusion in his 1960 collection of Bultmann's writings,* Existence and Faith.

I SOURCES

The sources for a historical knowledge of Paul are essentially his genuine letters; these include Romans, I and II Corinthians, Galatians, Philippians, I Thessalonians, and Philemon. These letters come from a limited period in his life and, as occasional writings, contain only a few notices and intimations about his life; on the other hand, they give a rich picture of his views and intentions. So far as the outer course of his life is concerned, Acts provides much good material in its sources, even if alongside of these it also provides legendary tradition. As far as possible, its information must be controlled by Paul's own letters. The later Christian tradition, to which the spurious Pauline letters in the New Testament already belong, contains only a few reliable statements in addition to legendary information. Paul is not mentioned at all in heathen literature, although he is perhaps referred to in certain Jewish writings.

II LIFE

1. Background and Training

Paul was the child of a true Jewish family of the tribe of Benjamin (Rom. 11:1; II Cor. 11:22; Gal. 2:15; Phil. 3:5). According to Acts 22:3 (cf. 9:11, 21:39), he was born and raised in Tarsus in Cilicia and thus came from a Hellenistic city in which there was a mingling of Oriental and Greek populations. Tarsus was significant as a commercial city and was also a place where Greek science (and especially Stoic philosophy) was carried on. If Paul speaks of himself in Phil. 3:5 as a "Hebrew of Hebrews", this can be taken to suggest that his family had strictly preserved its Palestinian character (especially the Aramaic language) in the Diaspora. Whether his parents actually migrated to Tarsus from Gischala in Judaea — and, indeed, whether he himself was born in Gischala (Hieronymus) — is uncertain and is hardly confirmed simply because in Acts 23:16 ff. the son of his sister appears in Jerusalem. In fact, it seems rather improbable, if Acts (22:28, cf. 16:37) is correct in handing down that he was born a Roman citizen and had the civic rights of a citizen of Tarsus (21:39). If he was born a Roman citizen, then he had the name Paul (the only name he ever uses in his letters) from birth, while his Jewish name was Saul. Moreover, this means that he cannot have belonged to the lower social classes. In any case, his letters show that he was a Hellenistic Jew, i.e., that in his training Jewish tradition and Greek culture were combined. And if his scientific development was not anywhere near as comprehensive as that, say, of Philo, he still had mastered the Greek language to a high degree; not only are many of the techniques of rhetoric and of popular philosophy ("diatribe") familiar to him, but he is also acquainted with certain concepts and ideas of Stoic philosophy (e.g., the concepts of "conscience", "freedom", and "duty"). He obviously had enjoyed a systematic training in Jewish scribism, as is evident not only from his having belonged to the company of the Pharisees (Phil. 3:5; cf. Gal. 1:14), but especially from the style of his thinking, his argumentation, and his exegesis. According to Acts 22:3, he had studied in Jerusalem with Gamaliel the elder. But this is hardly correct, since one must surely conclude from Gal. 1:22 that prior to his conversion he had never resided for any length of time in Jerusalem (although this naturally would not exclude occasional trips for religious festivals). As a rabbi Paul practiced a trade (according to Acts 18:3, he was a tentmaker), for he frequently makes reference to his work (I Thess. 2:9; I Cor. 9:6 ff.; II. Cor. 11:12). His world of ideas gives evidence of an acquaintance with heathen cults and with Oriental and Gnostic mythology. To what extent this stems from the views that he acquired in his youth or from his later travels cannot be said; it would have been mediated to him in part through his Jewish connections, among whom, in addition to scribism, apocalyptic and mythological speculations were also carried on. In any case, his christology did not grow entirely from Christian ideas, but rather presupposes the concepts of a mythological-apocalyptic expectation of Messiah and redeemer in which he already lived as a Jew.

2. Conversion

So far as the pre-Christian period of Paul's life is concerned, we know for certain only that as a Pharisee he was a zealous champion of the law and of the scribal tradition (Gal. 1:13f.; Phil. 3:6). It appears likely from Gal. 5:11 that even as a Jew he engaged in missionary activity among the heathen, apparently with the point of view that is characterized in Rom. 2:19f. In his zeal he became a persecutor of the Christian community (Gal. 1:13, 1:23; Phil. 3:6; cf. Acts 9:1ff., 22:4f., 26:9ff.). Since he cannot have resided in Jerusalem prior to his conversion (see above, II., 1.), this persecution cannot have taken place in Judaea; and his participation in the death of Stephen is a legend — a judgment that is also confirmed by a literary-critical investigation of Acts 7:58-8:3. From Gal. 1:17 one must infer that the scene of the persecution was either in or around Damascus. Moreover, the character of the persecution is considerably exaggerated in the account in Acts; for what was involved could not have been a carrying out of sentences of death, but only beating with rods and expulsion from the synagogue — or, in other words, the same kind of persecution that Paul himself subsequently experienced as a Christian missionary (II Cor. 11:24). But why did Paul persecute the church? Naturally, for him also it was scandalous that Christians proclaimed a crucified one as the Messiah (I Cor. 1:18ff.) and claimed that the time of salvation was already breaking in. But while in the judgment of Jews this would indeed be madness, it would not be a crime that was deserving of punishment. The Christian message first became a crime when, with the preaching of the crucified one, the validity of the law was also called in question. Thus when Paul characterizes himself in Gal. 1:13f. as a persecutor of the church and at the same time as one who was zealous for the law, he shows that he had come to know Christianity in a form in which it already stood over against the law in a critical way and to some extent had actually overcome it. This is also evident because for him the question concerning the acceptance of the Christian message is identical with the either/or decision between the law and Jesus Christ. And it is further confirmed because we know of different forms of Hellenistic Christianity, all of which to some degree pose this either/or and yet are not determined by Paul's characteristic teaching concerning the law. Therefore, Paul first came to know Christianity in its Hellenistic form; and he became a persecutor because he could not help seeing it as an attack on the law that was the holy will of God and "the embodiment of knowledge and truth" (Rom. 2:20).

It was as a persecutor that Paul experienced his conversion; and to be sure, as a psychic process this conversion was a vision of Christ (Gal. 1:15; I Cor. 9:1, 15:8; there is very likely an allusion also in II Cor. 4:6), which has been colored over with legendary features by Acts (9:1ff., 22:4ff., 26:9ff.). In view of the complete lack of biographical reports, nothing at all can be said about how this process is to be made psychologically understandable and thus how it was prepared by Paul's inner development. In particular, it is nothing other than sheer fantasy when one depicts the impression that was made on him by the persecuted Christians; and that he even saw Jesus and was impressed by him is also to be read out of II Cor. 5:16 only by fantasy. Paul himself had no interest in his personal development, but only in the theological meaning of his conversion; and it is solely the latter that we are in a position to know.

Especially may one not understand Rom. 7:7-25 as a biographical document of Paul's inner development; for the "I" of these verses is as little the individual "I" of Paul as is, for example, the "I" of I Cor. 13:11. On the contrary, Paul is there presenting the situation of the Jew under the law in the light of the real meaning of that situation as it is disclosed to the eye of faith. Moreover, the phrase "kicking against the goads", in Acts 26:14, does not refer to an inner struggle, but rather is a widespread proverbial expression that means that man cannot withstand the divine. It is completely clear from Paul's letters that his "conversion" was not a conversion of "repentance", in which after long suffering under an afflicted conscience and inner resistance he finally succeeded in confessing his guilt before God and thereby inwardly set himself free. For as one who has been converted, he does not look back on his past with a feeling of shame, as though it had been a time in which he was sunk in guilt, but rather views it with a feeling of pride (Gal. 1:13f.; Phil. 3:6). He has not been freed from a burden, but rather has sacrificed a proud past (Phil. 3:6ff.). That he was a persecutor does not impress him as guilt, but merely provides a measure of the grace of the God who has called him (I Cor. 15:9f.). His conversion also does not appear to him as an enlightenment that emancipates him from an illusion, from the unbearable burden of works of the law and a false idea of God. For he never doubts that up to the time of "fulfillment", the way of the law was commanded by God and was meaningful (Gal. 3:23ff; even Rom. 7:7ff. is a defense of the law, not an attack on it!). Thus he knows nothing about the law's being a burden from the standpoint of the Jew's subjective experience; and at no time in his Christian polemic against the law does he represent faith as an emancipation from such a burden. Nor is what is meant by the "anxiety" in which man exists prior to faith the subjective feeling of anxiety that is caused by false religious ideas (see below, III., 2.). Faith is not the emancipation of a man who is yearning for freedom from chains that he himself experiences as oppressive; rather it is the resolution to surrender all that was man's pride, all self-glorification, all "boasting". This means, however, that Paul's conversion was the resolve to surrender his whole previous self-understanding, which was called in question by the Christian message, and to understand his existence anew. If God had already permitted the time of salvation to break in by sending the Messiah, then the way whereby man himself sought to achieve righteousness by means of works of the law was called in question. If God himself had introduced salvation by sending the Messiah and permitting him to be crucified, then he had destroyed the Jewish way of salvation and had thereby passed judgment against everything human, which had reached its highest point in Judaism. Thus what Paul was asked by the Christian proclamation was whether he was willing to see in a historical fact like the person and destiny of Jesus the breaking in of the time of salvation, the new creation that was being introduced by God. He was asked whether he was willing to acknowledge in the cross of Jesus the judgment against the previous self-understanding of the pious Jew and whether he was thus willing to understand himself anew and to accept the judgment of "sin and death" against his previous life. And this he affirmed in his conversion.

3. Career as Apostle

a. Paul apparently knew himself to be an apostle by his conversion (Gal. 1:15f.) and immediately engaged in missionary activity in Damascus and Arabia. After a brief visit to Jerusalem, he then worked in Syria and Cilicia (Gal. 1:21) and resided for a time in Tarsus, in order thence to be fetched by Barnabas to Antioch, where Hellenistic Jewish Christians who had been driven from Jerusalem had already established a congregation (Acts 11:19ff.). Since as a result of this Hellenistic mission there arose a Gentile Christianity that did not accept the law and specifically did not accept circumcision, a discussion with the primitive community, which remained faithful to the law, became inevitable. This took place at the so-called Apostolic Council, for which Paul and Barnabas went up to Jerusalem. They sought to see to it that the Gentile Christians' freedom from the law was acknowledged and thus were able to preserve the unity of the two early Christian groups; this was especially expressed by the determination that there should be a collection taken in the Gentile Christian congregations for the "poor" at Jerusalem (Gal. 2:1-10; the presentation in Acts 15 is legendary). Since, however, the question concerning the intercourse in mixed congregations (especially at table) of Jewish Christians who were faithful to the law and Gentile Christians who were free from it was apparently left undiscussed, there subsequently arose a conflict between Paul and Peter in Antioch, which also led to Paul's falling out with Barnabas (Gal. 2:11ff.). Later on, also, Paul's mission was occasionally interfered with by "Judaizers", i.e., by Jewish Christian missionaries who demanded from converted Gentiles an acceptance of the law or, at least, of circumcision. Paul struggled against such "Judaizers" in Galatia. However, the opinion, which has been influential ever since F. C. Baur, that throughout the whole field of

Paul's missionary activity there was a constant struggle between Paulinism and Judaizing Christianity is false. To be sure, in II Corinthians also Paul has to struggle with Jewish Christian adversaries; however, they clearly are not preachers of the law; and whether he is fighting against "Judaizers" or rather against Jews in Phil. 3:2ff. is disputed. In any case, his polemic in Romans is not directed against "Judaizers", but rather takes issue in principle with the Jewish position of legalistic piety.

The mission field that Paul undertook to serve after the Apostolic Council can be determined from Acts, which is frequently confirmed by statements in the letters. He first preached in Cyprus and in Pamphylia, Lycaonia, and Pisidia in Asia Minor (Acts 13 and 14, which are falsely placed before the Apostolic Council in ch. 15). Then, a subsequent journey led him from Syria-Cilicia clear across Asia Minor (the Galatian congregations were founded at that time; Acts 16) to Troas and thence to Macedonia (Philippi and Thessalonica) and back to Achaia. In Corinth, then, he tarried for a longer period and from there also established other congregations (Acts 15:40-18:22). After what seems to have been a short return trip to Antioch (Acts 18:22f.), he once again undertook a large-scale mission for which Ephesus was his headquarters. From there, after a trip through Macedonia to Corinth, he again went up to Jerusalem to deliver a collection (Acts 18:23-21:16). There, at the instigation of the Jews, he was arrested by the Romans because of a riot and then (the record is not clear) was brought to Rome for sentencing (Acts 21:17-28:31). Acts closes with the statement that he was imprisoned in Rome for two years. So far as the outcome of his trial is concerned, nothing certain is known; however, it is firmly fixed in the tradition that he died the death of a martyr. This is evidenced already by the intimations in Acts (especially 20:22ff., 21:10ff.), and it is specifically narrated in I Clement (ch. 5), which is apparently of the opinion that Paul, like Peter, was executed under Nero. According to I Clem. 5:7, before he died, Paul also preached in Spain, just as he says he had planned to do in Rom. 15:24f. Whether he actually did so, however (to do so he would have had to be freed from the Roman imprisonment that is reported by Acts), or whether the Spanish journey is a legend that has grown out of Rom. 15:24f. is a matter of dispute. It is certain, however, that he did not do any further work in the East, as is assumed by those scholars who argue for the Pauline authorship of the Pastorals in order to be able to maintain the statements that are contained in these letters concerning journeys that cannot be assigned to his career prior to his (first) Roman imprisonment.

b. Paul was not the first nor was he the only missionary of the apostolic age. Already before him, Hellenistic Jewish Christians, among them especially Barnabas, had engaged in missions to the Gentiles (Acts 11:19ff.), and in Damascus as well as in Antioch there existed Christian communities. Moreover, Paul did not found the congregation at Rome, any more than he established the Christianity of Alexandria, whose origins are in general unknown to us. Thus in addition to him and his fellow workers, there were both before and alongside of him a whole host of missionaries who are now forgotten. Whether some one of them envisaged the missionary task in the same way that Paul did, to carry the gospel to the ends of the earth until Christ returns (Rom. 15:17ff.), we do not know. In any case, Paul himself was sustained by a consciousness of this task; and he supposed that he was fulfilling it by founding congregations in the important cities, whence the faith might then be spread to the surrounding countrysides. His work as a missionary was his "boast", which, to be sure, was wrought by Christ; and he was proud of having only preached the gospel where it had not as yet been heard (Rom. 15:20; II Cor. 10:15f.), and also proud that he had renounced the right of the apostle to be supported by the congregations (I Cor. 9:15ff.; II Cor. 11:7ff.). All the same, however much he looked upon his work as a missionary as his life-task and however certain he was that the results of his mission had been prodigious — in his own conviction, the greatest of all (I Cor. 15:10) — it is not in his accomplishments as a missionary that his real significance lies. Nor does it lie in the fact that he not only won the Gentiles to the faith, but also organized viable congregations and inwardly and outwardly strengthened them by his letters and visits. In this respect, there may well have been others who were his equal. Moreover, his real historical accomplishment is not that he fought for and won freedom from the law for Gentile Christianity, even if his part in this was a prominent one. For there is little doubt that this also would have happened without him, even as it had been prepared for before him and was actually carried out alongside of him. Writings like Hebrews, Barnabas, and I Clement, which in one sense or another, although in an un-Pauline sense, are free from the law, show that in this connection there were several possibilities; indeed, this is even shown by the so-called "Apostolic decree", which was not concluded by Paul and the earliest apostles at the Apostolic Council, as Acts reports, but rather was afterwards agreed upon by the Jerusalem community and the Hellenistic Christians and then subsequently communicated to Paul (Acts 21:25). In this respect, the way had also been prepared by Hellenistic Judaism through reinterpreting the law and easing its requirements for proselytes. Thus there was hardly a danger that the Christian communities in the Greco-Roman world would become legalistic Jewish sects. However, there was considerable danger that they would become a passing phenomenon of Hellenistic syncretism, like the other religious communities that grouped themselves around the cult of some Oriental redeemer-deity. An essential part of Paul's accomplishment consists in his having joined the Christian communities into a firm unity and in seeing to it that there was no break with the mother community in Jerusalem. By teaching the individual churches to understand themselves as members of the one ecclesia and by helping those who had faith in Jesus Christ to see themselves as the true Israel, he gave the new religion a historical consciousness of itself as a church and also endowed it with the power that indwells such a consciousness. The Christian congregations were not only bound together, like the mystery congregations, by the same cult and the same theological or mythological ideas, but rather by the conviction that they stood at the end of a closed and unified history and thus also by a strong feeling that they belonged together and to Jerusalem. It is for this reason that Paul puts so much importance on what seems to be the most trivial stipulation of the Apostolic Council — namely, the collection; hence also his endeavor to bind the congregations together, not only by exchanging news and greetings between them, but also by impressing upon them their ties with Jerusalem (Gal. 2:10; I Cor. 16:1ff.; II Cor. 8 and 9; Rom. 15:25ff.). Thus, to a high degree, Paul's significance consists in his having given to Christianity not the consciousness of being a new "religion", but rather the consciousness of being a "church" in a sense that was unknown in the Hellenistic world. Nevertheless, this consciousness of being a church is but a recasting of the Jewish inheritance; for in Judaism also the idea of the church as the people of God was very much alive. And there undoubtedly were other Christian missionaries of Hellenistic-Jewish background who were also sustained by such a church consciousness (cf. again Hebrews, Barnabas, and I Clement), so that here, too, it is impossible to speak of an exclusive accomplishment of Paul. If, however, his accomplishment actually does tower above that of others, this is not only because the idea of the church was determinative in his work, but especially because as a writer he surpassed everyone else in quality and influence. Even if his letters are only occasional writings, still, in form as well as content, they are the surpassing monuments of early Christian literature (with the sole exception of John), which almost immediately were read in the church way beyond the congregations for which they were written, were subsequently collected together, and were also frequently imitated. However, even with this we still have not spoken of Paul's real significance. For this lies in the fact that as a *theologian* he gave to the Christian faith an adequate understanding of itself. However much his thought still moved within the mythological ideas of antiquity, still, on the one hand, he extricated Christian thinking from the realm of mythology and speculation and made it into an unfolding of the understanding of man, the world, and God that is given in faith itself; he based Christian knowing on our being known by God and defined its proper object as that which has been "bestowed" on us by God through grace (I Cor. 2:12); thus he understood knowing in its unity with the whole Christian life, so that knowing proves its legitimacy by realizing itself in unity with the obedience of faith and love as existential (*existentiell*) thinking. On the other hand, he also demonstrated the indispensability of such thinking for the life of faith and love, by showing that it preserves for this life a correct self-understanding, so that the latter does not fall away and is not led astray, whether by Jewish legalism or by the speculations of pneumatics and Gnostics. Paul finally performed the greatest service for the freeing of faith from the law and for uniting the congregations into a church because he gave a firm conceptual expression to the necessities that others also had more or less clearly recognized. This expression gave strength to the self-understanding and self-consciousness of the Christian community and determined Christian theological thinking forever after, again and again saving it from falling away into a false understanding of faith. And Paul's theology acquired such significance even where its propositions were passed on without their meaning's really being understood in its fullness, as was in fact immediately the case with his disciples and imitators; even as truths that were only half or badly understood they carried their corrective in themselves.

III THEOLOGY

1. Presuppositions

a. *Paul's Personality and Conversion*

If we are concerned to inquire about the actual content of Paul's theology, then it would be wrong to go back to his "personality" in order on that basis to understand his theology. For in the first place, a picture of his personality and his character can only be obtained by reconstructing it on the basis of having first understood his theological and non-theological statements; and so one deceives himself if he imagines that he can understand what Paul says by understanding his personality. In the second place, however, what one customarily refers to as the "character" of a man is not something outside of his work to which one can refer it in order to explain it; his "character" is as little this as, conversely, his work is something that is detached from his "character". Rather a man first acquires his "character" in his work, and his work is a presentation of his "character". Thus it is certainly correct to say that the prominent features in a picture of Paul are his concern with his subject and his passion, which together combine to make for a radicalism in thought and judgment. However, in saying this, one is not speaking about presuppositions from which his work has grown, but rather is characterizing that work itself. If, on the other hand, one means by the question concerning Paul's character the natural dispositions that were a given condition of his work, then indeed it is possible to say something about these on the basis of his letters; but what is said can never be of any use in making the content of his work understandable. For that Paul was temperamental, was given to brooding, had a sensitive feeling for life, was touchy, etc. are all things that he shared in common with countless other men. Therefore, while to draw this kind of a picture of his character can offer an aesthetic fascination, it is of no consequence whatever in understanding the subject matter with which he was concerned.

Likewise, it is a popular error to try to derive Paul's theology from his conversion experience. For this experience also can only be reconstructed by having first understood what he says. Thus the question about the actual content of his conversion is a question about his theology itself. His conversion was neither a conversion of repentance nor one of enlightenment (cf. above, II., 2.). And if one, by viewing it from the standpoint of the psychic course of his life, can speak of it in general as "a break in his development", this still does not say anything about its meaning. For what happened when Paul was changed from a persecutor into a faithful man was, in his view, only an extreme instance of what happens in principle whenever a man is smitten by the "word" and resolves to believe it, surrendering his old self and obediently placing himself under the grace of God. This is clearly shown by Phil. 3:4-16 and II Cor. 4:3-6. Indeed, Paul demands such a "break" from every man, although it is characteristic of him, in contradistinction to Hellenistic mysticism and pietistic and Methodist religiousness, that he says nothing about the psychic conditions of the "break" or about the forms of experience in which it takes place.

The presuppositions of Paul's theology which must be considered in order to understand it all have to do with the *actual subject matter* of his thought. Whoever would understand him must, on the one hand, become acquainted with the understanding that he had of himself (and thus also of God and the world) as a Jew under the law, and likewise with the word of the Christian proclamation that encountered him and constrained him to a yes or no decision. On the other hand, one must acquaint himself with the world-views (*Weltbild*) and the traditional modes of thinking and forming concepts in which Paul lived and in terms of which (or in opposition to which) he developed his new understanding of faith. It is only in this way that one can translate his statements into a modern conceptuality and yet at the same time avoid modernizing reinterpretations. In fact, of course, both types of presuppositions overlap; for the Jewish faith in God as well as the Christian kerygma were naturally expressed in a specific contemporary conceptuality.

b. *The Early Community and Jesus*

It is impossible here to present the Jewish faith in God and the Christian kerygma (cf. above, II., 2.). However, the one thing that must be emphasized is that Paul's theology cannot be understood as a further development in the "history of ideas" of the preaching of Jesus. It is not with the preaching of Jesus that he begins, but rather with the kerygma of the early community, the content of which is not Jesus' proclamation, but Jesus himself. It is the message that Jesus of Nazareth, the rabbi and prophet, the one who was crucified, has been raised by God and made Messiah; that he will shortly come as the "Son of Man" in order to hold judgment and to bring salvation. At the same time, it says that the community of his followers knows itself to be the congregation of saints of the end-time, the elected Israel, which is in possession of the Spirit, the promised gift of the last days. Therefore, the early community did not detach itself from the ordinances of life of Israel, but rather continued to move in them in the way that had been taught by Jesus, whose sayings it preserved. To be sure, it did define itself as a unique congregation within Judaism (without, however, segregating itself from the cult of the temple) by baptism, which it understood as the purifying bath for the penitent and those who were sanctified for the breaking in of the time of salvation. It also met together for common meals, although there was as yet no talk of cultic veneration of Jesus Christ. It is this community and its kerygma that is a basic presupposition of the theology of Paul. On the other hand, the preaching of Jesus is such a presupposition only insofar as it signified radical Judaism in the spirit of the old prophetic proclamation. Paul neither heard Jesus' preaching itself, nor did he permit it to be mediated to him by the first disciples, in relation to whom he knew himself to be completely independent (Gal. 1:1, 1:11ff.). To be sure, he did take over some of the sayings of Jesus (whether genuine sayings, or sayings created by the community) from the Palestinian tradition, namely, bits of regulation having to do with congregational order (I Cor. 7:10f., 9:14), which he, of course, regarded as words not of the "historical Jesus", but of the exalted Lord (cf. I Cor. 7:25). Perhaps I Thess. 4:15-17 also stems from traditional sayings of Jesus; but this is hardly true of I Cor. 11:23-5. It is also possible that certain sayings of the Lord are echoed in Paul's moral instruction (e.g., Rom. 12:4, 13:9f., 16:19; I Cor. 13:2); however, what is involved here is precisely a type of moral instruction which, with Jesus as well as with Paul, to some extent came from Jewish tradition or the Jewish spirit. In any case, Paul's real doctrine of salvation, with its anthropological and soteriological ideas, is not a continuation of the preaching of Jesus. This is clear, for example, from the fact that he never once appeals to a saying of Jesus in support of his teaching about freedom from the law. And if in his letters he makes reference to the tradition concerning Jesus' life (outside of I Cor. 11:23, where what is really involved, is the basing of a cultic feast in the destiny of the cult deity), then one may not say that he must have proceeded very differently from this in his missionary preaching and must have told a good deal about Jesus' life. (Nor may one appeal in support of such a statement to Gal. 3:1; for what is meant there is the preaching of the cross, as is indicated in Gal. 3:10ff., I Cor. 1:18ff., and elsewhere.) Whether Paul knew much or little of the tradition about Jesus' life, the content of that life as that of a teacher, a prophet, a miracle-worker, or one who had been crowned with thorns plays absolutely no role in his preaching of salvation. For him, the significance of Jesus' person lies in the latter's having been sent as the Son of God in human form in order through his death and resurrection to free men from the law and sin (Gal. 4:4f., etc.).

However, just as little as one may say that Paul's theology represents a development in the history of ideas of Jesus' preaching, so little, of course, may one say that, from the standpoint of the history of ideas, it stands in opposition to Jesus' message — as though the latter's piety, say, was a joyous faith in God the Father, whereas Paul's religion is to be characterized as an austere faith in redemption. Looked at in terms of the history of ideas, the proclamation of Jesus and that of Paul are essentially the same. Thus their idea of God is the same: God is the Judge and also the God of grace; and similar also is their view of man, who is obligated to obey the will of God and as a sinner is dependent on God's grace — who can exhibit no merit before God and also can make no claims on him. Neither for Jesus nor for Paul is God the immanent law of the world or the hypostatization of an eternal Idea of the Good. Rather he is the one who stands before man as he comes in judgment and grace; and for both men God deals with man in history. The difference, however, is that Jesus proclaims a final and decisive act of God, the Reign of God, as coming or, indeed, as now breaking in, while Paul affirms that the turn of the aeon has already taken place and, to be sure, with the coming, the death and the resurrection of Jesus. Thus, for Paul, it is Jesus' cross and resurrection that are the decisive event of salvation through which the forgiveness of sins, the reconciliation of man with God is effected, and with which, therefore, the new creation is introduced. Consequently, while the person and history of Jesus do indeed constitute a presupposition of his theology, they do not do so from the standpoint of their historical or ideal content, but rather as the act of God, as the occurrence of the revelation of salvation. Paul does not teach other and new *ideas* from those that Jesus teaches, but rather teaches us to understand an *event* in a new way. This he does by saying that the world is new since and because Jesus has come; now the reconciliation between God and man is established and the word that proclaims this reconciliation is instituted.

c. *The General Conditions in the History of Religion*

Outside of Paul's rabbinic training (cf. above II., 1.), the presuppositions from the history of religion that must be considered in relation to the formulation of his theological concepts and his explication of the kerygma are the following: (1) *The preaching of the one God and his judgment* that was characteristic of the propaganda both of Hellenistic Judaism and of pre-Pauline Christianity. Under the influence of the Greek enlightenment, there had taken place in Hellenistic Judaism a new conceptual formulation of monotheistic faith, together with a total interpretation of the world in the manner of the philosophy of religion and a critique of the polytheism and its cult as well as the moral life of the Gentiles. This tradition was directly taken over by Christianity; and Paul also stands within it when he makes use of the Stoic theory of a natural knowledge of God (Rom. 1:18ff.) or varies somewhat a Stoic formula concerning the divine omnipotence (Rom. 11:36; I Cor. 8:6), or when he applies the concepts of "conscience" (Rom. 2:15, etc.), "duty" (Rom. 1:28), "virtue" (Phil. 4:8), "nature" (I Cor. 11:14, etc.), or even when he interprets the heathen gods as demons (I Cor. 10:10) or as "elemental spirits of the world" (Gal. 4:3, 4:9). In all probability such ideas played an even larger role in his actual missionary preaching; thus they are presented also in Acts 14:17, 17:23ff. (2) *The discussion concerning the law* in Hellenistic Judiasm and in pre-Pauline Hellenistic Christianity. Here, too, there is a unified tradition running from the former to the latter, which attempts to demonstrate the moral character and universal scope of the divine demand. Insofar as this tradition practiced allegorical reinterpretation of the narratives and laws of the Old Testament, Paul also stands in it (cf., e.g., I Cor. 9:9f., 10:6ff.); however, insofar as it made a distinction between moral demands and cultic-ritual ones, he has left it behind, although he is still affected by it, as is shown by I Cor. 7:19. (This is probably a saying that Paul quotes and then modifies in his own sense in Gal. 5:6, 6:15). (3) *The Kyrios-cult and the sacraments* in pre-Pauline Hellenistic Christianity. If the early Palestinian community had expected Jesus the risen one as the coming Son of Man and if, accordingly, its messianic faith was essentially eschatological, there had already developed prior to Paul in the Hellenistic Christian communities in Syria (which did not participate in the Jewish temple cult and the ordinance of life that emanated from it) a cultic veneration of Christ as the "Lord". He was known to be present in the congregation's worship, dispensing supernatural powers to those who belonged to him. Baptism was understood in the sense of the Hellenistic mysteries as a sacrament that mysteriously unites the baptized person with Christ and thus grants him a share in the latter's death and resurrection. And the common meals of the early community became the "Lord's Supper", which likewise brings about sacramental communion with Christ. Naturally, the form of the kerygma corresponded to this, and already prior to Paul there were represented different interpretations of Jesus' death, which in part expressed the ideas of an atoning or covenantal sacrifice and in part the ideas of a cosmic process and a sacramental *communio*. This can be learned from the remarks concerning baptism in Rom.

6:3ff. and the saying concerning the Lord's Supper in I Cor. 11:23-5, which already combine different interpretations, as well as from the tradition to which Paul refers in I Cor. 15:3 and, likewise, for example, from the theology of Mark. For the rest, we can no longer prove which of the concepts that Paul uses to interpret Christ's death and resurrection were already in use prior to his time; it is clear, however, that the frequently encountered ideas of "for us", of an atoning sacrifice (Rom. 3:25), of reconciliation (Rom. 5:11; II Cor. 5:18ff.), of a ransom (Gal. 3:13, 4:4f.; I Cor. 6:20, 7:23), and of substitution (Gal. 3:13; II Cor. 5:14f.) all stem from this sphere in which the Jewish ideas of sacrifice and the notions of the Hellenistic mysteries were combined and from which Paul's formulations came to him. (4) *Gnosticism and pneumaticism.* In the syncretism of the Hellenistic-Oriental world and, of course, hardly ever sharply separated from the mystery cults (which, having originally been vegetation cults, celebrated the dying and rising of a deity in which the faithful were vouchsafed a share), there was a religion of redemption which had migrated to the West from Iran, combined itself with certain astrological ideas, and found its historically significant expressions in "Gnosticism". The cosmological and soteriological ideas of this religion give expression to a dualistic understanding of human existence. They teach, first of all, the heavenly origin of the soul, which has been banished to the body and the world of the senses, and then, second, the soul's redemption by a divine being, who disguised himself in human form, took upon himself all the misery of earthly life, thereby deceiving the demonic rulers of the world, and then after having brought revelation to "his own" through doctrines and rites, once again was exalted to the heavenly world, whither his own will subsequently follow him. According to the Gnostic or the pneumatic, whoever believes this revelation has knowledge and freedom. Hence his intense self-consciousness and peculiar way of life, which could lead either to asceticism or to libertinism. That such Gnosticism and pneumaticism had already prior to Paul or contemporaneously with him penetrated the Christian congregations is shown by his struggle against the pneumatics in Corinth. With them, apparently, such Gnosticism had been combined with Jewish theology, very much as also happened with Philo. But these Gnostic ideas had already influenced Jewish apocalypticism and in this way had also influenced Paul. For as much as he fights against the consequences of such pneumaticism, he still appropriates Gnosticism's concepts (e.g., the contrast between "spiritual" and "psychic", the concepts "knowledge", "freedom", or "authority")

217

and makes use of its mythology in his own doctrines. Thence stem the ideas of "this aeon" and the "coming aeon", the idea of Satan as the "god of this aeon" (II Cor. 4:3f.), of the "rulers" (I Cor. 2:6) and other spiritual powers. Thence also the notions of Adam as the first, and Christ as the new "man" (Rom. 5:12ff.; I Cor. 15:21f., 15:44ff.), of the giving of the law by angels (Gal. 3:19), of Christ's descent in the disguise of a man (I. Cor. 2:6ff.; Phil. 2:6ff.; II Cor. 8:9), and of redemption as a mighty cosmic drama (I Cor. 15:24f.; Rom. 8:18ff.).

2. Content

a. *Theology and Anthropology*

For Paul, *God* is not a metaphysical being and thus is not an object of speculation, but rather is the God whose action does not take place primarily in cosmic occurrences, but in relation to man in history. On the other hand, he does not understand *man* as an isolated being within the world, but rather always sees him in his relation to God. Therefore, it follows that what God and man mean for Paul can only be understood together as a unity and that his "theology" can be presented as anthropology.

And the same thing is true of his "christology"; for he also does not understand Christ primarily as a metaphysical being about whose "natures" he speculates, but rather understands him and his work as God's act of salvation in relation to man. Of course, one may not make a division between a "physical" anthropology that describes who man is "in himself" and an "ethical" anthropology that expresses how he stands in relation to God. For as Paul understands him, man is never what he is outside of his relation to God; and even general anthropological concepts like "body" and "soul" are decisively determined for Paul by man's standing before God. However, there *is* a division that arises because man has acquired a new possibility for relation with God through the revelation in Christ, namely, faith. Therefore, the arrangement must be as follows: (1) man prior to the revelation of faith; and (2) man under faith. It must be noted, however, that the being of man prior to faith first becomes visible in its true lineaments only from the standpoint of faith itself and that it is from this perspective alone that it can be understood.

218

b. *Man prior to the Revelation of Faith*

i. With the word "man" Paul can, of course, occasionally refer to one being in the world among others (e.g., angels; cf. I Cor. 4:9, 15:36ff.); but his more precise use of language is such that the title "man" characterizes man in his relation to God and, indeed, in such a way that before God all the differences and advantages of which individuals could boast disappear (Rom. 3:28f.; I Cor. 1:25; Gal. 1:1). "Man" designates man in his humanity before God. And this God before whom he stands is not a cosmic being that is separate from him; to be sure, there may also be such a being, but insofar as *God's* being is spoken about, it is not a being that is merely on hand, but rather a "being for us", so that in a precise sense God alone "is" (I Cor. 8:4-6). Man's being in relation to God is primarily a being claimed by God as the Creator. When Paul makes use of the Stoic theory of a natural knowledge of God (Rom. 1:20ff.), it does not serve him in order to conclude to God's being *in* the world and to the divinity of the world and the security of man by reason of divine providence, but rather in order to conclude to God's being *beyond* the world, to the world's creatureliness and to God's claim to be honored by man. Correspondingly, "world" for Paul means "creation" (Rom. 1:20; I Cor. 3:22). And, to be sure, it can mean the totality of what is created by God as that which surrounds man and concerns him; but it especially refers to the world of man himself (Rom. 3:19, 11:12; II Cor. 5:19, etc.), although not in the sense of a total class of beings on hand within the world, but rather as a community of creatures who are responsible to God. Insofar as men have withdrawn from this responsibility, have denied their creatureliness, and have made themselves independent of God, they are called "this world". This world (or "this aeon", as Paul can also say in order to express the notion that it is provisional) is at enmity with God and seeks its own glory; therefore, it stands under God's wrath and will be judged by him. That this "dualism", which is several times expressed in Gnostic terminology, is not meant in the cosmological sense of Gnosticism is shown by the counterconcept "new creation", with which Paul refers to the men who are reconciled and are faithful (II Cor. 5:17; Gal. 6:15). Thus "world" does not refer to men as a "what", but rather as a "how", as a "how" of their life and, to be sure, as a "how" that they themselves have created by turning away from God. As such it is a power that always already encompasses each individual, encountering him and taking him along with it, so that he cannot isolate himself from it (by believing, say, in his soul that has tragically fallen from the world of light and is imprisoned in "this world" or by imagining his free spiritual personality). And this "how" manifests itself in the "care" (I Cor. 7:29ff.) in which each man takes his life in his own hands and wills to secure it. From "care", then, grow "boasting" and "confidence", which base themselves on anything that, by man's estimation or accomplishment, passes for a work. Precisely this pride, whether it is based on national or social advantages, or on wisdom or works of the law is rebellion against God, before whom no man may boast (Rom. 2:17, 2:23, 3:27; I Cor. 1:29, 3:21, 4:7). The height of illusion is that man thinks he can separate himself from the "world" and bring himself to a being beyond it. The Jew who wills to earn "righteousness" before God is fallen under this illusion, even as is the pneumatic who imagines that he can become a "perfect one" by means of his "wisdom". The counterpart of such boasting and confidence is "anxiety" (Rom. 8:15); such a man is in fact a slave. For in his care and putting confidence in worldly values and accomplishments he lets these become lord over him, and because they are all transitory (I Cor. 7:31), he himself falls under death; by understanding himself in terms of the transitory and the provisional, his being is not authentic, but rather has fallen subject to what is passing away. In the mythological way of thinking of his time, Paul sees such an existence as an enslavement to spiritual powers, Satan and his hosts. Indeed, he can even speak of the law as having been given by such spiritual powers, insofar as man understands the law as a pretext for his own accomplishments; and he can also speak of the service of worship as a veneration of the "elemental spirits of the world" (Gal. 3:19ff., 4:8ff.). Nevertheless, how little these mythological notions have a speculative character, how little Paul wants to "explain" something by them, but rather makes use of them simply in order to express a certain understanding of human existence, is shown, for example, by his not tracing sin back to Satan (Rom. 5:12ff., 7:7ff.) and by his saying that such powers are no longer really of any concern to the man of faith because for him they no longer even "are" (I Cor. 8:4ff.); i.e., they no longer mean for him the lordship over the world under which he is fallen, but simply the quality of the world to tempt him; Satan is the "tempter" (I Cor. 7:5; I Thess. 3:5).

ii. It is on this basis that the individual anthropological concepts, like "body", "soul", and others, are also to be understood. They do not refer to *parts* of man, individual members or organs, but rather always mean *man as a whole* with respect to some specific possibility of his being. For this reason, Paul can also use almost every one of these concepts in the sense of "I" (cf., e.g., I Cor. 6:15 with 12:27; or I Cor. 13:3 with II Cor. 1:23, 12:15), and so also, the concepts can many times seem to flow into one another. One may not, for example, permit himself to be misled by I Cor. 15:35 and attempt to understand "body" as the form of man and "flesh" as his matter. In this passage, this meaning is of course present; but it is a mistake to take this passage as one's starting point because Paul here lets himself be misled by his adversary into speaking apologetically. Passages in which he speaks calmly, like Rom. 1:24, 6:12, 12:1; I Cor. 13:3, all clearly show that "body" for him does not mean "form" but rather refers to the whole man and, to be sure, insofar as, for others as well as for himself, man can be the object of observation and action. "Body" designates man insofar as something can be done to him or can happen to him, indeed, insofar as he is always exposed to such happenings and never freely has himself at his own disposal — and thus, for example, can become ill and die. Man is "body" in his temporality and historicity. That "body" is not thought of "dualistically" is made especially evident when Paul affirms the resurrecton of the body; i.e., to have a body for him is something that belongs to man as such, and he is as anxious about the prospect of being without a body as if it meant nothingness (II Cor. 5:1ff.). Thus the body is not some part of man in which the soul or the real I is stuck. And if man yearns to be free from "this body of death" (Rom. 7:24), he yearns to be freed from himself as he now is, to be "transformed", as Paul elsewhere puts it (II Cor. 3:18; Phil. 3:21; Rom. 8:29). The extent to which Paul has at the same time formulated his thought in terms of mythological ideas is unimportant, if one sees what the understanding of existence is that is hereby expressed.

So also "soul" is not a something *in* man — say, his better self — but rather is the whole man himself insofar as he is alive, is a living being (I Cor. 15:45). Therefore, "soul" for Paul is neither the bearer of spiritual life in the Greek sense nor our immortal self, the heavenly stranger in a darksome body, in the sense of Gnosticism; rather it is the vitality, the "life" (Rom. 11:3, 16:4; Phil. 2:30), which also belongs to animals in contradistinction to lifeless instruments (I Cor. 14:7). Precisely as such a vitality, however, the soul is not immortal, but mortal; it does not at all signify man's authentic being. But, of course, "soul" can also be the "I", for man is a living being (II Cor. 1:23, 12:15; I Thess. 2:8). As in the Old Testament, "every soul" means "every man" (Rom. 2:9, 13:1).

Insofar as the life of man is a conscious life, Paul can occasionally refer to it as "spirit" (I Cor. 2:11; Rom. 8:16; to be distinguished, of course, from the Spirit of God, the Holy Spirit, that is also referred to alongside of it!). And once again "spirit" also can mean simply "man", or "I" (Rom. 1:9; I Cor. 16:18; II Cor. 2:13; and in formulas of greeting). But the real word that Paul uses to refer to man as conscious is "mind"; it designates man insofar as he understands or knows something and, to be sure, insofar as he knows about his own possibilities and understands himself (e.g., Rom. 14:5). Since, however, man's being is a being before God, the knowledge about his own possibilities is at the same time the knowledge of the claim of God, of what man ought to do (Rom. 1:20, 7:23). And, further, since the specifically human knowing about oneself does not have the character of a theoretical, neutral confirmation that something is so, but rather also has the character of laying hold of a possibility, of willing (Rom. 7:15ff.), it follows that "mind" can be either a correct or a false self-understanding. The mind of the heathen is base (Rom. 1:28f.); their minds are blinded (II Cor. 4:4); on the other hand, the mind of Christians is renewed (Rom. 12:2). Paul can also speak of the mind as the "inner man" (Rom. 7:22; however, one may not draw on II Cor. 4:16 to explain this, for what is spoken of there is the man of faith!). But what is meant by this is not something like a better self "in" man; for in Rom. 7:13ff. the "mind" or the "inner man" is as much the "I" or self as is "flesh" (cf. below, III., 2., b., iii.). The wretchedness of man that is presented here does not consist in his better self's standing over against his worse material corporeality, but rather in his self's being split, in I standing over against I. Indeed, the essence of the unredeemed man is to be thus split.

In order to refer to man as one who has knowledge of himself, i.e., of his possibilities before God, and thus a knowledge that can also go astray, Paul likewise makes use of the Old Testament expression "heart" (e.g., Rom. 2:5, 8:27; II Cor. 4:6) and the Greek expression "conscience" (Rom. 2:15; I Cor. 8:7ff., 10:25ff., etc.).

What has been given now by this clarification of Paul's basic concepts is not anything like a "physical" anthropology; for the concepts "body" and "soul" refer to man in respect of his creatureliness, while the concepts "mind", "heart", and "conscience" speak of him in his responsibility before God.

iii. If man as having a body is withrawn from his own disposal and always stands in the context of a history, then, for Paul, there is only a twofold possibility for the determination of this history — by God or by sin. He expresses this either/or by means of the contrast between flesh and Spirit. And, to be sure, the being of man prior to faith is determined by the "flesh". This word means, first of all, the animated flesh of the body. But, then, just as "body" refers to man himself as object of an action or as subject of a happening, so also "flesh" refers to him in his pure being on hand in which he can become an object. Hence the concepts body and flesh can to a certain degree mean the same thing (II Cor. 4:10f.; I Cor. 6:16); illnesses and marks are in the body as well as in the flesh (Gal. 4:13f., 6:17; II Cor. 12:7). And as "body" can be the "I" or self, so also can "flesh" (II Cor. 7:5). Thus flesh is not a part of man, but man himself as he is actually found — as well or ill, as belonging to a nation or to a family. Abraham is the father of the Jews "according to the flesh", while Christ "according to the flesh" is a descendant of David (Rom. 4:1, 1:3, 9:5). The natural life of man is a life "in the flesh" (II Cor. 10:3; Gal. 2:20; Phil. 1:21ff.), and whatever belongs to such a life, like food or means, is called "fleshly" (Rom. 15:27; I Cor. 9:11). But in close connection with this, "flesh" acquires yet another meaning, which becomes clear when it is said that the man of faith no longer exists "in the flesh" or "according to the flesh". As the characteristic of a certain type of demeanor (boasting, knowing, walking, etc., I Cor. 11:18, 5:16, 10:2), "according to the flesh" does not designate man as he appears to others, but as he understands himself, namely, on the basis of what he is found to be, of what is immediately evident (Rom. 2:28). "To be according to the flesh" means "to be intent on what is fleshly" (Rom. 8:5). This does not mean to be determined by what is fleshly in the sense of the life of impulse or of the senses, but rather to be determined by anything in the entire sphere of what is immediately evident, whether this be national advantage, legal correctness, the accomplishments of the man who exists under the law, or human wisdom. All of this is "flesh" (Phil. 3:4ff.; Gal. 3:3; I Cor. 1:26); therefore, works righteousness is included under the concept as surely as are vices. No man can get out of the flesh as existence in what is immediately evident; but the question with which he is faced is whether he will understand himself in terms of it and put his "confidence" in it — whether as one who is situated in the flesh he also wants to walk according to it (II Cor. 10:3). To understand oneself in terms of the "flesh", however, is "sin"; for sin is the care, boasting, and confidence of the man who forgets his creatureliness and tries to secure his own existence. It reaches its acme in the Jew; for to pursue one's own righteousness means precisely to put one's confidence in the flesh (Phil. 3:4-9); it is similar, however, with those who are "wise according to the flesh"; for they, too, do not honor God, but boast of themselves

(I Cor. 1:18-31). Sin is falsely wanting to be oneself; and there is the deep connection between the flesh and sin that the man who thus wills to be himself can only do so by understanding his existence in terms of what is on hand, what has been accomplished, what can be grasped and proven — in short, in terms of the "flesh". And so also there is a connection between flesh and sin *and* "death"; for each man understands himself in terms of what is transitory, what is fallen under death, and so death is already at work in him (Rom. 7:5). For everyone, on the other hand, who no longer understands himself on the basis of the flesh, or of what is visible, but rather understands himself on the basis of the invisible, and walks accordingly, flesh, sin, and death have come to an end (Rom. 8:9, 6:2, 6:10f.; Gal. 5:24; I Cor. 15:56f.). Thus, for Paul, flesh is neither matter in the Greek sense, i.e., the material has to be given shape by spirit as the power of form, or the life of the senses that must be educated, nor is it matter in the sense of Gnosticism (even if he is influenced by the latter's terminology), i.e., the inferior, evil realm of the senses, which is opposed to the soul. Rather it is the world of what is on hand, which first becomes the sphere of sin through the attitude of man, just as the creation only becomes "this world" through men's falling away from God.

But now Paul does not look upon sin as something accidental, which is present here and there or even in most places; rather he views it as the attitude that man necessarily has since the first sin of Adam; i.e., he sees that every man is already guided by a false understanding of human existence and that the man who wants to free himself from this world only becomes the more entrapped in it because he but repeats the primal sin of wanting to be himself. In order to illustrate this fact of sin's sovereignty, Paul makes use of the Gnostic myth of the primal man and interprets it in terms of the contrast between Adam and Christ (Rom. 5:12ff.; I Cor. 15:20ff., 15:44ff.). And from the crossing of his own ideas with the notions of the myth there arise confusions that cannot be considered here. The one thing that we must note, however, is that he never traces sin back to something that is not yet sin; rather sin has come into the world through sin, although it has thereby become an absolute and all-dominating power (Rom. 5:12). Even in Rom. 7:7ff. sin is not referred to the flesh as matter or as a mythical power, but rather to the sinner, to the man who lives according to the flesh. What Paul means becomes clear when it is recognized that for him the sole way of becoming free from sin is forgiveness; i.e., if man has sinned, then he *is* a sinner. What has happened in his past is not an individual fact that has now been left behind, but rather is present in that it qualifies him as guilty before God. Neither man nor mankind can become free from the past by their own self-will; on the contrary, they bring the past with them into every present. However, because sin is guilt before God there is also the possibility that God will free man from the past, that man will become new. But this can only become clear when the final factor that determines the existence of man prior to faith has been taken into consideration.

iv. The "law" means that there is a fact in the existence of the sinful man that, in spite of his false understanding of himself, again and again makes audible to him the claim of God. This fact is given in the concrete demands that always encounter man and point out to him that he does not belong to himself. From the standpoint of his Christian understanding of the law, Paul sees that these concrete demands actually grow out of man's constantly being bound together with other men at whose disposal he ought to place himself. For it seems to him that the final meaning of all of the specific requirements of the law is that man should love his neighbor as himself (Rom. 13:8ff.; Gal. 5:14, cf. 6:2). That the Gentiles also hear such demands is indicated by Paul in the letters that we have only in Rom. 2:14f. Thus it is with reference to the Jews that he develops his detailed consideration of man's situation under the law, because being himself a Jew, he naturally assumes that the true embodiment of the law is the law of Moses. From this it becomes clear, first of all, that for him the law of God is not the eternal moral law, not the Idea of the Good that springs from the human spirit as the idea of its perfection and at the same time is its norm. Rather the law is the whole complex of concrete, historically given moral and ritual demands that encounter the Jew in his actual historical community. It is characteristic of Paul that, unlike the prophets and Jesus, he does not distinguish between cultic-ritual demands, formal-legal demands, and moral demands; for man prior to faith, the law is the "letter" that kills (II Cor. 3:6) even in its moral demands. Paul does not criticize the law from the standpoint of its *content*, but with respect to its *significance* for man; i.e., he criticizes it as it appears from the standpoint of the Jewish understanding. In the law, man is confronted by the demand of God, obedience to which would bring life, for God is the Judge (Gal. 3:12; Rom. 2:10, 2:13, 10:5). Moreover, the demand of the law is also valid for the Christian, for it is once again taken up in the commandment to love; and for the Christian also God is the Judge (I Cor. 1:8, 3:12ff.; II Cor. 5:10, etc.). Therefore, the situation of man prior to faith is not so frightful because the law is inferior, but because man does not fulfill it, because at best he wills it, but does not do it (Rom. 7:11f.). Nevertheless, Paul not only says that man *can* not be rightwised [justified] by the law, but also that he *should* not be rightwised by it. And he also says that although the law is indeed the holy will of God, which is valid also for Christians, it still is something provisional that is done away with for the man of faith (Rom. 7:1-6, 10:4). The apparent contradiction is simply resolved. Since in fact every man is a sinner (Rom. 3:9-20), it is an illusion to want to earn righteousness by works of the law, as the Jews suppose they can do. For what is evident in such a supposition is not only that they regard sin as an individual work that can also be abstained from or, in any case, can be compensated for, but also that they understand obedience to the law as the accomplishment of individual works of which they can boast before God. In other words, they are not obedient at all in the genuine sense; and the law ought not to meet men in the way in which it meets them. The way of the law, when it is understood as a means of earning righteousness, is false. Thus the sin of the Jews is the failure to appreciate that man owes God an absolute obedience and therefore is dependent on him, on his forgiving grace; the real sin is "boasting". And insofar as it is precisely the law that provokes this extreme possibility in the man who has a false self-understanding, the law is what allows him thus to founder, so that he can understand what grace is in case it encounters him. So the law becomes the "taskmaster to bring us to Christ" (Gal. 3:24) and finds its end in him (Rom. 10:4). So also, in accordance with God's plan, sin has increased so that grace might increase all the more (Rom. 5:20; Gal. 3:19). Precisely because under the law man is driven to his most extreme possibility, there also develops under it an understanding for Christ. Therefore, the unity of man in the history that leads through his sin and redemption is clear. Redemption is as little a magical transformation of his "nature", or his endowment with a higher "nature", as it is enlightenment. It is forgiveness, through which he is brought from bondage to freedom, from anxiety to joy, and from disobedience to obedience. And equally clear is the unity of the will of God that encounters man in law and grace; for just as the law demands obedience, so also does the message of God's gracious act (cf. below, III., 2., c.).

However much Paul's doctrine of the law is polemic in character, it is by no means something occasional and secondary, but rather contains his central thoughts. This becomes especially evident when he struggles against the Gnostic pneumatics in Corinth on the basis of the

226

same fundamental ideas. As the Jews use the law in order to boast, so also do the pneumatics use the gospel and imagine that they are able thereby to lift themselves above the ranks of a sinful humanity. They forget that man himself does not build his life, but that everything that he has has been received as a gift (I Cor. 4:7) and that he may boast of nothing save of the Lord (I Cor. 1:31). Jews and pneumatics alike repeat the world's primal sin of not honoring God as God (Rom. 1:21).

c. *Man under Faith*

i. Like every man, Paul knows that human life is governed by the image of salvation, by an ideal, a state or a condition in which all of man's questions and grievances and anxiety have ceased — or, in purely formal terms, that it is governed by the image of man's authenticity. And he fully agrees with Judaism in understanding this authenticity as "righteousness". Man ought and wants to be "righteous"; as righteous he can stand before God, and the pious Jew hungers and thirsts for the day in which God will pronounce him righteous in the judgment. As for Judaism, "righteousness" for Paul is primarily a forensic and eschatological concept; i.e., it does not mean, first of all, man's moral uprightness, a human quality, but rather the position that he has in his relations with and before others, and pre-eminently before God in the judgment. His righteousness is his "acceptance", which is granted to him by others and especially by God. Paul entirely agrees with Judaism that man can finally receive his acceptance only from God in the last judgment (Rom. 2:13, 3:20, 4:3, 4:6, etc.). However, he differs from Judaism at two points: (1) He says that God's eschatological sentence of judgment *has already been passed,* namely, in the death and resurrection of Christ; we are already righteous if we have faith in this act of salvation (Rom. 4:25, 5:1, 5:17, etc.). This does not mean that the faithful have a new quality, that they are ethically perfect, or that, their guilt having been canceled, they must now take care for themselves. Rather it simply means that God accepts them as they are. On the other hand, this does not mean that God merely regards the faithful man "as if" he were righteous; on the contrary, by accepting me, God takes me to be a different person than I am; and if I (in faith) let go of what I am in myself, if I affirm God's judgment and understand myself in terms of him, then I really *am* a different person, namely, the one that he takes me to be. (2) Judaism regarded fulfillment of the law as the condition of God's eschatological verdict; according to Paul, however, God pronounces the faithful man righteous entirely without conditions (Rom. 3:21ff., 10:4ff.; Gal. 2:16ff., etc.). Thus, for him, righteousness is not something that is merited, but rather is utterly the gift of God. Consequently, he refers to it in contrast to one's "own" righteousness, i.e., the acceptance merited by one's own accomplishments, as the "righteousness of God", i.e., the acceptance that God freely gives. Its sole basis is in God's freedom and grace, and so Paul can also speak of the "reconciliation" that God has established (Rom. 5:10f.; II Cor. 5:18ff.).

ii. The meaning of the saving act of God through which he actualizes righteousness for men is forgiveness. However, according to Paul, this forgiveness is carried out by God in the death and resurrection of Jesus Christ as the Son of God who became man (I Cor. 1:18ff., 15:3; Gal. 3:1; Phil. 2:6ff.; Rom. 3:24f., 4.24f., etc.). Thus, for Paul, Christ is significant neither as teacher and prophet nor as example and hero. His humanity and his destiny come into question only insofar as in them he realizes his obedience, *and*, to be sure, this is the obedience of the pre-existent Son of God (Phil. 2:6ff.; Rom. 5:28f.). However, the idea of pre-existence for Paul is not a speculative theory about a divine being, nor does it stand in the context of a cosmological mythology, as it does in Gnosticism (even if materially this is whence it stems). Rather it has the significance of saying that what has happened in Christ is not a human or earthly event in the continuum of such earthly occurrences, but rather is the act of God. In what has happened in Christ, *God* has acted, God's act of love has taken place. This act, however, is completely unapparent, and it also is not made apparent by the different images, drawn from cult and myth, in which Paul describes it (cf. above, III., 1., c.). These all say only one thing, that the historical fact of the cross is God's judgment against sin and the world and that therefore whoever accepts this judgment in faith is free from sin (Rom. 6:10f.; Gal. 6:14). And so also can one believe in Christ's resurrection; for however much Paul thinks of the latter also as a cosmic event, he still endeavors to understand it as an occurrence in which the believer himself participates. He tries to understand it as the making possible of a new humanity that is not caught in what is provisional and in death, but rather has the future and *life* (I Cor. 15:20-2; Rom. 5:12ff., 8:29).

In actual fact, faith does not relate itself to historical or cosmic processes that could be established as free from doubt, but rather to the *preaching* behind which faith cannot go and which says to man that he must understand the cross as God's act of salvation and believe in the resurrection. Only in preaching is the cross God's saving act, and therefore the preaching that is based on the cross is itself God's act of salvation and revelation. Faith comes from preaching (Rom. 10:10-17), and God's act of salvation is the institution of the "word" of reconciliation (II Cor. 5:18f.). It is in the preaching of the gospel that the righteousness of God is revealed (Rom. 1:17); and in the preaching of the apostle, what is encountered is the word of God itself (II Cor. 5:20) or the actual speaking of Christ (Rom. 15:18). This preaching of God's saving act, however, is not a communication about events that one can also establish outside of faith; rather in speaking of God's act of salvation, it at the same time addresses the conscience of the hearer and asks him whether he is willing to understand the occurrence that it proclaims as occurring to him himself and thereby to understand his existence in its light. For this reason, preaching has the possibility of working death as well as life (II Cor. 2:14-16, 4:1-6). Thus the event of preaching is itself the eschatological event of salvation (II Cor. 6:1f.).

As the preaching has its basis in what has happened in Christ, so also does the "church". For Paul, "church" is the community of the faithful, the central point in the life of which is the worshiping congregation; and, to be sure, it is the community of all those who are called by God, which is represented in each individual congregation. As the community of those who are called, it is constituted by the "word", and likewise by the sacraments of baptism and the Lord's Supper, which, like preaching, make the salvation-event something present and thus are also a kind of proclamation (cf. I Cor. 11:26). Therefore, the church is neither an association that constitutes itself nor a crowd of pneumatic individuals. As established by Christ and the word, it is itself an eschatological fact; those who belong to it are the "saints" of the last days who are already taken out of "this world". Since the last days have been introduced by Christ, the church is nothing other than the continuation of the Christ-event. It is his "body" (I Cor. 12:12ff.), and he is its "Lord", i.e., the one to whom the individual comes to belong in baptism (I Cor. 6:11, 12:13f.; Gal. 3:27f.), at whose table one eats the "Lord's Supper" (I Cor. 10:21, 11:20), and who is present with all his power in the congregation (I Cor. 5:4). The congregation is "in him" (Rom. 12:5; Gal. 3:28); it acknowledges him as its Lord and at the same time as the Lord of all (Rom. 10:9; I Cor. 12:3; Phil. 2:11). So also, then, does each individual belong to Christ, since he is baptized in him (Rom. 6:3; I Cor. 12:13; Gal. 3:27); he is "in him", i.e., he belongs to him (Gal. 3:28f., 5:24; Rom. 8:9, 14:7ff.), he belongs to the new world as a "new creation" (II Cor.

5:17). Thus the meaning of the salvation-occurrence is that the act of God that takes place in Christ continues in preaching and in the church, that the "world" has come to an end, and that the time of salvation has already become a reality for faith. Just how what is wrought by his occurrence can actually be understood as the possibility of a new human existence must now be made clear by an elucidation of the concept of faith.

iii. "Faith", first of all, is the obedient hearing of the word of proclamation. It is "obedience" because it is the subjection of oneself to the act of God that is proclaimed and realized in the word (Rom. 1:15, 10:3, 11:30; cf. Rom. 1:8 and I Thess. 1:8 with Rom. 15:18, 16:19; further, II Cor. 10:5f. with 10:15, etc.). As obedience, faith is the exact opposite of a "work", and Paul takes great pains to show that faith is not a "condition" of salvation in the sense of an accomplishment (Rom. 3:28, 4:5f., 9:31f.; Gal. 2:16, 3:2, etc.). But although it is not an accomplishment, it is an *act* of genuine obedience, in which man radically renounces his own existence and gives glory to God alone (Rom. 3:27, 4:20f.). Therefore, faith for Paul is not a psychic state or a spiritual attitude, as it is for Philo. Nor is it trust in God in general. Rather it is obedience toward a specific act of God that is proclaimed to man. It is faith *in* . . . , namely, in Jesus Christ, i.e., in the saving act of God that has occurred in Christ. Thus it is not "piety", but rather a specific "confession" (Rom. 10:9). And since the righteousness that is awarded to it (cf. above, III., 2., c., i.) is not an individual attribute, which the believer obtains and possesses, but rather is the acceptance that is awarded to it by the judgment of God, faith is never closed, but is always simultaneously "hope". Indeed, the proclamation does not say that the image of God's wrath is false, but rather that whoever believes escapes from his wrath. But the wrath itself abides (Rom. 2:5, 2:8, 5:9; I Thess. 1:10); for it is not God's "attribute" or his "affect", but his rule as Judge; and God's grace has its character precisely in that he is and remains the Judge. It is the grace of the Judge, i.e., it is forgiveness; and it can only be understood as grace where God's verdict as judge is simultaneously seen with it. If for the faithful, anxiety is a thing of the past, this is not so with the "fear of God", which rather belongs to faith itself (Rom. 11:20f.; II Cor. 5:10f.; Phil. 2:12f.). Only so is the "trust" that also belongs to faith (Rom. 4:5, 4:17, 4:20, 6:8) genuine trust, in which man utterly looks away from himself and completely surrenders himself to God (II Cor. 1:9). Faith is also a "knowledge" in that it knows about the saving act of God that is proclaimed to it. However, it is not knowledge in the sense of speculation about some historical or cosmic event, but rather a knowledge in which the man of faith also knows about himself and understands himself anew, in that he understands the saving act as a gift and himself as one to whom it has been given (I Cor. 3:12). God's revelation in Christ is not the communication of knowledge as such, but rather an occurrence for man and in man that places him in a new situation and thereby also opens up to him a new understanding of himself (cf. especially II Cor. 2:14-4:6). Thus his knowing has its basis in his being known by God (I Cor. 8:2f., 13:12; Gal. 4:9). So it is that faith is the new possibility for existence before God; it is created by God's saving act, is laid hold of in obedience, and manifests itself as confession and hope, as fear and trust — in short, as a new understanding of oneself. That faith actually is such a new possibility of existence comes to expression when Paul can say not only that the righteousness of God was revealed (Rom. 1:17, 3:21), but also that faith was revealed (Gal. 3:23-5).

In its unity of obedience, confession, and hope, of fear and trust, faith as a new self-understanding is not the once for all resolve to join the Christian religion or a once accepted world-view. Rather it has reality only as the *obedience of faith that is always new*. However much such faith may begin with a foundational resolve and confession, the existence of the faithful man is not at all the simple state that is thereby established or the natural development that is thus begun. For if it were, faith as an act would become a process in the past and would be understood as a "work", which by its very essence it is not. It is only faith if it always remains faith, i.e., if the individual with his entire existence always realizes his obedience anew. This comes to expression (1) when Paul again and again admonishes his hearers to examine themselves and to stand fast in faith (I Cor. 10:12, 11:28, 16:15; II Cor. 13:5; Rom. 14:4, 14:22; Gal. 5:1, 6:3f., etc.), inasmuch as fear of God belongs to faith (Rom. 11:20f.; Phil. 2:12, etc.); (2) in the statements concerning the individual possibilities of faith; i.e., faith can be weak or strong (Rom. 14:1, 15:13f.; I Thess. 3:10; II Cor. 10:15, etc.), and from it can arise both this judgment and that (Rom. 14:2, 14:22f.). Thus the man of faith also still stands in a life in which it is necessary to judge and to act, and all this should be determined by faith (Rom. 12:6), for otherwise it is sin (Rom. 14:23). So, then, faith also "abides" (I Cor. 13:13); for no future can be imagined in which the Christian could understand himself otherwise than as having his basis in the saving act of God; the same thing follows (3) from the fact that the relation to the Lord that is acquired through faith and baptism is also thought of as a determination of one's entire life (Gal. 2:20). To die with Christ in baptism means a life-long crucifixion with him (Rom. 6:6; cf. Gal. 5:24, 6:14), so that henceforth his life and sufferings are at work in the ministry and sufferings of the man of faith (Rom. 8:17; II Cor. 1:5, 4:7ff., 13:3f.; Phil. 3:10). If this consciousness of being bound to the Lord occasionally found expression with Paul himself in mystic or ecstatic experiences (II Cor. 12:12ff.), still being "in Christ" is in principle not mysticism, but rather precisely life in the new historical possibility that is determined by Christ. One "stands fast" in the Lord just as he "stands fast" in faith (I Thess. 3:8; Phil. 4:1), and as there are levels of faith, so also are there levels of being in Christ (Rom. 16:10; I Cor. 3:1, 4:10) and individually different ways of manifesting one's life in him (I Thess. 5:12; Rom. 16:2, 16:8, 16:12, 16:22; I Cor. 15:58, 16:19, 16:24; Phil. 1:13, 2:1, 2:5, 4:2; II Cor. 2:17, 12:19; Philem. 8). In life and in death, the man of faith belongs to Christ (Rom. 14:7-9); I Cor. 15:18; I Thess. 4:16), and this communion, which can also be designated as Christ's being in the believer (Rom. 8:10; II Cor. 13:3, 13:5; Gal. 2:20, 4:19), is never completed, but is a constant striving forward; it is the determination of a life that is free from the past and open for the future (Phil. 3:12-14) because it is no longer dominated by the will to be oneself (Gal. 2:19f.).

iv. Paul can designate this new life in still a different way and thereby further describe it by the concept of the "Spirit". Just as "flesh" signifies the determination of life by what is on hand (cf. above, III., 2., b., iii.), so "Spirit" signifies its determination by what is *not* on hand, not produced, not disposable — by what is invisible, miraculous, and solely the object of faith. In the popular image of the Spirit with which Paul makes contact, the idea of "miracle" as a power that determines man's existence is already laid out, although it is thought of somewhat primitively in that remarkable phenomena, and especially psychic ones, are understood as miraculous and wrought by the Spirit. Paul radicalizes this idea by showing that all the phenomena that can be grasped on the plane of what is on hand are ambiguous and as such do not attest the Spirit of God. This they do only when they stand within a specific life-context (I Cor. 12). The only miracle is that which transforms man in his entire existence and, of course, also attests itself in all of the concrete expressions of his life. Therefore, for Paul, Spirit is the "how", the determination of the new life, which is not produced by man himself, but is given to him. Thus, on the one hand, Paul speaks of the Spirit as the gift that is given to the faithful man (Rom. 5:5; I Cor. 2:12; II Cor. 1:22, etc.), the gift of the last days in which the final consummation is already guaranteed (Rom. 8:23; II Cor. 1:22, 5:5); on the other hand, he speaks of it as the determination of the new life, which must be laid hold of in faith and which proves itself in the concrete way in which one leads his life (Gal. 5:25; Rom. 8:12-14). Spirit is the determination of heart and conscience, of walking and striving, of joy and of love (Rom. 5:5; Gal. 4:6; Rom. 9:1, 8:4-11; Gal. 5:16; Rom. 14:17, 15:30). The life of the man of faith is one of being led by the Spirit (Rom. 8:14), a constant bearing of fruit and being transformed (Gal. 5:22f.; II Cor. 3:18). Since this new possibility of life that is designated by "Spirit" must be expressly laid hold of, and since, further, it is faith that is the laying hold of it, Paul also does not refer faith to the activity of the Spirit, but rather, conversely, refers the reception of the Spirit to faith or to baptism. This clearly shows that he has no need of the wonderful or the miraculous for the purpose of explanation (Gal. 3:2, 3:5, 3:14; II Cor. 1:21f.). Insofar, however, as the resolve of faith must maintain itself as the determination of one's entire life, a life in the Spirit and a life in faith are one and the same. And as faith brings one into communion with the Lord, so this communion with the *Lord* is nothing other than being determined by the *Spirit*. Hence Paul can say that where in the Old Testament "Lord" is spoken of, what is meant is the "Spirit" (II Cor. 3:17). Lord and Spirit almost coincide (II Cor. 3:17f.; Rom. 8:9-11, 9:1, 15:18; cf. Rom. 8:8f. with I Cor. 15:5; Phil. 2:6, etc.); both terms designate the new eschatological mode of existence in which the faithful stand.

Both designate the "freedom" of the faithful (II Cor. 3:17; Gal. 5:1). This freedom is (1) *freedom from sin* (Rom. 6:18, 6:22, 8:2), i.e., not a sinless state, but rather the opening up of the possibility of new life through forgiveness; it is freedom for God's claim, for the imperative (Rom. 6:11ff.; Gal. 5:13f.; I Cor. 5:7f.), which did not exist before (Rom. 7:13ff.), but exists now (Rom. 7:4ff.). Thereby it is also (2) *freedom from the law* (Gal. 2:4, 5:18, 5:23; Rom. 6:14, 7:1ff.; II Cor. 3:7-18, etc.) and (3) *freedom from men* and their standards (I Cor. 7:21-3, 9:1, 9:19, 10:29; Gal. 3:28) and, finally, (4) *freedom from death* (Rom. 8:2), which receives its power precisely through sin and the law (I Cor. 15:56).

The new covenant is the covenant of "life" (II Cor. 3:7-18), and Romans 5 seeks to establish, in face of the claim of Judaism, that faith actually has the righteousness that is the substance of eschatological salvation because it has life, because it can live in hope. Faith has life not as a state in which dying has ceased, but as hope (Rom. 8:18-39), so that precisely every distress must serve as a confirmation of faith because it brings to mind that everything here and now, all that is simply on hand, is provisional (Rom. 5:3f., 8:19ff.; II Cor. 5:1ff.). Thus the believer who actually puts his hope in God alone (II Cor. 1:8f.) is raised above all the powers of natural life, yes, even above life and death themselves (II Cor. 5:6-9; Rom. 14:7-9; I Cor. 3:21f.). This never means, however, that he has salvation as a possession that is at his disposal or that he is perfected and can boast. On the contrary, he can boast solely of God and of what God gives him (I Cor. 1:29, 3:21; Rom. 5:11, 11:17f.) and, in a paradoxical way, of the cross of Christ and of his nothingness (Gal. 6:14; Rom. 5:3; II Cor. 11:16-12:13); for in this he becomes certain of the power of the Lord, which is made perfect in weakness (II Cor. 12:9f., 4:7). Indeed, he is not his own lord, but rather has his freedom precisely in that he no longer belongs to himself, but to another (I Cor. 6:19, 7:22; Rom. 7:4-6, 14:17-19; II Cor. 5:14f.; Gal. 2:19f.), that he obediently stands at the disposal of God (Rom. 6:13). Everything belongs to him because he belongs to Christ (I Cor. 3:22f.). Therefore, his freedom is not the right to indulge every caprice; for precisely such capriciousness would once again make him a slave to what is on hand, from which he has now become free.

If for the believer everything worldly and on hand that he encounters turns out to be radically indifferent, inasmuch as nothing can be held against him, this indifference nevertheless immediately disappears before the question of the individual's concrete responsibility (I Cor. 6:12, 8:1ff., 10:23). Service of Christ realizes itself in actual life as *service to the neighbor*, of whom precisely the man who is free, and only he, should and can make himself a genuine servant (I Cor. 9:19-22, cf. 8:9; Rom. 14:13ff., 15:1ff.; Gal. 5:13). Such service is the fulfillment of the "law of Christ" (Gal. 6:2); it is "love", which is the fulfillment of the law (Gal. 5:14; Rom. 13:8ff.), the love in which faith manifests itself as the determination of one's life (Gal. 5:6) and in which knowledge has the criterion of its genuineness (I Cor. 8:1ff.); the love that is higher than all of the other Spirit-wrought phenomena of the Christian life (I Cor. 12:31, 13:1ff.); the love in which the new creation becomes a reality (cf. Gal. 5:6 with 6:15) and which therefore never ends (I Cor. 13:8ff.). Naturally, for one who stands in love, an "ethic" is no longer necessary, however much brotherly admonition, such as Paul himself practices, can point out to another his responsibility and show him what he has to do (I Thess. 5:11f.; Rom. 12:8, 15:14).

All this, this life in the Spirit, in freedom and love, which is based in the faith that no longer seeks itself, but gives all glory to God, remains understandable and realizable only to him for whom the "glory of God" is indeed the final motive and the final goal. It is to the glory of God that Christ is confessed as Lord (Phil. 2:11); and the same thing is true of the life of the congregation (Rom. 15:6; II Cor. 1:20), our eating and drinking (I Cor. 10:31), the work of the apostle (II Cor. 4:15), and the works of love of the faithful (II Cor. 9:11-13). To God's glory, Christ accomplished his work (Rom. 15:7); for even as we belong to him, so also does he belong to God (I Cor. 3:23), and in the end he will relinquish his reign to God so that God may be all in all (I Cor. 15:28).

Existence and Faith, pp. 111-146.

*

"THE RELATION BETWEEN THEOLOGY AND PROCLAMATION"

Bultmann's consistent focus on the New Testament kerygma as the locus of faith suggested to some a very specific and limited formulation of that kerygma, as if it could be defined in terms of certain core New Testament beliefs: e.g., the confession that Jesus is Lord, that God has raised up this Jesus who was crucified, etc. Bultmann, however, rejected every effort to identify the kerygma with any particular past confession of faith. Since the kerygma is nothing else than God's word of address to a particular person, no formulation of it can ever be regarded as complete. It will always find expression in new forms of speech appropriate to the concrete situation of the person addressed. This brief selection first appeared as an essay, "Das Problem des Verhältnisses von Theologie und Verkündigung im Neuen Testament", in the 1950 Festschrift for Maurice Goguel, Aux Sources de la Tradition Chrétienne. Bultmann subsequently modified this essay for inclusion in the "Epilogue" to Volume 3, Theologie des Neuen Testaments (1953). This translation was done by Kendrick Grobel for the 1955 English version of Theology of the New Testament, Volume II.

The science called New Testament theology has the task of setting forth the theology of the New Testament; i.e. of setting forth *the theological thoughts of the New Testament writings*, both those that are explicitly developed (such as Paul's teaching on the Law, for example) and those that are implicitly at work in narrative or exhortation, in polemic or consolation. The question may be raised whether it is more appropriate to treat the theological thoughts of the New Testament writings as a systematically ordered *unity* — a New Testament system of dogmatics, so to say — or to treat them in their *variety*, each writing or group of writings by itself, in which case the individual writings can then be understood as members of an historical continuity.

The second procedure is the one chosen in the treatment here offered. By this choice the opinion is expressed that there can be no normative Christian dogmatics, in other words, that it is not possible to accomplish the theological task once for all — the task which consists of unfolding that understanding of God, and hence of the world and man, which arises from faith, for this task permits only ever-repeated solutions, or attempts at solution, each in its particular historical situation. Theology's continuity through the centuries consists not in holding fast to once formulated propositions but in the constant vitality with which faith, fed by its origin, understandingly masters its constantly new historical situation. It is of decisive importance that *the theological thoughts be conceived and explicated as thoughts of faith*, that is: *as thoughts in which faith's understanding of God, the world, and man is unfolding itself*— not as products of free speculation or of a scientific mastering of the problems involved in "God", "the world", and "man" carried out by the objectifying kind of thinking.

Theological propositions — even those of the New Testament — can never be the *object* of faith; they can only be the *explication* of the understanding which is inherent in faith itself. Being such explication, they are determined by the believer's situation and hence are necessarily incomplete. This *incompleteness*, however, is not a lack to be remedied by future generations, each generation supplying what is still lacking, so that by an ever-continued summation a complete dogmatics would finally result. Rather, the incompleteness has its cause in the inexhaustibility of believing comprehension, which must ever actualize itself anew; this incompleteness consequently signifies a task and a promise. Furthermore, my understanding of myself in my world of work and destiny by the light of a love conferred upon me or of a responsibility entrusted to me is necessarily always incomplete. It is self-evident, for example, that the New Testament's thought about the state and society are incomplete because the possibilities and the problems of forms of the state and society which history has introduced in the meantime could not be present to the minds of the New Testament authors. It is likewise clear that the world of modern science and technology imposes upon believing comprehension new tasks which could not yet occur to minds of the New Testament period. Therefore the theological thoughts of the New Testament can be normative only insofar as they lead the believer to develop out of his faith an understanding of God, the world, and man in his own concrete situation.

But from the fact that theological statements are by nature the explication of believing comprehension it also follows that *these statements may be only relatively appropriate, some more so, others less so.* The possibility exists that in some of them the believing comprehension may not be clearly developed, that it may be hindered — bound perhaps by a prefaith understanding of God, the world, and man and by a corresponding terminology — and consequently may speak of God's dealing and of the relation between God and man in juristic terms, for instance. Or it may speak of God's relation to the world in mythological or cosmological terms which are inappropriate to faith's understanding of God's transcendence. Or the consequence may be that it expresses God's transcendence in the terminology of mysticism or of idealistic thinking. From this possibility arises the task — even in the case of the New Testament writings — of *content-criticism* (Sachkritik) such as Luther, for example, exercised toward the Epistle of James and the Revelation of John.

But the most important thing is that basic insight that the theological thoughts of the New Testament are the unfolding of faith itself growing out of that new understanding of God, the world, and man which is conferred in and by faith — or, as it can also be phrased: *out of one's new self-understanding.* For by the believer's new understanding of himself we, of course, do not mean "understanding" as in a scientific anthropology which objectifies man into a phenomenon of the world, but we do mean an existential understanding of myself which is at one with and inseparable from my understanding of God and the world. For I am I, of course, not as an isolable and objectifiable world-phenomenon but I am I in my particular existence inseparably bound up with God and the world.

If the scientific presentation of the theological thoughts of the New Testament has the task of pointing them out as the unfolding of believing self-understanding, it then presents *not the object of faith but faith itself* in its own self-interpretation. But here arises the real problem of the presentation! For can one concentrate upon faith without seeing at the same time that toward which it is directed, its object and content?

For in the New Testament, faith is not understood as a self-understanding arising spontaneously out of human existence but as an understanding made possible by God, opened up by his dealing with men. Faith is not choosing to understand one's self in one of several possible ways that are universally available to man but is man's response to

God's word which encounters him in the proclamation of Jesus Christ. It is *faith in the kerygma,* which tells of God's dealing in the man Jesus of Nazareth.

When, therefore, the science of New Testament theology seeks to present faith as the origin of the theological statements, it obviously must present the kerygma and the self-understanding opened up by it in which faith unfolds itself. And that is just where the problem lurks! For both the kerygma and faith's self-understanding always appear in the texts, so far as they are expressed in words and sentences, already interpreted in some particular way — i.e. in theological thoughts. Although there are single statements in the New Testament which can be designated as specifically kerygmatic, even they are always formulated in a particular theological terminology — take, for instance, that simplest sentence, "Jesus, Lord" (II Cor. 4:5), for it presupposes a particular understanding of the term "Lord".

Therefore, it is *not possible simply and sharply to distinguish kerygmatic standards in the New Testament from theological ones,* nor to derive from the New Testament a self-understanding not formulated in theological statements. Nevertheless, he who sets forth a New Testament theology must have this distinction constantly in mind and must interpret the theological thoughts as the unfolding of the self-understanding awakened by the kerygma if he is to avoid conceiving them as an objectifying kind of thought cut loose from the act of living, no matter whether such thought be attributed to the intellect or to "revelation". For when revelation is conceived as an arrangement for the impartation of teachings, these teachings have the character of the objectifying thought of science, a kind of thought which dims their existential reference to living into a mere object of thought — but then they are pseudo-scientific teachings. Such a procedure leads to the misunderstanding that theology, conceived as the "right teaching", is the object and content of faith, when actually it is only the kerygma that may be regarded as the "right teaching" which is the object and content of faith. Though the propositions of philosophy, so far as they contain truth, are in themselves "right teaching", the propositions of theology are not themselves "right teaching" but, so far as they contain truth, teach what the "right teaching" is — a teaching which is not found by investigation but is given in the kerygma. But the kerygma is just what theology can never seize in definitive form; it can always take hold of it only as something conceptually stated, and that means as something already theologically interpreted.

This state of affairs reveals itself in its problematical character all the more when the theologian holds fast to the insight that faith can be nothing else but the response to the kerygma, and that the kerygma is nothing else than God's word addressing man as a questioning and promising word, a condemning and forgiving word. As such a word it does not offer itself to critical thought but speaks into one's concrete existence. That the kerygma never appears without already having been given some theological interpretation rests upon the fact that it can never be spoken except in a human language and formed by human thought. This very fact confirms its kerygmatic character; for it makes clear that the statements of the kerygma are not universal truths but are personal address in a concrete situation. Hence they can appear only in a form molded by an individual's understanding of his own existence or by his interpretation of that understanding. And correspondingly they are understandable only to him who is able to recognize the kerygma as a word addressed to him in his situation — to recognize it immediately only as a question asked him, a demand made of him.

Differently expressed: the kerygma is understandable as kerygma only when the self-understanding awakened by it is recognized to be a possibility of human self-understanding and thereby becomes the call to decision. For the theological investigator obviously cannot presuppose his own faith as an epistemological instrument and make use of it as a presupposition for methodical work. What he can and should do is keep himself ready, open, free. Or, better, keep himself questioning — or knowing the questionability of — all human self-understanding, in the knowledge that existential understanding of one's self (in distinction from existentialist interpretation of man's being) is real only in the act of existing and not in the isolated reflection of thought.

Theology of the New Testament II, pp. 237-241.

5

MODERNITY AND FAITH IN CONFLICT*

"THE CRISIS OF FAITH"

"The Crisis of Faith" was initially published as one of Three Marburg Lectures *(1931). All three were on the theme of crisis and the three authors were all faculty at Marburg University. The other two essays in this volume were: "The Crisis of the Church" by Hans von Soden and "The Crisis of Religion" by Heinrich Frick. Some aspects of Bultmann's essay still reflect its original relation to these other two essays: e.g., his distinction between the crisis of faith and the crisis of religion. In most of the essay the crisis of faith is depicted as an existential struggle calling for repeated decisions by each individual in any period of culture. Near the end, Bultmann introduces the differing ways in which modern culture complicates that struggle. The German original of this essay is available in* Glauben und Verstehen, II *(1952). James C. G. Greig first translated it into English with the misleading title, "The Crisis in Belief", in* Essays: Philosophical and Theological. *This translation is by Edward Hobbs. It was done for this volume of collected Bultmann essays and has not previously been published.*

If we speak of a "crisis of *faith*", we mean something other than when we speak of the crisis in *morality*, for example in trustworthiness and loyalty, in political conviction, or in respect for the law; indeed we even mean something other than a crisis in *religion*. For in all these cases the crisis is one of human attitude, of human character, and is concerned with the problem of a particular epoch or generation, with a sociological phenomenon. Even if faith is connected with morality and religion, if it is at the same time always a human attitude, it is nevertheless differentiated from them by its being a particular faith, faith in an otherness, in something beyond humanity. Faith is not religiosity, not a disposition of the soul to devotion, gratitude, reverence and awe for the world and life as a whole. Rather, it understands the world and life in terms of a reality beyond them, of a power beyond them, which is their origin and their Lord — i.e., in terms of God. A crisis of faith therefore arises when this unworldly reality has become questionable.

* See also pp. 33-39 above.

The situation is the same as in the relation of person to person, to which indeed we also apply the term "faith": the friend or the lover has faith in the other person. Faith here does not mean a loving attitude, for that can persist even when faith wavers or collapses. Nor does it mean an attribute of character, for that also can exist before and after love. Rather, faith is faith in a specific other person, who is seen as such in just this faithful love. Such faith undergoes a crisis when it turns out that the other person is not what faith in him made him appear to be.

Thus to speak of the crisis of faith in the realm of religion does not at all mean that we are speaking of a crisis of religion and religiosity, as, for example, in regard to their being shaken by events in world history or intellectual history, or to their awakening under these influences. Nor does it mean that we are speaking of indifference to religion; rather, we are speaking of the crisis of a specific faith. For us it is meaningful only to speak of the crisis of our own Christian faith.

I

GOD

What, then, is Christian faith whose crisis is our concern? What is that unworldly reality which is the object of Christian faith? *What is God in Christianity's sense?*

God in Christianity's sense is *nothing other than what he is to every faith* in which the idea of God is taken at all seriously. What, then, is signified by the idea "God"?

Every human being knows or can know about its *limitedness*, for — consciously or unconsciously — it is driven to and fro by its limitedness, as long as it exists. It is no more at its own disposal than it is its own creator. It is never complete, but is driven to and fro by *care* which reminds it of its limits, of its incompleteness:

> If no ear would hearken to me,
> In the heart 'twould echo surely;
> Changed in form before your eyes,
> Gruesome power I exercise.
> Vexing ever as your fellow
> On the pathway, on the billow;
> Ever found and never sought,
> Cursed when not with flattery bought . . .

He whom once I make my own
Might as well the world disown . . .
Fortune, failure stand revealed
As whims — he famishes though filled,
Joy or torment equally
Postponing to another day,
And as everything he leaves
For the future — naught achieves.

First of all there is *everyday care for the morrow.* One is occupied with the provision, procuring and preparation of the means of living. And yet in his heart he knows that he cannot secure his life with the means of living. Everyone understands the story of the rich farmer who wished to fill his barns with the rich harvest and then say to himself, "Soul, you have ample goods laid up for many years; take your ease, eat, drink, and be merry." But God said to him, "Fool! This night your soul is required of you; and the things you have prepared, whose will they be?" Everyone sees that the farmer was a fool. And this dark power — the power which limits one and is master of him even when he thinks he is his own master — is God, the master of one's future.

Or again, little as life can free itself from this care for the things of every day or for the morrow, it refuses to see in this care what gives life its meaning, but would go beyond it. Life is driven to and fro by the *longing for the true and the beautiful,* or even merely by that *indefinite longing* which awakes in the "deepest midnight" and in which it becomes clear that:

All pleasure craves eternity,
Craves utter, utter eternity.

And yet even in all its lofty moments human life is not granted this eternity of pleasure or this pleasure of eternity. Does it indeed know any hours in which it could say to the moment — "But tarry, you are so fair"? And even if it does — the moment just does not tarry! Mankind has no power over the temporal and the eternal. The power which has power over the temporal and eternal is God.

Or again, life is driven to and fro by the *longing for love,* and by the feeling that there is truth in what Karl Spitteler's Apollo says (in *Olympian Spring*) to Hera, who is haunted by anxiety over death, who would like to escape from death:

In Ananke's cruel domain
In vale or mountain flourishes no solace to remain,

Save the solace of the eyes — twin starts in friendship blest,
And the syllables of love, by grateful lips expressed.

Many a life is poor in friendship and in love, many another rich, but even the rich life is aware of a final solitude into which it is driven.

Can e'er man as he'd wish belong
On earth to his fellow?
In the long night I thought of it and could but answer: No!

The power which drives mankind into this final solitude is God.

Or again, life is moved by the *impulse toward knowledge* and is led to admit, "I see that we can nothing know." Or is it *the impulse to action, to work?* That in fact is the way in which Faust finally sought to reach that moment to which he could say, "But tarry, you are so fair!" Yet behind want, guilt, and care, to which access to it [the moment] or mastery over it is denied, comes "the brother, Death". And when the blind Faust takes delight in the clanking of the spades, they are not the spades which are accomplishing his work and bringing it to completion, but the spades which are digging his grave; and it is the *fore*taste of sublime happiness which is the highest and final moment. The power which sets a limit to knowing and doing is God.

Or, finally, existence is dominated by the *idea of duty*, by knowledge of the principle that "You can, for you ought." But it is well aware that life in accordance with the "You ought" is a struggle, in which it is a matter of mastering oneself. It knows the call of *conscience* which summons to duty, and recalls from thoughtlessness and aberration to everyday things, and pronounces the verdict "Guilty!" on wasted time and lost opportunity, impure thoughts and mean actions. The summons of the "You ought", divesting one of his willfulness, the call of conscience showing one his pettiness, incompleteness, and wretchedness, is God.

God is what limits mankind, who makes a comedy of his care, who allows his longing to miscarry, who casts him into solitude, who sets a limit to his knowing and doing, who calls him to duty, and who gives the guilty over to torment. And yet at the same time it is God who forces one into life and drives him into care; who puts longing and the desire for love in his heart; who gives him thoughts and strength for his work, and who places him in the eternal struggle between willfulness and duty. God is the enigmatic power beyond time, yet master of the temporal; beyond existence, yet at work in it.

II

FAITH IN GOD

But what we have said is not adequate as a description of the Christian idea of God, nor indeed of the idea of God at all. *For why do we call this dark power "God"?* Why give the enigma, the mystery which drives us this way and that and hedges us in, any other name than simply "the enigma", or "fate"? Does the name "God" not gloss over the fact that we are in the dark, and are at the mercy of fate? Or, if there must be a name, why not equally well that of the devil? Does not this power play a cruel game with us, destroying and annihilating? Is not unfulfillment the mark of every life? Is not death, nothingness the end?

> It's over, then! what moral have we won?
> It's just as if life never had begun,
> Though going full circle just as if it had.
> Give me eternal nothingness instead —

thus speaks the devil, Mephistopheles. And is this true? Or, in view of this enigma and this finiteness of ours, does a diabolical temptation perhaps lie in this approach? And is it not to the point, in face of the enigma and the darkness, to insist on the meaning of life with a cry of "Nevertheless!"?

However that may be, this "Nevertheless" is in any event the meaning of faith in God. It is the courage to designate that dark enigma, that sovereign power as God, as my God. It is the courage to assert that in the knowledge of this power every being acquires its meaning, that in knowing this power I also realize I belong to it, and that the limit which fences my being about is inwardly removed. This will, of course, happen when I give up my pretense to make my own way; when I submit to this power as that which brought me into existence, when I can say "Yes" to it. Faith in God is the courage which utters this "Nevertheless": "Nevertheless I am continually with you: you hold me by my right hand." [Psalm 73:23]

For such faith, harassing care loses its anxiety, for in it one attains to a peculiar detachment from care. Then are "they that weep, as though they wept not; and they that rejoice, as though they rejoiced not" (I Cor. 7:30), yet without ceasing to weep or rejoice. Then, whatever one has it will be as if one did not, in fact, have it. For this faith, longing loses its torture, for in the very longing, one frees himself from the illusion that the here and now could ever bring fulfillment, and longing is seen to go beyond time and into eternity. For this faith, the light of joy flashes out

244

of the darkness of solitude:

> Cannot I be as I would be
> With God in full community?
> What's to prevent my being so today?

For this faith the question is not of bringing knowing and doing to an end, but of being grateful for the power to investigate and to work; and for it the "You ought", the voice of conscience, is what brings one to oneself by limiting and judging him. And for this faith, what one says in the face of death is not at all, "It's over, then!", "It's just as if life never had begun!"

If the faith which says "Nevertheless!" is faith in God, then we must clearly distinguish *genuine faith in God* from what is usually termed a *world-view* [*Weltanschauung*].[93] Knowledge of the power which creates and limits existence is not theoretical knowledge but is the knowledge which breaks in on us in critical moments of our existence itself. We never have it as a lasting possession or a latent insight; rather, it has to keep on making its way in the face of all temptations which continually arise out of existence, giving one the illusion that he is captain of his soul and master of his fate — even if by virtue of that very insight. Faith in God is continually being stifled by the cares of each day that lay hold of us, by wishes and plans, by the passions that drive us to pleasure, and from one pleasure to another; or by living together, which is always in danger of losing its real character as a community of free and solitary persons, and of deteriorating into a clamor of voices weakening us and deceiving us about our solitariness, a clamor in which we are distracted and lose ourselves and even join in it. Action and work continually make one their prisoner; one becomes an "expert", a slave to his work, whose pauses are for him not the achievement of composure, but distraction. Consciousness of doing one's duty gives a false security and an arrogance in which one is blinded to his own insignificance.

Real faith in God always grows out of the realization of the *questionableness* of existence, which cannot be learned and retained in the form of a proposition, but rather which comes to consciousness in the *moment* of living. Real faith in God is not a proposition which one can have available in order to evade the moment; rather, it must actually be grasped and confirmed in the moment, by holding to a proper detachment from things and by carrying out that humbling, that "Yes": "Not my will, but yours be done."

Real faith in God, therefore, is *not a general truth* at my disposal which I

245

perceive and apply; on the contrary, it is what it is only as something continually perceived anew and developing anew. God is not a natural law of the world, not a providence or a general cosmic purpose that will enable me, once I have recognized this law or meaning, to explain and understand the individual phenomena of history and of my own life; or at least, if not that, to be persuaded on general grounds as to their meaning. A "world-view" is a theory about the world and life, and about the unity of the world, its origin, purpose or worth, or about its worthlessness, about the meaning of life, or about its meaninglessness. What we call a theistic or Christian "world-view" makes God into a principle for understanding the world, into an idea. For faith, God is the incomprehensible, enigmatic power that governs my concrete life and limits it, a power which I can come to know only in and for itself. In a "world-view" it is a question of understanding my life and my destiny on the basis of a general conception of the world, always as an instance of the universal. In a "world-view" I simply escape from the reality of my existence, which is actually real only in the moment, in the question involved in the moment and in the decision called for by the moment. We can see in the longing for a "world-view" an escape from the enigma and from the decisive question of the moment. It is one's escape from himself; it is the effort to find security in generalizations, whereas insecurity is what characterizes the real nature of human existence. A "world-view" is an attempt to relieve one of a decision when consciousness of his insecurity breaks in on him from the situation of the moment, say, in the case of a moral conflict, through an ethical theory, or, in the case of death, through a psychological or cosmological theory. Thus a "world-view" stands in sharpest contrast to faith in God. This saying "Yes", this "Nevertheless!" does not mean elucidation of the enigma by the insight which comes from observation, but is born only of the moment, that is, from surrender to the claims of the moment, from the surrender of the self. This is how Luther describes it: "This is the supreme article of the creed of which we speak: I believe in God the Father Almighty, Maker of heaven and earth. And whoever rightly believes that is helped already, and is brought back to the point from which Adam fell. But those people are few, who come so far as to believe fully that he is the God who makes and creates all things. For such a person must have died to all things, to good and evil, to death and life, to hell and heaven, and must acknowledge in his heart that he can do nothing in his own strength." Such a faith can never be a well-conceived and well-grounded "world-view" nor one that can be permanently retained and applied, but rather it must constantly be re-won in the struggle with one's self-will.

Even as faith in God is not a world-view, interpreting everything in the world on the basis of a principle, neither is it a *mysticism* rising superior to the world and seeking God in timelessness. God is the mysterious, enigmatic power that meets us *in* the world and *in* time. His *otherness* is the otherness of one having power over the temporal and the eternal, the otherness of the *power* which creates and limits our life, not the otherness of a substance or of a void with which the soul unites and into which it is swallowed up as it soars above the world in devotion, abstraction and ecstasy. Faith knows that the human soul is not a special something in which one can free himself from involvement in the affairs of the world in order to fling himself into the arms of eternity. It knows that in all such attempts the one who wishes to escape from himself is only flung back on himself, that for all the joys and delights of mysticism he is simply human and nothing else. It knows that what one *has done* and *does,* his decisions, constitute him in his very being, that temporality is his *essence,* and that wishing to escape from the temporal simply means wishing to escape from his own reality, and therefore from God, who is met by him nowhere else but in this temporal reality. Mysticism seeks that detachment, that "having as though one did not have", by ignoring the "having", by its cancellation of world and time. Faith in God does not speak of soul-sparks and soul-rudiments, but of the *whole* person who stands in the world and in time, in community and in responsibility, who is always to hear in the call of the *moment* the call of God, and is always to carry out his obedience to God in *decision,* in *action.* In such *obedience* he is to gain his freedom from the world, from bondage to the world in anxiety and thoughtlessness, in self-deception and vanity — but not like the mystic, by escaping from practical thought, decision and action. To preserve precisely in the concreteness of life that detachment which takes decision and action with real seriousness, because in it one thinks and acts as a free agent — that is precisely what faith means.

III

CHRISTIAN FAITH IN GOD

Thus we can characterize Christian faith in God; but so also any faith in God at all can be characterized. What is specifically Christian faith in God? This question remains to be answered; but it finds its answer when we face the other pertinent question that is urgently raised by the character of faith. How far is such a faith, faith in *God?* Is it not simply *faith in humanity?* Are we not using the word God here to gloss over a fatal self-deception? Is not this "Nevertheless!" simply the Nevertheless of defiance, of the courage bred by despair? In fact: faith as it has been described need not be anything but faith in humanity, that is, fundamentally not a faith in an otherness, but a human attitude, a disposition of the soul, which in overcoming despair and resignation, stupidity and thoughtlessness, takes stock of the reality in which it exists, saying "Yes" to it in awe and gratitude, proudly and humbly at one and the same time, refusing to be discomfited, but, on the contrary, going on its way composedly and courageously. It is the attitude of the Stoic or of Faust:

In that direction all is lost to view;
A fool is he who turns there dazzled eyes,
To see his like above the cloudy skies.
Let him stand firm and look around on earth —
This world's not mute to him who is of worth.
Why need he roam into eternity?
For he can have what he can plainly see.
Thus let him wander on through all earth's day;
Though spirits haunt, still let him go his way:
Advancing let him find both pain and joy,
He whom, each moment, nought can satisfy.

Goethe's honesty sought to avoid the name "God" for the reality to which one bows in the knowledge that he is yoked to it:

Feeling's the thing;
Its name? — but sound and smoke
Enshrouding heavenly flame.

This faith does not take God to be a real otherness: God is not a "You" to it, and no prayer to him is possible, not even:

Send, Lord, what pleaseth thee —
Something of joy, of pain.
That from thy hands the twain
Should flow, sufficeth me.

Such faith of course speaks of God; indeed, it even speaks *to* God. But for it, God is the undefined, is fate, and in any event, is not the God of Christian faith. But, in speaking of God and to God, that faith knows what God is and wishes to speak to him. *May* it?

Christian faith has its distinctiveness in speaking of an event that gives it this right, in saying that it hears a *word* which demands that it should recognize God as an otherness. For Christianity faith in God is not faith and trust in God in general, but faith in a definite word proclaimed to it. The event is *Jesus Christ*, in whom, as the New Testament says, God has spoken, and whom the New Testament itself calls "the Word". That is, in what happened in and through Christ, God has decisively manifested himself to humanity, and in this event a message is grounded and legitimated which confronts one as *God's Word*, not teaching him a new concept of God, but giving him the right to have faith in the God in whom he would like to have faith.

It is for this very reason that the Word was needed. "If God's Word and sign are not there, or are not recognized, then it is of no avail even if God himself were there." "For outside Christianity, even if people have faith in and worship only a true God, yet they do not know what his intentions are towards them, and they cannot look to him for any love or good, as they remain under eternal wrath and damnation" (Luther).

It is this, then, that is distinctive about Christian faith and is also its scandal! And we must not make it inoffensive and harmless by developing the content of its conception of God alone, and abandoning the scandal. This lies in the very assertion that faith in God simply cannot and must not arise as a general human attitude, but only as a response to God's Word and that it is this *one* Word, found in the New Testament and based on the Christ-event, which is God's Word; this Word which is passed on by the preaching of the Church and which reassures each hearer that God *is*, that God is *his* God!

In order to understand this, however, we need to reflect further on *how* this Word tells one that he may have faith in God. It tells him by its promise of the *forgiveness of his sin;* and in saying so, it is also telling him that that submission to the power which calls us into life and makes us finite, and that saying "Yes", is only real and radical, and what it should be, when it is at once a confession of sin and a plea for grace. Here we are not to think of sin as immorality, but as the human claim to seek to exist in one's own right, to be one's own master, and to take one's life into one's own hands, *superbia*, wishing to be like God. The implementation of this claim has indeed driven one up against his limit and has made him conscious of it. But if in recognizing it he submits, then is not the limitation inwardly overcome, as we said? Has one not then found God?

Yes, he has if this submission is real and radical. But Christian faith asserts that such submission is impossible without the *confession of sin* and *forgiveness.* By confession of sin, then, more is understood than the acknowledgment of one's limitedness and subjection of oneself to it, thus more than a confession that the claim was a false one. What we actually should understand by it is that in the self-will that has so far ruled my life I have become guilty, that I cannot dispose of what lies behind me by becoming aware of my limit and acknowledging it; that, if it is in earnest, this very acknowledgment of limit is, rather, inevitably the confession of guilt before the power that limits me, and that guilt can only be wiped out by a word of forgiveness.

At the same time the Christian message says even more plainly *what sin is,* and how far I have become guilty through my *superbia.* That striving to implement one's own claims, that running up against the limit, is therefore in reality the guilt which gives one his character, because in this way one has become guilty *in relation to his fellow-creature.* The neighbor, the "You" with whom he is associated, is given to him as the real limit of his "I". That desire to be oneself, that *superbia,* is lovelessness. And the Christian conception of sin is characterized by taking the *command to love* as the command which dominates life, as the claim of God which is continually met in the moment. This surrender to the claims of the moment is not to be thought of simply as the abstract, negative recognition of human finiteness; on the contrary, it involves the positive recognition of the claim of the "You" as the criterion of my limitation, and its fulfillment as love. Neither is it to be thought of simply as the negative acknowledgment that I am not master of my own fate; rather it involves at the same time the positive recognition that I am there for the other person.

For this reason one's past characterizes one, a past in which this self-will has driven him about, because he did not hear the claims of the "You", and was caught up in a life of lovelessness and hate. He is guilty and impure because so much callousness and ingratitude, falsehood and meanness, thoughtless spoiling of the joys of others, and selfish neglect of the other person, so much coolness towards others and insistence on his own rights, all lie behind him. No, rather they do *not* lie *behind* him but cling to him unforgiven, and make him impure.

The significance of this may strike one who seeks to win another's love. He knows very well: What lies behind is actually not in the past, but I *am* the one who was thus and acted thus; and not I, but only the goodness and purity of the other person, can free me from it.

That my guilt, that — in God's eyes — my sin, is forgiven, is what the Word of the Christian proclamation says, and only to the one who accepts this forgiveness, submitting to its judgment and taking upon oneself the demand of love, does it give the right to speak of God and to God.

IV

THE CRISIS OF FATIH IS A *CONSTANT* CRISIS

If, then, this is the meaning of Christian faith in God: faith in God as the enigmatic power which calls me into life and limits me; in the God who in the word established in the world through Christ judges me as a sinner and forgives me my sin; in the God who directs me to the "You" and commands me to hear the claims of the moment in love — if so, what about the *crisis of faith?* Must we still discuss it in detail, or has it not become clear already in our characterization of faith?

If Christian faith in God, like faith in God in general, is silent and reverent submission to the power calling me into life and limiting me, if faith is the will to continue in this submission in each moment by acknowledging the claim of the moment, then *the crisis of faith is a constant one;* for this will must always be involved in a *struggle with the self-will* which refuses to recognize one's limits. The summons must always be heard anew. Faith in God, indeed, is never a possession, but rather always decision. One cannot therefore speak of a crisis of faith as one can of that in a scientific theory, which perhaps has guided research for a generation, whose fundamentals have to be put to the test so that the crisis will lead to new fundamentals and new theories. Nor can one speak of a crisis of faith as one would were it of one's image of the world (*Weltbild*) or one's conception of the state; nor again, as one would were it the crisis of institutions or organizations, whether it be the Church or the constitution, economics or the law that we have in mind. Such crises are sociological phenomena and are the problem of a generation or an age, their significance being to lay down new foundations for generations or ages to come. They emerge because an old possession has become insecure, and because a new possession has to be created. Faith is never simply the concern of a generation or an age, but is always *my* concern, never a possession, but always a decision, and its crisis is the constant struggle of self-will against the claim of the moment.

If in *Christian* faith in God we understand the claim of the moment as the claim of the "You", as the demand to *love*, then it is clear that its crisis is in the constant *struggle of hate against love*, and that this crisis becomes acute in every encounter with the "You", to whom we thoughtlessly or selfishly close our ears, maintaining our own rights and our own interests, in contempt or in open hate. For this reason Christianity speaks of *original sin*. By this it means nothing other than this: That we come into our own present situation as those seeking to make their own way; that we come out of a history and exist in a world which was and is guided by this understanding of community; and that the understanding which has guided us from the outset is that everyone seeks his own, and that no one listens seriously to others. It is a world of lovelessness. And people rise in revolt against this admission and this judgment again and again, even if only by blinding themselves to reality with illusions and by busying themselves in apparent love for mankind. For Christianity's love is not something that can be presented by programs, and implemented in organizations. It is rather something which always belongs to the moment, to *my* particular moment. It is quite true that in regard to particular ills and sufferings of the present, just such a love may demand a program of aid and an organization. Yet love is not exhausted and assured in them. On the contrary, programs, organizations and institutions can actually become a cloak for lovelessness, and can blind me to the real demand of the moment, and to the concrete "You" who encounters me. Lovelessness and pride, i.e., struggling against the judgment or sin, are the constant crisis of faith.

Further! If *the scandal of Christianity* lies in the proclamation of forgiveness in this single Word of Christ, and nowhere else, then faith stands in the constant crisis which this scandal creates: What right has this proclamation to be regarded as the only legitimate one? What right has an ordinary person whom I do not know, and who does not know me, to promise me in the name of God the forgiveness of my sins, merely because he happens to be appointed to the proclamation office of the Church? But does this mean anything other than that one is actually striving against the concrete, actual judgment that has been pronounced, pronounced against *him*? That he may be willing to accept it as a general judgment, and to tell himself that he will recognize forgiveness in this general way, whereas it is something which can only be accorded as something concrete, to him, who is himself a concrete person? And does that mean anything other than that he will perhaps recognize the *idea* of sin, the *idea* of forgiveness, the *idea* of God, but not God himself? That is what Christianity means by *God's incarnation:* the reality of God is not that of the idea but of the concrete happening; and the reality of his forgiveness is met with only in the concrete world legitimated by him.

But are there not crises of faith which belong specifically to a generation or an age? Crises induced by the transformation of science or by political revolutions? Apparently so.

The crisis or apparent crisis in which faith was placed by *modern natural science* has today almost played itself out — at least for so-called cultured people. There is the question whether this crisis has been overcome rightly, whether because of insight into the true nature of faith, or merely through the latest transformation in science and so-called world-view. Basically, the crisis consists in one's being confronted by natural science with the question whether he will understand his existence in terms of the reality lying open to scientific observation and research, the reality of the object perceived by the senses, the systematic integration of which is perceptible to the thinking mind, whose unity can be construed, or whether he will understand it in terms of the reality of the moment. I might even say, whether he will interpret the moment as deriving from the natural occurrence lying behind it in such a way as to see it as a necessary outcome therefrom; or whether he will acknowledge the *un*-derivedness of the moment, its openness for the future, its claim, its character as decision. Whether he is willing to acknowledge that the moment has a richer content than what can be established by observation, by measurement and calculation, rich in possibilities of joy and gratitude, pain and repentance, duty and love, possibilities which demand decision in the present, a decision no science can take from him, a decision in which one loses or gains his true existence. The question is, therefore, whether or not he acknowledges the responsibility of the present; and, if the claim of the present is the call to love, whether the voice of a natural science concerned with objective observation, or the call to love, grasps him more strongly. It is not particular results of natural science that produce a crisis of faith, but the natural science's way of looking at things, as such. Faith never has to struggle against the findings of natural science, but solely against its possible claim, in world-view fashion, to comprehend the meaning of human existence.

But in that case the crisis of faith which is produced by natural science is only one form of the crisis in which faith as such always and everywhere stands, admittedly a form characteristic of a particular age. Hidden by the claim of natural science is actually the human claim to exist by oneself and to understand and shape one's life in terms of what one can control, what by thought and by application one can master, or intends to master. Faith in God, and not only Christian faith, demands abandonment of this claim and acknowledgment of the enigmatic powers which in reality shape life, the acknowledgment of the moment with its responsibility. Christian faith in God clarifies any claim of natural science to be a world-view as a cloak for lovelessness, which is deaf to the moment's call for love.

Do we still need to speak about the crisis in which faith is placed by *historical science*, since this discipline deals critically with the New Testament, and makes our knowledge of the historical Jesus doubtful, and further, places the Christian religion in the context of the general history of religion, thus making it one more relative phenomenon among others?

In the Christian proclamation, however, there is no question of our being given an historical account about a part of the past which we might test or critically confirm or reject. We are told, on the contrary, that in what happened then, whatever the circumstances, God has acted and that through this action of God, the Word of divine judgment and forgiveness which now encounters us is legitimated; that this action of God is nothing other than the actual establishment of this Word, as the proclamation of this Word itself. No historical science can verify this assertion, either to confirm or to reject it. For it is beyond the sphere of historical observation to say that this Word and its proclamation are God's act.

Historical science becomes a crisis for faith only by virtue of the scandal that the Christian word of proclamation asserts itself as the authentic word of God; because humanity would like to check this uncheckable assertion, and lays claim to have criteria, where in the very nature of the matter there can be no criteria.

But the same scandal is also at the root of the crisis growing out of the viewpoint of the general history of religions. It is quite true that, in the eyes of history, Christianity is one relative phenomenon among others. But the scandalous Christian assertion is precisely that a relative, historical phenomenon, this particular proclamation is God's Word. And this crisis is a constant one.

The crises in which faith is placed by natural and historical science are only to be welcomed. They bring the constant and mostly latent crisis of faith into the open; they compel reflection on the nature of faith, posing the question of decision for or against faith. This question of decision is never a question of knowledge researched and possessed, but is always a question of will, of openness for the moment, which cannot therefore be decided by any science.

Faith also enters into such a crisis, especially, when it is confused with something else, when it is neither combated nor questioned, but is given up while one thinks one is holding fast to it or even deepening it. The usual confusion of faith is *its confusion with a world-view or with mystical religiosity*. To what extent this means a crisis for faith need not be spelled out in view of our earlier characterizations. Both certainly imply flight from the moment, from its enigma, from its claim, from decision, from love. It is precisely by means of them that, in fleeing from surrender to the moment, one tries to hold fast to oneself, to make himself secure and to be master of himself. In a world-view and in mysticism, at the deepest level it is one's faith in himself that prevails, and thus it is the opposite of faith in God. And one's faith in himself always means a crisis for faith in God. If faith in God understands the call of the moment as the claim of the "You" who confronts me, as the call to love, then the crisis of Christian faith in God is also always the crisis of love.

What is the relevance of a lecture on the crisis of faith in the framework of a lecture on civics? In civics we may be concerned with gaining knowledge that leads to action, or with achieving a consciousness to guide action. But to the question "What shall I do?", Christian faith has but a single answer: "You shall love the Lord your God with all your heart, and with all your soul, and with all your strength, and you shall love your neighbor as yourself!"

This Christian command of love is not a program, nor an ethical theory, nor a principle, from which individual moral demands that have universal validity could be developed. On the contrary, any such undertaking would only obscure what is at stake. The Christian command of love keeps directing me to my particular moment, so that I as one who loves can hear the claim of the "You" who confronts me, and can discover, as one who loves, what I have to do. If one still wants a rule, it can be very simply given by reference to the Ten Commandments. For everything they say is, according to the word of Paul (Rom. 13:9), summed up in the one word, "You shall love your neighbor as yourself". And whoever expects something more or greater may be reminded of that dialogue between father and son in Dostoyevsky's *A Raw Youth*. In the face of the frightening prospect of a world catastrophe the son asks:

"Yes, but then what is one to do?"

"Oh, God, don't be in such a hurry; it won't all happen so soon. But, generally, nothing is to be done, that's the best. At least one then has an easy conscience and can tell oneself he hasn't gotten involved."

"Enough! Stick to the subject. I want to know what I really should do, and how I should live."

"What you should do, my dear boy? Be honest, don't tell lies, don't covet your neighbor's house, in a word, read the Ten Commandments — it's all written down there once and for all."

"Cut it out, cut it out! That's all so old, and besides, it's mere words. What's needed here is some action!"

"Well, if boredom's too much for you, then try to win the love of somebody or something, or, simply put your heart into something."

"You're making fun of me! Besides, how can I start with just the Ten Commandments alone?"

"Merely carry them out, in spite of all your questions and doubts, and you will be a great man."

Only one who tries to live by the simple Ten Commandments, who takes the command to love seriously, will understand Christian faith, its crisis, and the overcoming of that crisis. *The Crisis of Faith*, trans. Edward Hobbs.

*

"THE QUESTION OF WONDER"

*Bultmann uses the term "wonder" (*Wunder*) in this essay as an alternative to "miracle". For him, "miracle" distorts the recognition of God's action by claiming that certain events can be seen and proven to be caused exclusively by an action of God. Such violations of the laws of nature, in his judgment, belonged to an ancient world view (Weltbild) and are no longer credible in the modern era. In contrast, wonder is an event which appears objectively and visibly to be consistent with known natural laws but, at the same time, is perceived by faith to be an act of God. There is also an existential difference between wonder and miracle. The concept of miracle grows out of our work world in which we seek ever greater knowledge and control of our surroundings, in which we think in terms of objective categories, clear perceptions and casual relationships. The concept of wonder, in contrast, reflects our historical experience as selves in which we find ourselves surprised by acts like love or friendship. Bultmann will repeatedly distinguish between the world of work, with its expectations of winning security through knowledge and control, and existential relationships, characterized by a confidence and trust called forth by others. For him, genuine faith in God is existential, not an achievement of our work. The essay was first published in *Glauben und Verstehen, I (1933). This translation is by Louise Pettibone Smith from* Faith and Understanding *(1963).*

The concept of *wonder* is understood in two ways. (1) A wonder is an act of God (of deity, of gods) as distinct from an occurrence which is the result of natural causes or of human will and effort. (2) A wonder is an amazing event contrary to nature (*contra naturam*) — "nature" connoting the regular orderly sequence of natural events.

In either sense, the idea of wonder can be further extended. On the basis of a wrongly understood idea of omnipotence, all that happens in the world is interpreted as God's action and thus the difference between the regular sequence of world events and God's action vanishes. Or, on the other hand, a wonder is equated with a supernatural event, or an event contrary to nature which is indeed ascribed to God but in a way which represents God merely as a supernatural causal agent and which precludes any real understanding of the event itself as an act of God. What one has is simply the idea of a *miracle*. In theological discussion these concepts are often set against one another; actually when applied to the idea of wonder they are closely inter-connected.

I. THE ABOLITION OF THE IDEA OF MIRACLE

The idea of wonder as miracle has become almost impossible for us today because we understand the processes of nature as governed by law. Wonder, as miracle, is therefore a violation of the conformity to law which governs all nature, and for us today this idea is no longer tenable. It is untenable, not because such an event would contradict all experience, but because the conformity to law which is a part of our conception of nature does not require proof but is presupposed as axiomatic, and because we cannot free ourselves from that presupposition at will.

The idea of conformity to law, the idea of "Nature", underlies explicitly or implicitly all of our ideas and actions which relate to this world. This conception is not "an interpretation of the world", "a judgment about the world", "a *Weltanschauung*"; it is not a conclusion about the world, either subjective or based on a conscious decision. It is *given in our existence in the world*.[94] We act always in reliance on a sequence of world events conforming to law. When we are acting responsibly we do not reckon on the possibility that God may suspend the law of gravity or the like. "The mere resolve to work includes the notion that the things on which we work will in their origin and activity obey laws which our thinking can comprehend."[95] Our intercourse with other men, when we show them something, ask them to do something, etc., takes for granted this conception of general conformity to natural law. We recognize as real in the world only what can be set in this context of the rule of law;

and we judge assertions which cannot be accommodated to this conception as fantasies.[96]

The notion of the universal validity of natural law, of nature's conformity to law, did not arise for the first time in modern science. It is a very primitive idea indeed, for it is a part of human existence. It is revealed in the fact that at the primitive stage, the concept of causality was applied also to wonder. Wonder was merely assigned to a causality different from that which produced the everyday events which man can control and which he puts to his own use for his living. Wonder depends on a causality which man — at least in the beginning — does not know. But the idea of two causalities, different in kind, working concurrently, is not really conceivable and indeed was not held. Rather, when divine action is believed to issue in a higher causality, God is thought of simply as a man who knows more and can do more than other men. If other men can just imitate the method (as, for example, a magician does), they can do the same.

The result of further cultural development is, of course, that more and more events which at first seemed supernatural are understood as conforming to law. The notion of universal conformity to law, which was implicitly present in the idea of everyday regularity, is developed more radically. In this way the idea of miracle becomes that of an occurrence contrary to natural law. At the same time, however, the impossibility of accepting such a miraculous event as real becomes increasingly clear.

The idea of miracle has, therefore, become untenable and *it must be abandoned.* But its abandonment is also required because in itself, it is not a notion of faith but a purely intellectual notion. As is well known, miracles can help or harm, can be desired or feared. As there is black and white magic, so also wonders can be done either by Satan or by God, by wizards or by prophets. The "higher" causality can be divine or demonic. And no specific miracle carries a label telling whether it proceeds from God or from the devil. One must know God beforehand, before the miracle happens, in order to be certain; one must have a criterion beforehand, in order to know whether a wonder comes from God or not. But to say that is to admit that understanding a wonder as a miracle is to abandon the idea of God's action as an inherent element in miracle.

Hence the Christian faith is apparently not concerned with miracles; rather it has cause to exclude the idea of miracle. No argument to the contrary can be based on the fact that *in the Bible* events are certainly

recorded which must be called *miracles*. That fact merely makes necessary the use of critical methods which show that the biblical writers, in
accordance with the presuppositions of their thinking, had not fully
apprehended the idea of miracle and its implications. The authority of
Scripture is not abandoned when the idea of miracle is relinquished.
The real meaning of Scripture can be rightly seen only after the idea of
wonder as God's action has been made clear.

II. ABOLITION OF THE OUTWORN CONCEPTION OF WONDER

There is now a different problem to consider. Faith is unquestionably
concerned with wonder, since "wonder" means God's action in distinction to the sequence of events in the natural world. The question therefore arises, *whether this concept of wonder does not involve miracle* and
whether if the concept of miracle is abandoned the concept of wonder is
not lost also. To guard against this loss is certainly the motive for refusing to discard miracles. One thing was accomplished with the concept
of miracle; it served to denote specifically an event which is not a part of
the natural world-process and thus apparently fits the requirement of
the concept of wonder. Can that concept be retained if the idea of
miracle is abandoned?

When the idea of miracle is given up, the procedure favored today is
also to abandon the definition of wonder as an action of God consum-
mated contrary to the natural sequence of world events and to assert,
with a reference to the belief in creation, that *everything that happens in the
world is a wonder*. "Wonder" then becomes "the religious designation for
event" (Schleiermacher). "This religious concept of wonder has nothing to do with contradiction of natural law. For it, the laws of nature are
the forms and instruments used in the fulfillment of God's works."[97]
This idea is suspiciously close to the Roman Catholic teaching according to which God, as the First Cause (*prima causa*), can use secondary
causes at his pleasure. But the conception is no longer tenable for anyone who has radically thought through the idea of nature and its conformity to law. If the specific character of the conception of wonder is that it
is God's action as distinct from natural world events, and if we can think
of that sequence only as governed by law, then *the idea of wonder contradicts nature absolutely* and I eliminate the idea of nature if I talk of wonder.

The *idea of creation* does not help at all, since that idea also eliminates
the notion of nature, as conforming to law. For in such a conception, the
world process is without spatial or temporal limit; but the idea of crea-

tion includes a beginning and an end. Therefore if one tries to apply the ideas of creation and wonder to the unending, law-conforming process which we call nature, the whole idea of wonder becomes meaningless. If all that happens is wonderful, then there is nothing further; God and world are equated. God, creation and wonder are then only edifying names for the factual complex of events which I confront concretely in my actual life, and with which I deal as parts of the scientifically discoverable, unending sequence of all happening, as nature and as natural events.

In such pantheistic dissolution of the idea of wonder there is a double error:

1. *The idea of creation and omnipotence is not an axiom of science,* under which the whole world process can be subsumed. It is not an intelligible, generally valid assertion which is discovered or perhaps believed and then held as proved. As an idea of faith, it is to be distinguished from a scientific idea, not because it is attained in an astonishing or non-rational way; that is, it is not differentiated by its origin (so far as origin is understood as a cause and therefore as a fact of the past); but because it can never be held as proven and applied like a scientific idea. It must always be won afresh; it can never be separated from its origin which is always present in it. It always is true only as it arises. But that means that I cannot achieve the idea apart from my own existence; I cannot understand or "interpret" something outside myself as creation of God or act of God. When I so speak, I am primarily saying something about myself.

But I am not saying something about myself as seen from the outside as an objective entity in the world. I am speaking only of my concrete existence here and now. I can speak of God's act of creation only if I know myself as a creature of God. And to see myself in this way involves, for example — since God's creation is good — seeing myself as good, as without sin. But that I can obviously never do at any time; and certainly that is not the way I act. Rather, I act habitually as if I were myself a creator. In my everyday work, in the use of my time, etc., I regard the world as at my own disposal. The world and my action in it are godless throughout. I can perhaps say that I *ought* to see the whole world as God's creation, that every event or act *ought* to be a wonder. But as actual fact, I do not find myself in a position to make that assertion.

2. The second error now becomes plain. The *idea of the world* is also mistaken. For if "wonder" means God's action in contradiction to the world-process which includes my own acts, then a specific understanding of the world is affirmed in it. World must then mean primarily not

nature, not the law-governed complex of all that happens, but the specific reality in which I live and act, *my* world. The thought of God and his action is primarily related to my life, to my existence, to the knowledge that this existence is godless, since I do not find God in it and cannot see him. He declares that I can only see him if he shows himself to me through his deed and that I have no right to speak of him at my own will and to explain whatever event I like as his action.

III. WONDER AS GOD'S ACTION

1. *Its Hiddenness*

First of all, it is now clear that faith is directed to wonder as an action of God which is different from the world process; faith can be established only through wonder; in truth, *faith in God and faith in the wonder are essentially the same.*

Therefore, just as every pantheistic concept of wonder is excluded, so also is every dogmatic concept. For example, considerations like the following are inadmissible: from the belief in God's omnipotence, it follows that he can do wonders. For since I have faith in God's omnipotence only through faith in wonder, I cannot use the omnipotence as apologetic to justify the belief in wonder. I can, of course, have the *idea* of the omnipotence of God, that is, I can depict God to myself as an omnipotent being (the godless can do that also). But in so doing, I do not yet have *God*, the Omnipotent — for I cannot have him otherwise than in wonder.

One certainty in regard to the concept of wonder is now attained. In no sense whatever is wonder as wonder an observable event in the world, not in any place nor at any time. To claim an event as an observable wonder would be to separate it from God and understand it as world. God is not provable by observation. *Wonder is hidden as wonder,* hidden from him who does not see God in it. Therefore it is also clear (1) that the wonder of which faith speaks cannot be a miracle, for a miracle is an observable event; and (2) that wonder is not the basis of faith in the sense that as an observable event it leads to the conclusion that the invisible God exists. For then God's hiddenness would be conceived in terms of the invisiblity of a natural force (something like electricity); God would be thought of as world. Faith can testify only to that on which it believes, never to something else because of which it believes.

But if the question of whether I see a wonder is identical with the question of whether I have faith — if, that is to say, it is the question of whether I will to have faith, will to see a wonder, and is therefore a question requiring immediate decision — then it is clear that *the hiddenness of the wonder as wonder counterpoises its visibility as a world event.* That is, the assertion that an event is a wonder is an express contradiction of the affirmation of it as a world event.[98] Faith is faith as opposed to sight; it is faith expressly contradicting all that I see. So, too, faith in wonder must mean the contradiction of all that I see in the world.

Since faith has this character because I am by nature godless, the impossibility of seeing world events as wonders must obviously have its cause in my godlessness. My inability to see world events as wonders has been developed and formulated in the *idea of nature* as a sequence governed by law; therefore this idea must obviously be adjudged *godless*. But that does not mean that I simply abandon it. I cannot do that. It merely becomes clear to me that godlessness is not something which man can discard by a strong act of will; on the contrary, godlessness is a mode of my being, my existence is determined by sin.

I understand very well what wonder means: God's action. I understand also that in the sequence of events in the world God's wonders ought to be visible to me. But I know that I do not see them. For the world appears to me as nature, conforming to law, and I cannot free myself from that view of it by deciding that it ought to look otherwise. And I must beware of inducing in myself the feeling that I could see it differently.

2. *The Reality of Wonder*

The *hiddenness of God* does not mean invisibility in general. It does not mean primarily that God is inaccessible to the senses, or to experiment. It means that he is hidden from *me*. No statement is being made about deity in general, about the nature of deity; no statements of a kind I could make without speaking of myself. Equally, to speak of wonder does not mean to speak of wonders in general and to discuss their possibility. To speak of wonder means to speak of my own existence; it means to declare that in my life God has become visible. Therefore it is to speak not about the universal visibility of God but about his revelation. If I see that God's hiddenness means that he is hidden *from me,* then I also see that his hiddenness means my godlessness and that I am a sinner. For he *ought* not to be hidden from me.

There is therefore only *one* wonder: the wonder of the *revelation,* the revelation of the grace of God for the godless, the revelation of forgiveness. But the forgiveness is understood strictly as *event;* it is not an *idea* of forgiveness, a *notion* of the grace of God as an attribute of the nature of God. Forgiveness is God's *act.* But this meaning needs to be more fully developed if it is to become clear: (1) that forgiveness is a wonder, in contradiction to the world process; and (2) what the reason is for the possibility of confusing wonder and miracle.

Why is asking for a *sign* characteristic of the Jews (I Cor. 1.22)? The reason is that in this desire the characteristic nature of their godlessness is so prominent — the seeking "their own righteousness". They estimate themselves by what they achieve and estimate others by what they achieve. And as they wish to certify themselves before God through their achievements, so God must certify himself to them through his achievement.

But that is basically the sin of the world in general: *to estimate itself and God by achievement and work.* Therefore, in so far as the world seeks God, miracle is an object of desire to the world; but *the* wonder, which does not have the character of a certifying achievement, is a stumbling-block. We have seen that the primitive notion of miracle fits into the understanding of the world as a working world in which we take for granted the regularity and the conformity to law of all that happens. Miracle is a violation of the law of this world, but it is thought of entirely in the terms of this world since it is a demonstrable achievement of God within it. But the concept of wonder radically negates the character of the world as the manageable world of everyday work. Wonder is not a demonstrable act of God; everyone is free to understand the event that is asserted to be a wonder as an occurrence which accords with natural law in the world.

Wonder confronts man with the critical question of how far he understands the world rightly when he understands it as the working world amenable to his control; how far he rightly understands himself when he estimates himself by his work and aims at making himself secure through his work. Thus the concept of wonder radically negates the character of the world as the controllable, working world, because it destroys man's understanding of himself as made secure through his work.

Our action can always be understood in two ways: as the production of something — that is, from the point of view of something which has been done; or as action now being done. Therefore we are also given two possible ways of understanding ourselves: *from what is done or from the doing.*

Our action, that is to say, occurs either as the fulfillment of the claim which confronts us, under which our *now* always stands — in which case the action is nothing but obedience; or it occurs so that something is produced or attained by it, and this something gives the action its meaning. If our act occurs as obedience, something is certainly produced or attained by it; the meaning of the act, however, does not lie in what is accomplished by it, but in the obedient doing of the act. In the same way, the meaning of a gift lies, not in the gift but in the act of giving.

When the latter understanding is really accepted, it includes the corollary that man, after he has acted, cannot remain with what he has done, stop at an attained goal and estimate himself by it. He can only say that as a servant he has done "only what was [his] duty" (Luke 17.10). He is not to look back on what he has done, but forward to what he still has to do. He must look forward, not because he wants to put this or that future task behind him and so looks in haste and anxiety; he looks forward simply in obedience.

If our action is action under the claim of God, then it is never completed. We produce no achievement after which we can stop, representing ourselves to ourselves as men who have in some sense finished their work. We must remain in the unremitting activity in which the claim of God sets us. This activity is the activity of *life*. No more than we are to look back should we keep looking forward to arrange a program for all that must still be done. For then we should be again estimating ourselves on the basis of what is done, is finished — even though the finishing is, of course, not yet accomplished. But all the same, we should be seeing ourselves as questioned about what has been finished, we should be estimating ourselves by what is accomplished. God's claim, however, brings us, not into the unrest of anxiety and care about something lying ahead of us which must be brought to completion; but to the unrest of life. It tears us loose from ourselves as we are, that is, from our past, and directs us to the future.

But since our action always does produce some effect, it carries within it the hidden temptation to estimate ourselves from what has been done and to attach ourselves to what has been done. In fact we are continually yielding to this temptation and so lapsing into the past — what is done is always past. When we estimate ourselves really from what is accomplished, though the accomplishment may be in the future, even our future action is already past, branded by sin and death. It confronts us actually as a work, as an established, attained position.[99] It is plain to us that we are all trapped in such an estimation of ourselves, since we all fear death. For this fear arises from the desire to keep ourselves as we are and the secret knowledge that we cannot do so.

We are all trapped in such an estimation of ourselves and we cannot by any exertion of our own free ourselves from this lapse into the past, into death. The freedom we are striving for would again by thought of as our own work, as the highest and best goal which we would win by our struggles. Such action would already belong to the past even before it was undertaken. Only if we could forget our own work, should we be free; only if we were acting solely from obedience.

The question is, therefore, how we can arrive at such obedience, at such true listening to God's claim. The question is really, *can* we so listen? Obviously we cannot simply make a resolution that we will hear; nor can we wait to find out whether we are hearing, for we are always already in the middle of some action through which we want to gain something. Every *now* to which we come is already distorted by the self-understanding we bring to it. Our past from which we come to the present moment always clings to us.

There is only one possible way to become free *from the past*, free for a true hearing of the claim which comes to us in the present moment; that freedom is given to us *through forgiveness*. For as temporal beings we cannot be free from the past in the sense that the past is simply canceled and ignored, that we receive something like a new nature — if we should receive it, we certainly could not keep ourselves in it. We always come to the present moment out of our past and bringing our past with us. For we are not plants, animals or machines; and our present is always qualified by our past. The critical question is whether our past is present in us as sinful or as forgiven. If the sin is forgiven, that means that we have freedom for the future; that we are really hearing God's claim and can yield ourselves to him as "his instruments" (Rom. 6.12ff.).

It has now become fully clear why *forgiveness* must be understood as *wonder* — that is, as God's action in contradiction to the world process. The world to which it stands in contradiction is our working world which lies at our disposal, in which from the beginning all action is understood as getting things done, as achievement; in which all that happens — even in the future — is always thought of in terms of the past. If God's forgiveness is a wonder, that is, if God in this wonder takes away our understanding of ourselves as achievers who as such are continually relapsing into the past, then simultaneously he has abolished the character of the world as the working world under our control.

Since in action something is always done, there is always the possibility of understanding all action as what has been done and all happening as what has happened. *For the eye of unbelief, God's action is also a world event which has happened.* And since the believer also knows that it can be so seen and that the possibility always exists for himself to see all that happens, he must when he speaks of God's action speak of it as a wonder which happens contrary to nature *(contra naturam).* He must say that when he speaks of a wonder he is nullifying the idea of conformity to natural law. But to apply the notions of wonder and of creation to the world understood as nature is senseless; for the world seen as past is not seen as creation. It preserves its character as creation only if we, as those who are forgiven, stand open to the future and can therefore see the world open before us as the field in which we are able to hear God's claim and to act under it.

To see the world in this way is *not* to have a "*world view*" [*Weltanschauung*]; it is not a theory about the world in general. The world is so seen only when the claim of God is heard on the basis of forgiveness. Hence the error of understanding ourselves and the world as past must be continually combated. This means that our "working ideas" in which we count the controllability of the world, that is, on its conformity to law, must always be limited by our "conceptions of faith". Furthermore, in our actual living, conceptions belonging to work and those belonging to faith are interchanged in such a way that the former are always delimited by the latter. For his working ideas, man needs the conception of nature. To what extent he must use it cannot be stated in general terms. He uses it in so far as he is required to use it in a specific task. If he lets it become his master, then the use becomes sin.

The *idea of miracle* is now understandable and so also is its amalgamation with the idea of wonder. Either, the idea is a despairing expression of the secret knowledge of relapse into the past; it has become impossible for man to understand the world as creation and to see God's action in it; when man speaks of God's action he can only conceive it on the analogy of the sequence of world events as a special achievement and he still remains wholly imprisoned in his old understanding of the world. Or, the conception of miracle is a primitive, unclear expression of the understanding that God's action is in contradiction to the world process, to all the activity of the world.

The *empty pantheistic concept of wonder*, too, is now understandable. The right motive is operative in it, the desire that faith be able to see the world as creation and to speak of ever new wonders because God's action can be seen in the world-process. But it is necessary to be on guard against the misunderstanding that the believer possesses a Christian world-view [*Weltanschauung*], which is at his disposal like a bill of exchange, so that he can now interpret all activity and every event as wonder. Faith must always be won afresh in the battle against the working conceptions which would corrupt it. Every wonder is visible only on the basis of the one wonder, forgiveness. But the wonder of forgiveness is not a fact of the past. I always have it only as a forgiveness just grasped. "It must always be believed" (*semper credendum*); the Christian always stands in "grace" (*gratia*).

But if that is so, then it is really possible for the Christian *continually to see new wonders*. This world process, which to the unbeliever must appear as a sequence of events governed by law, has for the Christian become a world in which God acts. And since he himself hears God's claim on him and acts in obedience, his own action is no longer a part of the world process; he is doing a wonder.

The reality of all wonder, therefore, depends on the relation of faith to the *one* wonder of forgiveness in Christ. It is then wrong to claim, apart from this relation of faith, a difference between the Christian and the pagan conception of wonder. Both can be primitive; both can be understood radically. Both can cling to miracle and in both the idea of God's action can be consistently developed. The difference between Christianity and paganism does not lie in a different idea of wonder — no more than it lies in a different idea of God. The difference is that Christianity speaks of the real God because it can speak of the real wonder.

IV. THE WONDERS OF THE NEW TESTAMENT

In the New Testament, wonders are recorded which have the characters of miracles — particularly wonders of Jesus. In so far as these are acts of Jesus (healing of the sick, etc.), they are acts which were important events for those immediately concerned. Even if all of them were historically verified (or so far as they are so verified), it is still true that as deeds of a man in the past they do not directly concern us. Seen as such they are not works of the Christ, if we understand by the work of Christ the work of redemption.[100]

Therefore, in any discussion, the "wonders of Jesus" are entirely open to critical investigation. It should be most strongly emphasized that Christian faith is not concerned with proving the possibility or the actuality of the wonders of Jesus as events of the past. On the contrary, such concern would be wrong.

If Christ is present for us as the preached Christ, then the wonders of Jesus are relevant only in so far as they are a part of that preaching, that is, as witnesses. And they are witnesses which reveal the whole *ambiguity of the Christian preaching.* They show that the wonders definitely are not to be understood as demonstrable events which provide a basis for faith, for every one is left free to explain them by a causality understandable to him. They are not secured against being explained as demonic activities (Mark 3.22) or as achievements by which Jesus guaranteed himself (Mark 8.11f.), on the basis of which the people want to make him king (John 6.14ff.), or as a means to be used in the service of individual lives (John 6.26). They therefore carry the same ambiguity as the wonder of Christ himself. For Jesus Christ is to the unbeliever a demonstrable fact of the past, historically involved in a specific situation of the past and historically comprehensible.

The question is simply whether we will to see him as a fact of the past, as an historical figure, as a personality or something of the sort; or to see him as the wonder of God, that is, to see him as the One who is here for us now as the Word of forgiveness spoken by God. There is always the temptation to transform his presence now into an objective presence in the past. Continually, the stumbling-block of the "was made flesh" must be overcome. Anyone who chooses to affirm God's revelation in the historical personality of Jesus lays himself open to Kierkegaard's taunt that he is smarter than God himself, who sent his Son in the *hiddenness* of the flesh. To apply the conception of revelation to the historically demonstrable personality of Jesus is as senseless as to apply the conception of creation and of wonder to the world seen as nature.

But the wonders of Jesus are also witnesses giving *evidence that the Christian faith in God is neither pantheism nor monism;* that it has no right to speak of God's act whenever it pleases, but can so speak only when it perceives God's action in the single concrete case. Christian faith in God is not a [general] world view. It is always won in the moment, and it says, "Lord, I believe, help my unbelief" (Mark 9.24). Therefore it is not a faith which consists in a man's spiritual attitude. It is always and only faith in God who does not stand, as does an entity in the world, available to the observation of men at their pleasure. It is faith in the God who is seen only when he wills to reveal himself.

Therefore doubt of God which asks for a criterion by which God can be demonstrated must be cast aside. Man must be led to *that* doubt in which he doubts himself. That is, he must come to doubt whether he can exercise control over himself and the world. He must despair.

Faith and Understanding, pp. 247-261.

*

"THE TASK OF THEOLOGY IN THE PRESENT SITUATION"

Bultmann's critique of modernity was not confined to the pretensions of a scientific-technological culture. As a German citizen and churchman he also experienced modernity in the form of the Nazi state, both its impressive economic and technological achievements and its destruction of whole human communities. "The Task of Theology in the Present Situation" is Bultmann's first lecture of the summer semester, 2 May 1933. On 30 January 1933 Adolf Hitler and the National Socialist Party had taken power in Berlin. On 27 February of that same year, the Reichstag (parliament building) was burned, providing a pretext for suppressing the political opposition and the press. By March, the "Law for the Reorganization of the Civil Service" was implemented to dismiss or transfer faculty who were not politically loyal to the state. By 25 April, an unknown naval chaplain was given full powers in church affairs by Hitler. This is the political context in which Bultmann gives this lecture. He reminds his students that "I have never spoken in my lectures about the politics of the day" and then cautions them against the dangers of the new political order and their own enthusiasm. In particular, he warns against the new spirit of denunciation which can only increase mistrust among all people and he deplores the injustice already instigated against German Jews by the defamation of their character. "Die Aufgabe der Theologie in der gegenwärtigen Situation" was published in the theological journal, Theologische Blätter *(1933). Schubert Ogden did this English translation for* Existence and Faith *(1960).*

Ladies and gentlemen! I have made a point never to speak about current politics in my lectures, and I think I also shall not do so in the future. However, it would seem to me unnatural were I to ignore today the political situation in which we begin this new semester. The significance of political happenings for our entire existence has been brought home to us in such a way that we cannot evade the duty of reflecting on the meaning of our theological work in this situation.

It should be emphasized, however, that what is at issue here is not the defense of a *political* point of view; nor can our purpose be either to repeat the "happy yes" to political events that is spoken all too quickly today or — depending on how we stand with respect to these events — to give voice to a sceptical or resentful criticism. Rather we must look at these events simply from the standpoint of their immense possibilities for the future and ask ourselves what our responsibility is *as theologians* in face of these possibilities.

Since, as theologians in the service of the church, we have to develop the basis and meaning of Christian faith for our generation, the first thing we must do is to reflect on what is in principle the relation of faith to nation and state, or the relation between the life of faith and the political order. This relation is determined by faith's being directed to the God who is Creator and Judge of the world and its Redeemer in Jesus Christ. This means that the relation of God to the world and therefore of faith to life in the world, and thus to political life, is a peculiarly two-sided one.

God is the *Creator;* i.e., the world is *his;* it is *his* gift that encounters us in the world in which we stand, in its goods and tasks, in its beneficient and frightening phenomena, in the events that make us both rich and poor. God is the Creator; this means that he is not the cause ($\alpha\iota\tau\iota\alpha$) to which thought refers the world, or the source ($\dot\alpha\varrho\chi\dot\eta$) in terms of which the happenings in the world can be grapsed in their unity and lawfulness by the understanding. Rather that God is the Creator means that he encounters us as Lord in our concrete world, in the world that is determined historically, in our actual life in the present. Faith in the Creator is not a philosophical theory or a world-view that one has in the background of his concrete experience and action, but rather is something that we are to realize precisely *in* our experience and action as obedience to our Lord. That God is the Creator means that man's action is not determined by timeless principles, but rather by the concrete situation of the moment.

This situation acquires its concreteness by means of a variety of factors. Included among them are what we speak of as the "ordinances of creation". By means of such ordinances we are not men in general who have to cultivate their humanity, but rather are this man or that man who belongs to this people or to that; we are male or female, parent or child, young or old, strong or weak, clever or dumb, etc. Also included in such ordinances of creation is our nationality and the political ordinance of the state, in which alone nationality can become the object of our concern and action. We do not need to reflect here on the place that nation and state occupy in the order of priority of the claims that encounter us; nor do we need to ask whether it even has meaning to speak of an order of priority here or whether such ordering of claims is precisely a question that can only be decided in the concrete moment. For the present it suffices to recognize that faith in God and nationality stand in a positive relation, insofar as God has placed us in our nation and state. It suffices to understand — in the words of F. K. Schumann — that "nationality means being subject to an original claim; that to stand in a nation or to be a member of a nation means to share a common destiny, to subject oneself to the claim of the past, to let one's own existence be determined by others, to be responsible for a common future, to receive oneself from others and thus also to be able to sacrifice oneself in return." It suffices to know that faith in God the Creator demands this of us.

But with this not everything has yet been said. For God is the *Creator*, i.e., he is not immanent in the ordinances of the world, and nothing that encounters us as a phenomenon within the world is *directly* divine. God stands beyond the world. Therefore, however much faith understands the world as his creation, indeed, precisely *because* it understands the world as his creation, it acquires a peculiar relation of distance to the world — the relation, namely, to which Paul refers by the peculiar phrase ὡς μή:

> I mean, brethren, the appointed time has grown very short. From now on, let those who have wives live as though they had none, and those who mourn as though they were not mourning, and those who rejoice as though they were not rejoicing, and those who buy as though they had no goods, and those who deal with the world as though they had no dealings with it. For the form of this world is passing away (I Cor. 7:29-31).

This does not mean that faith has a negative relation to the world, but rather that the positive relation that it has to it and to its ordinances is a *critical* one. For faith knows that God the Creator is also the Judge of the world. It knows that men always forget that the world's goods and ordinances summon man to service, point him to his tasks, and are not given for his possession and gratification. It knows that human striving, both individual and collective, is always directed toward disposing of the world and contriving security for the self. It knows that man forgets his creatureliness and wills to understand himself as the lord of his life. And through such sinful perversion of man's own self-understanding the ordinances of creation also become ordinances of sin, and, to be sure, all the more so, the more man veils the sinful tendency of his will and looks upon the ordinances in which he is placed as though they were directly divine. Everything, possessions and family, education and law, nation and state, can become sin at man's hands; i.e., it can become a means for pursuing his own interests and disposing of his existence.

Therefore, all of the ordinances in which we find ourselves are *ambiguous.* They are *God's* ordinances, but only insofar as they call us to service in our concrete tasks. In their mere givenness, they are ordinances of *sin.*

In order to make this clear I need only remind you how different are the positions of the Old Testament prophets and Jesus with respect to justice. In an age that imagined it satisfied its duty to God by pompously carrying on the cult and that permitted unrestrained self-will to rule the common life, the prophets proclaimed the demand for justice and righteousness as the demand of God. For justice puts a check upon man's self-will. Think, for example, of some of the laws to which Jesus makes reference in the Sermon on the Mount. The law regulating divorce insures the wife against the arbitrariness of the husband, in that it places the latter under certain limits of justice. The *jus talionis* ("an eye for an eye, a tooth for a tooth") limits the thirst for revenge to an extent that is bearable for political life. Likewise, the commandment "You shall love your neighbor and hate your enemy" puts a check on the blind hate that sees the enemy in every adversary, and gives legal recognition to the concept of the "neighbor". On the other hand, Jesus' own "But I say to you" opens our eyes to how human sin turns justice to its own ends, how the restraints of justice are interpreted as concessions: "I *may* divorce my wife", "I *may* seek revenge", "I *may* hate" — in short, by preserving a formal legality I can at the same time leave room for my self-will. Thus Jesus protests against ordinances of justice that have become ordinances of sin. Everyone who dismisses his wife is an adulterer! If anyone strikes you on the right cheek, turn to him the other also! Love your enemies!

This does not mean that Jesus demands anarchism; for his protest is against ordinances of justice only insofar as they have become ordinances of sin. A life of justice that is determined by the thought of service and fulfills the original purpose of justice to bind man to his fellow men is not touched by his polemic. On the contrary, he affirms that God demands justice and righteousness.

The situation is such, however, that every ordinance of justice has the double possibility of being placed either in the service of sin or in the service of God. All ordinances are ambiguous, and our understanding of the ordinances in which we find ourselves is always already conditioned by the history out of which we come. And all our human history is likewise ambiguous. At one and the same time it presents us with a great inheritance of possibilities for free and noble action *and* temptations to act slavishly and meanly. All history conceals within itself both deeds of heroism and sacrificial courage *and* the war of all against all. All history is infected with sin, and from the beginning every human action is guided by that sinful self-understanding in which man wills to pursue his own interests and to dispose of his existence. Consequently, the power for every great and good deed must be acquired by overcoming the self. No state and no nation is so unambiguous an entity, is so free from sin, that the will of God can be read off unambiguously from its bare existence. No nation is so pure and clean that one may explain every stirring of the national will as a direct demand of God. As nature and all our personal relations with one another have become uncanny as a result of sin, so also has nationality. From it emerge deeds of beauty and nobility; but there also breaks out of it the demonry of sin. Every state and every nation bears within itself not only the possibilities and tasks of the good and the beautiful, but also the temptations to the evil and the mean.

In a day when the nation has again been generally recognized as an ordinance of creation, the Christian faith has to prove its critical power precisely by continuing to insist that the nation is ambiguous and that, just for the sake of obedience to the nation as an ordinance of creation, the question must continue to be asked what is and what is not the nation's true demand. Indeed, precisely in this time of crisis we are sensible that we must once again seek and find the true meaning of possessions and the family, the true ordinance with respect to the sexes and age levels, and the true meaning of authority and education. And so also it is necessary to ask what is the true and normative meaning of the nation. To be sure, there is given to man an original knowledge of such matters, which we can speak of as an "instinct" of nationality. However, in this instance, as everywhere else, this original instinct is obstructed and spoiled, warped and distorted by the history of sin out of which we come.

Christian faith must be a critical power in the present discussion, and it must prove its essentially *positive* character precisely in its *critical* stance. How can it do this? Well, it can do it because it knows not only about sin, but also about *grace* — because it knows God not only as the Judge, but also as the Redeemer, who through Jesus Christ restores his original creation. Redemption through Jesus Christ means the forgiveness of sins through the revelation of the love of God, and therefore also means the freeing of man to love in return.

Only he who knows the transcendent God who speaks his word of love to the world in Christ is able to extricate himself from this sinful world and to achieve a perspective from which the world's ordinances can really be known as ordinances of creation — i.e., ordinances for which he must gratefully rejoice and in which he must silently suffer and serve as one who loves. He alone has a critical perspective over against the loud demands of the day, in that he measures the good and evil in such demands by asking whether and to what extent they serve the command of love. And he alone has a critical perspective with respect to himself, which enables him to ask whether his own action is really selfless service.

Such a critical perspective will never permit the struggle for state and nation to become a struggle for *abstractions*. For we may never overlook that state and nation are made up of concrete human beings who are our neighbors. Like humanity, nationality is always in danger of losing its concreteness and becoming a mere abstraction. Is our present struggle on behalf of the ideal of nationality a struggle for an abstraction or for something concrete? The criterion for each one of us is whether, in his struggle, he is really sustained by love, i.e., by the love that not only looks to the future in which it hopes to realize its ideal, but also sees the concrete neighbor to whom we are now bound in the present by all the common-place ties of life. To be sure, every struggle involves severity and demands sacrifice. But the right to demand sacrifice and to exercise severity belongs only to him who sees his neighbor in those who are affected by what he does! He alone will discover the kind and manner and also the limit of his action. The only man who can truly serve his nation is he who has been freed to love by receiving the love of God in Christ.

Ladies and gentlemen! There cannot be the slightest doubt that this is the meaning and the demand of the Christian faith, and that these are the thoughts that the theologian has to advocate. For what I have said is simply taken from the thoughts of the New Testament and the Reformers. Thus while it may be comforting or disturbing, this is in any event the way it is; and it is not my task to expound how we might wish things to be, but only how they actually are, according to the teaching of the church.

We have attempted in face of the immense possibilities that are now open to us to understand our responsibility as it becomes clear to us through the critical power of the Christian faith. We must not close our eyes to the fact that with these possibilities we are also presented with temptations; indeed, it is precisely our duty as theologians to point this out, so that the joy over the new situation will be pure and the faith in the new possibilities, honorable.

Will we preserve the power of our critical perspective and not succumb to the temptations, so that we may work together for Germany's future with clean hands and believe in this future honorably? Must I point out that in this critical hour the demonry of sin also lies in wait? "We want to abolish lies!" — so runs a great and beautiful slogan from the recent demonstration of German students. But it also belongs to lying to hide the truth from oneself. And I want to show quite openly by referring to three examples what our responsibility is as protagonists of the new Germany in face of these temptations. The examples are "the advance laurels", the practice of denunciation, and the use of defamation as a means for winning the struggle.

The first example is comparatively harmless. If Adolf Hitler, in a very gratifying decree, exhorted us not to change the old names of streets and squares, then the new Marburg town council should be ashamed of itself that, at its first session, it could find no more urgent a duty in the new situation than to give new names to some of our streets and squares. Indeed, the matter is not nearly as harmless as it may first appear. For by means of such a process of awarding laurels in advance one feeds a peculiar feeling of security that is not to be confused with "faith" in the future. Faith involves *seriousness,* and seriousness knows what Hitler again emphasized in his speech yesterday, that we are only at the beginning and that infinitely much is still required of us in the way of patient work and a willingness to sacrifice. And I hardly need to point out how quickly such light-minded security will turn to disillusionment when our leaders demand sacrifice. As over against this temptation of light-mindedness we have to emphasize the seriousness of the task.

The second example is much worse, and the government's repeated demonstrations against the practice of denunciation is sufficient evidence of the danger that lurks here. I happen to know, for example, that the Minister of Religious Affairs receives daily baskets full of denunciations; happily, I also know that these find their well-deserved places in the waste basket! But the issue here is not only the eventual result of the denunciations; rather the worst of it is that such a practice of informing against others poisons the atmosphere, establishes mistrust between fellow countrymen, and suppresses a man's free and honest word. "We want to abolish lies" — fine, but it also belongs to this that one respects the free word, even when it expresses something other than what he wishes to hear. Otherwise one educates men to lie.

This already brings us to the third example. The defamation of a person who thinks differently from you is not a noble means for winning a struggle. And once again I may appeal to a statement of Hitler, that those who think differently should not be suppressed, but rather won over. By defamation one does not convince his adversaries and win them to his point of view, but merely repulses the best of them. One really wins only by a struggle of the *spirit* in which he respects his adversary. As a Christian, I must deplore the injustice that is also being done precisely to German Jews by means of such defamation. I am well aware of the complicated character of the Jewish problem in Germany. But, "We want to abolish lies!" — and so I must say in all honesty that the defamation of the Jews that took place in the very demonstration that gave rise to this beautiful sentiment was not sustained by the spirit of love. Keep the struggle for the German nation pure, and take care that noble intentions to serve truth and country are not marred by demonic distortions!

But there is yet this final word. If we have correctly understood the meaning and the demand of the Christian faith, then it is quite clear that, *in face of the voices of the present, this Christian faith itself is being called in question*. In other words, it is clear that we have to decide whether Christian faith is to be valid for us or not. It, for its part, can relinquish nothing of its nature and claim; for *"verbum Domini manet in aeternum"*. And we should as scrupulously guard ourselves against falsifications of the faith by national religiosity as against a falsification of national piety by Christian trimmings. The issue is either/or!

The brief words of this hour can only remind us of this decision. But the work of the semester will again and again bring the question to our attention and clarify it in such a way that the requisite decision can be clearly and conscientiously made. *Existence and Faith*, pp. 158-165.

*

"SERMON ON MATTHEW 6:25-33"

While Rudolf Bultmann was not an ordained minister, he did understand preaching to be a continuing responsibility as a Christian layman and Professor of Theology. At the time of his death on 30 July 1976, he left over one hundred and twenty-five different sermon manuscripts which he had preached during a period of more than fifty years, from his earliest in 1906 to the latest in March 1959 in Syracuse NY. This sermon is from a 1956 collection of twenty-one Marburg sermons. In it Bultmann weaves together New Testament themes and existentialist concepts in a critique of the middle-class work ethos. He links the theme of anxiety, as developed by Heidegger — the unnamed "philosopher of our day" — with the words of Jesus, "do not be anxious". While he, like Heidegger, recognizes anxious care as a fundamental fact of life, manifest most obviously in our efforts to provide for our future through our work, faith commends a way of working not driven by anxiety. Harold Knight translated this sermon for the English volume, This World and the Beyond.

"Therefore I tell you, do not be anxious about your life, what you shall eat or what you shall drink, nor about your body, what you shall put on. Is not life more than food, and the body more than clothing? Look at the birds of the air: they neither sow nor reap nor gather into barns, and yet your heavenly Father feeds them. Are you not of more value than they? And which of you by being anxious can add one cubit to his span of life [*marginal note*, to his stature]? And why are you anxious about clothing? Consider the lilies of the field, how they grow; they neither toil nor spin; yet I tell you, even Solomon in all his glory was not arrayed like one of these. But if God so clothes the grass of the field, which today is alive and tomorrow is thrown into the oven, will he not much more clothe you, O men of little faith? Therefore do not be anxious, saying, "What shall we eat?" or "What shall we drink?" or "What shall we wear?" For the Gentiles seek all these things; and your heavenly Father knows that you need them all. But seek first his kingdom and his righteousness, and all these things shall be yours as well."

The text exhorts us thus: "Do not be anxious!"

I have chosen this text because the time in which we live is full of care and anxiety; but also because this text is difficult to understand. To some it is puzzling and offensive and to others it is even an occasion for mockery.

I

Such an exhortation sounds strange and perplexing. For it seems inevitable that human life should be full of care, should be motivated by anxieties of one sort or another, to such an extent in fact that a philosopher of our day has gone so far as to describe care as the fundamental temper of human life. Man is indeed a creature immersed in time; his present is ever confronted by a future and is accordingly always inspired by the question: What will the future bring? This is not always a question of arousing joyful expectation; it is often one of distressing anxiety. Shall we pull through? our nation asks. Will my work by successful? This we ask when heavy duties lie upon us. Will my toil bear fruit? So asks the man who has to maintain himself and his family. Will the loved one about whom I am worrying be preserved for me? So we ask when the life of one we love is in danger. I suppose everyone knows the anxiety which robs our nights of sleep.

And not only so. Does not the future demand of us — even at times when the skies are brighter for us — that we should be anxious for the morrow? that we should be concerned about our food and drink, and as to how we shall be clothed? Unceasing care about ourselves and those we love!

Hence how can Jesus exhort us: "Do not be anxious"? Of course we should like very much to be able to follow that advice. We should like very much to be without a care in the world. As every man is urged by anxiety, so everyone knows the desire for a carefree life. In legend and fairy tale a fanciful imagination has always delighted to depict a wonderland in which no one needs to care any longer about sordid and material things.

For everyone feels how care, which directs our attention from the present to the future, impoverishes and devalues the present moment; how through care the center of gravity of our life is transferred to something which has not yet sprung into existence, which may not be tomorrow or the day after, and which for ever eludes us until the "last syllable of recorded time". Hence Goethe makes "Care" address Faust thus:

"Whom I make my own with loathing,
Counts the whole wide world as nothing.
His eternal gloom surpriseth,
With each outer sense excelling,
In his breast hath darkness dwelling.
He may not by any measures,
Make him lord of all his treasures.

God and ill become caprices,
Him midst fullness famine seizes;
Puts him off unto the morrow,
On the future ever waiteth,
So that naught he consummateth."

Of course care does not dominate every personality to the same degree, nor does it influence us equally at all times. There are "happy natures" which do not allow themselves to be assailed by anxiety; and no doubt we all have moments when we are able to forget our worries. Yes, just that: forget! Hence fundamentally they are still there! And is it not more honest not to banish them from our minds, but to look them straight in the face and to refuse to foster illusions about the realities of life? And if we cannot sustain this effort constantly but need hours of forgetfulness and refreshment — do we not need them precisely in order to strengthen ourselves that we may once more shoulder the burden of the cares which are waiting for us? And if we blame a man as being frivolous when he blinds himself to the future and its cares, do we not by implication recognize that care is an integral part of the genuinely human life?

Of human life! For we are not plants and animals which do not need to care like ourselves about food and clothing: which do not, like us, have to face the future clear-eyed, but live and grow according to natural instinct: which do not have to bear like us responsibility for others, anxiety and toil for others. Hence, how can Jesus exhort us: "Look at the birds of the air!" "Consider the lilies of the field!"? Yes, of course, they neither toil nor spin, nor do they need to; but how could we learn from them that we do not need to worry?

II

More closely considered, however, our text shows that Jesus is by no means overlooking the distinction between man and the plant or animal kingdoms, and that he certainly does not mean that we should live a life like that of plants or animals, should close our eyes to the future with its destiny and responsibility. For what does our text say exactly? "Look at the birds of the air; they neither sow nor reap nor gather into barns! . . . Consider the lilies of the field, how they grow; they neither toil nor spin." They do not do any of the things which man does to secure his future. And naturally Jesus does not propose to say: "You must do the same, that is, neither sow nor reap nor work". Rather he is assuming that men do all these things. But with this presupposition in mind he wishes to say: "You should imitate them by not fretting and worrying!" For if plants and animals which cannot make provision for the future are yet without anxiety about it, how should men worry who are skilled in making provision? Precisely because you men sow and reap, toil and spin, for just that reason you should not be anxious!

But does not our sowing and reaping and all our toil take place because we are made anxious by the question: What shall we eat, what shall we drink, and what shall we put on? Now, if Jesus is assuming that by our work we make provision for our food and clothing, and yet says that we must not be anxious, it is obvious that he is making a distinction between different kinds of anxiety. Care for the needs of the future is not rejected but is taken for granted. And if Jesus says that we who are daily providing for the future ought not to be anxious, then he understands by this anxiety, from which we should be released, an anxiety of a different kind. Of what kind? Well, at bottom, it is not a different type of anxiety that is in question, but his meaning is simply this: we must not allow anxiety for the future, which of course impels us as human beings to make due provision, to become master of our lives. For as soon as that happens, its character changes and from being a natural providential care it becomes an anxious consuming care, and the question, what shall we . . .? becomes a question laden with fretful anxiety.

Hence such questioning may be right and proper, but it is also may be quite false and wrong. It is right and proper when it concerns our daily work, and our provision for future needs. That is a matter of obligation for us if we do not want to be a burden to others and leave them to do our work, which it is incumbent on us to do because we ourselves have to bear a burden of responsibility for others. But such questioning is false when we go further than this and question with fretful anxiety; when we do not simply allow our work to give an answer to our question; when in spite of everything we can find no rest and torture ourselves with the anxious question: What shall we . . .?

Hence the first thing that we should learn from plants and animals is this: we can do what they cannot — namely, provide for our future by our work; and hence we should not encumber ourselves with further tormenting worries when even plants and animals live free from care.

III

But we must think more precisely about the words of Jesus. For if they said nothing more than this: you do not need to worry because you can work, there are many to whom his advice would be inapplicable. For there are many people who cannot work, and cannot make provision for their future, while there are others who indeed can and do work, but who in spite of all their labor have ill success and can only look to the future with distressing anxiety. May we reproach them with their anxiety and invoke the words: "Do not be anxious! Look at the birds of the air! Consider the lilies of the field!" What are we to say in face of the situation of such people? Well, in the first place, it is quite obvious that Jesus is not addressing his exhortation to such unfortunate ones, who on the whole are the exceptions; he is speaking rather to average humanity to whom it is true that they can work and can thus provide for their future needs, just as he is speaking of the average case in the kingdom of plants and animals where it is true also that occasionally a beast perishes or a plant dies for want of nourishment.

And further, Jesus is taking it for granted that if a man is in need, others should come to his assistance. Had we said to Jesus: "How can you say in general terms, that we ought not to be anxious: do you not see the many people whose lives are inevitably clouded by anxiety?" he might well have replied: "I do indeed see them; but do not you see them too? And do you not realize what is your duty in the circumstances?" And he might have gone on to say: "Look at the birds: consider the lilies . . .! They have no laws and are not organized into a state: they do not live in a community in which each is responsible for other lives and each is dependent on others. And you have your laws and your state organization, you live in fellowship and community, where each is responsible towards others and all are mutually interdependent, you cannot even banish needless anxiety from your community life which implies mutual help and support."

Hence if anyone would answer: the words of Jesus are pointless, because there is so much acute need in the context of which they are quite inappropriate, then these words of the Master become for such a one an admonition as to his responsibilities, or even an accusation suggesting that he has not done all that he might have done to ensure that such words can be suitably addressed to all mankind.

IV

Yet having said so much, we have not said all. For if we who can work and make reasonable provision for the future consider in our minds whether we are really obeying the Master's injunction, and can really live a life free from fretful anxiety, we are beset by doubts. For do we know whether we shall always be able to work? Or whether the fruit of our labors may not be destroyed? Whether the resources which we have already garnered for the future may not be wiped out? Are we secure?

Of course if we understood the words of Jesus to imply that we can secure our future by our own active provision then we should be making a great mistake. For if we consider the matter well, we come to realize that we can never make ourselves secure by work and toil, and such a realization is apt to bring renewed anxiety to many people. There are no doubt others who do not reflect on the constant uncertainties of life or else soon forget them, who work with eager industry, assemble their resources and, looking with pride on what they have amassed, live with the feeling of absolute security. The words of Jesus apply to both groups: to those who are only too painfully aware of their fundamental insecurity, and to those who, always aiming at profit, live comfortably with the sense of long-term security. To both he says: "Abandon your anxieties! They cannot help you at all, neither the anxiety which springs from painful awareness of the truth, nor the anxieties of money-making. Both kinds of anxiety are useless." To both groups his ironic word applies: "Which of you by being anxious can add one cubit to his stature?" Hence something which to many people may perhaps seem desirable but at bottom is a ridiculously trivial matter, our height, cannot be altered in the smallest degree by any amount of anxiety. How much less can our busy carefulness avail to make our lives basically secure! What then is the point of living in fretful anxiety when such an attitude is from the outset certain to effect nothing? Or what is the point of worrying about money-making when after all it can never bring ultimate security? You, who cannot add to your stature by one cubit, nor make one hair of your head black or white (Matt. 5:36) — you imagine that you must or can make your future secure!

Both types of men are alluded to in this message; fundamentally both have the same way of thinking, that of the man who thinks he must at all costs make his future secure, and who is either distressed because he cannot do so or imagines that by his busy activities he can do so. In both cases, anxiety has become man's tyrant; in both cases, life is absorbed in care about the material means of life, while in reality life itself slips from their grasp.

"Therefore I tell you: do not be anxious about your life, what you shall eat or what you shall drink, nor about your body, what you shall put on! Is not life more than food and the body more than clothing?" Some, of course, will feel inclined to reply that it is precisely for life and body that they are caring when they toil for their food and clothing. But they do not notice that in fretful anxiety or busy care they are consuming themselves by concern about the material basis of life, that in one way or the other they are becoming mastered by the illusion that if only they are assured of material resources, they have no further need to worry. They are losing their souls and their true life because they are forgetting that there are far more serious concerns than those about material subsistence; concerns in comparison with which the concern for means of subsistence becomes trivial.

Jesus wishes to lead men's minds to realize the centrality of this most serious concern by impressing upon them that their anxieties about material resources are at bottom useless. No doubt man has this advantage over plants and animals that by a little forethought he can provide for his future. But in order that this concern may not assume control of his life, he must become aware of the truth that he can never make his life secure by his anxiety to provide for the material basis of living.

V

Jesus, however, adopts another method of approach when he says: this fretful anxiety or busy care is not necessary either, since God cares for us: "Look at the birds of the air: they neither sow nor reap nor gather into barns, and yet your heavenly Father feeds them. Are you not of more value than they? . . . Consider the lilies of the field, how they grow: they neither toil nor spin: yet I tell you, even Solomon in all his glory was not arrayed like one of these. But if God so clothes the grass of the field, which today is alive and tomorrow is thrown into the oven, will he not much more clothe you, O men of little faith?" How are we to understand this thought? For many people it contains the most obnoxious element in this phrase of the teaching of Jesus. For is it really true that we can firmly rely on the providence of God to provide us always with food and clothing just as certainly as the bird finds its nourishment and the flower receives its garb of color? Are we meant to learn from plants and animals that our life is secure through God's unceasing providence? Of course we are to learn such a lesson. But if it is clearly a mistake to suppose that our life is thus secured in the same way as that of the plants and animals, namely, by the constant provision of food and clothing without any care or trouble on our part — then our true life which is assured by God's merciful providence is obviously of a different kind from that of plants and animals; of a different kind, indeed, from a life whose wants are supplied by the provision of food and clothing. And what we are to learn is this: so certainly as God provides in the realm of nature for the real need and the good of his creatures, so certainly he provides for our needs on a deeper level of life.

283

For there is a difference between the life of nature and that of humanity. No doubt in nature too not every single living creature is made secure. There are birds which die of hunger and flowers which perish through frost. Jesus too knows that some sparrows fall to the ground (Matt. 10:29) and that not every seed brings forth grain (Mark 4:3ff.). Nevertheless he can say that the animals find their food and the flowers are clothed in splendor. he views nature as a whole as we also are accustomed to do. When we view the life of nature thus, we see that while there is decay, there is also a constant renewal of life, so that decay and growth form the rhythmic pulsation of the flow of natural life, in which destructive forces also have their appointed place, and promote the vitality of the whole. The life of nature thus appears as a purposefully ordered whole, within the pattern of which each part is provided for, so that no part need grow anxious.

Are we to understand the message of Jesus in the sense that human life is integrated with the structure of the natural life? It would be a great self-delusion to think so. There was indeed a period of thought when it ws considered that the life of man could be viewed as forming a unity with the life of nature, and the intelligent design which nature reveals could be equated with God's providential care for humanity. This type of piety was impressed by the orderly pattern and purpose which nature disclosed and believed that such design suggested a self-revelation of God, the revelation of his watchful care. Of course, such an outlook has by no means died out completely; but in the days when it was predominant it received a terrible shock from that great natural calamity, the earthquake of Lisbon, in which thousands of people perished. We can still see from Goethe's *Poetry and Truth* how this event disturbed and agitated the minds of men. The belief in a providential design, which had grown up from a consideration of the intelligent patterns of nature, collapsed.

No; we cannot in this way arrive at an understanding of the working of God's providential care for humanity. For the life of man cannot be resolved into the processes of the life of nature, because it is simply not to be equated with the life of plants and animals. It is impossible for man to accept the facts of his transience and death without question, and to comfort himself by the consideration that in the course of nature new growth follows upon decay. For him transience and death mean real annihilation; and the fact that his life is so closely entwined with the processes of nature is no appeasement to his spirit but rather a torturing mystery. No doubt nature offers him the means of subsistence; but often too she denies them. No doubt she offers him the raw material of his labor; but also she often destroys his labor. No doubt she presents herself to his contemplation as an image of beauty and orderliness; but at the same time she may cruelly assemble her sinister forces and swallow up his life.

What then is the underlying implication when Jesus points to the birds of the air and the lilies of the field? He does not wish us to equate our life with the life of nature, but rather he insists on the qualitative distinction which differentiates us from nature: "Are you not of more value than they?" If God clearly cares for the life of nature so that what is necessary to sustain it is always there and it may live free from fear, how much more shall we not live without fear in the assurance that God will unfailingly supply what we need? The insecurity of our life should not tempt us to be anxious: for what is decisively necessary is not affected by this insecurity. Hence in the midst of our insecurity we should know ourselves to be secure, whatever may happen to us. We are to realize that even the hairs of our head are all numbered (Matt. 10:30). Jesus speaks this word in exhorting the disciples not to allow themselves to be dismayed by the prospect of persecution, imprisonment and death. The fact that the hairs of our head are numbered does not mean that nothing untoward can happen to us, but that it cannot happen without the will of God, just as certainly as no sparrow falls to the ground without the divine will and knowledge. Hence we must not be mastered by the tormenting fear. "What shall we . . .?" "The Gentiles seek all these things; and your heavenly Father knows that you need them all." If therefore he sometimes withdraws such things from us, he also knows why.

Often we ourselves do not know why. But although we are puzzled, we must not be anxious but rejoice in the assurance that God cares about what is fundamentally necessary and right for us. And we shall have this trust and be free from the mastery of fear about the material things of life only when we are dominated by a far more important concern, when a very different question presses more closely on our minds. What question is that?

VI

Jesus tells us that when in conclusion he enjoins us to seek first the kingdom of God and his righteousness. Our lives must be controlled by the concern for God's kingdom. The sovereignty of God and the will of God must be placed first in our lives. We are to learn that in the last resort our concern should not be for the material aspect of life; that it is vain to try to make ourselves secure through material resources, and unnecessary because God cares for us, but that there is one supreme thing we should seek and care about with all the energies of our being — namely, that we might be able to stand in the presence of God. If this really becomes our controlling care then anxiety about sustenance and clothing will disappear.

On a purely human level we find it is true that material concerns take second place for anyone who is moved and mastered by higher thoughts and aims. For instance, the man who is gripped by the inspiration of some great task, some life work whose importance for him is so overwhelming and obvious that he is prepared to sacrifice everything for it — comfort and security and in certain circumstances life itself. Or one who has encountered friendship and love, the gift of which makes everything else seem a matter of indifference, and who is now moved by higher cares than material ones, by concern for the beloved — friend for friend, husband for wife, mother for child — for the sake of which he is prepared for any deprivation or insecurity or self-sacrifice.

If we find this to be true in human relationships, must we not understand that it is still more true of our relationship to God? Shall we love and worship God only if he first guarantees us peace and security of life? Or does not belief in God mean abandoning the pressing care for peace and security of life? Does it not mean to be ready for self-devotion and self-sacrifice? We are only seeking the kingdom of God and his righteousness when we are asking what God requires of us, for what purpose he needs us, and when the anxious question "What shall we . . .?" is silent.

And if we are really putting first this central aim, we shall understand when Jesus continues: "All these things shall be yours as well." Then God will provide what is necessary for our outward life too. This, of course, does not mean that material security is guaranteed us. But we can then leave the care of it to God with the consolation of trust. He needs us when and where he wills; and so long as he is using us, he will also maintain our lives. And if he sends us distress and want, he knows why even though we do not know. It is impossible for us to solve the riddles of life. Neither can we attain by a perspicacious solution of all the problems of the universe the proof that the reins of government are in the hands of God, who guides all things well; nor have we in our religious faith the means of solving these problems. The will of God suffers no question. But we can win the strength to bear the burden of these mysteries, if we do not allow ourselves to be mastered by tormenting fears about the material side of life, but rather seek with all our hearts and minds the kingdom of God and his righteousness. In that case we shall not only gather the strength to bear the burden of the mystery but more and more shall we come to realize what gift God wishes to bestow on us through the burden of the mystery: inner freedom and peace. And we shall become ever more aware what gift he has bestowed on us in Jesus Christ, who in his word calls us to this freedom of the spirit.

This World and Beyond, pp. 23-35.

6

DEMYTHOLOGIZING: CONTROVERSIAL SLOGAN AND THEOLOGICAL FOCUS*

"JESUS CHRIST AND MYTHOLOGY"

Bultmann first offered his controversial proposal on demythologizing in a 1941 lecture before a group of pastors of the Confessing Church in Frankfurt, Germany. (The "Confessing Church", of which Bultmann counted himself a member, consisted of German Christians opposed to the Nazi party in general, and its religious arm, the German Christian Church, in particular.) In that same year, Bultmann published a modified version of this lecture, "Neues Testament und Mythologie", in Offenbarung und Heilsgeschehen *(1941). The essay set off such a flurry of discussion, within the Confessing Church and even under wartime conditions, that shortly after World War II, it was re-issued in* Kerygma und Mythos *(1948). Three years later, in the Fall of 1951, Bultmann came to the United States to give a series of lectures on "demythologizing" at several American universities and divinity schools. These English language lectures, in revised form, constitute the text for the several chapters of* Jesus Christ and Mythology *(1958). (A German translation of this volume was not published until 1964.) It is the most fully developed of Bultmann's theological writings, and his most careful and clear statement on demythologizing. He restates his original proposal, incorporates clarifications developed in response to his critics, and continues his dialogue with major opponents. Readers of this volume will also recognize many themes first articulated in earlier essays: e.g., New Testament eschatology, biblical interpretation or hermeneutics, miracles and faith.*

I THE MESSAGE OF JESUS AND THE PROBLEM OF MYTHOLOGY

1

The heart of the preaching of Jesus Christ is the Kingdom of God. During the nineteenth century exegesis and theology understood the Kingdom of God as a spiritual community consisting of men joined

---

* See also pp. 39-43 above.

together by obedience to the will of God which ruled in their wills. By such obedience they sought to enlarge the sphere of his rule in the world. They were building, it was said, the Kingdom of God as a realm which is spiritual but within the world, active and effective in this world, unfolding in the history of this world.

The year 1892 saw the publication of *The Preaching of Jesus about the Kingdom of God* by Johannes Weiss. This epoch-making book refuted the interpretation which was hitherto generally accepted. Weiss showed that the Kingdom of God is not immanent in the world and does not grow as part of the world's history, but is rather eschatological; i.e., the Kingdom of God transcends the historical order. It will come into being not through the moral endeavor of man, but solely through the supernatural action of God. God will suddenly put an end to the world and to history, and he will bring in a new world, the world of eternal blessedness.

This conception of the Kingdom of God was not an invention of Jesus. It was a conception familiar in certain circles of Jews who were waiting for the end of this world. This picture of the eschatological drama was drawn in Jewish apocalyptic literature, of which the book of Daniel is the earliest still extant. The preaching of Jesus is distinguished from the typical apocalyptic pictures of the eschatological drama and of the blessedness of the coming new age in so far as Jesus refrained from drawing detailed pictures. He confined himself to the statement that the Kingdom of God will come and that men must be prepared to face the coming judgment. Otherwise he shared the eschatological expectations of his contemporaries. That is why he taught his disciples to pray,

Hallowed be thy name,
Thy Kingdom come,
Thy will be done on earth as it is in heaven.

Jesus expected that this would take place soon, in the immediate future, and he said that the dawning of that age could already be perceived in the signs and wonders which he performed, especially in his casting out of demons. Jesus envisaged the inauguration of the Kingdom of God as a tremendous cosmic drama. The Son of Man will come with the clouds of heaven, the dead will be raised and the day of judgment will arrive; for the righteous the time of bliss will begin, whereas the damned will be delivered to the torments of hell.

When I began to study theology, theologians as well as laymen were excited and frightened by the theories of Johannes Weiss. I remember that Julius Kaftan, my teacher in dogmatics in Berlin, said: "If Johannes Weiss is right and the conception of the Kingdom of God is an eschatological one, then it is impossible to make use of this conception in dogmatics." But in the following years the theologians, J. Kaftan among them, became convinced that Weiss was correct. Perhaps I may here refer to Albert Schweitzer who carried the theory of Weiss to extremes. He maintains that not only the preaching and the self-consciousness of Jesus but also his day-to-day conduct of life were dominated by an eschatological expectation which amounted to an all-pervading eschatological dogma.

Today nobody doubts that Jesus' conception of the Kingdom of God is an eschatological one — at least in European theology and, as far as I can see, also among American New Testament scholars. Indeed, it has become more and more clear that the eschatological expectation and hope is the core of the New Testament preaching throughout.

The earliest Christian community understood the Kingdom of God in the same sense as Jesus. It, too, expected the Kingdom of God to come in the immediate future. So Paul, too, thought that he would still be alive when the end of this world was to come and the dead were to be raised. This general conviction is confirmed by the voices of impatience, of anxiety and of doubt which are already audible in the synoptic gospels and which echo a little later and louder, for example, in the Second Epistle of Peter. Christianity has always retained the hope that the Kingdom of God will come in the immediate future, although it has waited in vain. We may cite Mark 9:1, which is not a genuine saying of Jesus but was ascribed to him by the earliest community: "Truly, I say to you, there are some standing here who will not taste death before they see the Kingdom of God come with power." Is not the meaning of this verse clear? Though many of the contemporaries of Jesus are already dead, the hope must nevertheless be retained that the Kingdom of God will still come in this generation.

2

This hope of Jesus and of the early Christian community was not fulfilled. The same world still exists and history continues. The course of history has refuted mythology. For the conception "Kingdom of God" is mythological, as is the conception of the eschatological drama. Just as mythological are the presuppositions of the expectation of the Kingdom of God, namely, the theory that the world, although created by God, is ruled by the devil, Satan, and that his army, the demons, is the cause of all evil, sin and disease. The whole conception of the world which is presupposed in the preaching of Jesus as in the New Testament generally is mythological; i.e., the conception of the world as being structured in three stories, heaven, earth and hell; the conception of the intervention of supernatural powers in the course of events; and the conception of miracles, especially the conception of the intervention of supernatural powers in the inner life of the soul, the conception that men can be tempted and corrupted by the devil and possessed by evil spirits. This conception of the world we call mythological because it is different from the conception of the world which has been formed and developed by science since its inception in ancient Greece and which has been accepted by all modern men. In this modern conception of the world the cause-and-effect nexus is fundamental. Although modern physical theories take account of chance in the chain of cause and effect in subatomic phenomena, our daily living, purposes and actions are not affected. In any case, modern science does not believe that the course of nature can be interrupted or, so to speak, perforated, by supernatural powers.

The same is true of the modern study of history, which does not take into account any intervention of God or of the devil or of demons in the course of history. Instead, the course of history is considered to be an unbroken whole, complete in itself, though differing from the course of nature because there are in history spiritual powers which influence the will of persons. Granted that not all historical events are determined by physical necessity and that persons are responsible for their actions, nevertheless nothing happens without rational motivation. Otherwise, responsibility would be dissolved. Of course, there are still many superstitions among modern men, but they are exceptions or even anomalies. Modern men take it for granted that the course of nature and of history, like their own inner life and their practical life, is nowhere interrupted by the intervention of supernatural powers.

Then the question inevitably arises: is it possible that Jesus' preaching of the Kingdom of God still has any importance for modern men and the preaching of the New Testament as a whole is still important for modern men? The preaching of the New Testament proclaims Jesus Christ, not only his preaching of the Kingdom of God but first of all his person, which was mythologized from the very beginnings of earliest

Christianity. New Testament scholars are at variance as to whether Jesus himself claimed to be the Messiah, the King of the time of blessedness, whether he believed himself to be the Son of Man who would come on the clouds of heaven. If so, Jesus understood himself in the light of mythology. We need not, at this point, decide one way or the other. At any rate, the early Christian community thus regarded him as a mythological figure. It expected him to return as the Son of Man on the clouds of heaven to bring salvation and damnation as judge of the world. His person is viewed in the light of mythology when he is said to have been begotten of the Holy Spirit and born of a virgin, and this becomes clearer still in Hellenistic Christian communities where he is understood to be the Son of God in a metaphysical sense, a great, pre-existent heavenly being who became man for the sake of our redemption and took on himself suffering, even the suffering of the cross. It is evident that such conceptions are mythological, for they were widespread in the mythologies of Jews and Gentiles and then were transferred to the historical person of Jesus. Particularly the conception of the pre-existent Son of God who descended in human guise into the world to redeem mankind is part of the Gnostic doctrine of redemption, and nobody hesitates to call this doctrine mythological. This raises in an acute form the question: *what is the importance of the preaching of Jesus and of the preaching of the New Testament as a whole for modern man?*

For modern man the mythological conception of the world, the conceptions of eschatology, of redeemer and of redemption, are over and done with. Is it possible to expect that we shall make a sacrifice of understanding, *sacrificium intellectus*, in order to accept what we cannot sincerely consider true — merely because such conceptions are suggested by the Bible? Or ought we to pass over those sayings of the New Testament which contain such mythological conceptions and to select other sayings which are not such stumbling-blocks to modern man? In fact, the preaching of Jesus is not confined to eschatological sayings. He proclaimed also the will of God, which is God's demand, the demand for the good. Jesus demands truthfulness and purity, readiness to sacrifice and to love. He demands that the whole man be obedient to God, and he protests against the delusion that one's duty to God can be fulfilled by obeying certain external commandments. If the ethical demands of Jesus are stumbling-blocks to modern man, then it is to his selfish will, not to his understanding, that they are stumbling-blocks.

What follows from all this? Shall we retain the ethical preaching of Jesus and abandon his eschatological preaching? Shall we reduce his preaching of the Kingdom of God to the so-called social gospel? Or is there a third possibility? We must ask whether the eschatological preaching and the mythological sayings as a whole contain a still deeper meaning which is concealed under the cover of mythology. If that is so, let us abandon the mythological conceptions precisely because we want to retain their deeper meaning. This method of interpretation of the New Testament which tries to recover the deeper meaning behind the mythological conceptions I call *de-mythologizing* — an unsatisfactory word, to be sure. Its aim is not to eliminate the mythological statements but to interpret them. It is a method of hermeneutics. The meaning of this method will be best understood when we make clear the meaning of mythology in general.

3

It is often said that mythology is a primitive science, the intention of which is to explain phenomena and incidents which are strange, curious, surprising, or frightening, by attributing them to supernatural causes, to gods or to demons. So it is in part, for example, when it attributes phenomena like eclipses of the sun or of the moon to such causes; but there is more than this in mythology. Myths speak about gods and demons as powers on which man knows himself to be dependent, powers whose favor he needs, powers whose wrath he fears. Myths express the knowledge that man is not master of the world and of his life, that the world within which he lives is full of riddles and mysteries and that human life also is full of riddles and mysteries.

Mythology expresses a certain understanding of human existence. It believes that the world and human life have their ground and their limits in a power which is beyond all that we can calculate or control. Mythology speaks about this power inadequately and insufficiently because it speaks about it as if it were a worldly power. It speaks of gods who represent the power beyond the visible, comprehensible world. It speaks of gods as if they were men and of their actions as human actions, although it conceives of the gods as endowed with superhuman power and of their actions as incalculable, as capable of breaking the normal, ordinary order of events. It may be said that myths give to the transcendent reality an immanent, this-worldly objectivity. Myths give worldly objectivity to that which is unworldly. (In German one would say, "Der Mythos objektiviert das Jenseitige zum Diesseitigen.")

All this holds true also of the mythological conceptions found in the

Bible. According to mythological thinking, God has his domicile in heaven. What is the meaning of this statement? The meaning is quite clear. In a crude manner it expresses the idea that God is beyond the world, that he is transcendent. The thinking which is not yet capable of forming the abstract idea of transcendence expresses its intention in the category of space; the transcendent God is imagined as being at an immense spatial distance, far above the world: for above this world is the world of the stars, of the light which enlightens and makes glad the life of men. When mythological thinking forms the conception of hell, it expresses the idea of the transcendence of evil as the tremendous power which again and again afflicts mankind. The location of hell and of men whom hell has seized is below the earth in darkness, because darkness is tremendous and terrible to men.

These mythological conceptions of heaven and hell are no longer acceptable for modern men since for scientific thinking to speak of "above" and "below" in the universe has lost all meaning, but the idea of the transcendence of God and of evil is still significant.

Another example is the conception of Satan and the evil spirits into whose power men are delivered. This conception rests upon the experience, quite apart from the inexplicable evils arising outside ourselves to which we are exposed, that our own actions are often so puzzling; men are often carried away by their passions and are no longer master of themselves, with the result that inconceivable wickedness breaks forth from them. Again, the conception of Satan as ruler over the world expresses a deep insight, namely, the insight that evil is not only to be found here and there in the world, but that all particular evils make up one single power which in the last analysis grows from the very actions of men, which form an atmosphere, a spiritual tradition, which overwhelms every man. The consequences and effects of our sins become a power dominating us, and we cannot free ourselves from them. Particularly in our day and generation, although we no longer think mythologically, we often speak of demonic powers which rule history, corrupting political and social life. Such language is metaphorical, a figure of speech, but in it is expressed the knowledge, the insight, that the evil for which every man is responsible individually has nevertheless become a power which mysteriously enslaves every member of the human race.

Now the question arises: is it possible to de-mythologize the message of Jesus and the preaching of the early Christian community? Since this preaching was shaped by the eschatological belief, the first question is this: *What is the meaning of eschatology in general?*

II THE INTERPRETATION OF MYTHOLOGICAL ESCHATOLOGY

1

In the language of traditional theology eschatology is the doctrine of the last things, and "last" means last in the course of time, that is, the end of the world which is imminent as the future is to our present. But in the actual preaching of the prophets and of Jesus this "last" has a further meaning. As in the conception of heaven the transcendence of God is imagined by means of the category of space, so in the conception of the end of the world, the idea of the transcendence of God is imagined by means of the category of time. However, it is not simply the idea of transcendence as such, but of the importance of the transcendence of God, of God who is never present as a familiar phenomenon but who is always the coming God, who is veiled by the unknown future. Eschatological preaching views the present time in the light of the future and it says to men that this present world, the world of nature and history, the world in which we live our lives and make our plans is not the only world; that this world is temporal and transitory, yes, ultimately empty and unreal in the face of eternity.

This understanding is not peculiar to mythical eschatology. It is the knowledge to which Shakespeare gives grand expression:

The cloud-capp'd towers, the gorgeous palaces,
The solemn temples, the great globe itself,
Yea, all which it inherit, shall dissolve,
And like this insubstantial pageant faded,
Leave not a rack behind. We are such stuff
As dreams are made on; and our little life
Is rounded with a sleep. . . .

Tempest IV, 1

It is the same understanding which was current among the Greeks who did not share the eschatology which was common to the prophets and to Jesus. Permit me to quote from a hymn of Pindar:

Creatures of a day, what is anyone? what is he not?
Man is but a dream of a shadow.

Pythian Odes 8, 95-96

and from Sophocles:

Alas! we living mortals, what are we
But phantoms all or unsubstantial shades?

Ajax 125-126

The perception of the boundary of human life warns against "presumption" (ὕβρις) and calls to "thoughtfulness" and "awe" (σωφροσύνη and αἰδώς). "Nothing too much" (μηδὲν ἄγαν), "of strength do not boast" (ἐπὶ ῥώμη μὴ χαυχῶ) are sayings of Greek wisdom. Greek tragedy shows the truth of such proverbs in its representations of human destiny. From the soldiers slain in the Battle of Plataeae we should learn, as Aeschylus says, that

> Mortal man needs must not vaunt him overmuch. . . .
> Zeus, of a truth, is a chastiser of overweening pride
> And corrects with heavy hand.
>
> *Persians 820-828*

And again in the *Ajax* of Sophocles Athene says of the mad Ajax,

> Warned by these sights, Odysseus, see that thou
> Utter no boastful word against the gods,
> Nor swell with pride if haply might of arm
> Exalt thee o'er thy fellows, or vast wealth.
> A day can prostrate and a day upraise
> And that is mortal; but the gods approve
> Sobriety and frowardness abhor.
>
> *127-133*

2

If it is true that the general human understanding of the insecurity of the present in the face of the future has found expression in eschatological thought, then we must ask, *what is the difference between the Greek and the Biblical understanding?* The Greeks found the immanent power of the beyond, of the gods compared with whom all human affairs are empty, in "destiny". They do not share the mythological conception of eschatology as a cosmic event at the end of time; and it may well be said that Greek thought is more similar to that of modern man than to the Biblical conception, since for modern man mythological eschatology has passed away. It is possible that the Biblical eschatology may rise again. It will not rise in its old mythological form but from the terrifying vision that modern technology, especially atomic science, may bring about the destruction of our earth through the abuse of human science and technology. When we ponder this possibility, we can feel the terror and the anxiety which were evoked by the eschatological preaching of the imminent end of the world. To be sure, that preaching was developed in conceptions which are no longer intelligible today, but they do express the knowledge of the finiteness of the world, and of the end which is imminent to us all because we all are beings of this finite world. This is the insight to which as a rule we turn a blind eye, but which may be brought to light by modern technology. It is precisely the intensity of this insight which explains why Jesus, like the Old Testament prophets, expected the end of the world to occur in the immediate future. The majesty of God and the inescapability of his judgment, and over against these the emptiness of the world and of men were felt with such an intensity that it seemed that the world was at an end, and that the hour of crisis was present. Jesus proclaims the will of God and the responsibility of man, pointing towards the eschatological events, but it is not because he is an eschatologist that he proclaims the will of God. On the contrary, he is an eschatologist because he proclaims the will of God.

The difference between the Biblical and the Greek understanding of the human situation regarding the unknown future can now be seen in a clearer light. It consists in the fact that in the thinking of the prophets and of Jesus the nature of God involves more than simply his omnipotence and his judgment touches not only the man who offends him by presumption and boasting. For the prophets and for Jesus God is the Holy One, who demands right and righteousness, who demands love of neighbor and who therefore is the judge of all human thoughts and actions. The world is empty not only because it is transitory but because men have turned it into a place in which evil spreads and sin rules. The end of the world, therefore, is the judgment of God; that is, the eschatological preaching not only brings to consciousness the emptiness of the human situation and calls men, as was the case among the Greeks, to moderation, humility and resignation; it calls men first and foremost to responsibility toward God and to repentance. It calls them to perform the will of God. Thus, the characteristic difference between the eschatological preaching of Jesus and that of the Jewish apocalypses becomes evident. All the pictures of future happiness in which apocalypticism excels are lacking in the preaching of Jesus.

The difference between the [Biblical and Greek] conception is due to different theories of human nature. Plato conceives the realm of spirit as a realm without time and without history because he conceives human nature as not subject to time and history. The Christian conception of the human being is that man is essentially a temporal being, which means that he is an historical being who has a past which shapes his character and who has a future which always brings forth new encounters. Therefore the future after death and beyond this world is a future of the totally new. This is the *totaliter aliter*. Then there will be "a new heaven and a new earth" (Rev. 21:1, II Peter 3:13). The seer of the future Jerusalem hears a voice, "Behold, I make all things new" (Rev. 21:5). Paul and John anticipate this newness. Paul says, "If any one is in Christ, he is a new creation; the old has passed away, behold, the new has come" (II Cor. 5:17), and John says, "I am writing you a new commandment, which is true in him and in you, because the darkness is passing away and the true light is already shining" (I John 2:8). But that newness is not a visible one, for our new life "is hid with Christ in God" (Col. 3:3), "it does not yet appear what we shall be" (I John 3:2). In a certain manner this unknown future is present in the holiness and love which characterize the believers in the Holy Spirit which inspired them, and in the worship of the Church. It cannot be described except in symbolic pictures: "for in this hope we were saved. Now hope that is seen is not hope. For who hopes for what he sees? But if we hope for what we do not see, we wait for it with patience" (Rom. 8:24-5). Therefore, this hope or this faith may be called readiness for the unknown future that God will give. In brief, it means to be open to God's future in the face of death and darkness.

This, then, is the deeper meaning of the mythological preaching of Jesus — to be open to God's future which is really imminent for every one of us; to be prepared for this future which can come as a thief in the night when we do not expect it; to be prepared, because this future will be a judgment on all men who have bound themselves to this world and are not free, not open to God's future.

3

The eschatological preaching of Jesus was retained and continued by the early Christian community in its mythological form. But very soon the process of de-mythologizing began, partially with Paul, and radically with John. The decisive step was taken when Paul declared that the turning point from the old world to the new was not a matter of the future but did take place in the coming of Jesus Christ. "But when the time had fully come, God sent forth his Son" (Gal. 4:4). To be sure, Paul still expected the end of the world as a cosmic drama, the *parousia* of Christ on the clouds of heaven, the resurrection from the dead, the final judgment, but with the resurrection of Christ the decisive event has already happened. The Church is the eschatological community of the elect, of the saints who are already justified and are alive because they are in Christ, in Christ who as the second Adam abolished death and brought life and immortality to light through the gospel (Rom. 5:12-14; II Tim. 1:10). "Death is swallowed up in victory" (I Cor. 15:54). There-fore, Paul can say that the expectations and promises of the ancient prophets are fulfilled when the gospel is proclaimed: "Behold, now is the acceptable time [about which Isaiah spoke]; behold, now is the day of salvation" (II Cor. 6:2). The Holy Spirit who was expected as the gift of the time of blessedness has already been given. In this manner the future is anticipated.

This de-mythologizing may be observed in a particular instance. In the Jewish apocalyptic expectations, the expectation of the Messianic kingdom played a role. The Messianic kingdom is, so to speak, an *inter-regnum* between the old world time (*οὖτος ὁ αἰών*) and the new age (*ὁ μέλλων αἰών*). Paul explains this apocalyptic, mythological idea of the Messianic *interregnum*, at the end of which Christ will deliver the Kingdom to God the Father, as the present time between the resurrec-tion of Christ and his coming *parousia* (I Cor. 15:24); that means, the present time of preaching the gospel is really the formerly expected time of the Kingdom of the Messiah. Jesus is now the Messiah, the Lord.

After Paul, John de-mythologized the eschatology in a radical man-ner. For John the coming and departing of Jesus is the eschatological event. "And this is the judgment, that the light has come into the world, and men loved darkness rather than light, because their deeds were evil" (John 3:19). "Now is the judgment of this world, now shall the ruler of this world be cast out" (12:31). For John the resurrection of Jesus, Pentecost and the *parousia* of Jesus are one and the same event, and those who believe have already eternal life. "He who believes in him is not condemned; he who does not believe is condemned already" (3:18). "He who believes in the Son has eternal life; he who does not obey the Son shall not see life, but the wrath of God rests upon him" (3:36). "Truly, truly, I say to you, the hour is coming, and now is, when the dead will hear the voice of the Son of God, and those who hear will live" (5:25). "I am the resurrection and the life; he who believes in me, though he die, yet shall he live, and whoever lives and believes in me shall never die" (11:25f.).

As in Paul, so in John de-mythologizing may be further observed in a particular instance. In Jewish eschatological expectations we find that the figure of the anti-Christ is a thoroughly mythological figure as it is described, for example, in II Thessalonians (2:7-12). In John false teachers play the role of this mythological figure. Mythology has been transposed into history. These examples show, it seems to me, that de-mythologizing has its beginning in the New Testament itself, and therefore our task of de-mythologizing today is justified.

III THE CHRISTIAN MESSAGE AND
THE MODERN WORLD-VIEW [WELTBILD]

1

An objection often heard against the attempt to de-mythologize is that it takes the modern world-view as the criterion of the interpretation of the Scripture and the Christian message and that Scripture and Christian message are not allowed to say anything that is in contradiction with the modern world-view.

It is, of course, true that de-mythologizing takes the modern world-view as a criterion. To de-mythologize is to reject not Scripture or the Christian message as a whole, but the world-view of Scripture, which is the world-view of a past epoch, which all too often is retained in Christian dogmatics and in the preaching of the Church. To de-mythologize is to deny that the message of Scripture and of the Church is bound to an ancient world-view which is obsolete.

The attempt to de-mythologize begins with this important insight: Christian preaching, in so far as it is preaching of the Word of God by God's command and in his name, does not offer a doctrine which can be accepted either by reason or by a *sacrificium intellectus*. Christian preaching is *kerygma*, that is, a proclamation addressed not to the theoretical reason, but to the hearer as a self. In this manner Paul commends himself to every man's conscience in the sight of God (II Cor. 4:2). De-mythologizing will make clear this function of preaching as a personal message, and in doing so it will eliminate a false stumbling-block and bring into sharp focus the real stumbling-block, the word of the cross.

For the world-view of the Scripture is mythological and is therefore unacceptable to modern man whose thinking has been shaped by science and is therefore no longer mythological. Modern man always makes use of technical means which are the result of science. In case of illness modern man has recourse to physicians, to medical science. In case of economic and political affairs, he makes use of the results of psychological, social, economic and political sciences, and so on. Nobody reckons with direct intervention by transcendent powers.

Of course, there are today some survivals and revivals of primitive thinking and superstition. But the preaching of the Church would make a disastrous mistake if it looked to such revivals and conformed to them. The nature of man is to be seen in modern literature, as, for instance, in the novels of Thomas Mann, Ernst Jünger, Thornton Wilder, Ernest Hemingway, William Faulkner, Graham Greene and Albert Camus, or in the plays of Jean-Paul Sartre, Jean Anouilh, Jean Giraudoux, etc. Or let us think simply of the newspapers. Have you read anywhere in them that political or social or economic events are performed by supernatural powers such as God, angels or demons? Such events are always ascribed to natural powers, or to good or bad will on the part of men, or to human wisdom or stupidity.

The science of today is no longer the same as it was in the nineteenth century, and to be sure, all the results of science are relative, and no world-view of yesterday or today or tomorrow is definitive. The main point, however, is not the concrete results of scientific research and the contents of a world-view, but the method of thinking from which world-views follow. For example, it makes no difference in principle whether the earth rotates round the sun or the sun rotates round the earth, but it does make a decisive difference that modern man understands the motion of the universe as a motion which obeys a cosmic law, a law of nature which human reason can discover. Therefore, modern man acknowledges as reality only such phenomena or events as are comprehensible within the framework of the rational order of the universe. He does not acknowledge miracles because they do not fit into this lawful order. When a strange or marvelous accident occurs, he does not rest until he has found a rational cause.

The contrast between the ancient world-view of the Bible and the modern world-view is the contrast between two ways of thinking, the mythological and the scientific. The method of scientific thinking and inquiry is in principle the same today as it was at the beginning of methodical and critical science in ancient Greece. It begins with the question about the $\dot{\alpha} \varrho \chi \acute{\eta}$ (origin) from which the world is conceivable as unity, as $\kappa \acute{o} \sigma \mu o \varsigma$, as systematic order and harmony. It begins therefore also with the attempt to give reasonable proofs for every statement ($\lambda \acute{o} \gamma o \nu \, \delta \iota \delta \acute{o} \nu \alpha \iota$). These principles are the same in modern science, and it does not matter that the results of scientific research are changing over and over again, since the change itself results from the permanent principles.

Certainly it is a philosophical problem whether the scientific world-view can perceive the whole reality of the world and of human life. There are reasons for doubting whether it can do so, and we shall have to say more about this problem in the following chapters. But for present purposes it is enough to say that the thinking of modern men is really shaped by the scientific world-view, and that modern men need it for their daily lives.

2

Therefore, it is mere wishful thinking to suppose that the ancient world-view of the Bible can be renewed. It is the radical abandonment and the conscious critique of the mythological world-view of the Bible which bring the real stumbling-block into sharp focus. This stumbling-block is that the Word of God calls man out of all man-made security. The scientific world-view engenders a great temptation, namely, that man strive for mastery over the world and over his own life. He knows the laws of nature and can use the powers of nature according to his plans and desires. He discovers more and more accurately the laws of social and of economic life, and thus organizes the life of the community more and more effectively — as Sophocles said in the famous chorus from *Antigone*.

Many wonders there be,
but nought more wondrous than man.
(332-333)

Thus modern man is in danger of forgetting two things: first, that his plans and undertakings should be guided not by his own desires for happiness and security, usefulness and profit, but rather by obedient response to the challenge of goodness, truth and love, by obedience to the commandment of God which man forgets in his selfishness and presumption; and secondly, that it is an illusion to suppose that real security can be gained by men organizing their own personal and community life. There are encounters and destinies which man cannot master. He cannot secure endurance for his works. His life is fleeting and its end is death. History goes on and pulls down all the towers of Babel again and again. There is no real, definitive security, and it is precisely this illusion to which men are prone to succumb in their yearning for security.

What is the underlying reason for this yearning? It is the sorrow, the secret anxiety which moves in the depths of the soul at the very moment when man thinks that he must obtain security for himself.

It is the word of God which calls man away from his selfishness and from the illusory security which he has built up for himself. It calls him to God, who is beyond the world and beyond scientific thinking. At the same time, it calls man to his true self. For the self of man, his inner life, his personal existence is also beyond the visible world and beyond rational thinking. The Word of God addresses man in his personal existence and thereby it gives him freedom from the world and from the sorrow and anxiety which overwhelm him when he forgets the beyond. By means of science men try to take possession of the world, but in fact the world gets possession of men. We can see in our times to what degree men are dependent on technology, and to what degree technology brings with it terrible consequences. To believe in the Word of God means to abandon all merely human security and thus to overcome the despair which arises from the attempt to find security, an attempt which is always vain.

Faith in this sense is both the demand of and the gift offered by preaching. Faith is the answer to the message. Faith is the abandonment of man's own security and the readiness to find security only in the unseen beyond, in God. This means that faith is security where no security can be seen; it is, as Luther said, the readiness to enter confidently into the darkness of the future. Faith in God who has power over time and eternity, and who calls me and who has acted and now is acting on me — this faith can become real only in its "nevertheless" against the world. For in the world nothing of God and of his action is visible or can be visible to men who seek security in the world. We may say that the Word of God addresses man in his insecurity and calls him into freedom, for man loses his freedom in his very yearning for security. This formulation may sound paradoxical, but it becomes clear when we consider the meaning of freedom.

Genuine freedom is not subjective arbitrariness. It is freedom in obedience. The freedom of subjective arbitrariness is a delusion, for it delivers man up to his drives, to do in any moment what lust and passion dictate. This hollow freedom is in reality dependence on the lust and passion of the moment. Genuine freedom is freedom from the motivation of the moment; it is freedom which withstands the clamor and pressure of momentary motivations. It is possible only when conduct is determined by a motive which transcends the present moment, that is, by law. Freedom is obedience to a law of which the validity is recognized and accepted, which man recognizes as the law of his own being. This can only be a law which has its origin and reason in the beyond. We may call it the law of spirit or, in Christian language, the law of God.

This idea of freedom, constituted by law, this free obedience or obedient freedom was well known both to ancient Greek philosophy and to Christianity. In modern times, however, this conception vanished and was replaced by the illusory idea of freedom as subjective arbitrariness which does not acknowledge a norm, a law from beyond. There ensues a relativism which does not acknowledge absolute ethical demands and absolute truths. The end of this development is nihilism.

There are several reasons for this development. The first is the development of science and technology which procures the illusion that man is master over the world and his life. Then there is the historical relativism which grew out of the Romantic Movement. It contends that our reason does not perceive eternal or absolute truths but is subject to historical development, that every truth has only a relative validity for a given time, race or culture, and thus, in the end, the search for truth becomes meaningless.

There is still another reason for the change from genuine freedom to the freedom of subjectivism. This deepest reason is anxiety in the face of real freedom, the yearning for security. Genuine freedom, it is true, is freedom within laws, but it is not freedom in security, because it is always freedom gained in responsibility and decision, and therefore it is freedom in insecurity. Freedom of subjective arbitrariness believes itself to be secure precisely because it is not responsible to a transcendent power, because it believes itself to be master of the world through science and technology. Subjective freedom grows out of the desire for security; it is in fact anxiety in the face of genuine freedom.

Now it is the Word of God which calls man into genuine freedom, into free obedience, and the task of de-mythologizing has no other purpose but to make clear the call of the Word of God. It will interpret the Scripture, asking for the deeper meaning of mythological conceptions and freeing the Word of God from a by-gone world-view.

3

Thus it follows that the objection is raised by a mistake, namely, the objection that de-mythologizing means rationalizing the Christian message, that de-mythologizing dissolves the message into a product of human rational thinking, and that the mystery of God is destroyed by de-mythologizing. Not at all! On the contrary, de-mythologizing makes clear the true meaning of God's mystery. The incomprehensibility of

God lies not in the sphere of theoretical thought but in the sphere of personal existence. Not what God is in himself, but how he acts with men, is the mystery in which faith is interested. This is a mystery not to theoretical thought, but to the natural wills and desires of men.

God's Word is not a mystery to my understanding. On the contrary, I cannot truly believe in the Word without understanding it. But to understand does not mean to explain rationally. I can understand, for example, what friendship, love and faithfulness mean, and precisely by genuinely understanding I know that the friendship, love and faithfulness which I personally enjoy are a mystery which I cannot but thankfully receive. For I perceive them neither by my rational thinking, nor by psychological, nor by anthropological analysis but only in open readiness to personal encounters. In this readiness I can understand them in a certain way already before I am given them because my personal existence needs them. Then I understand them in searching for them, in asking for them. Nevertheless, the fact itself that my yearning is fulfilled, that a friend comes to me, remains a mystery.

In the same manner I can understand what God's grace means, asking for it as long as it does not come to me, accepting it thankfully when it does come to me. The fact that it comes to me, that the gracious God is my God, remains forever a mystery, not because God performs in an irrational manner something that interrupts the natural course of events, but because it is inconceivable that he should encounter me in his Word as the gracious God.

IV   MODERN BIBLICAL INTERPRETATION AND EXISTENTIALIST PHILOSOPHY

1

Over and over again I hear the objection that de-mythologizing transforms Christian faith into philosophy. This objection arises from the fact that I call de-mythologizing an interpretation, an existentialist interpretation, and that I make use of conceptions developed especially by Martin Heidegger in existentialist philosophy.

We can understand the problem best when we remember that *de-mythologizing is an hermeneutic method,* that is, a method of interpretation, of exegesis. "Hermeneutics" means the art of exegesis.

Reflection on the art of hermeneutics has been increasingly neglected, at least in German theology, since Schleiermacher, who himself was interested in it and wrote important treatises on it. Only since the First World War has the interest in hermeneutics revived, when the work of the great German philosopher Wilhelm Dilthey become effective.[101]

Reflection on hermeneutics (the method of interpretation) makes it clear that interpretation, that is, exegesis, is always based on principles and conceptions which guide exegesis as presuppositions, although interpreters are often not aware of this fact.

To illustrate the point we may take as an example the understanding of the New Testament conception of "spirit" ($\pi\nu\varepsilon\tilde{\upsilon}\mu\alpha$). During the nineteenth century the philosophies of Kant and Hegel profoundly influenced theologians and shaped their anthropological and ethical conceptions. Therefore, "spirit" in the New Testament was understood to mean spirit in the idealistic sense, based on the tradition of humanistic thinking which goes back to Greek idealistic philosophy. "Spirit" was thus understood to be the power of reason ($\lambda\acute{o}\gamma o\varsigma$, $\nu o\tilde{\upsilon}\varsigma$), in the inclusive sense as the power which works not only in rational thinking, in logic, but also in ethics, in moral judgments and behavior and in the field of art and poetry. "Spirit" was thought of as dwelling in the soul of men. In a certain sense spirit was thought to be a power from beyond, from beyond the individual subject. The spirit within the soul was part of the divine spirit which was cosmic reason. Therefore the spirit was for the individual subject the guide to living a truly human life. Man had to realize by education the possibilities given him by the spirit. This conception was generally dominant in philosophy as well as in theology during the nineteenth century.

The conception of "spirit" in the New Testament, especially in the Pauline epistles, was understood in this sense that spirit is the power of moral judgment and behavior; and the attribute "holy" was understood in the sense of moral purity. Further, spirit was understood as the power of knowledge from which creedal and dogmatic statements grow. Of course, the spirit was thought to be the gift of God, but it was understood in the idealistic sense. Then Hermann Gunkel, in his little book *Die Wirkungen des Heiligen Geistes* (1st ed. 1888), pointed out the error of this interpretation. He showed that "spirit" in the New Testament means a divine power which does not belong to the human soul or reason but which is supernatural, a surprising, amazing power which causes marvelous psychological phenomena such as glossolalia, prophecy, etc. While the earlier interpretation was guided by idealistic conceptions, Gunkel's was guided by psychological conceptions. Psychological conceptions dominated the so-called *religionsgeschichtliche Schule* in general. Because these scholars were aware of psychological phenomena they recognized important thoughts in the New Testament which had hitherto been overlooked or undervalued. They recognized, for example, the importance of enthusiastic and cultic piety and of cultic assemblies; they understood in a new way the conception of knowledge (γνῶσις) which as a rule does not mean theoretical, rational knowledge, but mystical intuition or vision, a mystical union with Christ. In this respect Wilhelm Bousset's *Kyrios Christos* (1st ed. 1913) was a landmark in New Testament research.

I need not continue this review. It will be clear that *every interpreter brings with him certain conceptions, perhaps idealistic or psychological, as presuppositions of his exegesis,* in most cases unconsciously. But then the question arises, which conceptions are right and adequate? Which presuppositions are right and adequate? Or is it perhaps impossible to give an answer to these questions?

I may illustrate the embarrassment (ἀπορία) by a further example. According to Paul, the believer who has received baptism is free from sin; he can no longer commit sin. "We know that our old self was crucified with him [i.e., by baptism] so that the sinful body might be destroyed, and we might no longer be enslaved to sin. For he who has died is freed from sin" (Rom. 6:6-7). How must we then understand the warnings and admonitions against sin contained in Paul's exhortations? How can the imperative "you shall not sin" be reconciled with the indicative "you are freed from sin"? Paul Wernle's book *Der Christ und die Sünde bei Paulus* (1897) gave the answer that they cannot be reconciled; there is a contradiction in Paul; in theory all Christians are free from sin, but in practice Christians still commit sin, and therefore Paul must make exhortations. But is Wernle right? Is it possible to attribute to Paul such a contradiction? I do not think so. For Paul there is an inner connection between indicative and imperative, since in some sayings he lays stress on the connection. For example, "Cleanse out the old leaven that you may be fresh dough, as you really are unleavened" (I. Cor. 5:7); or: "If we live by the Spirit, let us also walk by the Spirit" (Gal. 5:25). These sayings show clearly, it seems to me, the inner connection between indicative and imperative, namely, that the indicative is the ground of the imperative.

Now we return to our question: Which are the right conceptions? Which are the adequate presuppositions, if they are available at all? Should we perhaps say that we must interpret without any presupposition; that the text itself provides the conceptions of exegesis? This is sometimes asserted, but it is impossible. To be sure, our exegesis must be without presuppositions with regard to the results of our exegesis. We cannot know in advance what the text will say; on the contrary, we must learn from it. An exegesis which, for example, makes the presupposition that its results must agree with some dogmatic statement is not a real and fair exegesis. There is, however, a difference in principle between presuppositions in respect of results and presuppositions in respect of method. It can be said that method is nothing other than a kind of questioning, a way of putting questions. This means that I cannot understand a given text without asking certain questions of it. The questions may differ very widely. If you are interested in psychology, you will read the Bible — or any other literature — asking questions about psychological phenomena. You may read texts to gain knowledge of individual or of social psychology, or of the psychology of poetry, of religion, of technology, etc.

In this case you have certain conceptions by which you understand psychological life and by which you interpret the texts. Whence do you obtain these conceptions? This question calls attention to another important fact, to another presupposition of interpretation. You obtain the conceptions from your own psychical life. The resulting or corresponding presupposition of exegesis is that you do have a relation to the subject-matter (*Sache*) — in this case to the psychical life — about which you interrogate a given text. I call this relation the "life relation". In this relation you have a certain understanding of the matter in question, and from this understanding grow the conceptions of exegesis. From reading the texts you will learn, and your understanding will be enriched and corrected. Without such a relation and such previous understanding (*Vorverständnis*) it is impossible to understand any text.

It is easy to see that you cannot understand any text of which the theme is music unless you are musical. You cannot understand a paper or a book on mathematics unless you can think mathematically, or a book on philosophy unless you can think philosophically. You cannot understand an historical text unless you yourself live historically and can therefore understand the life of history, that is, the powers and motives which give content and motion to history as the will to power, the state, laws, etc. You cannot understand a novel unless you know from your own life what love or friendship, hate or jealousy, etc., are.

This is, then, the basic presupposition for every form of exegesis: that your own relation to the subject-matter prompts the question you bring to the text and elicits the answers you obtain from the text.

I have tried to analyze the situation of the interpreter by using the example of psychological interpretation. You can read and interpret a text with other interests, for example, with aesthetical or with historical interest, with the interest in political or cultural history of states, etc. With regard to historical interpretation there are two possibilities. First, your interest may be to give a picture of a past time, to reconstruct the past; second, your interest may be to learn from historical documents what you need for your present practical life. For example, you can interpret Plato as an interesting figure of the culture of fifth century Athenian Greece, but you can also interpret Plato to learn through him the truth about human life. In the latter case your interpretation is not motivated by interest in a past epoch of history, but by your search for the truth.

Now, when we interpret the Bible, what is our interest? Certainly the Bible is an historical document and we must interpret the Bible by the methods of historical research. We must study the language of the Bible, the historical situation of the biblical authors, etc. But what is our true and real interest? Are we to read the Bible only as an historical document in order to reconstruct an epoch of past history for which the Bible serves as a "source"? Or is it more than a source? I think our interest is really to hear what the Bible has to say for our actual present, to hear what is the truth about our life and about our soul.

2

Now the question arises as to which is the adequate method, which are the adequate conceptions? And also, which is the relation, the "life-relation", which we have in advance, to the theme (*Sache*) of the Bible from which our questions and our conceptions arise? Must we say that we do not have such relation in advance, since the theme of the Bible is the revelation of God, and we can gain a relation to God only by his revelation and not in advance of it?

Indeed, there are theologians who have argued in this manner, but it seems to me that they are in error. Man does have in advance a relation to God which has found its classical expression in the words of Augustine: "Tu nos fecisti ad te, et cor nostrum inquietum est, donec requiescat in te" (Thou hast made us for Thyself, and our heart is restless, until it rests in Thee). Man has a knowledge of God in advance, though not of the revelation of God, that is, of his action in Christ. He has a relation to

God in his search for God, conscious or unconscious. Man's life is moved by the search for God because it is always moved, consciously or unconsciously, by the question about his own personal existence. The question of God and the question of myself are identical.

Now we have found the adequate way to put the question when we interpret the Bible. This question is, *how is man's existence understood in the Bible?* I approach the Biblical texts with this question for the same reason which supplies the deepest motive for all historical reasearch and for all interpretation of historical documents. It is that by understanding history I can gain an understanding of the possibilities of human life and thereby of the possibilities of my own life. The ultimate reason for studying history is to become conscious of the possibilities of human existence.

The interpretation of the Biblical scriptures, however, has a special motive. The tradition and the preaching of the Church tells us that we are to hear in the Bible authoritative words about our existence. What distinguishes the Bible from other literature is that in the Bible a certain possibility of existence is shown to me not as something which I am free to choose or to refuse. Rather, the Bible becomes for me a word addressed personally to me, which not only informs me about existence in general, but gives me real existence. This, however, is a possibility on which I cannot count in advance. It is not a methodological presupposition by means of which I can understand the Bible. For this possibility can become a reality only when I understand the word.

Our task, therefore, is to discover the hermeneutical principle by which we can understand what is said in the Bible. It is not permissible to evade this question, since in principle every historical document raises it, namely, what possibility of understanding human existence is shown and offered in each document of the Bible? In critical study of the Bible I can do no more than search for an answer to this question. It is beyond the competence of critical study that I should hear the word of the Bible as a word addressed personally to me and that I should believe in it. This personal understanding, in traditional terminology, is imparted by the Holy Spirit, who is not at my disposal. On the other hand, we can discover the adequate hermeneutical principle, the right way to ask the right questions, only by objective, critical reflection. If it is true that the right questions are concerned with the possibilities of understanding human existence, then it is necessary to discover the adequate conceptions by which such understanding is to be expressed. To discover these conceptions is the task of philosophy.

But now the objection is brought forward that exegesis falls under the control of philosophy. This is the case indeed, but we must ask in what sense it is so. It is an illusion to hold that any exegesis can be independent of secular conceptions. Every interpreter is inescapably dependent on conceptions which he has inherited from a tradition, consciously or unconsciously, and every tradition is dependent on some philosophy or other. In this way, for example, much of the exegesis of the nineteenth century was dependent on idealistic philosophy and on its conceptions, on its understanding of human existence. Such idealistic conceptions still influence many interpreters today. It follows, then, that historical and exegetical study should not be practiced without reflection and without giving an account of the conceptions which guide the exegesis. In other words, the question of the "right" philosophy arises.

3

At this point we must realize that there will never be a right philosophy in the sense of an absolutely perfect system, a philosophy which could give answers to all questions and clear up all riddles of human existence. Our question is simply which philosophy today offers the most adequate perspective and conceptions for understanding human existence. Here it seems to me that we should learn from existentialist philosophy, because in this philosophical school human existence is directly the object of attention.

We would learn little if existential philosophy, as many people suppose, attempted to offer an ideal pattern of human existence. The concept of "truth of existence" (*Eigentlichkeit*) does not furnish such a pattern. Existentialist philosophy does not say to me "in such and such a way you must exist"; it says only "you must exist"; or, since even this claim may be too large, it shows me what it means to exist. Existentialist philosophy tries to show what it means to exist by distinguishing between man's being as "existence" and the being of all worldly beings which are not "existing" but only "extant" (*vorhanden*). (This technical use of the word "existence" goes back to Kierkegaard.) Only men can have an existence, because they are historical beings. That is to say, every man has his own history. Always his present comes out of his past and leads into his future. He realizes his existence if he is aware that each "now" is the moment of free decision: What element in his past is to retain value? What is his responsibility toward his future, since no one can take the place of another? No one can take another's place, since

311

every man must die his own death. In his loneliness every man realizes his existence.

Of course, I cannot here carry out the existentialist analysis in detail. It may be enough to say that existentialist philosophy shows human existence to be true only in the act of existing. Existentialist philosophy is far from pretending that it secures for man a self-understanding of his own personal existence. For this self-understanding of my very personal existence can only be realized in the concrete moments of my "here" and "now". Existentialist philosophy, while it gives no answer to the question of my personal existence, makes personal existence my own personal responsibility, and by doing so it helps to make me open to the word of the Bible. It is clear, of course, that existentialist philosophy has its origin in the personal-existential question about existence and its possibilities. For how could it know about existence except from its own existential awareness, provided that existentialist philosophy is not identified with traditional anthropology? Thus it follows that existentialist philosophy can offer adequate conceptions for the interpretation of the Bible, since the interpretation of the Bible is concerned with the understanding of existence.

Once again we ask, does the existentialist understanding of existence and the existentialist analysis of that understanding already include a decision in favor of a particular understanding? Certainly such a decision is included, but what decision? Precisely the decision of which I have already spoken: "You must exist." Without this decision, without the readiness to be a human being, a person who in responsibility takes it upon himself to be, no one can understand a single word of the Bible as speaking to his own personal existence. While this decision does not require philosophical knowledge, scientific interpretation of the Bible does require the existentialist conceptions in order to explain the Biblical understanding of human existence. Thus only does it become clear that the hearing of the word of the Bible can take place only in personal decision.

That existentialist philosophy does not furnish a pattern of ideal existence may be illustrated by an example. Existentialist analysis describes particular phenomena of existence, for example, the phenomenon of love. It would be a misunderstanding to think that the existentialist analysis of love can lead me to understand how I must love here and now. The existentialist analysis can do nothing more than make it clear to me that I can understand love only by loving. No analysis can take the place of my duty to understand my love as an encounter in my own personal existence.

To be sure, philosophical analysis presupposes the judgment that it is possible to analyze human existence without reflection on the relation between man and God. But to understand human existence in its relation to God can only mean to understand my personal existence, and philosophical analysis does not claim to instruct me about my personal self-understanding. The purely formal analysis of existence does not take into account the relation between man and God, because it does not take into account the concrete events of the personal life, the concrete encounters which constitute personal existence. If it is true that the revelation of God is realized only in the concrete events of life here and now, and that the analysis of existence is confined to man's temporal life with its series of here and now, then this analysis unveils a sphere which faith alone can understand as the sphere of the relation between man and God.

The judgment that man's existence can be analyzed without taking into account his relation with God may be called an existential decision, but the elimination is not a matter of subjective preference; it is grounded in the existential insight that the idea of God is not at our disposal when we construct a theory of man's existence. Moreover, the judgment points to the idea of absolute freedom, whether this idea be accepted as true or rejected as absurd. We can also put it this way: that the elimination of man's relation with God is the expression of my personal knowledge of myself, the acknowledgment that I cannot find God by looking at or into myself. Thus, this elimination itself gives to the analysis of existence its neutrality. In the fact that existentialist philosophy does not take into account the relation between man and God, the confession is implied that I cannot speak of God as my God by looking into myself. My personal relation with God can be made real by God only, by the acting God who meets me in his Word.

V THE MEANING OF GOD AS ACTING

1

It is often said that it is impossible to carry through de-mythologizing consistently, since, if the message of the New Testament is to be retained at all, we are bound to speak of God as acting. In such speech there remains a mythological residue. For is it not mythological to speak of God as acting? This objection may also take the form that, since demythologizing as such is not consistent with speaking of God as acting, Christian preaching must always remain mythological as was the preaching of the New Testament in general. But are such arguments valid? We must ask whether we are really speaking mythologically when we speak of God as acting. We must ask in what case and under what conditions is such speaking mythological. Let us consider how God's action is understood in mythological thinking.

In mythological thinking the action of God, whether in nature, history, human fortune, or the inner life of the soul, is understood as an action which intervenes between the natural, or historical, or psychological course of events; it breaks and links them at the same time. The divine causality is inserted as a link in the chain of the events which follow one another according to the causal nexus. This is meant by the popular notion that a miraculous event cannot be understood except as a miracle, that is, as the effect of a supernatural cause. In such thinking the action of God is indeed conceived in the same way as secular actions or events are conceived, for the divine power which effects miracles is considered as a natural power. In fact, however, a miracle in the sense of an action of God cannot be thought of as an event which happens on the level of secular (worldly) events. It is not visible, not capable of objective, scientific proof which is possible only within an objective view of the world. To the scientific, objective observer God's action is a mystery.

The thought of the action of God as an unworldly and transcendent action can be protected from misunderstanding only if it is not thought of as an action which happens between the worldly actions or events, but as happening within them. The close connection between natural and historical events remain intact as it presents itself to the observer. The action of God is hidden from every eye except the eye of faith. Only the so-called natural, secular (worldly) events are visible to every man and capable of proof. It is *within* them that God's hidden action is taking place.

If someone now insists that to speak in this sense of God as acting is to speak mythologically, I have no objection, since in this case myth is something very different from what it is as the object of de-mythologizing. When we speak of God as acting, we do not speak mythologically in the objectifying sense.

2

Now another question arises: If faith maintains that God's hidden action is at work within the chain of secular events, faith may be suspected of being pantheistic piety. As we reflect on this problem, we can further clarify the sense in which we must understand God's action. Faith insists not on the direct identity of God's action with worldly events, but, if I may be permitted to put it so, on the paradoxical identity which can be believed only here and now against the appearance of non-identity. In faith I can understand an accident with which I meet as a gracious gift of God or as his punishment, or as his chastisement. On the other hand, I can understand the same accident as a link in the chain of the natural course of events. If, for example, my child has recovered from a dangerous illness, I give thanks to God because he has saved my child. By faith I can accept a thought or a resolution as a divine inspiration without removing the thought or the resolution from its connection with psychological motivation. It is possible, for example, that a decision which seemed insignificant when I made it, is seen later on to have marked a decisive and fruitful "turning point" in my life. Then I give thanks to God who inspired the decision. The creedal belief in God as creator is not a guarantee given in advance by means of which I am permitted to understand any event as wrought by God. The understanding of God as creator is genuine only when I understand myself here and now as the creature of God. This existential understanding does not need to express itself in my consciousness as explicit knowledge. In any case the belief in the almighty God is not the conviction given in advance that there exists an almighty Being who is able to do all things. Belief in the almighty God is genuine only when it actually takes place in my very existence, as I surrender myself to the power of God who overwhelms me here and now. Once more this does not mean that the belief must express itself in my consciousness as explicit knowledge; it does mean, however, that the statements of belief are not general statements. For example, Luther's statement *terra ubique domini* is not genuine as a dogmatic statement but only here and now when spoken in the decision of my very existence. This distinction, I think, can be best understood today by one for whom the dogmatic statement has become doubtful, that is, in the misery of imprisonment in Russia.

We may conclude that pantheism is indeed a conviction given in advance, a general world-view (*Weltanschauung*), which affirms that every event in the world is the work of God because God is immanent in the

315

world. Christian faith, by contrast, holds that God acts on me, speaks to me, here and now. The Christian believes this because he knows that he is addressed by the grace of God which meets him in the Word of God, in Jesus Christ. God's grace opens his eyes to see that "in everything God works for good with those who love him" (Rom. 8:28). This faith is not a knowledge possessed once for all; it is not a general world-view. It can be realized only here and now. It can be a living faith only when the believer is always asking what God is telling him here and now. God's action generally, in nature and history, is hidden from the believer just as much as from the non-believer. But in so far as he sees what comes upon him here and now in the light of the divine word, he can and must take it as God's action. Pantheism can say "there divinity is working" with regard to any event, whatever it may be, without taking into account the importance of what happens for my personal existence. Christian faith can only say, "I trust that God is working here and there, but his action is hidden, for it is not directly identical with the visible event. What it is that he is doing I do not yet know, and perhaps I never shall know it, but faithfully I trust that it is important for my personal existence, and I must ask what it is that God says to me. Perhaps it may be only that I must endure and be silent".

What follows from all this? In faith I deny the closed connection of the worldly events, the chain of cause and effect as it presents itself to the neutral observer. I deny the interconnection of the worldly events not as mythology does, which by breaking the connection places supernatural events into the chain of natural events; I deny the worldly connection as a whole when I speak of God. I deny the worldly connection of events when I speak of myself, for in this connection of worldly events, my self, my personal existence, my own personal life, is no more visible and capable of proof than is God as acting.

In faith I realize that the scientific world-view [*Weltbild*] does not comprehend the whole reality of the world and of human life, but faith does not offer another general world-view [*Weltanschuung*] which corrects science in its statements on its own level. Rather faith acknowledges that the world-view given by science is a necessary means for doing our work within the world. Indeed, I need to see the worldly events as linked by cause and effect not only as a scientific observer, but also in my daily living. In doing so there remains no room for God's working. This is the paradox of faith, that faith "nevertheless" understands as God's action here and now an event which is completely intelligible in the natural or historical connection of events. This "nevertheless" is inseparable from faith. This "nevertheless" (the German *dennoch* of Ps. 73:23; and Paul Tillich's *in spite of*) is inseparable from faith. Only this is real faith in miracle. He who thinks that it is possible to speak of miracles as of demonstrable events capable of proof offends against the thought of God as acting in hidden ways. He subjects God's action to the control of objective observation. He delivers up the faith in miracles to the criticism of science and in so doing validates such criticism.

3

Here another question arises. If God's action must be thought of as hidden, how is it possible to speak of it except in purely negative statements? Is the conception of transcendence an exclusively negative conception? It would be if to speak of God did not also mean to speak of our personal existence. If we speak of God as acting in general, transcendence would indeed be a purely negative conception, since every positive description of transcendence transposes it into this world. It is wrong to speak of God as acting in general statements, in terms of the formal analysis of man's existence. It is precisely the formal, existentialist analysis of human existence which shows that it is indeed impossible to speak of our personal existence in general statements. I can speak of my personal existence only here and now in the concrete situation of my life. To be sure, I can explicate in general statements the meaning, the sense of the conception of God and of God's action in so far as I can say that God is the power which bestows upon me life and existence, and in so far as I can describe these actions as the encounter which demands my own personal decision. By doing so I acknowledge that I cannot speak of God's action in general statements; I can speak only of what he does here and now with me, of what he speaks here and now to me. Even if we do not speak of God in general terms but rather of his action here and now on us, we must speak in terms of general conceptions, for all of our language employs conceptions, but it does not follow that the issue in hand is a general one.

4

Now we may ask once more whether it is possible to speak of God as acting without falling into mythological speech. It is often asserted that the language of the Christian faith must of necessity be mythological language. This assertion must be examined carefully. First, even if we concede that the language of faith is really the language of myth, we must ask how this fact affects the program of de-mythologizing. This concession is by no means a valid argument against de-mythologizing, for the language of myth, when it serves as the language of faith, loses its mythological sense. To speak, for example, of God as creator, no longer involves speaking of his creatorship in the sense of the old myth. Mythological conceptions can be used as symbols or images which are perhaps necessary to the language of religion and therefore also of the Christian faith. Thus it becomes evident that the use of mythological language, far from being an objection to de-mythologizing, positively demands it.

Second, the assertion that the language of faith needs the language of myth can be validated only if a further qualification is taken into account. If it is true that mythological conceptions are necessary as symbols or images, we must ask what it is that is now expressed by such symbols or images. Surely it is impossible that their meaning within the language of faith should be expressed in terms of mythological conceptions. Their meaning can and must be stated without recourse to mythological terms.

Third, to speak of God as acting does not necessarily mean to speak in symbols or images. Such speech must be able to convey its full, direct meaning. How, then, must we speak of God as acting if our speech is not to be understood as mythological speech? God as acting does not refer to an event which can be perceived by me without myself being drawn into the event as into God's action, without myself taking part in it as being acted upon. In other words, to speak of God as acting involves the events of personal existence. The encounter with God can be an event for man only here and now, since man lives within the limits of space and time. When we speak of God as acting, we mean that we are confronted with God, addressed, asked, judged, or blessed by God. Therefore, to speak in this manner is not to speak in symbols or images, but to speak analogically. For when we speak in this manner of God as acting, we conceive God's action as an analogue to the actions taking place between men. Moreover, we conceive the communion between God and man as an analogue to the communion between man and man.[102] It is in this analogical sense that we speak of God's love and care for men, of his demands and of his wrath, of his promise and grace, and it is in this analogical sense that we call him Father. We are not only justified in speaking thus, but we must do so, since now we are not speaking of an idea about God, but of God himself. Thus, God's love and care, etc., are not images or symbols; these conceptions mean real experiences of God as acting here and now. Especially in the conception of God as Father the mythological sense vanished long ago. We can understand the meaning of the term Father as applied to God by considering what it means when we speak to our fathers or when our children speak to us as their fathers. As applied to God the physical import of the term father has disappeared completely; it expresses a purely personal relationship. It is in this analogical sense that we speak of God as Father.

From this view of the situation some important conclusions follow. First, only such statements about God are legitimate as express the existential relation between God and man. Statements which speak of God's actions as cosmic events are illegitimate. The affirmation that God is creator cannot be a theoretical statement about God as *creator mundi* in a general sense. The affirmation can only be a personal confession that I understand myself to be a creature which owes its existence to God. It cannot be made as a neutral statement, but only as thanksgiving and surrender. Moreover, statements which describe God's action as cultic action, for example, that he offered his Son as a sacrificial victim, are not legitimate, unless they are understood in a purely symbolic sense. Second, the so-called images which describe God as acting are legitimate only if they mean that God is a personal being acting on persons. Therefore, political and juridical conceptions are not permissible, unless they are understood purely as symbols.

5

At this point a really important objection arises. If what we have said is correct, does it not follow that God's action is deprived of objective reality, that it is reduced to a purely subjective, psychological experience (*Erlebnis*); that God exists only as an inner event in the soul, whereas faith has real meaning only if God exists outside the believer? Such objections are brought forward again and again, and the shades of Schleiermacher and Feuerbach are conjured up in this controversy. *Erlebnis* (psychological experience) was indeed a popular catchword in German theology before the First World War. Faith was often described as *Erlebnis*. It was on this catch-word that Karl Barth and the so-called dialectical theologians made an all-out attack.

When we say that to speak of God means to speak of our own personal existence, the meaning is a totally different one. The objection which I have just summarized suffers from a psychological misunderstanding of the life of the soul. From the statement that to speak of God is to speak of myself, it by no means follows that God is not outside the believer. (This would be the case only if faith is interpreted as a purely psychological event.) When man is understood in the genuine sense as an historical being which has its reality in concrete situations and decisions, in the very encounters of life,[103] it is clear, on the one hand, that faith, speaking of God as acting, cannot defend itself against the charge of being an illusion, and, on the other hand, that faith does not mean a psychologically subjective event.

Is it enough to say that faith grows out of the encounter with the Holy Scriptures as the Word of God, that faith is nothing but simple hearing? The answer is yes. But this answer is valid only if the Scriptures are understood neither as a manual of doctrine nor as a record of witnesses to a faith which I interpret by sympathy and empathy. On the contrary, to hear the Scriptures as the Word of God means to hear them as a word which is addressed to me, as *kerygma*, as a proclamation. Then my understanding is not a neutral one, but rather my response to a call. The fact that the word of the Scriptures is God's Word cannot be demonstrated objectively; it is an event which happens here and now. God's Word is hidden in the Scriptures as each action of God is hidden everywhere.

I have said that faith grows out of the encounters which are the substance of our personal lives as historical lives. Its meaning is readily understood when we reflect upon the simple phenomena of our personal lives. The love of my friend, my wife, my children, meets me genuinely only here and now as an event. Such love cannot be observed by objective methods but only by personal experience and response. From the outside, for example, by psychological observation, it cannot be perceived as love, but only as an interesting detail of psychological processes which are open to different interpretations. Thus, the fact that God cannot be seen or apprehended apart from faith does not mean that he does not exist apart from faith.

We must remember, however, that the affirmations of faith in its relation to its object, to God, cannot be proved objectively. This is not a weakness of faith; it is its true strength, as my teacher Wilhelm Herrmann insisted. For if the relation between faith and God could be proved as the relation between subject and object in worldly situations can be proved, then he would be placed on the same level as the world, within which the demand for proof is legitimate.

May we then say that God has "proved" himself by the "facts of redemption" (*Heilstatsachen*)? By no means. For what we call facts of redemption are themselves objects of faith and are apprehended as such only by the eye of faith. They cannot be perceived apart from faith, as if faith could be based on data in the same way as the natural sciences are based on data which are open to empirical observation. To be sure, the facts of redemption constitute the grounds of faith, but only as perceived by faith itself. The principle is the same in our personal relationship as persons with persons. Trust in a friend can rest solely on the personality of my friend which I can perceive only when I trust him. There cannot be any trust or love without risk. It is true, as Wilhelm Herrmann taught us, that the ground and the object of faith are identical. They are one and the same thing, because we cannot speak of what God is in himself but only of what he is doing to us and with us.

6

Now another question can be answered. If we hold that God's action is not visible, not capable of proof; that the events of redemption cannot be demonstrated, that the spirit with which the believers are endowed is not an object visible to objective observation; if we hold that we can speak of all such matters only when we are concerned with our personal existence, then it can be said that faith is a new understanding of personal existence. In other words, God's action bestows upon us a new understanding of ourselves.

The objection may be raised that in this case the event of God's revelation is nothing but the occasion which gives us understanding of ourselves and that the occasion is not recognized as an action which occurs in our actual lives and transforms them. In short, revelation is not recognized as a wonder. Then, the objection goes on, nothing happens but understanding or consciousness of the self; the content of the self-understanding is a timeless truth; once perceived it remains valid without regard to the occasion, namely, revelation, which has given rise to it.

This objection is based on a confusion to which I have referred above (p. 317), i.e., self-understanding of personal existence is confused with the philosophical analysis of man. The existential understanding (*das Existentiell*) is confused with the existentialist understanding (*das Existential*). Of philosophical analysis it may well be said that its statements are statements of timeless truth, not answers to the questions of the actual moment. But it is precisely this philosophical analysis of man, the *existentialist* understanding, which shows that the self-understanding —

the existential understanding — becomes realized only here and now as my own self-understanding. Philosophical analysis shows what existence in the abstract means. By contrast, existential, personal self-understanding does not say what existence means in the abstract, but points to my life as a concrete person in the here and now. It is an act of understanding in which my very self and the relationships in which I am involved are understood together.

Such existential, personal understanding need not take place on the level of consciousness, and this, indeed, is rare. But such personal self-understanding, albeit unconscious, dominates, or exercises a powerful influence upon, all our sorrows and cares, ambitions, joys and anxieties. Moreover, this personal self-understanding is put to the test, is called into question (*ist in Frage gestellt*) in every situation of encounter. As my life goes on, my self-understanding may prove inadequate or it may become clearer and deeper as the result of further experiences and encounters. This change may be due to radical self-examination or it may occur unconsciously, when, for example, my life is led out of the darkness of distress into the light of happiness or when the opposite experience comes to me. Entering into decisive encounters I may achieve a totally new self-understanding as a result of the love which is bestowed upon me when, for example, I marry or make a new friend. Even a little child unconsciously manifests such self-understanding in so far as he realizes that he is a child and that he therefore stands in a special relationship to his parents. His self-understanding expresses itself in his love, trust, feeling of security, thankfulness, etc.

In my personal existence, I am isolated neither from my environment nor from my own past and future. When, for example, I achieve through love a new self-understanding, what takes place is not an isolated psychological act of coming to consciousness; my whole situation is transformed. In understanding myself, I understand other people and at the same time the whole world takes on a new character. I see it, as we say, in a new light, and so it really is a new world. I achieve a new insight into my past and my future. I recognize new demands and am open to encounters in a new manner. My past and future become more than pure time as it is marked on a calendar or timetable. Now it should be clear that I cannot possess this self-understanding as a timeless truth, a conviction accepted once and for all. For my new self-understanding, by its very nature, must be renewed day by day, so that I understand the imperative self which is included in it.

Mutatis mutandis we may here apply the saying, "if we live by the Spirit, let us also walk by the Spirit" (Gal. 5:25). For indeed the saying is applicable to the self-understanding of faith, which is a response to our encounter with the word of God. In faith man understands himself anew. As Luther says in his interpretation of the Epistle to the Romans, "God going out from himself brings it about that we go into ourselves; and making himself known to us, he makes us known to ourselves". In faith man understands himself ever anew. This new self-understanding can be maintained only as a continual response to the word of God which proclaims his action in Jesus Christ. It is the same in ordinary human life. The new self-understanding which grows out of the encounter of man with man can be maintained only if the actual relation between man and man is maintained. "The kindness of God is new every morning"; yes, provided I perceive it anew every morning. For this is not a timeless truth, like a mathematical statement. I can speak of the kindness of God which is new every morning only if I myself am renewed every morning.

These considerations in turn throw light on the paradoxical juxtaposition of indicative and imperative in Paul to which I just referred above (Gal. 5:25). We now see that the indicative calls forth the imperative. The indicative gives expression to the new self-understanidng of the believer, for the statement "I am freed from sin" is not a dogmatic one, but an existential one. It is the believer's confession that his whole existence is renewed. Since his existence includes his will, the imperative reminds him that he is free from sin, provided that his will is renewed in obedience to the commandment of God.

7

A further objection which may arise is that the future action of God is eliminated by de-mythologizing. I reply that it is precisely de-mythologizing which makes clear the true meaning of God as acting in the future. Faith includes free and complete openness to the future. Philosophical analysis of existence shows that openness to the future is an essential feature of man's existence. But can philosophical analysis endow the concretely existing man with the openness? By no means. It can no more do this than it can bestow existence upon us. Philosophical analysis, as Heidegger has shown, can do no more than explain that man, if he is willing to exist in a full personal sense, must be open to the future. It can call attention to the effect, stimulating or frightening, of this perception when it affirms that for philosophical analysis the future cannot be characterized otherwise than as nothing.

Therefore, free openness to the future is freedom to take anxiety upon ourselves (*Angstbereitschaft*), i.e., to decide for it. If it is true that the Christian faith involves free openness to the future, then it is freedom from anxiety in the face of the Nothing. For this freedom nobody can decide of his own will; it can only be given, in faith. Faith as openness to the future is freedom from the past, because it is faith in the forgiveness of sins; it is freedom from the enslaving chains of the past. It is freedom *from* ourselves as the old selves, and *for* ourselves as the new selves. It is freedom from the illusion, grounded in sin, that we can establish our personal existence through our own decision. It is the free openness to the future which Paul acclaims in saying that "death is swallowed up in victory" (I Cor. 15:54).

8

Here a final and crucial question arises. If we must speak of God as acting only in the sense that he acts with me here and now, can we still believe that God has acted once for all on behalf of the whole world? Are we not in danger of eliminating this "once for all" of Paul's (Rom. 6:10)? Are we not in danger of relegating the divine dispensation, the history of salvation, to the dimension of timelessness? It should be clear from what we have said that we are not speaking of an idea of God but of the living God in whose hands our time lies, and who encounters us here and now. Therefore, we can make our answer to the objection in the single affirmation that God meets us in his Word, in a concrete word, the preaching instituted in Jesus Christ. While it may be said that God meets us always and everywhere, we do not see and hear him always and everywhere, unless his Word supervenes and enables us to understand the moment here and now, as Luther so often insisted. The idea of the omnipresent and almighty God becomes real in my personal existence only by his Word spoken here and now. Accordingly it must be said that the Word of God is what it is only in the moment in which it is spoken. The Word of God is not a timeless statement but a concrete word addressed to men here and now. To be sure God's Word is his eternal Word, but this eternity must not be conceived as timelessness, but as his presence always actualized here and now. It is his Word as an event, in an encounter, not as a set of ideas, not, for example, as a statement about God's kindness and grace in general, although such a statement may be otherwise correct, but only as addressed to me, as an event happening and meeting me as his mercy. Only thus is it the *verbum externum*, the word from the outside. Not as a knowledge possessed once for all, but precisely as meeting me over and over again is it really the *verbum externum*.

From this it follows that God's Word is a real word spoken to me in human language, whether in the preaching of the Church or in the Bible, in the sense that the Bible is not viewed merely as an interesting collection of sources for the history of religion, but that the Bible is transmitted through the Church as a word addressing us. This living Word of God is not invented by the human spirit and by human sagacity; it rises up in history. Its origin is an historical event, by which the speaking of this word, the preaching, is rendered authoritative and legitimate. This event is Jesus Christ.

We may say that this assertion is paradoxical. For what God has done in Jesus Christ is not an historical fact which is capable of historical proof. The objectifying historian as such cannot see that an historical person (Jesus of Nazareth) is the eternal Logos, the Word. It is precisely the mythological description of Jesus Christ in the New Testament which makes it clear that the figure and the work of Jesus Christ must be understood in a manner which is beyond the categories by which the objective historian understands world-history, if the figure and the work of Jesus Christ are to be understood as the divine work of redemption. That is the real paradox. Jesus is a human, historical person from Nazareth in Galilee. His work and destiny happened within world-history and as such come under the scrutiny of the historian who can understand them as part of the nexus of history. Nevertheless, such detached historical inquiry cannot become aware of what God has wrought in Christ, that is, of the eschatological event.

According to the New Testament the decisive significance of Jesus Christ is that he — in his person, his coming, his passion, and his glorification — is the eschatological event. He is the one "who is to come", and we are not to "look for another" (Matt. 11:3). "When the time had fully come, God sent forth his Son" (Gal. 4:4). "This is the judgment, that the light has come into the world" (John 3:19). "The hour is coming, and now is, when the dead will hear the voice of the Son of God, and those who hear will live" (John 5:25). All these sayings declare that Jesus Christ is the eschatological event. The crucial question for de-mythologizing is whether this understanding of Jesus Christ as the eschatological event is inextricably bound up with the conceptions of cosmological eschatology as it is in the New Testament, with the single exception of the Fourth Gospel.

In the Fourth Gospel, as we have seen, the cosmological eschatology is understood, from our point of view, as an historical eschatology. We have also seen that for Paul the believer is already a new creation, "the old has passed away, behold, the new has come" (II Cor. 5:17). We must, therefore, say that to live in faith is to live an eschatological existence, to live beyond the world, to have passed from death to life (cf. John 5:24; I John 3:14). Certainly the eschatological existence is already realized in anticipation, for "we walk by faith, not by sight" (II Cor. 5:7). This means that the eschatological existence of the believer is not a worldly phenomenon, but is realized in the new self-understanding. This self-understanding, as we have seen before, grows out of the Word. The eschatological event which is Jesus Christ happens here and now as the Word is being preached (II Cor. 6:2; John 5:24) regardless of whether this Word is accepted or rejected. The believer has passed from death to life, and the unbeliever is judged; the wrath of God rests upon him, says John (John 3:18, 36; 9:39). The word of the preaching spreads death and life, says Paul (II Cor. 2:15f.).

Thus, the "once for all" is now understood in its genuine sense, namely, as the "once for all" of the eschatological event. For this "once for all" is not the uniqueness of an historical event but means that a particular historical event, that is, Jesus Christ, is to be understood as the eschatological "once for all". As an eschatological event this "once for all" is always present in the proclaimed word, not as a timeless truth, but as happening here and now. Certainly the Word says to me that God's grace is a prevenient grace which has already acted for me; but not in such a way that I can look back on it as an historical event of the past. The acting grace is present now as the eschatological event. The word of God is Word of God only as it happens here and now. The paradox is that the word which is always happening here and now is one and the same with the first word of the apostolic preaching crystallized in the Scriptures of the New Testament and delivered by men again and again, the word whose content may be formulated in general statements. It cannot be the one without the other. This is the sense of the "once for all". It is the eschatological once-for-all because the word becomes event here and now in the living voice of the preaching.

The word of God and the Church belong together, because it is by the word that the Church is constituted as the community of the called, in so far as the preaching is not a lecture comprised of general propositions

326

but the message which is proclaimed by authorized, legitimate messengers (II Cor. 5:18-20). As the word is God's word only as an event, the Church is genuine Church only as an event which happens each time here and now; for the Church is the eschatological community of the saints, and it is only in a paradoxical way identical with the ecclesiastical institutions which we observe as social phenomena of secular history.

9

We have seen that the task of de-mythologizing received its first impulse from the conflict between the mythological views of the world contained in the Bible and the modern views of the world which are influenced by scientific thinking, and it has become evident that faith itself demands to be freed from any world-view produced by man's thought, whether mythological or scientific. For all human world-views objectivize the world and ignore or eliminate the significance of the encounters in our personal existence. This conflict shows that in our age faith has not yet found adequate forms of expression; that our age has not yet become aware of the identity of its ground and object; that it has not yet genuinely understood the transcendence and hiddenness of God as acting. It is not yet aware of its own "nevertheless", or of its "in spite of"; over and over again it yields to the temptation to objectivize God and his action. Therefore, the criticism of the mythological world-view of Biblical and ecclesiastical preaching renders a valuable service to faith, for it recalls faith to radical reflection on its own nature. The task of de-mythologizing has no other purpose than to take up this challenge. The invisibility of God excludes every myth which tries to make God and his action visible; God withholds himself from view and observation. We can believe in God only in spite of experience, just as we can accept justification only in spite of conscience. Indeed, de-mythologizing is a task parallel to that performed by Paul and Luther in their doctrine of justification by faith alone without the works of law. More precisely, de-mythologizing is the radical application of the doctrine of justification by faith to the sphere of knowledge and thought. Like the doctrine of justification, de-mythologizing destroys every longing for security. There is no difference between security based on good works and security built on objectifying knowledge. The man who desires to believe in God must know that he has nothing at his own disposal on which to build his faith, that he is, so to speak, in a vacuum. He who abandons every form of security shall find the true security. Man before

RUDOLF BULTMANN: INTERPRETING FAITH FOR THE MODERN ERA

God has always empty hands. He who gives up, he who loses every security shall find security. Faith in God, like faith in justification, refuses to single out qualified or definable actions as holy actions. Correspondingly, faith in God, like faith in creation, refuses to single out qualified and definable realms from among the observable realities of nature and history. Luther has taught us that there are no holy places in the world, that the world as a whole is indeed a profane place. This is true in spite of Luther's "the earth everywhere is the Lord's" (*terra ubique Domini*), for this, too, can be believed only in spite of all the evidence. It is not the consecration of the priest but the proclaimed word which makes holy the house of God. In the same way, the whole of nature and history is profane. It is only in the light of the proclaimed word that what has happened or is happening here or there assumes the character of God's action for the believer. It is precisely by faith that the world becomes a profane place and is thus restored to its true place as the sphere of man's action.

Nevertheless, the world is God's world and the sphere of God as acting. Therefore, our relation to the world as believers is paradoxical. As Paul puts it in I Cor. 7:29-31, "Let those who have wives live as though they had none, and those who mourn as though they were not mourning, and those who rejoice as though they were not rejoicing, and those who buy as though they had no goods, and those who deal with the world as though they had no dealings with it." In terms of this book, we may say, "let those who have the modern world-view live as though they had none."

Jesus Christ and Mythology, pp. 11-27, 30-85.

SELECT BIBLIOGRAPHY

An incomplete bibliography of Rudolf Bultmann's publications up to 1965, in both German and English, is available in: *The Theology of Rudolf Bultmann*, Charles W. Kegley, ed. (New York: Harper & Row, 1966).

I. BULTMANN'S PUBLICATIONS IN ENGLISH
(in chronological order of publication in English)

"The New Approach to the Synoptic Problem", *The Journal of Religion*, VI (1926) 337-362.

Jesus and the Word, Louise Pettibone Smith and Erminie Huntress, trans. (New York: Scribners, 1934).

"The Study of the Synoptic Gospels", *Form Criticism*, Fredrick C. Grant, trans. (New York: Willett, Clark & Company, 1934).

"How does God Speak to us through the Bible?" *The Student World*, XXVII, 2 (1934) 108-112.

"To Love Your Neighbour", *Scottish Periodical*, I, (1947) 42-56.

Theology of the New Testament, Kendrick Grobel, trans. (New York: Scribners, 1951 [vol. I] and 1955 [vol. II]).

"Humanism and Christianity", *Journal of Religion*, XXXII (1952), 77-86.

"New Testament and Mythology",
"A Reply to the Theses of J. Schniewind",
"Bultmann Replies to His Critics", *Kerygma and Myth*, Hans Werner Bartsch, ed., Reginald H. Fuller, trans. (London: SPCK, 1953.)
[For a more recent and complete translation, see Ogden, 1984 below.]

"The Christian Hope and the Problem of Demythologizing", *The Expository Times*, LXV (1954).

"History and Eschatology in the New Testament", *New Testament Studies*, I, (1954) 5-16.

Essays: Philosophical and Theological, James C. G. Greig, trans. (London: SCM Press, 1955). [Essays from *Glauben und Verstehen*, II.]

"The Transformation of the Idea of the Church in Early Christianity", *Canadian Journal of Theology*, I, (1955) 73-81.

Primitive Christianity in its Contemporary Setting, R. H. Fuller, trans. (New York: Meridian Books, 1957).

History and Eschatology (Edinburgh: The University Press, 1957).
The Presence of Eternity is the same book published in America the same year by Harpers under a different title.

"Introduction", *What is Christianity?* by Adolf Harnack (New York: Harpers, 1957).

"Theology for Freedom and Responsibility", *Christian Century*, LXXV, (1958) 967-969.

Jesus Christ and Mythology (New York: Scribners, 1958).

"On Behalf of Christian Freedom", *The Journal of Religion*, XL (1960), 1, 95-99.

Existence and Faith: Shorter Writings of Rudolf Bultmann, Schubert Ogden, trans. (New York: Meridian, 1960).

This World and the Beyond: Marburg Sermons, Harold Knight, trans. (New York: Scribners, 1960).

"The Case for Demythologizing", *Kerygma and Myth*, II, Hans Werner Bartsch, ed., Reginald H. Fuller, trans. (London: SPCK, 1962).

The History of the Synoptic Tradition, John Marsh, trans. (New York: Harper & Row, 1963).

"The Primitive Christian Kerygma and the Historical Jesus", *The Historical Jesus and the Kerygmatic Christ*, Carl E. Braaten and Roy A. Harrisville, trans. (Nashville: Abingdon Press, 1964).

"The Idea of God and Modern Man", *Translating Theology into the Modern Age* (New York: Harper & Row, 1965).

The Old and New Man, Keith R. Crim, trans. (Richmond, VA: John Knox Press, 1967).

"The Problem of a Theological Exegesis of the New Testament",
Review, Karl Barth's *Epistle to the Romans* (second edition),
"Religion and Culture",
"Ethical and Mystical Religion in Primitive Christianity",
"The Question of a Dialectic Theology: A Discussion with Peterson",
The Beginnings of Dialectic Theology, James M. Robinson, ed. (Richmond, VA: John Knox Press, 1968).

Faith and Understanding, Louise Pettibone Smith, trans. (New York: Harper & Row, 1969). [Essays from *Glauben und Verstehen*, I]. Reissued with same English title (Philadelphia: Fortress Press, 1987).

The Gospel of John: a Commentary, G. R. Beasley-Murray, trans. (Oxford: Blackwell, 1971).

The Johannine Epistles: a Commentary, R. Philip O'Hara, trans. (Philadelphia: Fortress Press, 1973).

Karl Barth—Rudolf Bultmann Letters: 1922-1966, Bernd Jaspert, ed., Geoffrey W. Bromiley, trans. (Grand Rapids, MI: Eerdmans Press, 1981).

New Testament and Mythology and Other Basic Writings, Schubert Ogden, trans. (Philadelphia: Fortress Press, 1984).

The Second Letter to the Corinthians, Roy A. Harrisville, trans. (Minneapolis: Augsburg Press, 1985).

[Twenty-seven articles on Greek word-clusters from *Theologisches Wörterbuch zum Neuen Testament* (1933-1973), G. Kittel and G. Friedrich, eds., appear in excellent translation in the ten-volume *Theological Dictionary of the New Testament*, Geoffrey Bromiley, trans. (Grand Rapids, MI: Eerdmans, 1964-1976). Their locations are as follows: I: 19-21; 115-121; 169-171; 189-191; 238-251; 343-344; 367; 509-512; 689-719; II: 61-62; 477-487; 517-523, 529-535; 751-754; 772-775; 832-843, 849-851, 855-875; III: 7-25; 297-300; 645-654; IV: 313-324; 589-593; 892-895; V: 159-161; VI: 1-11; 40-43; 174-182, 197-228; IX: 1-10.]

II. SELECTED WRITINGS ABOUT BULTMANN

Hobbs, Edward C., ed., *Bultmann, Retrospect and Prospect: The Centenary Symposium at Wellesley* (Philadelphia, PA: Fortress Press, 1985).

Johnson, Roger A., *The Origins of Demythologizing* (Leiden: Brill, 1973).

Kegley, Charles W., ed., *The Theology of Rudolf Bultmann* (New York: Harper & Row, 1966).

Ogden, Schubert, *Christ Without Myth* (New York: Harper, 1961).

Perrin, Norman, *The Promise of Bultmann* (Philadelphia, PA: Lippincott, 1969).

Robinson, James M., *The Future of Our Religious Past: Essays in Honor of Rudolf Bultmann* (New York: Harper & Row, 1971).

Schmithals, Walter, *An Introduction to the Theology of Rudolf Bultmann* (Minneapolis, MN: Augsburg Press, 1968).

NOTES TO THE INTRODUCTION

[1] The centenary of Bultmann's birth, in the Fall of 1984, was observed with an academic conference and several publications. A three-day symposium was held at Wellesley College, which had been the academic home of Louise Pettibone Smith, Bultmann's first translator. Papers from this conference have been published in *Bultmann, Retrospect and Prospect: The Centenary Symposium at Wellesley*, Edward C. Hobbs, ed. (Philadelphia, PA: Fortress Press, 1985). In that same year, Schubert Ogden brought out a volume of new translations: *New Testament and Mythology and Other Basic Writings* (Philadelphia, PA: Fortress Press, 1984). In Germany, Bernd Jaspert edited a volume of collected essays: *Rudolf Bultmann's Werk und Wirkung* (Darmstadt: Wissenschaftliche Buchgesellschaft, 1984) and Erich Graesser brought together thirty-four of Bultmann's previously unpublished sermons: *Das verkündigte Wort* (Tübingen: J. C. B. Mohr, 1984).

[2] *Die Christliche Welt* was a liberal Protestant journal in which Bultmann published several of his early essays.

[3] This biographical information is taken from a brief sketch, "Autobiographical Reflections of Rudolf Bultmann", which first appeared in *Existence and Faith* (1960) and subsequently in *The Theology of Rudolf Bultmann* (1966). Bultmann was an extraordinarily modest man who did not wish to call attention to himself. While such modesty is a virtue in the man, it can contribute to a liability for the author writing about Bultmann. The lives of Bultmann's theological peers, like Karl Barth, Dietrich Bonhoeffer or Paul Tillich, are all documented in substantial biographies. We have no biography of Bultmann.

[4] Liberal Theology included many elements: the historical-critical study of the bible, a focus on the historical Jesus as God's decisive revelation to humanity, an identification of God with moral goodness, and confidence in humanity as God's fit partner for the building of the Kingdom. Some of these elements of Liberal Theology were already called into question by Bultmann in the 1917 sermon included in this volume. In the light of World War I (1914-1918), he rejected any glib identification of God with moral goodness, since the destructive powers released in that war also belonged, in some way, to the reality of God. The war also led him, and many others, to doubt the moral capacities of human nature to build an ideal society. However, in his published writings, Bultmann did not link such views with an explicit critique of Liberal Theology until this 1920 essay.

[5] Bultmann, "Ethical and Mystical Religion in Primitive Christianity", *The Beginnings of Dialectic Theology*, James M. Robinson, ed. (Richmond, VA: John Knox Press, 1968), p. 221.

[6] English translation of this essay by Carl E. Braaten and Roy A. Harrisville, ed., in *The Historical Jesus and the Kerygmatic Christ* (Nashville, TN: Abingdon Press, 1964).

[7] *The Beginnings of Dialectic Theology*, p. 235.

[8] In a letter of December 1923, Bultmann expressed his mixed reaction to Barth in terms of his appreciation for Barth's questions while rejecting the methods and results of his exegesis. "In my exegesis course, I am discussing Barth again. His *Epistle to the Romans* is certainly an amazing work, and though I find its exegesis artificial and allegorizing, I find its questions most fruitful for any effort of interpretation." Cited in "Bultmann's Papers", Antje Bultmann Lemke, *Bultmann, Retrospect and Prospect*, p. 9.

[9] Cited in Walter Schmithals, *An Introduction to the Theology of Rudolf Bultmann* (Minneapolis, MN: Augsburg Press, 1968), pp. 9-10.

[10] As indicated in a letter of December 1923, Bultmann also appreciated Heidegger's knowledge of Luther, as well as his familiarity with contemporary theologians, especially Herrmann, Gogarten and Barth. Already in December 1923, Bultmann reports that "This seminar [on Paul] is especially instructive because our new philosopher, Heidegger, participates in it". Antje Bultmann Lemke, "Bultmann's Papers", *Bultmann, Retrospect and Prospect*, pp. 9-10.

[11] In appreciation for their years of fruitful work together, Bultmann dedicated his first volume of collected essays, *Glauben und Verstehen* (1933), to Heidegger.

[12] Hermann Cohen and Paul Natorp were the most significant philosophical sources for Marburg Neo-Kantianism; Wilhelm Herrmann was its most prominent theological spokesman. While Cohen had retired from the Marburg faculty in 1912, Natorp and Herrmann were still there in 1921 when Bultmann returned as Professor of New Testament.

[13] Bultmann first set forth his view of the fundamental dichotomy between objectifying thinking and religion in a 1920 essay, "Religion and Culture", *The Beginnings of Dialectic Theology*, pp. 205-220. "Thus the basic difference [of religion] from culture becomes clear: Religion is not available in objective formulations as is culture, but only in being realized; that is, in that which happens with the individual. The meaning of religion is the being, the life, of the individual" (*ibid.*, p. 211). "If the religious life is to be found not in objective formulations, but in individual life, there cannot be a history of religion" (*ibid.*, p. 214). At this early date, Bultmann did not have an "existentialist conceptuality" available as an alternative for his rejected objectifying conceptuality. He could only appeal to the "inner life and experience of the individual". However, he was already convinced that any objectifying mode of thought necessarily introduced confusion and distortion in theology.

[14] For a philosophical discussion of this concept of objectifying, see the chapter on Marburg Neo-Kantianism, *The Origins of Demythologizing*, Roger A. Johnson (Leiden: E. J. Brill, 1974).

[15] When Bultmann published his demythologizing proposal in 1941, it created a sensation that generated two decades of theological controversy and many volumes of debate. The strong response was somewhat ironic since so much of demythologizing was not new. Bultmann's objection to any theological use of an objectifying mode of thought was a constant in his writings, from 1920 on.

[16] Some theological conversations deserve a special note in the history of theology. In the midst of their changing positions and much mutual criticism, Barth and Bultmann continued to respond actively to the others' theology. This appears in their correspondence: *Karl Barth—Rudolf Bultmann Letters: 1922-1966*, Bernd Jaspert ed. (Grand Rapids, MI: Eerdmans Press, 1981). Barth also wrote a single book on the subject: *Rudolf Bultmann: An Attempt to Understand Him*, as printed in *Kerygma and Myth*, II, pp. 83-132. The critical comments of the one concerning the theological work of the other needs to be understood in the context of their long standing personal friendship.

[17] The study of a religious movement known as the "Mandaeans" was one of Bultmann's history-of-religions projects. In the mid-twenties he was already loaning manuscripts on the Mandaeans to Karl Barth. Unlike his other writings of the twenties, collected together for the 1933 *Glauben und Verstehen*, Bultmann's research in the history-of-religions did not appear in a single volume until a 1967 edition, *Exegetica: Aufsätze zur Erforschung des Neuen Testaments* edited by Erich Dinkler. That volume has not yet been translated into English. For Bultmann's history-of-religions research, see Helmut Koes-

ter, "Early Christianity from the Perspective of the History of Religion", *Bultmann, Retrospect and Prospect.*

[18] For a systematic interpretation of Gnosticism as an existential phenomenon, see the work of Hans Jonas, especially *The Gnostic Religion* (Boston: Beacon Press, 1963). Bultmann and Jonas worked closely together at Marburg before Jonas was forced to leave Germany because he was Jewish. While it was against Nazi law for any German author to cite by name a Jewish emigre, Bultmann continued to acknowledge, in lectures and in published texts, the contribution of Jonas to his own thought.

[19] In *Jesus Christ and Mythology* (1958), Bultmann used the single English phrase 'world view' to express the meaning of two distinct but related German concepts: *Weltbild* and *Weltanschauung*. *Weltbild* refers to a model of external reality which people use in their practical dealings with the world; *Weltanschauung* is a more comprehensive category, a total belief system, including human beings, which answers to questions of meaning and value. In his English version, Bultmann distinguished between these two uses of "world view" by modifiers. "World view" in the sense of *Weltanschauung* was either preceded by "general" or followed by the German original. "World view" in the sense of *Weltbild* was most often preceded by "scientific" or "ancient". Bultmann's translators often rendered *Weltbild* not as "world view" but in a variety of other ways: e.g., "picture of the world", "world picture", "view of the world", or "conception of the world". In this volume, Bultmann's practice has been followed; his qualifying terms, including in some cases the German original, have been added to older translations so that readers can clearly distinguish between "world view" as *Weltbild* or as *Weltanschauung*. While this practice loses something in semantic clarity, with one English phrase representing two German terms, it does accurately express the existential ambiguity intended by Bultmann. While a *Weltbild*, in itself, should be merely a mental tool for one's dealing with the world, in actuality it is often taken to be much more than this: i.e., as an all inclusive understanding of the whole of reality. As such, it is a *Weltanschauung*, a substitute for faith in God, and a construct of sin.

[20] *Kerygma and Myth*, Hans Werner Bartsch, ed. (London: SPCK, 1957), volume I, p. 5.

[21] *Kerygma and Myth*, I, 3.

[22] *Kerygma und Mythos*, II, 180.

[23] "Mythus und Mythologie im Neuen Testament", *Die Religion in Geschichte und Gegenwart* (1930), vol. IV.

[24] *Kerygma and Myth*, I, 1.

[25] The German term *Entmythologisierung*, translated here as "demythologizing", was first coined by Hans Jonas in his 1930 publication, *Augustin und das paulinische Freiheitsproblem*. Bultmann borrowed the term from Jonas, one of his graduate students, as well as some of the presuppositions from historical Idealism which were basic to the early writings of Jonas: e.g., *Geist*, or Spirit, which first broke through to a new understanding of itself in the religious and philosophical objectivations of the Hellenistic era, subsequently had to pass through a stage of alienated objectivity before being reappropriated in a conceptuality appropriate to it, that is, existentialism. For a discussion of Jonas' contribution to Bultmann's proposal of demythologizing, see "The Existentialist Formulation of Myth", *The Origins of Demythologizing* (1974), Roger A. Johnson.

[26] Bultmann's 1941 essay, "New Testament and Mythology", is available in a new English translation by Schubert Ogden, *New Testament and Mythology* (1984). That volume also includes two of Bultmann's responses to his critics: "On the Problem of Demytholo-

gizing" (1952) and a second essay with the same title from 1961. Another major English language source for the demythologizing debate is: *Kerygma and Myth*, II, Hans-Werner Bartsch, ed. (1962). This volume includes Karl Barth's monograph, "Rudolf Bultmann — An Attempt to Understand Him", the exchange between Bultmann and the philosopher Karl Jaspers, and a lengthy summary of "The Present State of the Debate" by Hans-Werner Bartsch.

[27] For example, Enrico Castelli edited three volumes of essays (in French, German and Italian) published in 1961, 1962, and 1963. During this same period of time, a growing body of literature was appearing in Japanese, both translations of Bultmann and new works by Japanese theologians and philosophers dealing with the issues of demythologizing and existentialist interpretation.

NOTES TO SELECTED TEXTS

[*Editorial note (RAJ): Any text prefaced by the phrase "Editorial Note" is not by Bultmann. Initials within parentheses identify the editor and/or translator who is the source of that note. All other notes are from Bultmann.*]

1 Ich will dich kennen, Unbekannter,
  Du tief in meine Seele Greifender,
  Mein Leben wie ein Sturm Durchschweifender,
  Du Unfassbarer, mir Verwandter!
  Ich will dich kennen, selbst dir dienen!
    (Friedrich Nietzsche, *"Dem unbekannten Gott"*)
2 Du bist der Wald der Widersprüche.
  Ich darf dich wiegen wie ein Kind,
  Und doch vollziehn sich deine Flüche,
  Die über Völkern furchtbar sind.
    (Rainer Maria Rilke, *"Studenbuch"*)
3 Ja, alles ist in dir, was nur das Weltall beut,
  Der Himmel und die Höll, Gericht und Ewigkeit.

4 Editorial Note (KC): quoted material is Keith Crim's translation. Page numbers refer to Barth's *The Epistle to the Romans* (London: Oxford University Press, 1933), translated by Edwyn C. Hoskyns from the 6th edition of *Der Römerbrief*.

5 What Herrmann called "experience" is not that against which Barth polemizes. And Herrmann's polemic against the philosophy and psychology of religion as opposed to mysticism was no less radical than that of Barth.

6 Editorial Note (JR): Bultmann has written me that he would now replace here "consciousness" with "concrete existence".

7 Barth will in part take from what is said here and in part will say to himself that, in that which involves the philological historical explanation and in what concerns the evaluation of the content of Romans and of Paul, I largely follow what Jülicher said concerning the first edition.

8 In this article (based on a previous lecture), I have confined myself to a discussion of the movement as represented by Barth and Gogarten only. My reason for so limiting myself in a treatment of the "latest theological movement" is that I find that both the recognition of our present theological situation and the efforts to overcome the difficulties it presents have been most fruitful in their work. I do not overlook the fact that similar incentives are operative elsewhere and that important statements are being made by others.

9 Editorial Note (RAJ): "The Significance of the Historical Jesus for Faith" is available in English in Robert Morgan and Michael Pye (eds.), *Ernst Troeltsch: Writings on Theology and Religion* (London 1977).

10 This idea finds naïve expression on page 398 of *Morgenandachten*, published in 1909 by the Friends of the Christian World. After a polemic against the idea of "the splendid sins" (*splendida vitia*) of the heathen, we read, "It cannot be denied that the spirit of the

336

noblest nations of antiquity, which also is a spirit given by God, built the road for the ideas of the Christian world and helped the progress upward towards freedom".

[11] I am concerned — especially because of the voices raised in certain circles since Heitmüller's call to Tübingen — to emphasize once more that this whole discussion is directed against a theological trend and not against individual theologians. The statements I cite are characteristic of that position, not of Heitmüller individually. It would be very unfair to label his work as a whole "liberal theology".

[12] Barth, *Der Römerbrief*, 3rd ed., p. 276; (cf. ET, *The Epistle to the Romans*, p. 293).

[13] Gogarten, *ZZ* 2, (1923), p. 21.

[14] *Die Soziallehren der christlichen Kirchen und Gruppen*, Tübingen, 1912; ET, *The Social Teaching of the Christian Churches*, London and New York, 1931.

[15] Cf. Luther, *Genesisvorlesungen* 1535-45 on Gen. 1.2, Weimar ed., vol. 42, p. 12; for English edition see J. Pelikan, ed., *Luther's Works*, vol. 1: *Lectures on Genesis*, St. Louis, 1958.

[16] Eduard Thurneysen, *Dostojewski*, München, 1921, p. 53.

[17] Cf. W. Herrmann, *Realencyc.*, I³, p. 498, lines 29ff. "Where we ourselves are, there is the world. The man who seeks to reach God beyond this world is therefore attempting the impossible. When he thinks he has found God, he has got hold of nothing more than a fragment of the world or a world conceived as abstractly as possible, divested of its perceptual concreteness."

[18] W. Herrmann, *Die Wirklichkeit Gottes*, Tübingen, 1914, p. 42.

[19] Literally, "neither as dæmonic nor as fascinating".

[20] Editorial Note (KG): Quotations from the New Testament are given according to the Revised Standard Version (1946), with the kind permission of the copyright owner, Division of Christian Education, National Council of the Churches of Christ in the U.S.A., unless there is an indication to the contrary. "Blt." (= Bultmann's version) means that the author himself translated the passage into German, for which an English equivalent is here offered; "tr." (= translator's version) means that the author quoted only the Greek text, which I, Kendrick Grobel, felt compelled to translate anew in the sense implied by the author's context. Rarely King James or a modern private translation is quoted, and always by name.

[21] Formulations presumably due to the Church, or words edited by the evangelists are placed in brackets. Lk. 17:30 is perhaps original.

[22] Not by Lk. 17:21 either. On the meaning of this saying, see p. 106 above.

[23] *Cf.* espec. IV Esdras 8:20ff.

[24] Disregarding the distinction between Messiah and Son of Man; after all, both mean the eschatological bringer of salvation.

[25] *Cf.* the substitution of the word "king" Βασιλεύς Mk. 15:2, 9, 18, 26, 32; Jn. 1:49; Ps. Sol. 17:23, etc. See P. Volz, *Die Eschatologie der jüdischen Gemeinde im neutestamentl. Zeitalter* (1934), 173f.; W. Staerk, *Soter* I (1933), 48ff.

[26] Hans Walter Wolff attempts to prove the opposite in his Halle dissertation: *Jesaja 53 im Urchristentum* (1942). The attempt is scarcely successful.

[27] Editorial Note (RAJ): Bultmann's use of the German concepts, *Existentiell* and *Existential*, is clarified in the Introduction, above, pp. 22-24.

[28] Preface to the Third Edition of his *Epistle to the Romans* (1923). Editorial Note (RAJ): In this reference to "other spirits in the text", Barth is responding to the last few lines of Bultmann's review of *Epistle to the Romans*, above, pp. 64-65. In his review Bultmann spoke of spirits in the text other than the "Spirit of Christ" (ibid.).

[29] W. Dilthey, *Die Entstehung der Hermeneutik* (1900), published with additions from the manuscripts in the *Gesammelte Schriften*, 5 (1924), 317-83. The passages quoted are from pp. 332-33 and 317.

[30] Ibid., 317, 334.

[31] Ibid., 319.

[32] The presentation of hermeneutics in the substantial article by G. Heinrici in the *Realenzyklopädie für protestantisch Theologie und Kirche*, 7 (1899), 718-50, is limited to the development of the traditional hermeneutical rules. The same is true of F. Torm's *Hermeneutik des Neuen Testaments* (1930), while E. Fascher, in *Vom Verstehen des Neuen Testaments* (1930), seeks to go further without, in my opinion, ever finding a clear direction. Joachim Wach portrays the "basic features of a history of hermeneutical theory in the nineteenth century" in his great work, *Das Verstehen*, 3 vols. (1926, 1929, 1933), which is an extraordinarily careful inventory, but in my judgment is far too reserved in taking a position that could have critically illumined the history. The hermeneutical principles that Wach sketches in the *Journal of Biblical Literature* 55 (1936): 59-63 are also merely the old hermeneutical rules, augmented only by the "necessity of psychological understanding", by which he evidently intends to validate Schleiermacher's demand, but without further developing it by consistently working out Dilthey's suggestions. Also, his article on "understanding" in *Religion in Geschichte und Gegenwart*, 5 (2d ed., 1931), 1570-73 is — understandably enough — too sketchy. Fritz Buri engages the discussion of the problem of hermeneutics in contemporary Protestant theology in a critical way in *Schweizerische theologische Umschau, Festgabe für Martin Werner zum 60. Geburtstag* (1947). I find myself close to him both in his struggle for a historical-critical understanding of scripture and in his rejection of a "pneumatic-superhistorical understanding of scripture" and a so-called theological hermeneutics by means of which one practices a "christological exegesis" of the Old Testament. That he has not correctly understood my own efforts is certainly due in part to my not having previously distinguished clearly between a scientific understanding of scripture and obedience to the kerygma. But it is due, above all, to his not having grasped the distinction between existentialist and existential understanding, as becomes clear when he speaks of my attempt at an "existential exegesis", against which I can only protest. He cites my statement from *Offenbarung und Heilsgeschehen* (1941), 41 that there should be an "existentialist" interpretation of New Testament mythology by writing "existential" in place of "existentialist".

[33] See Dilthey, *Gesammelte Schriften*, 5 (1924), 321, and for what follows, 321ff.

[34] H. Patzer, "Der Humanismus als Methodenproblem der klassischen Philologie", *Studium Generale* 1 (1948), 84-92.

[35] Aside from Dilthey, see especially Wach, *Das Verstehen*, 1 (1926), 83ff., 102ff., 143, 148-49.

[36] The formulations follow Dilthey's characterization in *Gesammelte Schriften*, 5 (1924), 327-28; see also 328, 335.

[37] Ibid., 329. See Wach, *Das Verstehen*, 1 (1926), 141. Schleiermacher grounded the process of divinatory understanding in the fact that while each human being is unique, he or she also has a "receptiveness" for all others.

[38] Dilthey, *Gesammelte Schriften*, 5 (1924), 329-30, 334, 332.

[39] Ibid., 326-27.

[40] G. Misch, *Geschichte der Autobiographie*, 1 (1907).

[41] The formula according to which the real goal of exegesis is understanding the author and his or her work (H. Gunkel, *Monatsschrift für die kirchliche Praxis* [1904]:

552), is correct insofar as it denies that exegesis should (or may) be guided by dogmatic or practical interests. But for the rest, it says nothing whatever about the hermeneutical problem, which begins at this very point. For what undertanding of the author is meant? A psychological one? A biographical one? etc. And how is the work to be understood? As belonging to the history of some problem? Aesthetically? etc.

⁴² This insight is obviously intended in the "idealistic metaphysics of understanding, according to which historical understanding is possible only on the basis of an identity of the human spirit in its diverse objectifications and of this spirit with the absolute Spirit" (Buri, *Schweizerische theologische Umschau* [1947]: 25). But even J. C. K. von Hofmann sees in his way what is decisive here when he says that biblical hermeneutics does not pretend to be an independent science closed in upon itself but rather presupposes general hermeneutics, even though in doing so it does not consist simply in applying general hermeneutics to the Bible but presupposes a relation to the Bible's contents (*Biblische Hermeneutik* [1880], 1ff.). On Hofmann, see also Wach, *Das Verstehen*, 2 (1929), 365, 369-70.

⁴³ This is the sense in which the "congeniality" demanded of the historian by Wilhelm von Humboldt, August Boeckh, and especially Johann Gustav Droysen is also understood. On this, see H. Astholz, *Das Problem "Geschichte" untersucht bei Johann Gustav Droysen* (1933); she cites, among other things, Droysen's characteristic statement that "every human being is indeed a historian, but whoever makes ἱστορεῖν his or her vocation has something to do that is in a special degree human" (97-98).

⁴⁴ N. Söderblom, *Das Werden des Gottesglaubens* (1916), 41ff.

⁴⁵ Patzer, *Studium Generale* 1 (1948): 90.

⁴⁶ K. Reinhardt, *Sophokles* 2d ed., 1943); P. Friedländer, *Platon*, 2: *Die platonischen Schriften* (1930). I may also refer to Reinhardt's lectures and essays, which appeared under the title *Von Werken und Formen* (1948).

⁴⁷ *Theologische Rundschau*, N.F. 2 (1930): 44-46.

⁴⁸ E. Auerbach, *Mimesis, Dargestellte Wirklichkeit in der abendländischen Literatur* (1946). In his *Bildnisstudien* (1947), E. Buschor attempts to make stylistic analysis serviceable for what one may well call an existentialist interpretation, even if its categories are insufficiently clear.

⁴⁹ F. Blättner, "Das Griechenbild J. J. Winckelmanns", *Jahrbuch "Antike und Abendland"* 1 (1944): 121-32.

⁵⁰ See Wach, *Das Verstehen*, 1 (1926), 106, 185.

⁵¹ See R. Buchwald's Foreword to the essays of Hermann Grimm that have appeared under the title *Deutsche Künstler*.

⁵² The formulations follow Dilthey, *Gesammelte Schriften*, 5 (1924), 317, 328, and the survey by F. Kaufmann, "Geschichtsphilosophie der Gegenwart", *Philosophische Forschungsberichte* 10 (1931): 109-17.

⁵³ See Kaufmann, *Philosophische Forschungsberichte* 10 (1931): 54-55 for a discussion with Simmel about being personally related to the occurrence of history. On hearing the claim of history in Droysen, see Astholz, *Das Problem "Geschichte" undersucht bei J. G. Droysen* (1933), 106, and 120-21 on understanding as a concern of life and as an act.

⁵⁴ *Briefwechsel zwischen Wilhelm Dilthey und dem Grafen Paul Yorck von Wartenburg 1877-1897* (1923), 60.

⁵⁵ Ibid., 120.

⁵⁶ M. Heidegger, *Sein und Zeit*, 1 (1927), especially paragraphs 31 and 32. Concerning Heidegger, see Kaufmann, *Philosophische Forschungsberichte* 10 (1931): 118ff.

[57] See Kaufmann, *Philosophische Forschungsberichte* 10 (1931): 41: Understanding a historical context of life is understanding "how human existence once understood or misunderstood its own problem, either standing up to it or fleeing from it". See also Droysen in Astholz, *Das Problem "Geschichte" untersucht bei J. G. Droysen* (1933), 121.

[58] Insofar as it is not the forced and accidental choice of a theme for dissertation.

[59] Kaufmann, *Philosophische Forschungsberichte* 10 (1931): 41.

[60] K. Barth, *Die kirchliche Dogmatik*, 3/2 (1948), 534.

[61] Ibid., 535.

[62] Ibid., 535-36.

[63] Ibid., 536.

[64] Ibid., 536-37.

[65] Walter Klaas, *Der moderne Mensch in der Theologie Rudolf Bultmanns* (1947), 29. This writing is a pertinent and sympathetic contribution to the discussion. It is to be regretted only that the author clearly has not understood the meaning of "demythologizing" as a hermeneutical principle and does not know to distinguish between existential and existentialist understanding.

[66] In the Old Testament Satan has not yet become the Devil. The figure of the Devil entered Judaism from Iranian sources, and appears here under various names, of which "Satan" is only one (meaning enemy or accuser).

[67] From the "Assumption of Moses", an apocalyptic document, which, however, emanates from the first (or second) century A.D. Eng. Trans. by R. H. Charles, in Charles, *Apocrypha and Pseudepigrapha of the Old Testament*, Vol. II, 1913, pp. 407-24.

[68] Texts from IV Esra are quoted from translations by G. H. Box in Charles, op. cit., pp. 542-624, and of the Syrian Apocalypse of Baruch from the translation by R. H. Charles, op. cit., pp. 470-526.

[69] Owing to the slavish translation of the Aramaic term for "man" by the Greek ὁ υἱὸς τοῦ ἀνθώςπου, the designation "Son of Man" has become traditional.

[70] Literature: Franz Cumont, *The Oriental Religions in Roman Paganism*, Chicago, 1911. Edwyn Bevan, *Stoics and Sceptics*, Oxford, 1913; also his *Later Greek Religion*, London, Dent, 1927. Franz Boll, *Sternglaube und Sterndeutung* (Aus Natur und Geisteswelt 638), 2nd Ed., 1926. Hugo Gressmann, *Die hellenistische Gestirnreligion* (Beih. zum Alten Orient, 5), 1925. Wilhelm Gundel, *Sternglaube, Sternreligion und Sternorakel* (Wissensch. und Bildung, 288), 1933. Viktor Stegemann, "Fatum und Freiheit im Hellenismus und in der Spätantike". *Das Gymnasium* 50 (1939), pp. 165-91. Franz Boll, *Sternglaube und Sterndeutung*, 4th Ed. (no longer in "Aus Natur und Geisteswelt"), by W. Gundel, 1931. Dom Jacques Dupont, O.S.B., *Gnosis. La connaissance religieuse dans les Epitres de Saint Paul* (1949), C. VII, §1. Cf. Rudolf Bultmann, "Zur Geschichte der Lichtsymbolik im Altertum," *Philologus*, 97 (1948), p. 1-36.

[71] Cumont, op. cit., p. 134, cf. also pp. 207f.

[72] Pliny, *nat. hist.*, II, 22. Trans. H. Rackham (Loeb).

[73] Sen., *de prov.*, 5, 7f. Trans. J. W. Basore (Loeb).

[74] Sen., *ad Helv.*, 8. 5. Trans. R. M. Gummere. Cf. Corp, Herm. 5, 3-5.

[75] Sen., *ad Marc.*, 18.5f. (Is Poseidonius the basis of this? Cf. also Cicero *de nat. deor.*, II, 56; *Tusc.*, I, 19, 44.).

[76] Sen., *Ep.*, 102, 21-9: the trans. are all from the Loeb edition. Cf. also the description of the beatific vision in Plut., *de genio Socr.*, 590bff., and see Bultmann, op. cit. (see n. 70), pp. 26-9.

[77] Apul., *Met.*, XI, 15. Trans. S. Gaselee (Loeb).

[78] Clem Alex. *Exc. ex Theod,* 71f. Trans. R. P. Casey.

[79] Editorial Note (RAJ): A detailed account of the history of the study of Gnosticism is given in Hans Jonas *The Gnostic Religion* (Boston: Beacon Press, 1963).

[80] Ibid.

[81] I Cor. 2.14, 15.44, 46; Jas. 3.15; Jude 19.

[82] The separation of the concepts of εἱμαρμένη and πρόνοια is characteristic in Stoicism they are used synonymously to designate the law and order of the universe or the rule of φύσις. In Gnosticism εἱμαρθένη is the law and order of the universe, while πρόνοια is divine providence, which has no longer a cosmological but and soteriological import, leading the Gnostics to σωτηρία. Cf. Jonas, op. cit., pp. 172-8 Equally characteristic is the change in the meaning of πέρας and ἄπειρον; see Jonas, p. 163, 1.

[83] God is characterized by attributes such as ἄγνωστος, ἀκατονόμαστος, ἀποκεκρυμμένος, ξένος, etc.; his nature is characterized, not by λόγος, but by σιγή. Cf. W. Bousset, *Hauptprobleme der Gnosis,* 1907, p. 84; Jonas, op. cit., pp. 243-51.

[84] *Corp. Herm.,* I, 27f.; 7, 1-3.

[85] Thus e.g., the process of "rebirth" or deification is accomplished in the hearing (or reading) of the word which communicates the λόγος τῆς παλιγγενεσίας. *Corp. Herm.,* 13. On this, see R. Reitzenstein, *Die hellenist. Mysterienreligionen,* 3rd ed., 1927, pp. 52, 64.

[86] Odes of Solomon, 25. The song is also found in the Gnostic document *"Pistis Sophia",* Ch. 69. Eng. Trans. G. S. Meade, London, 1921, and G. Horner, S.P.C.K., 1924.

[87] The characterization of Christianity as a syncretistic religion derives from Hermann Gunkel, *Zum religionsgeschichtlichen Verständnis des Neuen Testaments,* 2nd ed., 1910.

[88] The people who denied the resurrection whom Paul is combating in I Cor. 15 are clearly Gnosticizing Christians. They did not, as Paul supposes, deny a continuation of the life of the baptized after death (he admits that they had themselves baptized for the dead in v. 29), but maintained the standpoint of the false teachers attacked in II Tim. 2.18, who said "the resurrection is passed already".

[89] That in Phil. 2.6-11 Paul is quoting a traditional Christological hymn has been demonstrated by Ernst Lohmeyer (*Kyrios Jesus,* Sitzungsber. der Heidelb. Ak. d. Wiss., Phil.-Hist. Kl., 1927-8, 4. Abh., 1928).

[90] The radical elimination of apocalyptic eschatology in the Fourth Gospel has to some extent been redressed by the ecclesiastical redaction which the Gospel has undergone. This redaction sought to reintroduce the traditional view. Hence 5.28f., 6.51-8 and further minor additions.

[91] Cf. Rom. 7.5: ὅτε γὰρ ἦμεν ἐν τῇ σαρκί.

[92] For Paul the primary meaning of faith (πίστις) is obedience (ὑπακοή). E.g. what Rom. 1.8 and I Thess. 1.8 call the "faith" of the churches, which has become known everywhere, is in Rom. 16.19 called their "obedience". It is the ministry of the apostle to produce the "obedience of the Gentiles". Unbelief is disobedience; cf. Rom. 10.3, 16, 11.30-2, etc. Thus Paul can coin the term, "obedience of faith" (ὑπακοή πίστεως) (Rom. 1.5).

[93] Editorial Note (RAJ): In this essay, "world view" is used only to translate *Weltanschauung.*

[94] Wilhelm Herrmann, *Offenbarung und Wunder,* Giessen, 1908, pp. 39f.

[95] Ibid. p. 36f.

[96] Unintentionally, the defenders of miracle provide evidence of this attitude when they try to prove that a miracle has really occurred. They attach the "miracle" directly to the sequence of world events by asserting that this or that event cannot be understood without positing a wonder, that observation of the event concerned leads to the X, called

wonder. They themselves, therefore, subordinate the "wonder" to the notion of conformity to law and thereby nullify the concept of wonder.

[97] H. Schuster, *Lebenskunde*, 1927, p. 8.

[98] Cf. Luther on Rom. 8.26 (Ficker, p. 204, lines 11ff.): "For it is necessary that a work of God be hidden and not understood at the time when it is done. But it is not hidden otherwise than under the contrary aspect of our conception or way of thinking."

[99] Luther on Rom. 8.26 (Ficker, p. 205, lines 5f.): "It always happens that we know our own work before it is done; but God's work we do not know until it has been done."

[100] Luther on Gal. 4f. (Weimar ed. XL, I, p. 568, lines 9ff.): "Christ also gives commandments, but that is not his real office; it is incidental even as are his benefits: teaching, comforting, helping. These are not works peculiar to Christ. For the prophets also taught and did wonders. But Christ is God and man, who submits to the law of Moses and foreign tyranny, conquers Moses and that tyranny, contends with the law and suffers and afterwards in his resurrection damns and destroys our enemy." Those other acts are "common acts".

[101] As an example I may call attention to the great work of Joachim Wach, *Das Verstehen*, Vols. I-III (Leipzig, 1926-33). The more recent book by Christian Hartlich and Walter Sachs, *Der Ursprung des Mythosbegriffes in der modernen Bibelwissenschaft* (Tübingen, 1952) is especially important for our problem.

[102] See the discussion of analogy by the late Erich Frank in his *Philosophical Understanding and Religious Truth* (New York, 1945).

[103] Man is a historical being not only in so far as he is enmeshed in the course of the world-history, but particularly in so far as he has a personal history of his own.

SUBJECT INDEX

INDEX OF NAMES